T0323438

CONSUMER PSYCHOLOGY

Sara Miller McCune founded SAGE Publishing in 1965 to support the dissemination of usable knowledge and educate a global community. SAGE publishes more than 1000 journals and over 800 new books each year, spanning a wide range of subject areas. Our growing selection of library products includes archives, data, case studies and video. SAGE remains majority owned by our founder and after her lifetime will become owned by a charitable trust that secures the company's continued independence.

Los Angeles | London | New Delhi | Singapore | Washington DC | Melbourne

Hazel Huang

CONSUMER PSYCHOLOGY

Theories & Applications

⑤SAGE

Los Angeles | London | New Delhi
Singapore | Washington DC | Melbourne

Los Angeles | London | New Delhi
Singapore | Washington DC | Melbourne

SAGE Publications Ltd
1 Oliver's Yard
55 City Road
London EC1Y 1SP

SAGE Publications Inc.
2455 Teller Road
Thousand Oaks, California 91320

SAGE Publications India Pvt Ltd
B 1/I 1 Mohan Cooperative Industrial Area
Mathura Road
New Delhi 110 044

SAGE Publications Asia-Pacific Pte Ltd
3 Church Street
#10-04 Samsung Hub
Singapore 049483

Editor: Matthew Waters
Editorial assistant: Charlotte Hanson
Production editor: Victoria Nicholas
Copyeditor: Neil Dowden
Proofreader: Christine Bitten
Indexer: David Rudeforth
Marketing manager: Kimberley Simpson
Cover design: Francis Kenney
Typeset by: C&M Digitals (P) Ltd, Chennai India

Library of Congress Control Number: 2022943985

British Library Cataloguing in Publication data

A catalogue record for this book is available from the British Library

ISBN 978-1-4739-0697-6
ISBN 978-1-4739-0698-3 (pbk)

Contents

Online Resources	xi
About the Author	xiii
Preface	xv
Acknowledgements	xix

1 Introduction — **1**

1.1 Main schools of psychology	1
A brief history of psychology as an academic discipline	1
Functionalism	4
Behaviourism	4
Humanistic psychology	6
Cognitivism	7
Social psychology	8
1.2 Development of consumer psychology	9
A brief historical account	9
The evolution of the theoretical development in consumer psychology	11
1.3 Outline of this book	16
1.4 Summary	17
Discussion questions	18
Further reading	19
Notes	19

2 Consumer Knowledge — **27**

2.1 Introduction	27
2.2 Memory	28
Sensory memory	29
Short-term (working) memory	31
Long-term memory	34

2.3 Knowledge   38
      The psychological basis   38
      Implications for consumer behaviour   39
2.4 Summary   41
Discussion questions   43
Further reading   43
Notes   44

3   Consumer Inference and Evaluation   53

3.1 Introduction   53
3.2 Category-based inferences   54
      The psychological basis   54
      Implications for consumer behaviour   55
3.3 Causal inferences   57
      The psychological basis   57
      Implications for consumer behaviour   58
3.4 Cognitive illusion: the framing effect   61
      The psychological basis   61
      Implications for consumer behaviour   64
3.5 Summary   67
Discussion questions   68
Further reading   68
Notes   68

4   Consumer Implicit Cognition   77

4.1 Introduction   77
4.2 The basics: the implicit–explicit distinction   78
4.3 Implicit knowledge   79
      The psychological basis   79
      Implications for consumer behaviour   80
4.4 Implicit learning   84
      The influence at cognitive level   84
      Perception without awareness   84
      The limitations   86
4.5 Summary   87
Discussion questions   88
Further reading   88
Notes   89

5   Consumer Development and Socialisation   **95**

5.1 Introduction   96
5.2 Children consumers: from childhood to adolescence   96
       The psychological basis   96
       Implications for consumer behaviour   98
5.3 Ageing consumers   107
       The increasing importance of ageing consumers   107
       Physiological changes   108
       Changes in decision-making   110
       The limitations   112
5.4 Summary   112
Discussion questions   114
Further reading   114
Notes   114

6   Emotions in Consumer Behaviour   **125**

6.1 Introduction   126
6.2 The basics of emotions   126
       A brief introduction of emotion   126
       How do emotions influence?   128
6.3 Positive emotions   129
       Happiness   129
       Pride   131
6.4 Negative emotions   133
       Fear   133
       Anger   135
       Regret   137
6.5 Summary   139
Discussion questions   141
Further reading   141
Notes   141

7   Consumer Motivation   **151**

7.1 Introduction   152
7.2 Motivation: a top-down perspective   152
       The psychological basis   152
       Implications for consumer behaviour   154

7.3 Motivation: a bottom-up perspective   156
    The psychological basis   156
    Implications for consumer behaviour   157
7.4 Self-regulation   159
    Self-regulation   159
    Self-regulation failure   160
    The regulatory focus theory   165
7.5 Summary   167
Discussion questions   168
Further reading   169
Notes   169

8 Consumer Identity – I Shop; Therefore, I am   **179**

8.1 Introduction   179
8.2 Self-identity   181
    William James's empirical self   181
    Brand-as-person   184
    Higgins's self-discrepancy theory   190
8.3 Social identity   191
    The psychological basis   191
    Implications for consumer behaviour   192
8.4 Culture and the self: self-construal   194
    The psychological basis   194
    Implications for consumer behaviour   195
8.5 Summary   197
Discussion questions   198
Further reading   199
Notes   199

9 Environmental Psychology and Consumer Behaviour   **211**

9.1 Introduction   212
9.2 Key models of environmental psychology in
    consumer behaviour   212
    Key theories of environmental psychology   212
    The Mehrabian–Russell Model   213
    Bitner's model of servicescape   216
9.3 Music   217
    The psychological basis   217
    Implications for consumer behaviour   220

9.4 Scent   223
　　The psychological basis   223
　　Implications for consumer behaviour   224
9.5 Lighting   225
　　The psychological basis   225
　　Implications for consumer behaviour   226
9.6 Touch   227
　　The psychological basis   227
　　Implications for consumer behaviour   228
9.7 Summary   230
Discussion questions   232
Further reading   233
Notes   233

10 Evolutionary Psychology and Consumer Behaviour   243

10.1 Introduction   243
10.2 The basics of evolutionary psychology   244
　　Charles Darwin's theory of evolution   244
　　What is evolutionary psychology?   246
10.3 The survival drives – self-protection   247
　　The psychological basis   247
　　Implications for consumer behaviour   248
10.4 The mating drives   249
　　Mate attraction   249
　　Mate retention   252
10.5 The affiliation drives   254
　　The theory of reciprocal altruism   254
　　Status   254
10.6 Reflection   256
10.7 Summary   256
Discussion questions   258
Further reading   259
Notes   259

11 Consumer Well-Being   269

11.1 Introduction   269
11.2 Self-esteem   270
　　The psychological basis   270
　　Implications for consumer behaviour   271

11.3 Pleasure   276
      The psychological basis   276
      Implications for consumer behaviour   277
11.4 Summary   282
Discussion questions   284
Further reading   284
Notes   284

12 Research Methods in Consumer Psychology   **295**

12.1 Introduction   296
12.2 Before choosing a method   296
12.3 Qualitative methods   299
      Key methods   299
      Sampling   307
      Data analysis   308
      Reporting   311
12.4 Quantitative methods   312
      Key methods   313
      Sampling   325
      Data analysis   328
      Reporting   331
12.5 Ethical issues in research   334
12.6 Summary   335
Discussion questions   338
Further reading   338
Notes   338

Index   341

Online Resources

This textbook is accompanied by online resources to aid teaching and support learning. To access these resources, visit: https://study.sagepub.com/huang. Please note that lecturers will require a SAGE account in order to access the lecturer resources. An account can be created via the above link.

FOR LECTURERS

- **PowerPoints** that can be downloaded and adapted to suit individual teaching needs
- A **Teaching Guide** providing practical guidance and support and additional materials for lecturers using this textbook in their teaching
- **Supplementary Materials** to be used alongside the textbook

About the Author

Hazel Huang is an Assistant Professor in Marketing at Durham University Business School, England. Coming from Taiwan, she holds a PhD degree from Warwick University, and is a Chartered Marketer at the Chartered Institute of Marketing. Her research interests lie in consumer behaviour, in particular symbolic consumption, and she specialises in quantitative methods. She has presented her work at prestige international conferences, such as ACR, SCP, and EMAC, and has published in *Psychology & Marketing*, *Computers in Human Behaviour*, and *Journal of Consumer Behaviour*. Before embarking on her academic career, she had worked in industry for approximately ten years. She started her career as a junior buyer at FIC (once the world's largest motherboard supplier), and later on moved to the roles of sales, branding, and marketing. Her experiences in the real world crossed various industries, including IT (Acer), retailing (Carrefour), and FMCG (J&J).

Preface

The idea of writing a consumer psychology textbook started back in 2010 when I was teaching a consumer psychology module at Durham University. Searching on the market, I was unable to identify a suitable textbook. On the one hand, the majority of the books were overly basic. For example, whilst there were many consumer behaviour textbooks, the consumer psychology module was positioned as an advanced consumer behaviour module. Students taking consumer psychology had consumer behaviour as a prerequisite course. This positioning rendered the use of consumer behaviour books unsuitable. On the other hand, there were two handbooks that were very theoretical:

- *Perspectives in Consumer Behaviour* edited by Kassarjian and Robertson (1991)[1]
- *Handbook of Consumer Psychology* edited by Haugtvedt, Herr, and Kardes (2008)[2]

Whilst these books provide systematic literature reviews, the language and the depth of discussion is not student-friendly, and they are more suitable for researchers whose interests lie in consumer psychology. More than ten years have passed, and during this time we have observed a surge in researchers' interests in consumer psychology with Haugtvedt, Herr, and Kardes updating their highly valued *Handbook of Consumer Psychology*, and publishing its second edition in 2023, and four more handbooks are now also available on the market: *The Cambridge Handbook of Consumer Psychology*,[3] *Routledge International Handbook of Consumer Psychology*,[4] *Handbook of Research Methods in Consumer Psychology*,[5] and *APA Handbook of Consumer Psychology*.[6]

Not only has a growth in researching consumer psychology been observed, but we have also seen a rise in the numbers of marketing students and in specialised marketing programmes both at undergraduate and master's levels. The demand for a suitable consumer psychology textbook can be reflected from the launch of the second edition of the only consumer psychology textbook (that is still in print and not out of date) on the market by Jansson-Boyd (2019),[7] nine years after its first edition. Different from Jansson-Boyd's consumer psychology book, a small book containing a short introduction to the selected theories and applications of consumer psychology, the current book encompasses a broader and more systematic application of the psychological theories in consumer behaviour. When I discussed with Matthew Waters, the editor at SAGE, about my idea of writing a consumer psychology textbook at the EMAC conference in 2013, he was thrilled and welcomed the idea of having a consumer psychology textbook that is aimed at advanced marketing students. With his and his team's help, the inception of this book is now materialised.

Unlike other consumer psychology books, this book is written for students as well as for their tutors by touching upon the key and various theoretical concepts in different schools of psychological thought:

- *Cognitive psychology*: consumer knowledge (Chapter 2), consumer inference and evaluation (Chapter 3), consumer development and socialisation (Chapter 5), and consumer emotions (Chapter 6)
- *Behaviourism* (combined with the viewpoints from cognitive and social psychology): consumer implicit cognition (Chapter 4), consumer emotions (Chapter 6), consumer motivation (Chapter 7), and environmental psychology and consumer behaviour (Chapter 9)
- *Humanistic psychology*: consumer motivation (Chapter 7) and consumer identity (Chapter 8)
- *Social psychology*: consumer development and socialisation (Chapter 5), consumer identity (Chapter 8), and consumer well-being (Chapter 11)
- *Biological psychology*: consumer development and socialisation (Chapter 5) evolutionary psychology and consumer behaviour (Chapter 10)

As consumer psychology is applied psychology, each key topic is opened with an introduction of the psychological basis prior to discussing the application of the psychological concepts in consumer psychology. The introduction of the psychological basis provides a brief, yet solid, background information to students without a psychology education, and at the same time offers a quick refresher to those with a background in psychology. This structure helps students grasp the importance of the development in psychology on which consumer psychology heavily relies. Additional, supplementary information is also available through SAGE for instructors to help customise the design of their module. This book concludes with the chapter "Research Methods in Consumer Psychology", which is based on my experience of supervising dissertation students, and focuses on the commonly made mistakes and frequently asked questions to provide students with a reference guide, regardless of whether they choose a qualitative or a quantitative approach. This chapter can help instructors who supervise dissertation topics on consumer psychology to provide their students with useful references in a structured manner.

The writing of this book was delayed many times because of my health conditions. However, writing this book has helped keep me going, mentally, if not physically. I thoroughly enjoyed writing this book, as I had learned a lot beyond what I could have imagined if I had only focused on conducting original research. I hope you will not only learn something about consumer psychology from this book, but also enjoy reading it.

NOTES

1. Kassarjian, H. H., & Robertson, T. S. (eds). (1991). *Perspectives in Consumer Behavior* (fourth edn). Englewood Cliffs, NJ: Prentice-Hall.
2. Haugtvedt, C. P., Herr, P. M., & Kardes, F. R. (eds). (2008). *Handbook of Consumer Psychology*. New York: Psychology Press.
3. Norton, M. I., Rucker, D. D., & Lamberton, C. (eds). (2016). *The Cambridge Handbook of Consumer Psychology*. New York: Cambridge University Press.
4. Jansson-Boyd, C. V., & Zawisza, M. J. (eds). (2017). *Routledge International Handbook of Consumer Psychology*. Abingdon: Routledge.
5. Kardes, F. R., Herr, P. M., & Schwarz, N. (eds). (2019). *Handbook of Research Methods in Consumer Psychology*. New York: Routledge.
6. Kahle, L. R., Lowrey, T. M., & Huber, J. (eds). (2022). *APA Handbook of Consumer Psychology*. Washington: American Psychological Association.
7. Jansson-Boyd, C. V. (2019). *Consumer Psychology* (second edn). Maidenhead: Open University Press.

Acknowledgements

This book would not have been completed without the help of some people. First and foremost, I owe my thanks to Matthew Waters and his team (Charlotte Hanson, Jasleen Kaur, and Nina Smith) at SAGE who have shown great patience in waiting for me to complete this book. The book contract came at the most challenging time because of my health problems, and I would have given up without Matt's encouragement and patience. Second, my gratitude goes to two of the anonymous reviewers, whose constructive and positive evaluations of the earlier drafts have greatly helped me restructure the content and encouraged me to continue to write. In particular, their suggestion of splitting the psychological basis from implications for consumer behaviour reshaped the entire book. Finally, I thank three special friends: Mary Lynn Mundell, Keith Bartram, and Su Stewart. Mary Lynn, who I co-developed the consumer psychology module in 2011 at Durham, generously shared her teaching materials on evolutionary psychology and environmental psychology, and the classic readings speeded up the preparation of my manuscript. Keith proofread two of my chapters and gave me great encouragement by saying how much the content reflected his shopping experience. Last, but not the least, Su painstakingly proofread the first drafts of every chapter of the book. With a background in medical physics and experience with teaching university students, her feedback allowed me to make the book more accessible, not to mention her interest in the book that had greatly boosted my confidence. With their help, this book has now materialised.

1

INTRODUCTION

─Learning objectives─

To explore, understand, and explain:

- the main schools of psychological thought
- the development of consumer psychology as a discipline

1.1 MAIN SCHOOLS OF PSYCHOLOGY

A brief history of psychology as an academic discipline

The word "psychology" is derived from two Greek words, *psyche* and *logos*, to indicate the study of mind. In a broad sense, psychology has existed for a really long time: psychology was intertwined with philosophy and can be traced back to Plato and Aristotle's debate of mind versus body. Psychology, as an independent and scientific discipline separated from philosophy, was not established until the nineteenth century when empirical evidence became critical in the pursuit of psychological knowledge through endeavours to develop rigorous research methods.[1] In particular, it was the development of the quantitative methods during this time that marked the nineteenth century as the beginning of scientific psychology. The significant developments were threefold:

1. the use of experiments
2. the invention of measurements measuring psychological constructs
3. the development of statistics

Specifically, G. T. Fechner (1801–1887), the first psychologist to invent statistical methods to measure psychological constructs,[2] paved the way for Wilhelm Wundt (1832–1920), the father of experimental psychology, to found the first psychology lab and establish psychology as an independent academic discipline.[3] He inspired many psychologists to dedicate themselves to improving experimental procedures for studying psychological issues. During this time, statistical development joined in to accelerate psychological methodology and enabled it to claim its status as a science. That is, Sir Francis Galton (1822–1911) invented the survey method[4] and the idea of the correlation coefficient.[5] It was also Galton who inspired Karl Pearson (1857–1936), a mathematical biologist, to develop statistical techniques including, among others, the Pearson correlation, chi-square, and regression,[6] on which we have heavily relied for quantitative studies not just in psychology, but also in other disciplines.

Box 1.1

The contribution of qualitative methods in psychology

Although it was the quantitative methods that led to the recognition of scientific psychology, the contributions of qualitative methods cannot be ignored. For example, Sir Francis Galton (1822-1911) invented the free association technique for studying memory[7] and the introspection method for studying higher mental processes.[8] These methods were improved, used, and advocated by the founder of psychoanalysis, Sigmund Freud (1856-1939),[9] who invented the dream analysis[10] and projective technique.[11] Most notable among Freud's contributions is his use of case studies[12] which deepened our understanding of the psychological issues of patients with unique traumas; for example, Genie's case in developmental psychology[13] and H.M.'s case in cognitive psychology.[14]

The nineteenth century was not just the time when the rigorous and various research methods were developed as different schools of psychological thought also flourished at that time. Figure 1.1 shows the main schools of psychology. Although some schools of thought dominated at different times during the development of psychology, many modern psychologists have acknowledged the fact that the complicated human mind cannot be fully understood without input from all the schools of thought.[15] This acknowledgement has led to an integrated model of psychological thought that takes into account the biological, psychological, and social factors.[16]

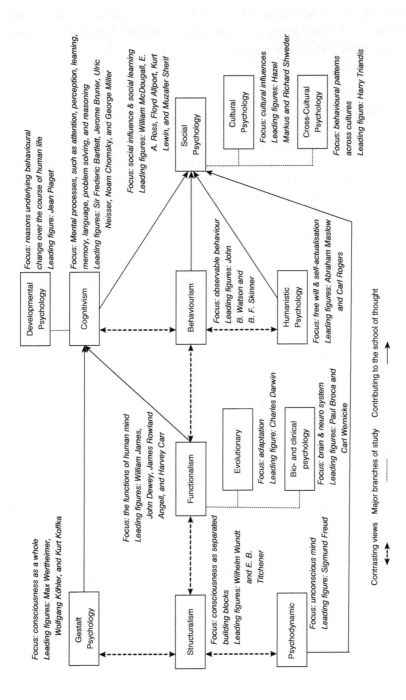

Figure 1.1 Main schools of psychological thought

Gestalt Psychology

Focus: consciousness as a whole
Leading figures: Max Wertheimer,
Wolfgang Köhler, and Kurt Koffka

Developmental Psychology

Focus: reasons underlying behavioural
change over the course of human life
Leading figure: Jean Piaget

Cognitivism

Focus: Mental processes, such as attention, perception, learning,
memory, language, problem solving, and reasoning
Leading figures: Sir Frederic Bartlett, Jerome Bruner, Ulric
Neisser, Noam Chomsky, and George Miller

Social Psychology

Focus: social influence & social learning
Leading figures: William McDougall, E.
A. Ross, Floyd Allport, Kurt
Lewin, and Muzafer Sherif

Cultural Psychology

Focus: cultural influences
Leading figures: Hazel
Markus and Richard Shweder

Cross-Cultural Psychology

Focus: behavioural patterns
across cultures
Leading figure: Harry Triandis

Behaviourism

Focus: observable behaviour
Leading figures: John
B. Watson and
B. F. Skinner

Humanistic Psychology

Focus: free will & self-actualisation
Leading figures: Abraham Maslow
and Carl Rogers

Functionalism

Focus: the functions of human mind
Leading figures: William James,
John Dewey, James Rowland
Angell, and Harvey Carr

Evolutionary

Focus: adaptation
Leading figure: Charles Darwin

Bio- and clinical psychology

Focus: brain & neuro system
Leading figures: Paul Broca and
Carl Wernicke

Structuralism

Focus: consciousness as separated
building blocks
Leading figures: Wilhelm Wundt
and E. B.
Titchener

Psychodynamic

Focus: unconscious mind
Leading figure: Sigmund Freud

Contrasting views   Major branches of study   Contributing to the school of thought

Among all the schools of psychological thought, five schools that are the most relevant to consumer behaviour are briefly introduced below: functionalism, behaviourism, humanistic psychology, cognitivism, and social psychology.

Functionalism

The primary interest of functionalism lies in the functions of the human mind. Functionalists believe that mind activities are a stream of ongoing processes, which cannot be broken down to static conscious states and it is this point where functionalists diverged from structuralists (Figure 1.1; later functionalism gradually replaced structuralism). These ongoing processes are revealed in habits, knowledge, and perception, and are constantly engaged in reacting to the environment.[17] Ongoing mental processes are therefore useful, and functionalists are interested in how they are used in guiding behaviour.[18]

Functionalism is closely related to evolutionary psychology, bio-psychology, and clinical psychology; all of which are rooted in biology and all of which focus on the functions of the human mind.

- *Evolutionary psychology*: with the focus on the adaptation of the human mind to its environment (which can be applied to explain consumer behaviour; see Chapter 10 in this book)
- *Bio-psychology*: with the focus on brain and neuroscience that explores how biological factors, such as genes, hormones, and the nervous system, influence mental processes and behaviour
- *Clinical psychology*: a branch of bio-psychology, but with the focus on mental illness or brain injury

This heavy emphasis on biology was because early psychologists were physicians, and in the nineteenth century psychology was often referred to as psychophysics. As a matter of fact, "psychology as we know it today is an offspring of the marriage of philosophy and life sciences".[19] To the modern day, bio-psychology lays the foundations for the neurosciences, relying on such methods as brain imaging techniques (e.g. EEG, fMRI), eye tracking, and biometric techniques (e.g. heart rate, blood pressure), to study the relationship between stimuli and brain functions.

Behaviourism

Behaviourism started its development in the 1910s, and dominated the landscape of psychology in the US from the 1920s to 1950s. Behaviourism rejects the study of mind and consciousness, because behaviourists believe that scientific, objective psychology should focus on the study of behaviour, which is observable.[20] Psychology, therefore, is the science of behaviour, rather than the science of mind. To behaviourists, behaviour is learned and determined (i.e. controlled) by the environment,[21] and as a result free will is a myth and has no place in our understanding of behaviour.[22] Chapter 4 ("Consumer Implicit Cognition") and Chapter 9 ("Environmental Psychology and Consumer Behaviour") in this book give a flavour of behaviourism.

Box 1.2

Key concepts in behaviourism

Conditioning, or learning, is at the heart of behaviourism. How is a behaviour learned? To behaviourists, behaviour is learned via classical conditioning or operant conditioning (also known as instrumental conditioning):

Classical conditioning is a reflex-like behaviour that can occur in response to an unrelated stimulus after the subject learns that the occurrence of the unrelated stimulus is paired with a related stimulus.[23] The most notable research was Pavlov's experiment with dog salivation.[24] Every time before Pavlov fed his dog, he rang a bell, and over time, the dog learned that food would be presented after the bell rang. The dog would, therefore, start salivating every time it heard the bell ringing even without the food being present (Figure 1.2).

Salivation is a reflex behaviour in the presence of food . . .

To train the "conditioned stimulus" is to pair the stimulus with the unconditioned stimulus

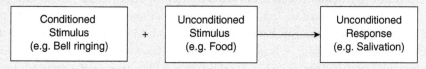

Over time, the "conditioned stimulus" will be learned, and the unconditioned response will become conditioned. That is, the response will occur in the presence of the conditioned stimulus without the unconditioned stimulus.

Figure 1.2 Mechanism of classical conditioning

(Continued)

Operant conditioning extends classical conditioning by focusing on the experiences that follow the action, for it is these experiences that provide a learning mechanism and result in behaviour. These experiences are called "reinforcement".[25] To put it simply, good behaviour earns rewards, which result in good experiences that make it more likely that one will maintain the same good behaviour in the future (Figure 1.3). On the other hand, poor behaviour brings punishment, which makes it more likely that one will try to avoid in the future by stopping the poor behaviour (Figure 1.3). Over time, the association between the cue (the situation) and the response (the behaviour) is presented as a habit,[26] and various habits comprise a repertoire of behavioural patterns, which Skinner[27] referred to as personality.

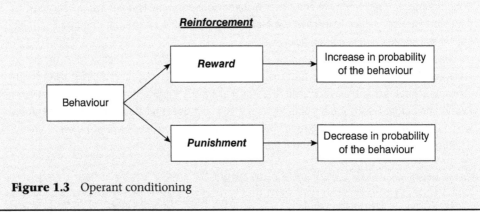

Figure 1.3   Operant conditioning

Humanistic psychology

Humanistic psychology rejects behaviourism's view of determinism. Humanistic psychologists believe that people have an "actualising tendency", a tendency to move toward fulfilment of potential by closing the gap between their actual and ideal self.[28] In Maslow's terminology, it is called self-actualising.[29] Rogers' and Maslow's humanistic views suggest that people are inherently good, and motivated for good behaviour. Ill behaviour, if it occurs, is because people try to adapt to an environment over which they do not have control. May, however, extends humanistic psychology by arguing that people are capable of creating environments.[30] In this case, good or poor behaviour is in the hands of the actor, rather than the environment, and we are not the victim of our environments because an alternative choice is always available.[31] Regardless of whether people are inherently good or not, humanistic psychologists stress people's unique freedom of will to act. We are able to decide how to act (or not to act) and how we act, and our behaviour is not determined for us by the environment we are in. See Chapter 7 ("Consumer Motivation") and Chapter 8 ("Consumer Identity") of this book to see traces of the humanistic view of psychology.

Cognitivism

The cognitive perspective of psychology surpassed behaviourism to become the dominant school of thought in psychology between the 1950s and 1970s in the United States. This shift from behaviourism to cognitivism is often referred to as the cognitive revolution, and marks the birth of cognitive science;[32] however, cognitivism emerged long before the cognitive revolution. Psychology in Europe was not as heavily impacted on by behaviourism as in the US, so the cognitive revolution was more of a phenomenon in the US, but it did start to bring together the psychologists in the US and Europe.[33] For example, the pioneering work of Sir Frederic Bartlett (1886–1969), from Cambridge, on memory, Jean Piaget (1896–1980), from Geneva, on children's mind, and A. R. Luria (1902–1977), from Moscow, on neuropsychology inspired many cognitive psychologists in the US.

Cognitivism can be summarised in one word: thinking. This view firmly sits cognitivism in opposition to behaviourism, which claims human behaviour is a matter of conditioning, not a result of thinking. The cognitive view of psychology focuses on the conscious thought, and stresses the importance of thinking and reasoning, which is a characteristic unique to human beings. The cognitive perspective studies how our thoughts influence how we interpret different situations, and how our interpretation influences our behaviour. It is, therefore, sometimes referred to as information-processing psychology (Figure 1.4).

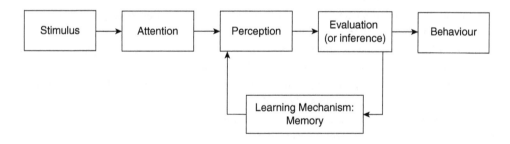

Figure 1.4 A cognitive model of information processing

The concept of information processing has influenced and also been influenced by the development of computer science on the areas of working memory (RAM in computer language), long-term memory (hard drives), and problem-solving (artificial intelligence). Cognitive psychology has significantly influenced how consumer psychology is understood, and details can be found in Chapter 2 ("Consumer Knowledge"), Chapter 3 ("Consumer Inference and Evaluation"), Chapter 4 ("Consumer Implicit Cognition"), and Chapter 6 ("Consumer Emotions"). Two disciplines closely related to cognitive psychology are:

- *Developmental psychology*: with the focus on cognitive and behavioural change over the course of human life (which can be applied to explain consumer behaviour; see Chapter 5 in this book)
- *Linguistics*: with the focus on language development (which can be applied to understand sound symbolism in Chapter 4, "Consumer Implicit Cognition")

Social psychology

Social psychology shares many views of cognitivism that stress the importance of thinking, but with a focus on how people interpret their *social* situation. Early social psychology topics focused on attitude and behavioural change,[34] impression formation,[35] and conformity,[36] and then later merged with the cognitive perspective to investigate attribution,[37] social learning,[38] and self-concept.[39]

Heavily influenced by sociology, social psychology became popular because of its usefulness in solving practical social problems. As a result, significant development and applications of social psychology took place around the time of significant social issues, such as the Great Depression in the 1930s and the Holocaust in the 1940s. However, issues of replicability and research ethics led social psychology to a crisis during the cognitive revolution. In particular, the replicability issues were concerned with the validity of the use of simulation, which is found to be difficult to re-create the real social situation, and therefore begs the question of whether the experimental results from social psychology would repeat in reality.[40] The other troubling issue is with ethics, as experiments in social psychology often used role-playing, which could potentially put participants in an unpleasant situation. For example, one of the most famous social psychology experiments, Zimbardo's Stanford prison experiment in 1971, involving students at Stanford University playing at being prison guards and inmates. The results not only failed to replicate in a BBC version of the original study with a more refined experimental procedure,[41] but the study also involved participants playing prison guards behaving aggressively and brutally, not to mention those playing inmates suffering pain and humiliation during the experiment.[42] Social psychology did not gain its rightful place until ethical guidelines improved and experimental procedures were refined (by borrowing from cognitive psychology) in the 1980s.[43] Since then, social psychology has been clearly distinct from sociology: the former examines micro social issues (i.e. how individuals behave within a society), whereas the latter investigates macro social issues (i.e. how entire social groups function within society).[44] It has also expanded to investigate cultural influences under the branch of cultural and cross-cultural psychology.

- *Cultural psychology*: with the focus on cultural influences on behaviour and mental processes. Culture refers to different social categories, including, race, ethnicity, socioeconomic class, and religion
- *Cross-cultural psychology*: with the focus on the similarities and differences in value and behavioural patterns across cultures

Social and cultural influences by and large are one and the same; therefore, social and cultural psychology are often combined and referred to as the sociocultural perspective of psychology.

1.2 DEVELOPMENT OF CONSUMER PSYCHOLOGY

A brief historical account

Consumer psychology, using psychological concepts and methods to understand consumer behaviour, is applied psychology. The first published work appeared in 1900 by Harlow Gale, the founder of the psychology of advertising, on advertising and psychology, and not long after that in 1903, the first book, *The Psychology of Advertising in Theory and Practice*, by Walter Dill Scott, was published.[45] They paved the way for the increased interest in consumer psychology that started from industry in around the 1920s, when media underwent a significant change (i.e. the evolution of newspaper print and the invention and commercial use of radio) and mass production became possible.[46] This interest grew out of the practicality of businesses wanting their advertisements to more effectively persuade consumers to buy, and also of some psychologists, including Daniel Starch,[47] Harry Hollingworth,[48] Albert T. Poffenberger,[49] and Howard K. Nixon,[50] who used psychological concepts to understand advertising effectiveness. Most notable was the founder of behaviourism, John B. Watson, who left academia in 1920 to join the then biggest advertising agency in the US, J. Walter Thompson, to use his earlier work on basic emotions (love, fear, and rage) in order to increase the effectiveness of advertisements.[51]

The increased interest in industry did not encourage psychologists to devote much scholarly attention to consumer psychology until the 1950s,[52] when the term "consumer psychology" started to be used.[53] Since then, academic research in consumer psychology had gradually gained a momentum that led to two significant developments in the 1960s – the American Psychological Association (APA) established Division 23 to focus on consumer psychology in 1962 (which later became an independent entity of the APA and was renamed as the Society for Consumer Psychology in 1988), and the flagship organisation in consumer research, the Association for Consumer Research (ACR), was founded in 1969. The ACR started the world's first annual conference focusing on consumer research in 1970 in the United States, and its annual conference is still the largest conference of consumer researchers from all over the world today. To extend the popularity of the ACR from North America, the ACR started its international spin-off groups and expanded to Europe in 1992, to Asia-Pacific in 1994, and to Latin America in 2006.

The first journal devoted to consumer research, *Journal of Consumer Research*, launched in 1974, was followed by *Psychology & Marketing* ten years later and *Journal of Consumer Psychology* in 1992. Many journals with strong applications of psychology were born to specialise in different areas of consumer behaviour (e.g. *Journal of Retailing* on the impact of shopping environment, *Journal of Services Marketing* on the impact of service encounters, and *Journal of Interactive Marketing* on the impact of interactive media) or different types of consumers (e.g. *International Marketing Review* on international consumers and *Tourism Management* on tourists). The annual *Consumer Psychology Review* launched in 2018, 68 years later than the first issue of the *Annual Review of Psychology*, a similar journal in psychology. See Figure 1.5 for the timeline of the development of consumer psychology. Compared with psychology, consumer psychology is a young discipline, but it has significantly benefited from the development of psychology.

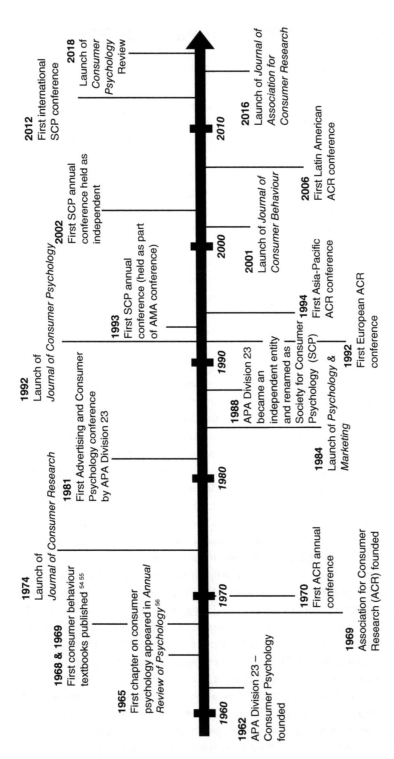

Figure 1.5 The development of consumer psychology since 1960s – timeline

The evolution of the theoretical development in consumer psychology

Prior to 1960

Heavily influenced by different schools of thought in psychology, early consumer psychologists shifted their theoretical attention with the development of the psychological concepts: from Wundt's focus on consciousness, to Watson's focus on behaviour and Freud's focus on motivation.[57]

1960s–1980s: classic attitude theories

The cognitive revolution significantly contributed to the development of the classic attitude theories that were heavily applied in consumer research. Influenced by the information processing theory of the cognitive psychology and economic theories,[58] the classic theories of attitudes assume that people are rational beings and take all available information into consideration. These assumptions are reflected in the early consumer decision-making models, including the Howard Sheth model of buyer behaviour,[59] the EKB (Engel–Kollat–Blackwell) model,[60] and the Bettman model.[61] These early consumer decision-making models considered various aspects, including actual and symbolic product attributes,[62] personal and social influences,[63] and internal and external information search.[64]

Despite the fact that these models make reasonable and conceptual sense, the complication of these models renders them difficult to apply in real situations and empirical evidence is hard to obtain. Besides, what consumer psychologists and advertising/marketing practitioners were most interested in was to determine how attitudes were formed and how they could be changed, as attitudes are strong predictors of behaviour. This is the evaluation stage in the consumer decision-making model (Figure 1.6) where consumers form their attitudes, or preferences, in order to decide which products or brands to purchase. Therefore, instead of using the earlier consumer decision-making models, researchers and practitioners became interested in the attitude-behaviour linkage, which resulted in applying the dominant theories of attitude – Fishbein's multi-attribute model of attitude[65] was the first, which was later replaced by Fishbein and Ajzen's theory of reasoned action[66] and then by Ajzen's theory of planned behaviour[67] (Box 1.3).

Box 1.3

Ajzen's Theory of Planned Behaviour

The theory of planned behaviour suggests three factors that determine our behavioural intentions, leading to our eventual behaviour:

(Continued)

1. our attitudes toward the behaviour;
2. social pressure we experience about the behaviour; and
3. perceived behavioural control, which suggests the degree to which we are able to perform a specific behaviour, which is similar to the concept of self-efficacy suggesting one's confidence in achieving a goal by performing a specific behaviour.[68] In Ajzen's conceptualisation, behaviour is not just a function of behavioural intention, but also a function of perceived behavioural control. In other words, perceived behavioural control both directly and indirectly predict our behaviour via behavioural intention.

The change to the theory of reasoned action helped better predict behaviour, which resulted in it becoming the dominant theory of attitudes in consumer research later on.[69]

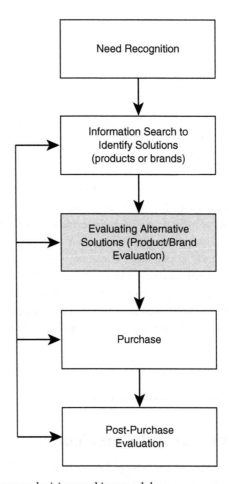

Figure 1.6   Classic consumer decision-making model

1980s-2000s: contemporary attitude theories

Since the late 1980s, many psychologists started to challenge the classic attitude theories by questioning the assumptions of these theories in that behaviour is not always rational and people may not be able to take all information available into consideration like a computer. For example, Kahneman and Tversky's prospect theory suggests that people's decision-making and information processing is easily subjected to manipulation (i.e. the framing effect; see Chapter 4), thereby placing a different weight on the same piece of information depending on how the information is presented.[70] Another example is Chaiken's proposal that information processing can be largely categorised as a heuristic or analytic information processing mode.[71]

This idea led to the development of the well-known elaboration likelihood model by Petty and Cacioppo who proposed that involvement determines whether people use an analytic information-processing mode by paying attention to the analytic-relevant (central) information, or use a heuristic information-processing mode by paying attention to the analytic-irrelevant (peripheral) information.[72] This idea was ground-breaking and took how consumers read advertisement information to the next level by emphasising the fact that, in an advertisement, the aesthetic aspects can be as important as the product attribute information,[73] and that pre-attention can play a significant role.[74] This stream of research laid down the foundation for later studies in automatic processing[75] and subliminal information processing[76] that stress the importance of nonconsciousness in information processing to attitude formation.

In addition to the contemporary attitude theories, another stream of research started to appear arguing for the role of the experiential aspects of consumption. Holbrook and Hirschman's seminar paper pioneered in this area,[77] and led to the development in consumer culture research, focusing on meaning, symbolism, and the ideology of consumption,[78] paved the way for research that shifted attention to experiences, satisfaction, and emotion, and laid the foundation for the acceptance of qualitative approaches to studying consumer behaviour in the 1990s and beyond.[79]

2000s-present

Two major developments took place in the late 1990s: (1) an integrative view of psychological thought appeared and (2) attention shifted from the comprehensive attitude or information-processing models to the more specific psychological theories for understanding consumer behaviour.[80] These two developments encouraged the application of more specific psychological theories to consumer psychology by integrating traditional thought with contemporary theories, and brought about a flourishing stream of research that can be roughly grouped into three areas.

Identity research

Benefiting from personality research[81] and symbolic consumption, an idea that consumption can be a representation of self-identity (i.e. we are what we shop),[82] identity research using self-congruity started to grow.[83] This growth led to Aaker's seminal development of the brand personality scale[84] that became one of the most popularly studied constructs in consumer psychology for at least two decades. Aaker's brand personality concept led to two other widespread areas of research: brand relationships and brand communities. Fournier extended Aaker's personification metaphor to the next level by using theories from the interpersonal relationship literature, and developed the idea of brand relationships,[85] which has been extensively studied and applied. Building on the branding literature and interpersonal relationship theories, Muñiz and O'Guinn shifted the attention from Fournier's brand–consumer relationships to consumer–consumer relationships centring on brands, and conceptualised the idea of brand communities.[86] Research attention originally focused on off-line brand communities, but the invention of social media in the mid-2000s has spurred the brand-community research into online applications.

Emotion

Attention on consumption experiences has led to research into consumer emotions. There are two streams of emotion research that have become widely investigated. One focuses on the basic emotions,[87] including happiness, anger, and fear; for example, how consumers respond to different kinds of happiness – excitement versus tranquillity, how anger shapes consumers' complaint behaviour in service encounters, or how mood (a low-intensity affective state, as opposed to high-intensity emotional state) changes consumer behaviour in a retailing environment. The other stream is extended from the research into brand relationships: brand emotions. This stream of research has encouraged the development in brand trust,[88] brand attachment,[89] brand love,[90] and brand hate[91] to name a few.

Motivation

Motivation research has revived since the 2000s. However, unlike the motivation research in the 1950s, it does not rely on Freud's psychoanalytic theories. Motivation research during these two decades focuses more on the impact of our goals on our attention and information processing.[92] Another growing area is motivation (1) for self-control through our regulatory focus – prevention versus promotion focus[93] and (2) for understanding the reasons for self-control failure.[94]

All these three areas of research are related to self-esteem, and, together with the growing interest in the subjective well-being, they contribute to the rise of research in consumer well-being (happiness), which may dominate the next era of consumer research.[95]

The evolution of research methods in consumer psychology

The survey method dominated consumer research in the initial development of consumer psychology, but in the 1990s–2000s, the experimental methods took over the survey method

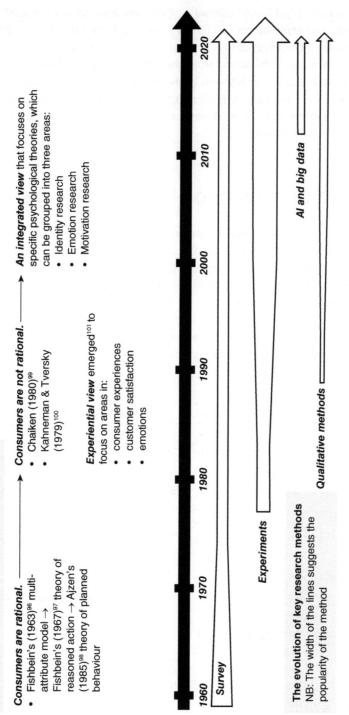

The evolution of key theoretical concepts adopted

Consumers are rational.
* Fishbein's (1963)[96] multi-attribute model →
  Fishbein's (1967)[97] theory of reasoned action → Ajzen's (1985)[98] theory of planned behaviour

Consumers are not rational. ——→
* Chaiken (1980)[99]
* Kahneman & Tversky (1979)[100]

Experiential view emerged[101] to focus on areas in:
* consumer experiences
* customer satisfaction
* emotions

An integrated view that focuses on specific psychological theories, which can be grouped into three areas:
* Identity research
* Emotion research
* Motivation research

The evolution of key research methods
NB: The width of the lines suggests the popularity of the method

1960   1970   1980   1990   2000   2010   2020

Survey

Experiments

Qualitative methods

AI and big data

Figure 1.7 The evolution of the theoretical and methodological development in consumer psychology

and became the predominant methodology; this trend can now be seen in the flagship journals in consumer psychology: *Journal of Consumer Research* and *Journal of Consumer Psychology*. Survey and experiments can both be commonly found in today's consumer psychology research with the experiments given more prestige status.[102] The slow, but steady, growth of qualitative methods started from the 1990s[103] with the launch of journals specialising in qualitative consumer research in the late 1990s, such as *Consumption Markets & Culture* and *Qualitative Market Research*. Currently, about 15–20% of publications adopt this methodology.[104] All of this development suggests that consumer psychologists have accepted the merit of the qualitative methods.

1.3 OUTLINE OF THIS BOOK

One of the key strengths of this book is a systematic inclusion of the main psychological theories that have been applied to consumer psychology. The inclusion is by no means exhaustive, as there are too many theories in the psychology literature to include them all. Nevertheless, this book introduces the key psychological theories that surround the evolution of the theoretical development in consumer psychology in order to provide a comprehensive understanding of the application of psychology in consumer studies. Therefore, the book deliberately includes a section on the underpinning psychological basis in each topic prior to discussing the applications in consumer behaviour, and the topics are summarised in Table 1.1.

Table 1.1   Outline of this book

Chapter Title	Psychological Theories	Topics to be discussed
Chapter 2 - Consumer Knowledge	Cognitive psychology - analytic mode of information processing	• Memory • Knowledge structure
Chapter 3 - Consumer Evaluation and Inferences	Cognitive psychology - dual information processing mode: analytic versus heuristic information processing	Analytic information processing: • Category-based inferences • Causal inferences Heuristic information processing: • Cognitive illusion (the framing effect)
Chapter 4 - Consumer Implicit Cognition	Cognitive psychology - heuristic information processing	• Automatic learning • Automatic information processing

Chapter 5 - Consumer Development and Socialisation	An integrated view of cognitive, social, and bio-psychology with a focus on the development of cognitive ability	• Young consumers
		  ○ 3-7 years old
		  ○ 7-11 years old
		  ○ 11-16 years old
		• Aging consumers (65+ years old)

Chapter Title	Psychological Theories	Topics to be discussed
Chapter 6 – Emotions in Consumer Behaviour	An integrated view of cognitive and social psychology	• Happiness • Pride • Sadness • Fear • Anger • Regret • Guilt
Chapter 7 – Consumer Motivation	An integrated view of cognitive psychology, humanistic psychology, and social psychology	• Expectancy-value theory of motivation • Maslow's hierarchy of needs • Goal-directed information processing • Self-regulation and self-regulation failure
Chapter 8 – Consumer Identity	An integrated view of cognitive and social psychology	• Self-identity • Social identity
Chapter 9 – Environmental Psychology and Consumer Behaviour	An integrated view of cognitive psychology (the emotional theories and implicit cognition) and behaviourism	• Music • Scent • Lighting • Touch • Crowding
Chapter 10 – Evolutionary Psychology and Consumer Behaviour	A functional view of psychology with bio-psychological influences	• The survival drives • The mating drives • The kin care drives • The affiliation drives
Chapter 11 – Consumer Well-Being	An integrated view of social psychology and bio-psychology	• Self-esteem • Pleasure

Chapter 12 – Research Methods in Consumer Psychology	n/a	• Qualitative research methods
		  o Interviews
		  o Netnography
		• Quantitative research methods
		  o Survey
		  o Experiments

1.4 SUMMARY

1. Separating psychology from philosophy, Wilhelm Wundt (1832–1920) established psychology as a scientific and independent academic discipline in 1920. The initial development of psychology benefited from medical sciences, as at that time psychologists were initially trained as physicians. The scientific status was given to

psychology because of the pioneers' efforts in developing rigorous methods, involving using experiments, objective measurements, and statistics.

2. The contemporary perception of psychology is an integrated view that combines the traditional schools of psychological thought depending on which aspect of psychology is under investigation. The main schools of psychological thought include functionalism (focusing on the functions of mind), behaviourism (focusing on overt behaviour), cognitivism (focusing on mental processes), humanistic psychology (focusing on self-actualisation), and social psychology (focusing on social influences and learning).

3. Although publications of consumer psychology appeared in the early 1900s, prior to the 1950s research in consumer psychology was limited. The growth of consumer psychology research contributed to the APA's (American Psychological Association) inception of Division 23, the first organisation that focused on consumer psychology, in 1962, and the initiation of Association for Consumer Research (ACR), the flagship organisation in consumer research, in 1969. Both organised annual conferences to gather thoughts on consumer psychology, which later led to the launch of the pioneering journals that solely focus on consumer psychology: *Journal of Consumer Research* in 1974 and *Journal of Consumer Psychology* in 1992.

4. Psychological theories have significantly contributed to the theoretical development of consumer psychology. In the 1960s–1980s, it was the classic attitude theories that dominated consumer psychology. They relied on the analytical model of information processing to focus on attention, memory, and evaluation. In the 1980s–2000s, the classic attitude theories gave way to the contemporary attitude theories, which challenged the view of rational consumers who take all available information into consideration like a computer. As a result, research on heuristic information processing and implicit cognition started to emerge and flourish. During this time, attention also shifted to stress the importance of consumer experience, which led to the development of research in areas of customer satisfaction and emotion. From the 2000s onward, an integrated view came into the spotlight and fostered research in the areas of identity, emotion, and motivation.

5. In the early days, the main research method was the survey, but from the 1990s experiments started to emerge and later took over the survey as the main and preferred methodology. Since the 1990s, academic journals started to accept qualitative research methods, although qualitative methods are still not the mainstream methodology (about 15–20% of consumer research papers adopt this methodology); however, their appearance in journals is now commonly accepted.

DISCUSSION QUESTIONS

1. Which school of psychological thought do you think is most relevant to consumer psychology? Discuss.

2. Discuss how psychological theories have influenced the development of consumer psychology.

FURTHER READING

- Kassarjian, H. H., & Goodstein, R. C. (2010). The Emergence of Consumer Research. In P. Maclaran, M. Saren, B. Stern, & M. Tadajewski (eds), *The SAGE Handbook of Marketing Theory* (pp. 59–88). Los Angeles: SAGE.
- Malter, M. S., Holbrook, M. B., Kahn, B. E., Parker, J. R., & Lehmann, D. R. (2020). The Past, Present, and Future of Consumer Research. *Marketing Letters, 31*(2), 137 –149.
- Pham, M. T. (2013). The Seven Sins of Consumer Psychology. *Journal of Consumer Psychology, 23*(4), 411–423.
- Schumann, D. W., Haugtvedt, C. P., & Davidson, E. (2008). History of Consumer Psychology. In C. P. Haugtvedt, Herr, P. M., & F. R. Kardes (eds), *Handbook of Consumer Psychology* (pp. 3–28). New York: Psychology Press.

NOTES

1. Toulmin, S., & Leary, D. E. (1985). The Cult of Empiricism in Psychology, and Beyond. In S. Koch & D. E. Leary (eds), *A Century of Psychology as Science* (pp. 594–617). New York: McGraw-Hill.
2. Gregory, R. L. (1981). *Mind in Science: A History of Explanations in Psychology and Physics.* London: Weidenfeld & Nicolson.
3. Goodwin, C. J. (1999). *A History of Modern Psychology.* New York: John Wiley & Sons.
4. Ibid.
5. Leahey, T. H. (1994). *A History of Modern Psychology* (second edn). Englewood Cliffs, NJ: Prentice-Hall.
6. Porter, T. M. (2004). *Karl Pearson: The Scientific Life in a Statistical Age.* Princeton, NJ: Princeton University Press.
7. Nelson, D. L., McEvoy, C. L., & Dennis, S. (2000). What Is Free Association and What Does It Measure? *Memory & Cognition, 28*(6), 887–899.
8. Grossman, W. I. (1967). Reflections on the Relationships of Introspection and Psychoanalysis. *International Journal of Psycho-Analysis, 48,* 16–31.
9. Ibid; Zilboorg, G. (1952). Some Sidelights on Free Associations. *International Journal of Psycho-Analysis, 33,* 489–495.
10. Gutheil, E. A. (ed.) (1951). *The Handbook of Dream Analysis.* Oxford: Liveright.
11. Mosak, H. H. (1958). Early Recollections as a Projective Technique. *Journal of Projective Techniques, 22*(3), 302–311.
12. Smith, J. A. (2004). Reflecting on the Development of Interpretative Phenomenological Analysis and Its Contribution to Qualitative Research in Psychology. *Qualitative Research in Psychology, 1*(1), 39–54.
13. Curtiss, S. (1977). *Genie: A Psycholinguistic Study of a Modern-Day 'Wild Child'.* New York: Academic Press.
14. Corkin, S. (2013). *Permanent Present Tense: The Man With No Memory, and What He Taught the World.* New York: Basic Books.

15. Chaplin, J. P., & Krawiec, T. S. (1968). *Systems and Theories of Psychology*. London: Holt, Rinehart and Winston.

16. Engel, G. L. (1977). The Need for a New Medical Model: A Challenge for Biomedicine. *Science, 196*(4286), 129–136.

17. James, W. (1890). *The Principles of Psychology* (Vol. I). New York: Henry Folt and Company.

18. Carr, H. A. (1925). *Psychology: A Study of Mental Activity*. New York: Longmans, Green and Co.

19. Page 108 in Hearnshaw, L. S. (1987). *The Shaping of Modern Psychology*. London: Routledge & Kegan Paul.

20. Watson, J. B. (1913). Psychology as the Behaviorist Views It. *Psychological Review, 20*(2), 158–177; Watson, J. B. (1919). *Psychology: From the Standpoint of a Behaviorist*. Philadelphia: J. B. Lippincott.

21. Skinner, B. F. (1953). *Science and Human Behaviour*. New York: Macmillan.

22. Skinner, B. F. (1987). Whatever Happened to Psychology as the Science of Behavior? *American Psychologist, 42*(August), 780–786.

23. Watson, J. B., & Rayner, R. (1920). Conditioned Emotional Reactions. *Journal of Experimental Psychology, 3*(February), 1–14.

24. Pavlov, I. P. (1927). *Conditioned Reflexes*. Oxford: Oxford University Press.

25. Skinner, B. F. (1963). Operant Behavior. *American Psychologist, 18*(August), 503–515.

26. Miller, N. E., & Dollard, J. (1945). *Social Learning and Imitation*. London: Butler & Tanner.

27. Skinner, B. F. (1974). *About Behaviourism*. New York: Knopf.

28. Rogers, C. R. (1959). A Theory of Therapy, Personality, and Interpersonal Relationships, as Developed in the Client-Centred Framework. In S. Koch (ed.), *Psychology: A Study of a Science* (Vol. 3: Formulation of the Person and the Social Context, pp. 184–256). New York: McGraw-Hill.

29. Maslow, A. H. (1968). *Toward a Psychology of Being*. New York: Van Nostrand Reinhold.

30. May, R. (1982). The Problem of Evil: An Open Letter to Carl Rogers. *Journal of Humanistic Psychology, 22*(3), 10–21.

31. Kelly, G. A. (1955). *The Psychology of Personal Constructs* (Vol. 1: A Theory of Personality). New York: W. W. Norton.

32. Miller, G. A. (2003). The Cognitive Revolution: A Historical Perspective. *Trends in Cognitive Sciences, 7*(3), 141–144; Sperry, R. W. (1993). The Impact and Promise of the Cognitive Revolution. *American Psychologist, 48*(8), 878; Greenwood, J. D. (1999). Understanding the "Cognitive Revolution" in Psychology. *Journal of the History of the Behavioral Sciences, 35*(1), 1–22.

33. Miller, The Cognitive Revolution.

34. Festinger, L. (1957). *Theory of Cognitive Dissonance*. Evanston: Peterson; Lewin, K. (1936). *Principles of Topological Psychology*. New York: McGraw-Hill; Allport, F. H. (1924). *Social Psychology*. Boston: Houghton Mifflin.

35. Allport, F. H. (1924). *Social Psychology*. Boston: Houghton Mifflin.

36. Ibid; Sherif, M. (1936). *The Psychology of Social Norms*. New York: Harper; Thibaut, J. W., & Kelley, H. H. (1959). *The Social Psychology of Groups*. New York: John Wiley & Sons.

37. Weiner, B. (1985). An Attributional Theory of Achievement Motivation and Emotion. *Psychological Review, 92*(4), 548–573.

38. Bandura, A. (1986). *Social Foundations of Thought and Action: A Social Cognitive Theory.* Englewood Cliffs, NJ: Prentice Hall.

39. Tajfel, H., & Turner, J. (1979). An Integrative Theory of Intergroup Conflict. In G. A. Williams & S. Worchel (eds), *The Social Psychology of Intergroup Relations* (pp. 33–47). Belmont, CA: Wadsworth; Tajfel, H. (1982). Social Psychology of Intergroup Relations. *Annual Review of Psychology, 33*, 1–39.

40. Maxwell, S. E., Lau, M. Y., & Howard, G. S. (2015). Is Psychology Suffering from a Replication Crisis? What Does "Failure to Replicate" Really Mean? *American Psychologist, 70*(6), 487–498; Shrout, P. E., & Rodgers, J. L. (2018). Psychology, Science, and Knowledge Construction: Broadening Perspectives from the Replication Crisis. *Annual Review of Psychology, 69*, 487–510; Earp, B. D., & Trafimow, D. (2015). Replication, Falsification, and the Crisis of Confidence in Social Psychology. *Frontiers in Psychology, 6*, 621.

41. Reicher, S., & Haslam, S. A. (2006). Rethinking the Psychology of Tyranny: The BBC Prison Study. *British Journal of Social Psychology, 45*(1), 1–40.

42. Zimbardo, P. G. (1973). On the Ethics of Intervention in Human Psychological Research: With Special Reference to the Stanford Prison Experiment. *Cognition, 2*(2), 243–256.

43. Jones, E. E. (1985). Major Developments in Social Psychology During the Last Five Decades. In G. Lindzey & E. Aronson (eds), *Handbook of Social Psychology* (Vol. 1, pp. 47–107). New York: Random House.

44. Smith, E. R., & Mackie, D. M. (2007). *Social Psychology* (third edn). New York: Psychology Press.

45. Jacoby, J. (2001). Consumer Psychology. In N. J. Smelser & P. B. Baltes (eds), *International Encyclopedia of the Social & Behavioral Sciences* (Vol. 4, pp. 2674–2678). Amsterdam: Elsevier.

46. Jansson-Boyd, C. V., & Marlow, N. (2017). The History of Consumer Psychology. In C. V. Jansson-Boyd & M. J. Zawisza (eds), *Routledge International Handbook of Consumer Psychology* (pp. 3–17). Abingdon: Routledge.

47. Starch, D. (1914). *Advertising: Its Principles, Practice, and Technique.* Chicago: Scott, Foresman; Starch, D. (1923). *Principles of Advertising.* New York: McGraw-Hill.

48. Hollingworth, H. L., & Poffenberger, A. T. (1917). *The Sense of Taste.* Moffat, NY: Yard; Hollingworth, H. L. (1913). *Advertising and Selling: Principles of Appeal and Response.* Cambridge, MA: D. Appleton.

49. Poffenberger, A. T. (1925). *Psychology in Advertising.* Chicago: AW Shaw Company; Poffenberger, A. T. (1927). *Applied Psychology: Its Principles and Methods.* New York: Appleton.

50. Nixon, H. K. (1926). *An Investigation of Attention to Advertisements.* New York: D. Appleton.

51. Cohen, D. (1979). *J. B. Watson, The Founder of Behaviourism: A Biography.* London: Routledge & Kegan Paul.

52. Jacoby, Consumer Psychology.

53. Schumann, D. W., Haugtvedt, C. P., & Davidson, E. (2008). History of Consumer Psychology. In C. P. Haugtvedt, Herr, P. M., & F. R. Kardes (eds), *Handbook of Consumer Psychology* (pp. 3–28). New York: Psychology Press.

54. Engel, J. F., Kollat, D. T., & Blackwell, R. D. (1968). *Consumer Behavior.* New York, NY: Holt, Rinehart, Winston.
55. Howard, J. A., & Sheth, J. N. (1969). *The Theory of Buyer Behavior.* New York: John Wiley & Sons.
56. Twedt, D. W. (1965). Consumer Psychology. *Annual Review of Psychology, 16*(1), 265–294.
57. Ibid.
58. Jacoby, Consumer Psychology.
59. Howard, J. A., & Sheth, J. N. (1969). *The Theory of Buyer Behavior.* New York: John Wiley & Sons.
60. Engel et al., *Consumer Behavior.*
61. Bettman, J. R. (1979). *An Information Processing Theory of Consumer Choice.* Reading, MA: Addison-Wesley Publishing.
62. Howard & Sheth, *The Theory of Buyer Behavior.*
63. Engel et al., *Consumer Behavior.*
64. Bettman, J. R. (1979). *An Information Processing Theory of Consumer Choice.* Reading, MA: Addison-Wesley Publishing.
65. Fishbein, M. (1963). An Investigation of the Relationships between Beliefs about an Object and the Attitude toward That Object. *Human Relations, 16*(3), 233–239.
66. Ajzen, I., & Fishbein, M. (1969). The Prediction of Behavioral Intentions in a Choice Situation. *Journal of Experimental Social Psychology, 5*(4), 400–416; Fishbein, M., & Ajzen, I. (1975). *Belief, Attitude, Intention and Behavior: An Introduction to Theory and Research.* Reading, MA: Addison-Wesley Publishing; Ajzen, I., & Fishbein, M. (1970). The Prediction of Behavior from Attitudinal and Normative Variables. *Journal of Experimental Social Psychology, 6*(4), 466–487; Ajzen, I., & Fishbein, M. (1972). Attitudes and Normative Beliefs as Factors Influencing Behavioral Intentions. *Journal of Personality and Social Psychology, 21*(1), 1; Ajzen, I., & Fishbein, M. (1973). Attitudinal and Normative Variables as Predictors of Specific Behavior. *Journal of Personality and Social Psychology, 27*(1), 41–57.
67. Ajzen, I. (1985). From Intentions to Actions: A Theory of Planned Behavior. In J. Kuhl & J. Beckmann (eds), *Action Control: From Cognition to Behavior* (pp. 11–39). Berlin: Springer-Verlag.
68. Bandura, A. (1977). Self-Efficacy: Toward a Unifying Theory of Behavioral Change. *Psychological Review, 84*(2), 191–215.
69. Notani, A. S. (1998). Moderators of Perceived Behavioral Control's Predictiveness in the Theory of Planned Behavior: A Meta-Analysis. *Journal of Consumer Psychology, 7*(3), 247–271; Godin, G., & Kok, G. (1996). The Theory of Planned Behavior: A Review of Its Applications to Health-Related Behaviors. *American Journal of Health Promotion, 11*(2), 87–98; Chang, M. K. (1998). Predicting Unethical Behavior: A Comparison of the Theory of Reasoned Action and the Theory of Planned Behavior. *Journal of Business Ethics, 17*(16), 1825–1834.
70. Kahneman, D., & Tversky, A. (1979). Prospect Theory: An Analysis of Decision Under Risk. *Econometrica, 47*(2), 263–291.
71. Chaiken, S. (1980). Heuristic Versus Systematic Information Processing and the Use of Source Versus Message Cues in Persuasion. *Journal of Personality and Social Psychology, 39*(5), 752–766.

72. Petty, R. E., & Cacioppo, J. T. (1979). Issue Involvement Can Increase or Decrease Persuasion by Enhancing Message-Relevant Cognitive Responses. *Journal of Personality and Social Psychology*, *37*(10), 1915–1926; Petty, R. E., & Cacioppo, J. T. (1981). Issue Involvement as a Moderator of the Effects on Attitude of Advertising Content and Context. In K. B. Monroe (ed.), *NA – Advances in Consumer Research* (Vol. 8, pp. 20–24). Ann Arbor, MI: Association of Consumer Research; Petty, R. E., & Cacioppo, J. T. (1981). *Attitudes and Persuasion: Classic and Contemporary Approaches*. Boulder, CO: Westview Press; Petty, R. E., & Cacioppo, J. T. (1986). The Elaboration Likelihood Model of Persuasion. In R. E. Petty & J. T. Cacioppo (eds), *Communication and Persuasion: Central and Peripheral Routes to Attitude Change* (pp. 1–24). New York: Springer.

73. Petty, R. E., Cacioppo, J. T., & Schumann, D. (1983). Central and Peripheral Routes to Advertising Effectiveness: The Moderating Role of Involvement. *Journal of Consumer Research*, *10*(September), 135–146.

74. Greenwald, A. G., & Leavitt, C. (1984). Audience Involvement in Advertising: Four Levels. *Journal of Consumer Research*, *11*(June), 581–592.

75. Bargh, J. A., & Chartrand, T. L. (1999). The Unbearable Automaticity of Being. *American Psychologist*, *54*(7), 462–479; Fitzsimons, G. J., & Williams, P. (2000). Asking Questions Can Change Choice Behavior: Does It Do So Automatically or Effortfully? *Journal of Experimental Psychology: Applied*, *6*(3), 195–206; Hofmann, W., Friese, M., Gschwendner, T., Wiers, R. W., & Schmitt, M. (2008). Working Memory Capacity and Self-Regulatory Behavior: Toward an Individual Differences Perspective on Behavior Determination by Automatic Versus Controlled Processes. *Journal of Personality and Social Psychology*, *95*(4), 962–977; Aggarwal, P., & McGill, A. L. (2012). When Brands Seem Human, Do Humans Act Like Brands? Automatic Behavioral Priming Effects of Brand Anthropomorphism. *Journal of Consumer Research*, *39*(2), 307–323.

76. Bornstein, R. F. (1992). Subliminal Mere Exposure Effects. In R. F. Bornstein & T. S. Pittman (eds), *Perception Without Awareness: Cognitive, Clinical, and Social Perspectives* (pp. 191–210). New York: Guilford Press; Smith, K. H., & Rogers, M. (1994). Effectiveness of Subliminal Messages in Television Commercials: Two Experiments. *Journal of Applied Psychology*, *79*(6), 866–874; Theus, K. T. (1994). Subliminal Advertising and the Psychology of Processing Unconscious Stimuli: A Review of Research. *Psychology & Marketing*, *11*(3), 271–290; Trappey, C. (1996). A Meta-Analysis of Consumer Choice and Subliminal Advertising. *Psychology & Marketing*, *13*(5), 517–530.

77. Holbrook, M. B., & Hirschman, E. C. (1982). The Experiential Aspects of Consumption: Consumer Fantasies, Feelings, and Fun. *Journal of Consumer Research*, *9*(September), 132–140.

78. Arnould, E. J., & Thompson, C. J. (2005). Consumer Culture Theory (CCT): Twenty Years of Research. *Journal of Consumer Research*, *31*(March), 868–882.

79. Malter, M. S., Holbrook, M. B., Kahn, B. E., Parker, J. R., & Lehmann, D. R. (2020). The Past, Present, and Future of Consumer Research. *Marketing Letters*, *31*(2), 137–149.

80. Wang, X. S., Bendle, N. T., Mai, F., & Cotte, J. (2015). The Journal of Consumer Research at 40: A Historical Analysis. *Journal of Consumer Research*, *42*(1), 5–18.

81. McCrae, R. R. (1982). Consensual Validation of Personality Traits: Evidence From Self-Reports and Ratings. *Journal of Personality and Social Psychology, 43*(2), 293–303; McCrae, R. R., & Costa, P. T., Jr. (1987). Validation of the Five-Factor Model of Personality across Instruments and Observers. *Journal of Personality and Social Psychology, 52*(1), 81–90; Goldberg, L. R. (1993). The Structure of Phenotypic Personality Traits. *American Psychologist, 48*(1), 26–34; Eysenck, H. J. (1947). *Dimensions of Personality*. London: Routledge; Eysenck, H. J. (1970). *The Structure of Human Personality* (third edn). London: Methuen; Pervin, L. A. (1990). A Brief History of Modern Personality Theory. In L. A. Pervin (ed.), *Handbook of Personality Theory and Research* (pp. 3–18). New York: Guilford Press.

82. Levy, S. J. (1959). Symbols for Sale. *Harvard Business Review, 37*(July–August), 117–124; Belk, R. W. (1988). Possessions and the Extended Self. *Journal of Consumer Research, 15*(September), 139–168; Sirgy, M. J. (1982). Self-Concept in Consumer Behavior: A Critical Review. *Journal of Consumer Research, 9*(December), 287–300.

83. Sirgy, M. J. (1985). Using Self-Congruity and Ideal Congruity to Predict Purchase Motivation. *Journal of Business Research, 13*(3), 195–206; Sirgy, M. J., Johar, J. S., Samli, A. C., & Claiborne, C. B. (1991). Self-Congruity versus Functional Congruity: Predictors of Consumer Behavior. *Journal of the Academy of Marketing Science, 19*(4), 363–375; Sirgy, M. J., Grewal, D., & Mangleburg, T. (2000). Retail Environment, Self-congruity, and Retail Patronage: An Integrative Model and a Research Agenda. *Journal of Business Research, 49*(2), 127–138.

84. Aaker, J. L. (1997). Dimensions of Brand Personality. *Journal of Marketing Research, 34*(August), 347–356.

85. Fournier, S. (1998). Consumer and Their Brands: Developing Relationship Theory in Consumer Research. *Journal of Consumer Research, 24*(March), 343–373.

86. Muñiz, A. M., Jr., & O'Guinn, T. C. (2001). Brand Community. *Journal of Consumer Research, 27*(4), 412–432.

87. Russell, J. A., & Barrett, L. F. (1999). Core Effect, Prototypical Emotional Episodes, and Other Things Called Emotion: Distracting the Elephant. *Journal of Personality and Social Psychology, 76*(5), 805–819.

88. Chaudhuri, A., & Holbrook, M. B. (2001). The Chain of Effects from Brand Trust and Brand Affect to Brand Performance: The Role of Brand Loyalty. *Journal of Marketing, 65*(April), 81–93.

89. Escalas, J. E. (2004). Narrative Processing: Building Consumer Connections to Brands. *Journal of Consumer Psychology, 14*(1&2), 168–180; Thomson, M., MacInnis, D., & Park, C. W. (2005). The Ties That Bind: Measuring the Strength of Consumers' Emotional Attachments to Brands. *Journal of Consumer Psychology, 15*(1), 77–91.

90. Carroll, B. A., & Ahuvia, A. C. (2006). Some Antecedents and Outcomes of Brand Love. *Marketing Letters, 17*(2), 79–89.

91. Grégoire, Y., Tripp, T. M., & Legoux, R. (2009). When Customer Love Turns into Lasting Hate: The Effects of Relationship Strength and Time on Customer Revenge and Avoidance. *Journal of Marketing, 73*(November), 18–32.

92. Mack, A., & Rock, I. (1998). *Inattentional Blindness*. Boston: MIT Press; Simons, D. J., & Levin, D. T. (1997). Change Blindness. *Trends in Cognitive Sciences, 1*(7), 261–267.

93. Higgins, E. T. (1998). Promotion and Prevention: Regulatory Focus as a Motivational Principle. *Advances in Experimental Social Psychology, 30*, 1–46.

94. Baumeister, R. F., & Heatherton, T. F. (1996). Self-Regulation Failure: An Overview. *Psychological Inquiry, 7*(1), 1–15.

95. Kassarjian, H. H., & Goodstein, R. C. (2010). The Emergence of Consumer Research. In P. Maclaran, M. Saren, B. Stern, & M. Tadajewski (eds), *The SAGE Handbook of Marketing Theory* (pp. 59–88). Los Angeles: SAGE.

96. Fishbein, An Investigation of the Relationships between Beliefs about an Object and the Attitude toward That Object.

97. Ajzen & Fishbein, The Prediction of Behavioral Intentions in a Choice Situation; Fishbein & Ajzen, *Belief, Attitude, Intention and Behavior*; Ajzen & Fishbein, The Prediction of Behavior from Attitudinal and Normative Variables; Ajzen & Fishbein, Attitudes and Normative Beliefs as Factors Influencing Behavioral Intentions; Ajzen & Fishbein, Attitudinal and Normative Variables as Predictors of Specific Behavior.

98. Ajzen, From Intentions to Actions: A Theory of Planned Behavior.

99. Chaiken, Heuristic Versus Systematic Information Processing and the Use of Source Versus Message Cues in Persuasion.

100. Kahneman & Tversky, Prospect Theory: An Analysis of Decision Under Risk.

101. Holbrook & Hirschman, The Experiential Aspects of Consumption.

102. Rapp, J. M., & Hill, R. P. (2015). "Lordy, Lordy, Look Who's 40!" The Journal of Consumer Research Reaches a Milestone. *Journal of Consumer Research, 42*(1), 19–29.

103. Ibid.

104. Jacoby, Consumer Psychology.

2

CONSUMER KNOWLEDGE

─ Learning objectives ─

To explore, understand, and explain:

- the psychological bases and implications for consumer behaviour based on three systems of memory:
  - o sensory memory
  - o short-term (working) memory
  - o long-term memory
- the role of knowledge in information processing and decision-making and how it can be applied to consumer behaviour

2.1 INTRODUCTION

Consumers rely on their knowledge to process information, evaluate their options, and to consequently make a decision.[1] Consumer knowledge is accumulated as a result of consumer learning, via product usage experience for example, and any effective learning depends on memory.[2]

> Memory is the record of our personal past . . . It also involves the capacity to learn, to be influenced by prior experience, and to behave differently in the future as a

consequence of an experience. [Thus,] memory is the controller of all acquired human behaviour, including speech, conceptual knowledge, skilled activities, social interactions, and consumer preferences.[3]

This chapter will discuss consumer knowledge from two different angles. First, memory will be introduced as a multi-store concept; that is, sensory memory, short-term (working) memory, and long-term memory. Following the discussion of different memory systems, the concept of knowledge will then be introduced. In particular, the effect of schema congruity will be discussed, and how consumer familiarity and expertise influence information processing and decision-making will be examined.

2.2 MEMORY

Human memory can be seen as a multi-store concept, including sensory memory, short-term (working) memory, and long-term memory.[4] Table 2.1 summarises the characteristics of these memory systems that are discussed in more detail in this section.

Table 2.1   Characteristics of sensory, short-term (working), and long-term memory

Type of Memory	Duration	Capacity	Sources	Function
Sensory memory	Very brief • Auditory info: 2 seconds[5] • Visual info: 0.5 second[6]	Large	5 senses: vision, touch, smell, taste, and hearing	• Forming impression

Short-term (working) memory	18 seconds[7]	3-5 chunks[8]	Sensory and long-term memory	• Carrying out tasks at hand, including
				  o Language comprehension
				  o Learning
				  o Reasoning

Long-term memory	From a few days to a lifetime[9]	Massive[10]	• Factual details • Personal experiences (learning)	• Using conceptual knowledge to carry out professional and personal activities • Using motor and perceptual skills to carry out daily activities

Sensory memory

The psychological basis

Sensory memory is a storage of sensory information, which comes from our five senses: vision (visual information), touch (tactile information), smell (olfactory information), taste (gustatory information), and hearing (auditory information) – see Chapter 9 for more information about how we process sensory information. Sensory information contributes to the formation of our perceptions,[11] which are recorded in our memory.[12] The capacity of sensory memory is relatively large, but the length of time information can be stored is quite short. For example, the duration for auditory information storage is about 2 seconds,[13] and stored visual information decays within about 0.5 second.[14] Because the duration of retained information is short, we are able to see cartoons, films, or TV programmes as unbroken motion, when in fact they consist of a series of single pictures, called film frames, which are shown in very quick succession: usually at a rate of 24 frames per second.[15] Even though during the transition from frame to frame there is nothing to be seen, our sensory memory edits out the very short time period between individual frames so that we perceive the movement in cartoons, for example, as a continuum.[16]

Broadbent's theory of attention

Broadbent's theory of attention suggests that we experience sensorial stimuli all the time, but the information is usually unprocessed, and therefore does not produce meanings to the individual who receives the information.[17] *The cocktail party phenomenon* explains why some sensory information is processed while some is not. This phenomenon, first observed by Cherry, suggests that we are able to follow one conversation even when several people are talking at the same time around us – which is usually the case at a party, hence it is called the cocktail party phenomenon.[18] This initial finding indicates that people have the ability to "tune in" and "tune out" to different sources of auditory information. Later research found that people tended to notice when their names were called even when their names were called in a noisy environment, for example at a party,[19] and this finding suggests that the key factor in tuning in to information for further processing is relevance.

Implications for consumer behaviour

Attention to print advertisements

Attention capture depends on the two factors:[20]

- The *extrinsic* factor: the design of the features in advertisements, including colour, intensity (complexity), and orientation (size and shape)

- The *intrinsic* factor: personal motivation to process information, including involvement and familiarity, or personal motivation, can also be influenced by advertising tactics; for example, the use of borrowed interest appeal such as using cute puppies or beautiful women/men as agents to attract attention.[21]

Research shows that each advertisement in a magazine, if it captured the attention of the subjects, is attended to for 1.73 seconds on average (0.7 seconds for text, 0.6 seconds for picture, and 0.4 seconds for brand).[22] There are three main effects accounting for attention capture in these advertisements (Figure 2.1):

- *Pictorial superiority effect*

    Compared with brand and text, pictures are superior in capturing readers' attention, regardless of their size.[23]

- *Text superiority effect*

    Changes in text size trump the changes in pictorial size and brand size in obtaining readers' attention; 70% of attention change comes from changes in text size.[24] Specifically, a 1% increase in text surface size increases attention selection by 0.5% and attention duration by 0.16%, which leads to a 0.85% increase in gaze duration.[25]

- *Brand superiority effect*

    If attention is first drawn to the brand, more attention can be drawn to the pictorial and text elements, compared with the amount of attention transfer from pictorial and text to brand.[26] Specifically, a 1% increase in attention to the brand increases attention to the pictorial by 0.22% and to the text by 0.51%.[27]

Attention to advertising banners on webpages

Many people claim that they intentionally block out advertisements when browsing websites – this behaviour is referred to as *banner blindness*. Research has suggested, however, that online advertisement avoidance is not as straightforward as it sounds. For example, an experiment featuring text-only banner advertisements found that more than 80% of the subjects paid attention to at least one of four advertisements when they browsed eight pages of web content.[28] This level of attention to online advertisements is consistent even if the advertisements contained animation.[29] Although animation can attract attention more easily, it is at the same time overly obvious so that the tendency to avoid looking at it directly can be more easily engaged. The potential increase in attention getting by animation is therefore offset by its obtrusive usage.

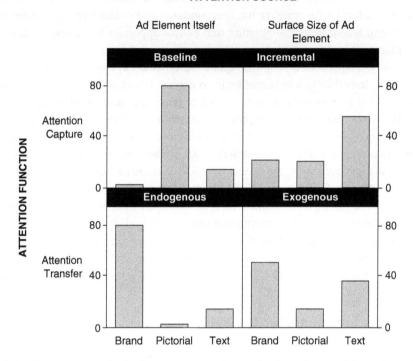

ATTENTION SOURCE

Figure 2.1   Comparison of attention capture and transfer: brand, pictorial, and text in advertisements.

Source: Pieters and Wedel[30]. Reprinted from *Journal of Marketing, 68*(2), Pieters and Wedel. Fear: Attention Capture and Transfer in Advertising: Brand, Pictorial, and Text-Size Effects, 36—50, Copyright (2004), with permission from SAGE.

Short-term (working) memory

The psychological basis

Short-term memory, also known as working memory[31] or primary memory,[32] is a temporary storage that is used to process necessary information in order to carry out tasks at hand, including language comprehension, learning, and reasoning. As it deals with information that is currently being processed, its capacity is limited. Miller suggests that the capacity for short-term memory is seven (which he called the *magical number seven*).[33] His classic paper reviewed studies on categorizing pitch, loudness, size, hue, brightness, et cetera and found that for people to be more accurate in categorising the selected objects, the average number of alternatives to be categorised is usually somewhere in the neighbourhood of seven; that is, the magical number seven, plus or minus two. This magical number is still frequently referred to even today, although the number has been updated and reduced to somewhere between three and five in recent years,[34] suggesting that people appear to be capable of dealing with even less information at any given time than formerly thought.

Although we are capable of dealing with limited information at any given time, we are able to put information into chunks which enables us to expand the capacity of our short-term memory. *Chunking* refers to grouping individual units into larger, and sometimes meaningful, units of information.[35] According to Miller, the process of forming chunks is called recoding, which is a fundamental process of memory and a very powerful means of increasing the amount of information we can process at a time.[36] For example, this 12-letter string *P P C C R M R O I W O M*, can be grouped into four chunks: PPC (pay per click), CRM (customer relationship management), ROI (return on investment), WOM (word-of-mouth), and therefore the likelihood to correctly recall this string would be higher for someone who is familiar with these abbreviations. Even if sometimes we are unable to recode the information into meaningful chunks, we are still able to use chunks to improve the capacity of our short-term memory. For example, instead of memorising a telephone number as a single unit, +447910807291, we could split the numbers into different chunks (units), such as +44-7910-807-291, so as to make the number easier to remember.

Implications for consumer behaviour

Advertising recall

There are two effects in advertising recall, the primacy effect and the recency effect:

- *The primacy effect:* we tend to better remember the first thing we are exposed to in a specified task, so the primacy effect is related to our long-term memory.[37]
- *The recency effect:* we tend to better remember the last thing we are exposed to in a specified task, so the recency effect is from our short-term memory.[38]

Because of the primacy and recency effect, it is more expensive for TV (or radio) advertisements to be aired at the beginning or end of a commercial block (that is, the advertisement right after the programmes go into commercials and the one right before the programmes start).[39] The primacy effect is, however, stronger than the recency effect.[40] The reason that the primacy effect is more pronounced is because our ability to retain information is more persistent for information stored in the long-term memory than in the short-term memory.[41]

Positioning strategy

One of the main principles in setting a good positioning strategy is "less for more" by focusing on limited benefits.[42] This less for more principle is born out of the limited capacity of our short-term memory. Hence, it explains why (good) advertising messages are usually highly simplified.[43]

Choice overload

Choice overload suggests that an increase in the number of options to choose from leads to adverse consequences, including a decrease in the motivation to choose,[44] in preference strength, and in satisfaction with the chosen option,[45] and an increase in negative emotions (confusion, disappointment, and regret[46]). These negative effects resulting from choice overload are termed as the "'too-much-choice'" effect.[47] Although it is difficult to determine how many choices is too many, research has generally used Miller's magical number seven as a benchmark,[48] while others have suggested the ideal number of choices depends on experiences and expectations.[49]

─Box 2.1─

Is too much choice always a bad thing?

Choice overload has been demonstrated in various product categories, including jam,[50] pens,[51] chocolates,[52] coffee,[53] and jelly beans.[54] Does it mean that too much choice is a bad thing in marketing?

It does not necessarily mean that. There are also some virtues pertaining to a large size of assortment, especially in retailing. Research has shown that consumers in general prefer to choose from a variety of options; hence, retailers who offer more choices seem to have a competitive advantage over those who offer less.[55] In addition to consumer preference in terms of variety, putting a large assortment together in the same place in a retailing environment implies that consumers' searching cost is reduced and a systematic and direct comparison between options is possible, which in turn leads to better-informed and more confident choice-making.[56] The critical issue is that when retailers wish to increase their assortment size, they should pay attention to the incremental effect of the increased assortment size which depends on the perceived quality of the increased offerings (e.g. to introduce fine distinctions within a product line[57]) and the perception of increased variety (e.g. to introduce categories to enhance variety perception[58]). If retailers neglect the importance of the incremental effect when considering assortment size, it is possible that sales could actually go up with a reduced assortment size.[59] Do not forget the fact that reduced assortment size contributes to a significant decrease in the operational costs for retailers. In other words, if an increase in assortment size cannot create the expected positive effect, retailers will be financially better off not to increase their assortment size.

Information overload

Similar to choice overload, information overload refers to the consumers' inability to deal with situations where too much information is presented. The implications include brand positioning,[60] the ideal amount of information,[61] and consumers' optimal decision-making.[62]

Selective information processing

Consumers use selective information processing to cope with information overload by selectively choosing which pieces of information to process.[63] Selective information processing has become more and more important as, thanks to the Internet technology, consumers face an ever-increasing amount of information to process in order to reach an optimal decision in today's market place. With the consumers' tendency to use selective information processing, customisation of information can help reduce information overload, and reduced information overload in an online environment can potentially increase the click-through rate by more than 60%.[64]

Relative importance of product attributes and optimal decisions

Research shows that people need to process more information for options that involve attributes with similar levels of importance than for those with attributes with dissimilar levels of importance in order to reach an optimal decision.[65] This is because for options with attributes that are more important, our information processing can selectively focus on those attributes, but for options with attributes that are equally important, our information processing has to be comprehensive.[66] This idea is especially important in an information-rich environment such as the Internet. For example, on comparison websites, it is crucial to make the ratings more distinguishable for the important attributes. Otherwise, they run a risk of information overload, which in turn will lead to less satisfied, less confident, and more confused consumers.[67]

Long-term memory

The psychological basis

As opposed to short-term (working) memory, whose main job is to process information for the task at hand, long-term memory deals with the rest of the absorbed information, which is stored in our brain, though not necessarily required for the current task. Long-term memory is sometimes referred to as secondary memory,[68] and can store an amazing amount of information; for example, it can contain details of our last holiday, facts on the Beijing Olympics in 2008, information about how to drive, and so on.

Broadly speaking, there are two different types of long-term memory: declarative and procedural memory (Table 2.2). *Declarative memory* is about *knowing what* the world presents to us, including knowledge of events, facts, and concepts. Access to declarative memory is usually a conscious act. On the other hand, *procedural memory* (or implicit memory) is about *knowing how*, including skills and conditioned emotional responses that are used to respond to the world. This knowing how is usually involved in actions at a nonconscious level, and we do not need to gain access to this information consciously in order to perform required tasks. 95% of our daily activities rely on procedural memory,[69] which will be discussed in Chapter 4, "Implicit Cognition". This section focuses on declarative memory.

Table 2.2 Types of long-term memory

Type of Long-Term Memory		Definition	Example

Declarative (explicit) memory	Episodic memory	• A storage of personal experiences, including
		  o What happened
		  o Where they happened
		  o When they happened
			• Going to Disneyland for a birthday celebration

	Semantic memory	• A storage of factual and conceptual knowledge • An internal representation of the world that is not perceptually present; [70] a bridge between declarative and procedural memory[71]	• Knowledge of what marketing strategies could be applied in different contexts
Procedural (implicit) memory	Skills	• Motor skills (also known as muscle memory) • Perceptual skills	• Driving • Writing
	Conditioned responses	• Conditioned emotional responses (via classical or operant conditioning)	• Fear response to spiders

Declarative memory involves forgetting and remembering. There are two fundamental assumptions for forgetting:[72]

1. Recent learning impairs previous learning.
2. Past learning inhibits our ability to learn new information.

Associated with forgetting is remembering, or memory retrieval. How do we enhance memory retrieval for things that we may forget? The answer is rehearsal, and there are two types of rehearsal:

• *Maintenance rehearsal* refers to repeating information within short-term memory by thinking or verbalising it.
• *Elaborative rehearsal* suggests that we establish associations between new information in the short-term memory (what we wish to remember) and what we have already remembered (that is stored in the long-term memory).

Elaborative rehearsal relies on a higher level of processing[73] by, for example, organising items into categories,[74] associating items with other known information,[75] or forming visual images.[76] In short, elaborative rehearsal reconstructs the memory pathways in our brain, thereby enhancing our ability to recall[77] – see Section 2.3. Therefore, elaborative rehearsal outperforms maintenance rehearsal in improving our long-term memory.[78]

Implications for consumer behaviour

Cues to retrieve consumer memory

Both verbal and visual information from advertisements can serve as cues at the point of purchase to retrieve memory of the advertisements from prior exposures.[79] However, the effect of memory retrieval is moderated by how competitive the advertising environment is. That is, if consumers are able to recall the competitive brands when cues are presented for these brands, then the focal brand would not benefit much by presenting cues.[80] On the other hand, if consumers are unable to recall the competitive brands, then the focal brand would benefit by presenting cues at the point of purchase.[81]

Advertising repetition

Advertising repetition has been used to enhance consumer memory,[82] and this tactic is based on maintenance rehearsal through an involuntary repetitive exposure to advertising messages. However, an effective use of advertising repetition is not only about memory. Rather, it is about creating positive consumer attitude through their memory. In other words, when the repetition of a certain advertisement becomes too much, this exposure may instigate consumer annoyance (Box 2.2). Because of this, the implications from advertising repetition are usually not as straightforward as what is suggested by maintenance rehearsal.

─Box 2.2─

Berlyne's two-factor theory

Based on Berlyne's two-factor theory, there are two phases in processing repetitive advertisements:[83]

1.   *The wearin phase:*

     Viewers are attracted to the novelty of the advertising messages, thereby developing positive habituation via repetition.[84]

2.   *The wearout phase:*

     Over time viewers develop boredom, resulting in the onset of tedium when exposed to repeated advertising messages. The build-up of negative emotions then leads to a decrease in advertising effectiveness[85] and encourages us to zap those annoying advertisements as much as we can.[86] In order to postpone or avoid the wearout effects, advertising repetition can adopt variation strategies, such as variations in advertisement materials and advertising channels.

Variation strategy: variation in advertisement materials

There are two main information processing routes: the central versus the peripheral route (Box 2.3). While it is important to encourage intentional processing (i.e. via the central route), it is equally important to facilitate incidental processing (i.e. via the peripheral route), as using a variety of routes can enhance memory via maintenance rehearsal (i.e. memory retrieval) and by elaborative rehearsal (i.e. memory reconstruction)[87] as well as increasing positive attitudes toward the advertisements and the brand.[88] In other words, a true variation (as opposed to cosmetic variation) in advertising suggests that consumers process the advertising information differently: via the central and peripheral routes. Therefore, with the true variation in advertising materials, consumers' memory is more lasting, and their positive attitudes towards the brand in the advertisements are able to withstand a competitive environment.[89]

─Box 2.3─

The elaboration likelihood model

The elaboration likelihood model suggests that there are two different information processes:[90]

- *The central route processing*

  o The information processing focus is on content-relevant information, such as product attributes
  o Relying more on cognitive efforts
  o Consumers are motivated to process more information.[91]

- *The peripheral route processing*

  o The information process focus is on content-irrelevant information
  o Minimum cognitive efforts are involved; relying more on System 1 for information processing (see Chapter 4)
  o Consumers are less motivated to process more information.[92]

Variation strategy: variation in advertising channels

There are many media in which advertisers can display their advertisements, including TV, radio, print, billboards, product placement, et cetera. Research shows that an effective repetition strategy focuses on spacing out the advertising messages through a combination of more involving media (e.g. TV commercials) and less involving media (e.g. product placement).[93] The effects of using a combination of different advertising channels are similar to those using a combination of different creative designs.[94]

Memory reconstruction via advertising

Advertising is able to activate elaborative rehearsal in order to remind consumers of their positive experiences with the brand.[95] Through elaborative rehearsal, we sometimes are able to reconstruct our memory. That is, advertising does not just reflect what we experienced, but also "tricks" us into remembering things differently from what actually happened,[96] thereby increasing our positive attitudes.[97] However, not all advertising cues are equivalent in their ability to conjure up the past. In fact, if consumers detect a discrepancy in their experience with the advertising cues, their recall ability can be inhibited and their attitudes towards the advertisement becomes negative.[98]

2.3 KNOWLEDGE

The psychological basis

Knowledge relies on memory to accumulate and develop, and is one of the key topics in developmental and educational psychology. Although heavily relying on memory, knowledge is not an exact copy of what is learned; rather, it is actively integrated into one's existing knowledge structures (i.e. a process called *memory reconstruction*) in order to reach comprehension.[99] In other words, remembering something does not guarantee accuracy or understanding.

Because of the close relationship between memory and knowledge, knowledge has three critical characteristics:

- Knowledge is *not* free of errors due to the susceptibility of human memories to errors.[100] This is contrary to common understanding of knowledge, because knowledge here denotes information stored in the knowledge structures in the human brain.
- Knowledge is updated frequently in order to adapt to the demands of the environment;[101] however, knowledge once gained can be resistant to change.[102]
- Existing knowledge facilitates processing new incoming information,[103] so people with different levels of knowledge process information differently.[104]

Schemata

Schemata, also known as knowledge frames,[105] are mental representations that organise knowledge of related concepts, and can be viewed as categories[106] (see Section 3.2, Category-based Inferences, for more details). Simply put, schemata are our expectations of objects, people, and events from our past experiences,[107] so schemata simplify the world by influencing what we pay attention to, thus helping us learn efficiently.[108] Therefore, schemata are something we all possess and continue to form and change throughout our lives.[109] However, schemata are easier to change during childhood, and become more and more resistant to change as we grow older,[110] thereby hindering our learning of new information. For example, prejudice, such as sexism, ageism, and racism, can be difficult to change in adults.[111]

Schema congruity effect

The schema congruity effect suggests that the greater the congruity between the features of a new stimulus and the category schema in which it belongs, the better the evaluations of the new stimulus will be.[112] This effect is attributed to *processing fluency* (i.e. the degree of easiness in information processing) resulting in the feeling of satisfaction because of the ease of understanding the stimulus due to the fit between the stimulus and the category schema.[113] However, if congruity is extremely high, the need for people to process information in order to make a judgement will be too low to sense satisfaction from processing fluency, resulting in only a mild positive response.[114] By contrast, if congruity is moderate, processing fluency is experienced, and at the same time, cognitive elaboration is activated to understand the incongruity, resulting in satisfaction from the discovery of the insight which together will generate a greater positive response.[115]

Implications for consumer behaviour

Consumer familiarity

Consumer familiarity refers to the level of product or brand related experiences consumers have accumulated,[116] and is composed of product familiarity and brand familiarity, which do not just suggest usage experiences, but include *any* experiences, such as exposures to advertisements[117] or discussions of products, brands, or advertisements in a social setting.[118]

Brand familiarity

Brand familiarity determines whether or not brands can be recalled from consumer memory. One of the main measures for brand recall is top-of-mind brand awareness, which indicates the first few brands (usually the first three brands) that come to consumers' mind when they are asked to name as many brands as they can in a specific product category. Top-of-mind brand awareness is a result of effective advertising,[119] and increases the likelihood of the brand being chosen.[120] As it takes time to develop brand familiarity, the existing brands have advantages over new brands because they enjoy better brand recall and advertising recall from consumers.[121]

Information processing

Consumers process information differently for familiar and unfamiliar brands. For unfamiliar brands, their goal of information processing is to form an accurate impression of the brand,[122] but for familiar brands, their information processing goal focuses on updating their existing knowledge.[123] As a result, for familiar brands, consumers engage in relatively less extensive, but more confirmation-based processing.[124] Perhaps because of this, brand familiarity enhances consumers' positive attitudes towards the brand's advertisements with increased advertising exposure, whereas their attitudes towards the advertisements for unfamiliar brands do not present such an effect.[125]

Expertise

Expertise is developed through familiarity,[126] but familiarity does not guarantee expertise.[127] For example, mere ownership of a motorcycle does not necessarily lead to the owners' knowledge in motorcycles, but their knowledge is directly and positively related to the amount of relevant information (such as motorcycle magazines) these owners have read.[128] In other words, expertise emphasises objective knowledge in a product category or a brand.

Objective versus subjective knowledge

Objective knowledge is what we know, whereas subjective knowledge is what we *think* we know.[129] Although there is a strong and positive relationship between objective and subjective knowledge, they are different. As a result, using subjective knowledge as a proxy to gauge objective knowledge may risk distorting the effects of objective knowledge.[130] "Experts" defined by subjective knowledge have good memories because their subjective knowledge is usually caused by their increased experience.[131] A true expert, however, is able to demonstrate not only memory superiority,[132] but also the ability to incorporate new information to old knowledge.[133] In a nutshell, the difference between objective and subjective knowledge suggests that we do not know what we *think* we know.

Information processing

Experts tend to use analytic information processing.[134] As consumer expertise increases, their perception of product complexity decreases, so does the negative effect of complexity,[135] thereby developing efficient strategies and behaviours, allowing them to make optimal decisions with reduced costs of information search and product usage.[136] That is, they are able to identify and use only relevant and diagnostic information while ignoring other information that may be salient but irrelevant,[137] and their doing so does not require much cognitive effort.[138]

Issue with subjective knowledge: overconfidence

Most consumer "experts" exhibit overconfidence in their objective knowledge.[139] Overconfidence often leads to reduced information search,[140] thereby resulting in an increase in inferior decisions.[141] The inferior decisions usually favour the current brand that the consumer "experts" use, so this type of inferior decision is also referred to as *incumbent bias*.[142]

The schema congruity effect

Product evaluation

Consumers prefer products that are moderately incongruent with the product schema[143] (see Product Categories on p.55); however, this preference is impacted on by the amount of their existing knowledge. That is, if they already possess extensive product knowledge, they are able to incorporate incongruent information into their existing knowledge structures with little effort and, therefore, their product evaluation is based on their inferences of product quality after analysing the new incoming information, and not on the schema congruity effect.[144] By contrast, those consumers without sufficient product knowledge are less able to understand incongruent information, thereby leading them to rely on the schema congruity effect for a heuristic judgement.[145]

Schema congruity between product and advertising designs

The schema congruity effect can be applied to aesthetic designs, and when it is applied to aesthetic designs, processing fluency is the key to obtain positive evaluations.[146] Therefore, for example, endorsers who match up with the products advertised, indicating a schema congruity between the endorsers and products, are effective in promoting the products (that is, *the match-up hypothesis*).[147] This effect can be taken further to have a congruent design between products and their advertisements. For example, consumers prefer products with human-like product features when their promotion messages evoke a human (versus object) schema,[148] and if the human-like product features or advertising messages evoke gender-schema, consumers prefer the products with the same gender to their own.[149]

2.4 SUMMARY

1. Sensory memory, a storage of sensory information (visual, tactile, olfactory, gustatory, and auditory information), contributes to the formation of perception and the explanation of attention catching. Broadbent's theory of attention suggests that we receive sensory information all the time, but we do not often process this information, and the key factor to what information we process is relevance (the cocktail party phenomenon). Similarly, we do not often process advertising information, but the key factors to increase our motivation to process are the advertisement design, consumer involvement, and familiarity. Information from pictures, texts, and brands in advertising contribute to capturing our attention, but even when we do process advertising information, attention to a print advertisement, for example, is brief (less than 2 seconds). In addition, we have the ability to actively block advertising information; for example, our ability to block animated online advertisements is better than for static advertisements, given the more obtrusive nature of animated advertisements.

2. Short-term memory is a temporary storage that is used to process necessary information in order to carry out tasks at hand, and its capacity is limited. How limited is the capacity of short-term memory? Miller's magical number seven suggests that we are able to process 7 units of information (+/– 2) at any one time, but this number has been updated and reduced to a range between 2 and 5. Because of the limited capacity of our short-term memory, the key implication in consumer behaviour is to address how to enhance advertising and brand recall. In order to enhance recall, we should focus on communicating a limited number of brand benefits in order to avoid information overload, and on offering a limited (or organised) product range in order to avoid choice overload.

3. Declarative (explicit) memory includes episodic and semantic memory. The former stores information about events that took place (both via personal experience and via knowing the events from other channels, such as news articles), and the latter stores information of factual and conceptual (abstract) knowledge. In order to enhance memory retrieval, we rely on rehearsals, especially the rehearsals that can help us reconstruct the memory pathways in our brain (i.e. elaborative rehearsals). The implication for elaborative rehearsals in advertising recall is to implement a variation strategy: variation in advertising materials that require the audience to view the brand from different angles and to process information differently (central versus peripheral information processing) and variation in advertising channels. Whilst a mere advertising repetition (repetition of the same advertisement; this repetition is classified as maintenance rehearsal) is able to enhance the audience's memory, such repetition can easily lead to a wearout effect that makes the audience feel annoyed. The true art of advertising is when advertising tricks us into remembering things differently from what actually happened, thereby increasing our positive attitude, but this strategy should be used with caution, since if consumers are not tricked, it may be counter-effective.

4. Knowledge relies on memory to accumulate and develop, and existing knowledge is able to facilitate processing new incoming information. Depending on the amount of knowledge consumers have, there are two broad dimensions: familiarity and expertise. Familiarity refers to consumers' product and brand-related experiences, and the degree of familiarity determines the rank in consumers' top-of-mind brand awareness. A brand reaching a higher rank (top three) increases the possibility that consumers purchase the brand, and the information processing goal is less extensive and focuses on knowledge updating. By contrast, for unfamiliar brands, consumers' information processing is more laborious as they would focus on forming an accurate impression of the brand. Brand familiarity also indicates consumers' expectations, which, if not met, will result in dissatisfaction and disappointment.

5. Consumer expertise is developed through familiarity, but expertise depends on consumers' objective knowledge (as opposed to subjective knowledge). Consumer expertise reflects their ability to incorporate new information into existing knowledge

by internalising relevant information with analytic information processing, thereby allowing them to make optimal decisions with decreased costs in information processing. If consumer expertise is masked by subjective knowledge, then their overconfidence may lead to reduced information search and increased inferior decisions, which tend to favour the current brand that the consumer "experts" use – this is referred to as the incumbent bias.

6. Schemata are mental representations that organise knowledge of related concepts, and reflections of our expectations of objects, people, and events from our experiences. The schema congruity effect suggests that the greater the congruity between the features of a new stimulus and the category schema in which the stimulus belongs, the better the evaluations of the new stimulus will be. This effect appears in the match-up between the schemata the product and advertising designs evoke. However, for new product evaluations, a moderate congruity (not extremely congruent, nor extremely incongruent) between the new product and the existing product category schema can better stimulate positive responses from consumers.

DISCUSSION QUESTIONS

1. What is sensory memory? How does it influence consumer behaviour?
2. What is short-term memory? How does it influence consumer behaviour?
3. What is long-term memory? How does it influence consumer behaviour?
4. What are schemata? How do schemata influence consumers' evaluation of products and advertisements?

FURTHER READING

- Alba, J. W., & Hutchinson, J. W. (1987). Dimensions of Consumer Expertise. *Journal of Consumer Research, 13*(4), 411–454.
- Alba, J. W., Hutchinson, J. W., & Lynch, J. G., Jr. (1991). Memory and Decision Making. In T. S. Robertson & H. H. Kassarjian (eds), *Handbook of Consumer Behavior* (pp. 1–49). Englewood Cliffs, NJ: Prentice Hall.
- Braun, K. A. (1999). Post-Experience Advertising Effects on Consumer Memory. *Journal of Consumer Research, 25*(4), 319–334.
- Hutchinson, J. W., & Eisenstein, E. M. (2008). Consumer Learning and Expertise. In C. P. Haugtvedt, P. M. Herr, & F. R. Kardes (eds), *Handbook of Consumer Psychology* (pp. 103–131). New York: Lawrence Erlbaum Associates.
- Pieters, R., & Wedel, M. (2004). Attention Capture and Transfer in Advertising: Brand, Pictorial, and Text-Size Effects. *Journal of Marketing, 68*(2), 36–50.

NOTES

1. Mandler, G. (1980). Recognizing: The Judgment of Previous Occurence. *Psychological Review, 87*(3), 252–271.
2. Hiebert, J., & Carpenter, T. P. (1992). Learning and Teaching with Understanding. In D. A. Grouws (ed.), *Handbook of Research on Mathematics Teaching and Learning: A Project of the National Council of Teachers of Mathematics* (pp. 65–97). New York: Macmillian; Myers, J., Shinjo, M., & Duffy, S. A. (1987). Degree of Causal Relatedness and Memory. *Journal of Memory and Language, 26*(4), 453–465.
3. Page 77 from Mantonakis, A., Whittlesea, W. A., & Yoon, C. (2008). Consumer Memory, Fluency, and Familiarity. In C. P. Haugtvedt, P. M. Herr, & F. R. Kardes (eds), *Handbook of Consumer Psychology* (pp. 77–102). New York: Lawrence Erlbaum Associates.
4. Atkinson, R. C., & Shiffrin, R. M. (1968). Human Memory: A Proposed System and Its Control Processes. *Psychology of Learning and Motivation, 2*, 89–195.
5. Treisman, A. (1964). Monitoring and Storage of Irrelevant Messages in Selective Attention. *Journal of Verbal Learning and Verbal Behavior, 3*(6), 449–459.
6. Sperling, G. (1960). The Information Available in Brief Visual Presentations. *Psychological Monographs: General and Applied, 74*(11), 1–29.
7. Peterson, L., & Peterson, M. J. (1959). Short-Term Retention of Individual Verbal Items. *Journal of Experimental Psychology, 58*(3), 193–198.
8. Chen, Z., & Cowan, N. (2009). Core Verbal Working Memory Capacity: The Limit in Words Retained Without Covert Articulation. *Quarterly Journal of Experimental Psychology, 62*(7), 1420–1429; Cowan, N. (2001). The Magical Number 4 in Short-Term Memory: A Reconsideration of Mental Storage Capacity. *Behavioral and Brain Science, 24*(1), 87–114; Cowan, N., Rouder, J. N., Blume, C. L., & Saults, J. S. (2012). Models of Verbal Working Memory Capacity: What Does It Take To Make Them Work? *Psychological Review, 119*(3), 480–499; Jarrold, C., Tam, H., Baddeley, A. D., & Harvey, C. E. (2010). The Nature and Position of Processing Determines Why Forgetting Occurs in Working Memory Tasks. *Psychonomic Bulletin & Review, 17*(6), 772–777; Luck, S. J., & Vogel, E. K. (1997). The Capacity of Visual Working Memory for Features and Conjunctions. *Nature, 390*(6657), 279–281.
9. Bahrick, H. P., Bahrick, P. O., & Wittlinger, R. P. (1975). Fifty Years of Memory for Names and Faces: A Cross-Sectional Approach. *Journal of Experimental Psychology: General, 104*(1), 54–75.
10. Brady, T. F., Konkle, T., Alvarez, G. A., & Oliva, A. (2008). Visual Long-Term Memory Has a Massive Storage Capacity for Object Details. *Proceedings of the National Academy of Sciences, 105*(38), 14325–14329.
11. Galotti, K. M. (2014). *Cognitive Psychology: In and Out of the Laboratory* (5th edn). Los Angeles: Sage.
12. Baddeley, A. D. (1990). *Human Memory: Theory and Practice.* Boston: Allyn & Bacon.
13. Treisman, A. M. (1964). Verbal Cues, Language, and Meaning in Selective Attention. *American Journal of Psychology, 77*(2), 206–219.

14. Sperling, G. (1960). The Information Available in Brief Visual Presentations. *Psychological Monographs: General and Applied, 74*(11), 1–29.
15. Smith, T. J., Levin, D., & Cutting, J. E. (2012). A Window on Reality: Perceiving Edited Moving Images. *Current Directions in Psychological Science, 21*(2), 107–113.
16. Raab, G., Goddard, G. J., Ajami, R. A., & Unger, A. (2010). *The Psychology of Marketing: Cross-Cultural Perspectives*. Farnham: Gower.
17. Broadbent, D. E. (1958). *Perception and Communication*. Oxford: Pergamon Press.
18. Cherry, E. C. (1953). Some Experiments on the Recognition of Speech with One and Two Ears. *Journal of the Acoustical Society of America, 25*(5), 975–979.
19. Moray, N. (1959). Attention in Dichotic Listening: Affective Cues and the Influence of Instructions. *Quarterly Journal of Experimental Psychology, 11*(1), 56–60.
20. Pieters, R., & Wedel, M. (2004). Attention Capture and Transfer in Advertising: Brand, Pictorial, and Text-Size Effects. *Journal of Marketing, 68*(2), 36–50.
21. Campbell, M. C. (1995). When Attention-Getting Advertising Tactics Elicit Consumer Inferences of Manipulative Intent: The Importance of Balancing Benefits and Investments. *Journal of Consumer Psychology, 4*(3), 225–254.
22. Pieters & Wedel, Attention Capture and Transfer in Advertising.
23. Ibid.
24. Ibid.
25. Ibid.
26. Ibid.
27. Ibid.
28. Hervet, G., Guérard, K., Tremblay, S., & Chtourou, M. S. (2011). Is Banner Blindness Genuine? Eye Tracking Internet Text Advertising. *Applied Cognitive Psychology, 25*(5), 708–716.
29. Lee, J., & Ahn, J.-H. (2012). Attention to Banner Ads and Their Effectiveness: An Eye-Tracking Approach. *International Journal of Electronic Commerce, 17*(1), 119–137.
30. Pieters & Wedel, Attention Capture and Transfer in Advertising.
31. Baddeley, A. D. (1992). Working Memory. *Science, 255*(5044), 556–559.
32. James, W. (1890). *The Principles of Psychology* (Vol. I). New York: Henry Folt and Company.
33. Miller, G. A. (1956). The Magical Number Seven, Plus or Minus Two: Some Limits on Our Capacity for Processing Information. *Psychological Review, 63*(2), 81–97.
34. Chen & Cowan, Core Verbal Working Memory Capacity; Cowan, The Magical Number 4 in Short-Term Memory; Cowan et al., Models of Verbal Working Memory Capacity; Jarrold et al., The Nature and Position of Processing Determines Why Forgetting Occurs in Working Memory Tasks; Luck & Vogel, The Capacity of Visual Working Memory for Features and Conjunctions.
35. Galotti, K. M. (2014). *Cognitive Psychology: In and Out of the Laboratory* (5th edn). Los Angeles: Sage; Jansson-Boyd, C. V. (2010). *Consumer Psychology*. Maidenhead: Open University Press.
36. Miller, The Magical Number Seven, Plus or Minus Two.
37. Glanzer, M., & Cunitz, A. R. (1966). Two Storage Mechanisms in Free Recall. *Journal of Verbal Learning and Verbal Behavior, 5*(4), 351–360.
38. Ibid.

39. Burke, R. R., & Srull, T. K. (1988). Competitive Interference and Consumer Memory for Advertising. *Journal of Consumer Research, 15*(1), 51–68; Stewart, D. W., Pechmann, C., Ratneshwar, S., Stroud, J., & Bryant, B. (1985). Methodological and Theoretical Foundations of Advertising Copytesting: A Review. *Current Issues and Research in Advertising, 8*(2), 1–74.

40. Peters, R. G. M., & Bijmolt, T. H. A. (1997). Consumer Memory for Television Advertising: A Field Study of Duration, Serial Position, and Competition Effects. *Journal of Consumer Research, 23*(4), 361–372.

41. Postman, L., & Stark, K. (1969). Role of Response Availability in Transfer and Interference. *Journal of Experimental Psychology, 79*(1), 161–177.

42. Keller, K. L. (2013). *Strategic Brand Management: Building, Measuring, and Managing Brand Equity (Global Edition)* (fourth edn). Harlow: Pearson.

43. Ries, A., & Trout, J. (2001). *Positioning: The Battle for Your Mind*. New York: McGraw-Hill.

44. Iyengar, S. S., & Lepper, M. R. (2000). When Choice is Demotivating: Can One Desire Too Much of a Good Thing? *Journal of Personality and Social Psychology, 79*(6), 991–1006; Kahn, B. E., & Wansink, B. (2004). The Influence of Assortment Structure on Perceived Variety and Consumption Quantities. *Journal of Consumer Research, 30*(March), 511–533.

45. Iyengar & Lepper, When Choice is Demotivating; Lee, B.-K., & Lee, W.-N. (2004). The Effect of Information Overload on Consumer Choice Quality in an On-Line Environment. *Psychology & Marketing, 21*(3), 151–183; Chernev, A. (2003). When More Is Less and Less Is More: The Role of Ideal Point Availability and Assortment in Consumer Choice. *Journal of Consumer Research, 30*(September), 170–183.

46. Lee & Lee, The Effect of Information Overload on Consumer Choice Quality in an On-Line Environment; Schwarz, B. (2000). Self-Determination: The Tyranny of Freedom. *American Psychologist, 55*(1), 71–88.

47. Scheibehenne, B., Greifeneder, R., & Todd, P. M. (2010). Can There Ever Be Too Many Options? A Meta-Analytic Review of Choice Overload. *Journal of Consumer Research, 37*(October), 401–425.

48. Iyengar & Lepper, When Choice is Demotivating; Kahn & Wansink, The Influence of Assortment Structure on Perceived Variety and Consumption Quantities.

49. Chernev, When More Is Less and Less Is More; Diehl, K., & Poynor, C. (2010). Great Expectations?! Assortment Size, Expectations, and Satisfaction. *Journal of Marketing Research, 47*(2), 311–322.

50. Iyengar & Lepper, When Choice is Demotivating.

51. Shah, A. M., & Wolford, G. (2007). Buying Behavior as a Function of Parametric Variation of Number of Choices. *Psychological Science, 18*(5), 361–370.

52. Chernev, When More Is Less and Less Is More.

53. Mogilner, C., Rudnick, T., & Iyengar, S. S. (2008). The Mere Categorization Effect: How the Presence of Categories Increases Choosers' Perceptions of Assortment Variety and Outcome Satisfaction. *Journal of Consumer Research, 35*(August), 201–215.

54. Kahn & Wansink, The Influence of Assortment Structure on Perceived Variety and Consumption Quantities

55. Bown, N. J., Read, D., & Summers, B. (2003). The Lure of Choice. *Journal of Behavioral Decision Making, 16*(4), 291–308; Oppewal, H., & Koelemeijer, K. (2005). More Choice Is Better: Effects of Assortment Size and Composition on Assortment Evaluation. *International Journal of Research in Marketing, 22*(1), 41–60.

56. Hutchinson, J. M. C. (2005). Is More Choice Always Desirable? Evidence and Arguments from Leks, Food Selection, and Environmental Enrichment. *Biological Reviews, 80*(1), 71–92.

57. Berger, J., Draganska, M., & Simonson, I. (2007). The Influence of Product Variety on Brand Perception and Choice. *Marketing Science, 26*(4), 461–472.

58. Kahn & Wansink, The Influence of Assortment Structure on Perceived Variety and Consumption Quantities; Mogilner et al., The Mere Categorization Effect.

59. Sloot, L. M., Fok, D., & Verhoef, P. C. (2006). The Short- and Long-Term Impact of an Assortment Reduction on Category Sales. *Journal of Marketing Research, 43*(4), 531–548.

60. Ries, A., & Trout, J. (2001). *Positioning: The Battle for Your Mind*. New York: McGraw-Hill.

61. Sicilia, M., & Ruiz, S. (2010). The Effects of the Amount of Information on Cognitive Responses in Online Purchasing Tasks. *Electronic Commerce Research and Applications, 9*(2), 181–191; Wang, K.-C., Chou, S.-H., Su, C.-J., & Tsai, H.-Y. (2007). More Information, Stronger Effectiveness? Different Group Package Tour Advertising Components on Web Page. *Journal of Business Research, 60*(4), 381–387.

62. Lee & Lee, The Effect of Information Overload on Consumer Choice Quality in an On-Line Environment; Lurie, N. H. (2004). Decision Making in Information-Rich Environments: The Role of Information Structure. *Journal of Consumer Research, 30*(March), 471–486.

63. Jacoby, J. (1984). Perspectives on Information Overload. *Journal of Consumer Research, 10*(March), 431–435.

64. Ansari, A., & Mela, C. F. (2003). E-Customization. *Journal of Marketing Research, 40*(2), 131–145.

65. Lurie, Decision Making in Information-Rich Environments.

66. West, P. M. (1996). Predicting Preferences: An Examination of Agent Learning. *Journal of Consumer Research, 23*(June), 68–80.

67. Lee & Lee, The Effect of Information Overload on Consumer Choice Quality in an On-Line Environment.

68. James, *The Principles of Psychology*.

69. Bargh, J. A., & Chartrand, T. L. (1999). The Unbearable Automaticity of Being. *American Psychologist, 54*(7), 461–479.

70. Tulving, E. (1985). How Many Memory Systems Are There? *American Psychologist, 40*(4), 385–398.

71. Ibid.

72. Underwood, B. J. (1957). Interference and Forgetting. *Psychological Review, 64*(1), 41–60; Postman, L., & Underwood, B. J. (1973). Critical Issues in Interference Theory. *Memory & Cognition, 1*(1), 11–40.

73. Craik, F., & Lockhart, R. S. (1972). Levels of Process: A Framework for Memory Research. *Journal of Verbal Learning and Verbal Behavior, 11*(6), 671–684.

74. Bousfield, W. A. (1953). The Occurrence of Clustering in the Recall of Randomly Arranged Associates. *Journal of General Psychology, 49*(2), 221–240.

75. Walker, Direct Retrieval from Elaborated Memory Traces.

76. Shepard, R. N. (1967). Recognition Memory for Words, Sentences, and Pictures. *Journal of Verbal Learning and Verbal Behavior, 6*(1), 151–163; Standing, L. (1973). Learning 10000 Pictures. *The Quarterly Journal of Experimental Psychology, 25*(2), 201–222; Weldon, M. S., Roediger, H. L., & Challis, B. H. (1989). The Properties of Retrieval Cues Constrain the Picture Superiority Effect. *Memory & Cognition, 17*(1), 91–105.

77. Walker, Direct Retrieval from Elaborated Memory Traces.

78. Glenberg, A., Smith, S. M., & Green, C. (1977). Type I Rehearsal: Maintenance and More. *Journal of Verbal Learning and Verbal Behavior, 16*(3), 331–352.

79. Keller, K. L. (1987). Memory Factors in Advertising: The Effect of Advertising Retrieval Cues on Brand Evaluations. *Journal of Consumer Research, 14*(December), 311–333.

80. Ibid.

81. Ibid.

82. MacKenzie, S. B., Lutz, R. J., & Belch, G. E. (1986). The Role of Attitude toward the Ad as a Mediator of Advertising Effectiveness: A Test of Competing Explanations. *Journal of Marketing Research, 23*(2), 131–143; Axelrod, J. N. (1968). Advertising Measures that Predict Purchase. *Journal of Advertising Research, 8*(March), 1–17.

83. Berlyne, D. E. (1970). Novelty, Complexity, and Hedonic Value. *Perception & Psychophysics, 8*(5), 279–286.

84. Cox, D. S., & Cox, A. D. (1988). What Does Familiarity Breed? Complexity as a Moderator of Repetition Effects in Ad Evaluation. *Journal of Consumer Research, 15*(June), 111–116.

85. Anand, P., & Sternthal, B. (1990). Ease of Message Processing as a Moderator of Repetition Effects in Advertising. *Journal of Marketing Research, 27*(3), 341–353; Blair, M. H., & Rabuck, M. J. (1998). Advertising Wearin and Wearout: Then Years Later – More Empirical Evidence and Successful Practice. *Journal of Advertising Research, 38*(September-October), 1–18.

86. Siddarth, S., & Chattopadhyay, A. (1998). To Zap or Not to Zap: A Study of the Determinants of Channel Switching During Commercials. *Marketing Science, 17*(2), 121–138.

87. Janiszewski, C., Noel, H., & Sawyer, A. G. (2003). A Meta-Analysis of the Spacing Effect in Verbal Learning: Implications for Research on Advertising Repetition and Consumer Memory. *Journal of Consumer Research, 30*(June), 131–149.

88. Haugtvedt, C. P., Schumann, D. W., Schneier, W. L., & Warren, W. L. (1994). Advertising Repetition and Variation Strategies: Implications for Understanding Attitude Strength. *Journal of Consumer Research, 21*(June), 171–189.

89. Ibid.

90. Petty, R. E., & Cacioppo, J. T. (1981). *Attitudes and Persuasion: Classic and Contemporary Approaches*. Boulder, CO: Westview Press

91. Petty, R. E., Cacioppo, J. T., & Schumann, D. (1983). Central and Peripheral Routes to Advertising Effectiveness: The Moderating Role of Involvement. *Journal of Consumer Research, 10*(September), 131–146.

92. Ibid.

93. Janiszewski, C., Noel, H., & Sawyer, A. G. (2003). A Meta-Analysis of the Spacing Effect in Verbal Learning: Implications for Research on Advertising Repetition and Consumer Memory. *Journal of Consumer Research, 30*(June), 131–149.

94. Ibid.

95. Wells, W. D. (1986). Three Useful Ideas. In R. J. Lutz (ed.), *Advances in Consumer Research* (Vol. 13, pp. 1–12). Provo, UT: Association for Consumer Research.

96. Braun, K. A. (1999). Post-Experience Advertising Effects on Consumer Memory. *Journal of Consumer Research, 25*(4), 311–334.

97. Braun-LaTour, K. A., LaTour, M. S., Pickrell, J. E., & Loftus, E. F. (2004). How And When Advertising Can Influence Memory for Consumer Experience. *Journal of Advertising, 33*(4), 1–25.

98. Ibid.

99. Bartlett, F. C. (1932). *Remembering: A Study in Experimental and Social Psychology*. Cambridge: Cambridge University Press.

100. Ibid.

101. Piaget, J. (1929). *The Child's Conception of the World*. New York: Harcourt Brace.

102. Padesky, C. A. (1994). Schema Change Processes in Cognitive Therapy. *Clinical Psychology & Psychotherapy, 1*(5), 261–278.

103. Brod, G., Werkle-Bergner, M., & Shing, Y. L. (2013). The Influence of Prior Knowledge on Memory: A Developmental Cognitive Neuroscience Perspective. *Frontiers in behavioral neuroscience, 7*, 139.

104. Snyder, M., & Stukas, A. A., Jr. (1999). Interpersonal Processes: The Interplay of Cognitive, Motivational, and Behavioral Activities in Social Interaction. *Annual Review of Psychology, 50*, 271–303; MacKenzie, S. B., & Spreng, R. A. (1992). How Does Motivation Moderate the Impact of Central and Peripheral Processing on Brand Attitudes and Intentions? *Journal of Consumer Research, 18*(March), 511–529.

105. Minsky, M. A. (1975). A Framework for Representing Knowledge. In P. H. Winston (ed.), *The Psychology of Computer Vision*. New York, NY: McGraw-Hill.

106. Bartlett, *Remembering: A Study in Experimental and Social Psychology*.

107. Baldwin, M. W. (1992). Relational Schemas and the Processing of Social Information. *Psychological Bulletin, 112*(3), 461–484.

108. Johnston, W. A., & Dark, V. J. (1986). Selective Attention. *Annual Review of Psychology, 37*, 41–75; Alba, J. W., & Hasher, L. (1983). Is Memory Schematic? *Psychological Bulletin, 93*(2), 201–231.

109. Piaget, J., & Inhelder, B. (1967). *The Child's Conception of Space*. New York: W. W. Norton.

110. Padesky, C. A. (1994). Schema Change Processes in Cognitive Therapy. *Clinical Psychology & Psychotherapy, 1*(5), 261–278.

111. Aosved, A. C., Long, P. J., & Voller, E. K. (2009). Measuring Sexism, Racism, Sexual Prejudice, Ageism, Classism, and Religious Intolerance: The Intolerant Schema Measure. *Journal of Applied Social Psychology, 39*(10), 2321–2354.

112. Fiske, S. T. (1982). Schema-Triggered Affect: Applications to Social Perception. In M. S. Clark & S. T. Fiske (eds), *Affect and Cognition: 17th Annual Carnegie Mellon Symposium on Cognition* (pp. 51–78). Hillsdale, NJ: Lawrence Erlbaum Associates.

113. Winkielman, P., Schwarz, N., Fazendeiro, T. A., & Reber, R. (2003). The Hedonic Marking of Processing Fluency: Implications for Evaluative Judgment. In J. Musch & K. C. Klauer (eds), *The Psychology of Evaluation: Affective Processes in Cognition and Emotion* (pp. 191–217). Mahwah, NJ: Lawrence Elrbaum Associates.

114. Mandler, M. (1982). The Structure of Value: Accounting for Taste. In M. S. Clark & S. T. Fiske (eds), *Affect and Cognition: 17th Annual Carnegie Mellon Symposium on Cognition* (pp. 1–36). Hillsdale, NJ: Lawrence Erlbaum Associates.

115. Alba, J. W., & Hutchinson, J. W. (1987). Dimensions of Consumer Expertise. *Journal of Consumer Research, 13*(March), 411–454.

116. Ibid.

117. MacKenzie et al., The Role of Attitude toward the Ad as a Mediator of Advertising Effectiveness; Axelrod, Advertising Measures that Predict Purchase.

118. Ritson, M., & Elliott, R. (1999). The Social Uses of Advertising: An Ethnographic Study of Adolescent Advertising Audiences. *Journal of Consumer Research, 26*(December), 261–277.

119. Alba, J. W., Hutchinson, J. W., & Lynch, J. G., Jr. (1991). Memory and Decision Making. In T. S. Robertson & H. H. Kassarjian (eds), *Handbook of Consumer Behavior* (pp. 1–49). Englewood Cliffs, NJ: Prentice Hall; Lavidge, R. J., & Steiner, G. A. (1961). A Model for Predictive Measurement of Advertising Effectiveness. *Journal of Marketing, 25*(October), 591–562; Ray, M. L., Sawyer, A. G., Rothschild, M. L., Heeler, R. M., Strong, E. C., & Reed, J. B. (1973). Marketing Communication and the Hierarchy-of-Effects. In P. Clarke (ed.), *New Models for Mass Communication Research* (pp. 141–176). Beverly Hills, CA: Sage.

120. Axelrod, Advertising Measures that Predict Purchase; Nedungadi, P., & Hutchinson, J. W. (1985). The Prototypicality of Brands: Relationships with Brand Awareness, Preference, and Usage. In E. Hirschman & M. B. Holbrook (eds), *Advances in Consumer Research* (Vol. 12, pp. 491–503). Provo, UT: Association for Consumer Research.

121. Kent, R. J., & Allen, C. T. (1994). Competitive Interference Effects in Consumer Memory for Advertising: The Role of Brand Familiarity. *Journal of Marketing, 58*(July), 91–105; Alpert, F. H., & Kamins, M. A. (1995). An Empirical Investigation of Consumer Memory, Attitude, and Perceptions toward Pioneer and Follower Brands. *Journal of Marketing, 59*(October), 31–45.

122. Hilton, J. L., & Darley, J. M. (1991). The Effects of Interaction Goals on Person Perception. In M. P. Zanna (ed.), *Advances in Experimental Social Psychology* (Vol. 24, pp. 231–267). New York: Academic Press.

123. Snyder & Stukas, Interpersonal Processes.

124. MacKenzie & Spreng (1992). How Does Motivation Moderate the Impact of Central and Peripheral Processing on Brand Attitudes and Intentions?

125. Campbell, M. C., & Keller, K. L. (2003). Brand Familiarity and Advertising Repetition Effects. *Journal of Consumer Research, 30*(September), 291–304.

126. Hutchinson, J. W., & Eisenstein, E. M. (2008). Consumer Learning and Expertise. In C. P. Haugtvedt, P. M. Herr, & F. R. Kardes (eds), *Handbook of Consumer Psychology* (pp. 101–131). New York: Lawrence Erlbaum Associates.

127. Mitchell, A. A., & Dacin, P. A. (1996). The Assessment of Alternative Measures of Consumer Expertise. *Journal of Consumer Research, 23*(3), 211–239.

128. Ibid.

129. Alba, J. W., & Hutchinson, J. W. (2000). Knowledge Calibration: What Consumers Know and What They Think They Know. *Journal of Consumer Research, 27*(September), 121–156.

130. Carlson, J. P., Vincent, L. H., Hardesty, D. M., & Bearden, W. O. (2009). Objective and Subjective Knowledge Relationships: A Quantitative Analysis of Consumer Research Findings. *Journal of Consumer Research, 35*(February), 861–876.

131. Mitchell, V. (1996). Assessing the Reliability and Validity of Questionnaires: An Empirical Example. *Journal of Applied Management Studies, 5*(2), 191–207.

132. Vicente, K. J., & Wang, J. H. (1998). An Ecological Theory of Expertise Effects in Memory Recall. *Psychological Review, 105*(1), 31–57.

133. Alba & Hutchinson, Dimensions of Consumer Expertise.

134. Hutchinson, J. W., & Alba, J. W. (1991). Ignoring Irrelevant Information: Situational Determinants of Consumer Learning. *Journal of Consumer Research, 18*(December), 321–345.

135. Dellaert, B. G. C., & Stremersch, S. (2005). Marketing Mass-Customized Products: Striking a Balance between Utility and Complexity. *Journal of Marketing Research, 42*(2), 211–227.

136. Hutchinson, J. W., & Eisenstein, E. M. (2008). Consumer Learning and Expertise. In C. P. Haugtvedt, P. M. Herr, & F. R. Kardes (eds), *Handbook of Consumer Psychology* (pp. 101–131). New York: Lawrence Erlbaum Associates.

137. Hutchinson, J. W., & Alba, J. W. (1991). Ignoring Irrelevant Information: Situational Determinants of Consumer Learning. *Journal of Consumer Research, 18*(December), 321–345.

138. Dellaert & Stremersch, Marketing Mass-Customized Products.

139. Wood, S. L., & Lynch, J. G., Jr. (2002). Prior Knowledge and Complacency in New Product Learning. *Journal of Consumer Research, 29*(3), 411–426.

140. Ibid.

141. Muthukrishnan, A. V. (1995). Decision Ambiguity and Incumbent Brand Advantage. *Journal of Consumer Research, 22*(June), 91–109.

142. Ibid.

143. Meyers-Levy, J., & Tybout, A. M. (1989). Schema Congruity as a Basis for Product Evaluation. *Journal of Consumer Research, 16*(June), 31–54.

144. Peracchio, L. A., & Tybout, A. M. (1996). The Moderating Role of Prior Knowledge in Schema-Based Product Evaluation. *Journal of Consumer Research, 23*(3), 171–192.

145. Ibid.

146. Reber, R., Schwarz, N., & Winkielman, P. (2004). Processing Fluency and Aesthetic Pleasure: Is Beauty in the Perceiver's Processing Experience? *Personality and Social Psychology Review, 8*(4), 361–382.

147. Kahle, L. R., & Homer, P. M. (1985). Physical Attractiveness of the Celebrity Endorser: A Social Adaptation Perspective. *Journal of Consumer Research, 11*(4), 951–961; Kamins, M. A. (1990). An Investigation into the "Match-Up" Hypothesis in Celebrity Advertising: When Beauty May Be Only Skin Deep. *Journal of Advertising, 19*(1), 1–13.

148. Aggarwal, P., & McGill, A. L. (2007). Is That Car Smiling at Me? Schema Congruity as a Basis for Evaluating Anthropomorphized Products. *Journal of Consumer Research, 34*(December), 461–479.

149. van den Hende, E. A., & Mugge, R. (2014). Investigating Gender-Schema Congruity Effects on Consumers' Evaluation of Anthropomorphized Products. *Psychology & Marketing, 31*(4), 261–277.

3

CONSUMER INFERENCE AND EVALUATION

3.1 INTRODUCTION

Consumer inference and evaluation mainly derive from reasoning, deduction, and judgement research in cognitive psychology. Customers rely on reasoning to infer and evaluate products or brands in order to make the right decisions based on the market information they are exposed to. However, market information is often presented in an incomplete or inconsistent manner, so how do consumers deal with this?

There are three purposes of studying consumer inference and evaluation. First, to understand "how [consumers] integrate multiple, incomplete, and sometimes conflicting cues to infer what is happening in the external world".[1] Second, to use such understanding to devise effective marketing activities in a marketer's daily practices. Last, but not the least, to avoid potential biases in our daily consumption decisions. This chapter will surprise you by how much our inference and evaluation can be influenced by the way information is presented to us! It is important to note that, although consumer inference and evaluation derive from reasoning and deduction, this does not necessarily imply that our inferences and evaluations are always rational or correct.

3.2 CATEGORY-BASED INFERENCES

The psychological basis

Category-based inferences are about how people conceptualise their knowledge.[2] That is, people conceptualise their knowledge based on *category representations*, referred to as the information stored in the cognitive system and later used to process for inference or evaluation.[3] To put it simply, category representations are classifications of objects or ideas.[4] For example, shoes belong to the category of clothing, whereas chairs belong to that of furniture. Using the categories the objects belong to can facilitate our information process and allow us to make sense of the information around us. There are three main ways in which the information is stored in the cognitive system:

1. *The prototype view*: The prototype view classifies objects based on their features or characteristics,[5] and the greater feature overlap between an object and the category, the more likely it is to be regarded as a member of that category.[6] Because of this, some category members are more representative (or typical) than other category members;[7] for example, crisps are more representative of the snack food category than fruits.
2. *The exemplar view*: The exemplar view suggests that people categorise new objects by comparing them to the instances previously stored in their memory, and these instances are called exemplars. The way the exemplars work in our cognition relies on cues to retrieve memories of similar exemplar representations in order to compare the cues to the existing exemplars and classify the new object accordingly.[8]
3. *The contingent view*: While the prototype view focuses on specific *features* that constitute membership in a given category and the exemplar view focuses on specific *examples* that classify membership, the contingency-based view suggests that it is not an either–or question. Rather, people are able to construct category membership based on both features and examples, stored in the individual's repertoire, and either might be used depending on the context.[9]

Similarity-based inferences

Similarity-based inferences underpin category-based inferences to determine the characteristics or evaluation of a new object or idea. That is, people perceive the accessible information regarding the new object/idea to be similar to the information ascribing an existing category. When the new object/idea is perceived as a category member for an existing category, the inferences people draw about the new member will be similar to what they know about the existing ones. These similarity-based inferences are rooted in the *assimilation effects*, which indicate that if an object/idea is perceived as similar to a category, it will be assimilated into that category,[10] thereby the features and subsequent emotions of the category will then also be applied to the object.[11]

Implications for consumer behaviour

Cultural/social categories

Cultural and social influences play a significant role in our cognition, emotion, and behaviour (see Sections 8.3 and 8.4). These influences are so strong that when we are reminded of our group membership, we are inclined to change our information processing to be consistent with that of the social groups we belong to,[12] and we subsequently draw similar inferences concerning other group members.[13] For example, people from independent cultures evaluate products more positively when the advertising messages focus on their benefits, whereas those from interdependent cultures judge the same products more favourable if they use risk-avoidance messages in advertising[14] (more details can be found in Section 8.4).

Product categories

Early research shows that a product with features that are similar to what consumers believe to be the typical features in the product category activates product category schema, which exerts a positive affect (called product category schema affect) leading to a favourable evaluation of the product[15] (see Section 2.3, "The schema congruity effect"). This evaluation is performed quickly because of a dependence on heuristics to make inferences.[16] However, more recent research suggests that it would be beneficial for new products to activate a more deliberate information processing, and to do so new products should adopt moderately incongruent product features.[17] After all, consumers experience less enjoyment when they see, evaluate, or consume many similar products in the same product category.[18]

Brand categories

Brand extensions

The perceived fit, or the extent to which consumers perceive the newly extended product to be similar to the existing products available under the parent brand name, activates similarity based inferences. There are two types of extension in general:

- Far extensions: when the extension is dissimilar to the existing products. For example, Häagen-Dazs product range extended to include cottage cheese would be seen as a far extension.[19]
- Near extensions: when the extension is similar to the existing products. For example, Häagen-Dazs product range extended to include candy bars would be seen as a near extension.[20]

Compared with far extensions, consumers are more able to activate similarity-based inferences by transferring the evaluations of the parent brand for near extensions.[21] However, there is one exception: quality perception. Research shows even for far extensions, if the parent brand's quality is believed to be high, most attributes in the parent brand are likely to transfer to the extended product line.[22]

Similarity-based inferences are viewed as heuristic in decision-making,[23] suggesting that the effects of perceived fit or quality perception diminish as the motivation to process or the exposure to the attribute information of the extension increases.[24]

In addition, similarity does not automatically result in a positive evaluation of brand extension. Rather, similarity-based inferences exist to minimize cognitive effort.[25] For example, research shows dissimilar movie sequels (movie extensions) are rated higher than similar sequels in terms of both story plots and name sequels.[26] That is, a different story plot to the parent movie is preferred and named sequels (e.g. *Die Hard with a Vengeance*) are also preferred to numbered sequels (e.g. *Spiderman 2*).

Brand competitions

Typicality

Typicality is referred to as the similarity of a brand to other category members. Research has shown that there is a positive relationship between a category member's typicality and the category member's evaluation; that is, more typical category members are better liked.[27] For example, if a market leader has a prestige reputation and premium pricing strategy, the new entrants will be better off if they imitate the market leader by setting a high/premium pricing strategy.[28] This is because, if the market leader brand is prominent, consumers will evaluate the category positively on the cue of the market leader. Therefore, if the new entrants are seen as similar to the market leader brand, the subsequent evaluation will be drawn from the market leader brand. This strategy is likely to result in perceptual prominence for the new brand.

However, typicality is not the panacea. For example, low typicality can be associated with positive emotions, such as excitement and romance in apparel shopping.[29] As consumers generally seek hedonic value in apparel shopping, they expect a more personally gratifying experience that may be stimulated by excitement experienced in an atypical store. This exception tells us that contexts are important in how consumers infer, evaluate, and judge.[30]

Brand differentiation

It would not be sufficient for the new entrants to *only* imitate what the market leader does;[31] it is essential to find ways to be differentiated from the market leader.[32] There are two main differentiation strategies:

- *Alignable differentiation: using features that are comparable or similar along the same dimension as its differentiation strategy*. As the market standard that has been established by the early entrants can be more easily recalled by the consumers,[33] the late entrants can benefit more by using comparable but enhanced features to differentiate their brand from the early entrants.[34] The principle of alignability also works for comparative advertising; that is, alignable comparative advertisements are more effective, compared with non-alignable comparative advertisements.[35]
- *Non-alignable differentiation: using unique features as a differentiation strategy*. The danger of using a non-alignable differentiation strategy is that consumers are less able to see the unique feature offered by the late entrant as superior because the unique feature is not comparable to the benchmark established by the early entrants.[36] However, radically new products, such as the invention of Dyson's bagless vacuum cleaner, have no other choice but to use this strategy. Perhaps because it is difficult for consumers to draw similarity-based inferences from their existing product repertoire, it usually takes a long time for radically new products to establish their initial market.

3.3 CAUSAL INFERENCES
The psychological basis

Causal inferences are formed based on people's "if–then" associations from information to conclusions, and these if–then associations are established based on individuals' subjective logic,[37] which involves a sense of uncertainty in reasoning and is the type of reasoning we encounter the most frequently in our daily life. For example, when we see a person eat a lot (information), we may infer that this person is hungry or that the food is delicious (conclusion). In order to produce a correct reasoning by reducing the level of uncertainty, subjective logic relies on the perception of plausibility to generate conclusions.[38] This process of using subjective logic to generate conclusions as accurately as possible can be explained by attribution theories.[39] There are two main attributional theories used in consumption contexts: correspondent inference theory and emotion and control theory.

Jones's correspondent inference theory

Jones's correspondent inference theory suggests that people's dispositions can be inferred from their behaviour;[40] that is, there is a "correspondence" between people's dispositions and their behaviour.[41] This theory was initially devised to examine impression formation of a person by associating his personality with his behaviour. This theory can be extended to examine how we form our impressions of brands and products through their "behaviour". This theory is subject to the *correspondence biases* that come into effect when one disregards the situational factors, has unrealistic expectations for behaviour, and inflates the effect of the correspondence between the situation and the behaviour.[42]

Weiner's affect and control theory

Weiner's affect and control theory suggests that behaviour is determined by an individual's expectancy and emotions.[43] Expectancy (or an inference) is associated with the causes of the outcome, and determined by three dimensions:[44]

1. Causal locus: internal factors versus external factors
2. Stability: enduring versus temporary
3. Controllability: controllable versus non-controllable

Accompanying expectancy are the emotions arising in response to the outcome (success or failure). That is, positive emotions, including pride, happiness, hopefulness, or gratitude, are associated with positive outcomes, whereas negative emotions, including embarrassment, anger, hopelessness, and guilt, are associated with negative outcomes. Emotions, together with expectancy, influence how people will behave in the future when a similar event occurs.

Implications for consumer behaviour

Endorsers and their endorsement

There is a correspondence between endorsers' dispositions and their endorsement behaviour. That is, consumers infer endorsers' personalities, attitudes, and preferences about the brands they endorse, and therefore transfer the personalities, attitudes, and preferences from the endorsers to the brands they endorse.[45] For example, seeing a celebrity endorse a brand leads us to infer that the celebrity likes and uses the brand.[46] In addition, it is not only the endorsers that would influence the brands they endorse; the brands they endorse would also influence the endorsers. That is, consumers also make inferences about the endorsers according to the brand they endorse. For example, endorsers acquire the brand personality of the brands they endorse.[47] Therefore, it is equally important for endorsers to carefully choose which brands they endorse.

Sponsored versus non-sponsored endorsement

Whether or not endorsement is undertaken in exchange for (monetary) compensation influences how consumers draw the correspondence between the endorser's personalities, attitudes, and preferences and those of the endorsed brand. Research shows, when a form of compensation is involved and disclosed, consumers' belief that the endorser likes and uses the endorsed brand is significantly lower than when there is no disclosed compensation.[48] This explains why many developed countries now require celebrities, influencers, and suchlike to disclose whether their promotion for products/brands involves monetary compensation, and this regulation is in place in the hope that consumers will be able to draw more accurate correspondence inferences by reducing the correspondence bias. However, even though the correspondence inference is weaker in the compensation situation, consumers will still make considerable correspondence inferences about the celebrity's attitudes and preferences for the endorsed brand,[49] suggesting the existence of a correspondence bias.

—Box 3.1—

Inferences about social media influencers

There are five levels of influencers depending on their popularity, which can be inferred from the number of followers they have:[50]

1. Nano-influencer: with less than 10,000 followers
2. Micro-influencer: with between 10,000 and 100,000 followers
3. Macro-influencer: with between 100,000 and 1 million followers
4. Mega-influencer: with more than 1 million followers
5. Celebrity-influencer: with more than 1 million followers

The difference between mega-influencers and celebrity-influencers is whether or not they had the celebrity status prior to their being influencers. In most cases, and reasonably, how much an influencer is liked can be deduced from their popularity: the more popular the influencer is, the more liked he or she will be.[51] However, when the influencer follows very few people, even if the influencer is very popular, how much the audience likes the influencer is likely to reduce.[52]

Although it seems that popularity is crucial for influencers to grow their business, research has shown that, in some cases, less is more, indicating that micro influencers can be more effective than macro influencers to promote a brand.[53] For example, a unique brand/product is more effectively promoted by micro influencers than by macro influencers,[54] because popularity would trigger the perception of the brand/product being popular rather than unique.[55] In addition, micro

(Continued)

influencers are able to instil more trust in their audience than macro influencers with their act to disclose that their posts or videos are sponsored, because the audience sees the disclosure as an attempt to be honest and open with their close and smaller number of fans.[56] However, this perception (or inference) disregards the fact that influencers are required to disclose this information, indicating that a correspondence bias is still at work.

Endorsing multiple brands

When a celebrity endorses multiple brands in various product categories, consumers are more likely to doubt the celebrity's trustworthiness and sincerity.[57] In other words, the effectiveness of celebrity advertising decreases, therefore, with the number of brands the celebrity endorses.

Negative reviews or information

Negative reviews or information (e.g. word-of-mouth) about a brand is not necessarily viewed as negative. That is, our evaluation depends on the extent to which we ascribe credibility of the purveyor of the negative word-of-mouth information.[58] Let's say, if we believe the communicator of the negative word-of-mouth messages to have a personal grudge, the negative word-of-mouth effect will then be discounted and our brand evaluation will not be influenced. However, if we believe it is the brand's responsibility that leads to the negative review, then our brand evaluation will be impacted and become negative. How we draw the inference of who is being responsible or negligent mainly depends on the two properties of Weiner's theory: causal locus and controllability.

—Box 3.2—

Inferences about online reviews

Buying online has become more and more common, and people tend to use information they find online to form quality perception and purchase intentions. The most often used information is online reviews, which usually involve a star rating and text review content, but in addition to these there are other cues indicating product quality, including price, number of ratings, and third-party product reviews (such as *Consumer Reports* in the US or *Which?* in the UK). How do consumers infer from all this information? An investigation of more than 1200 products across 120 different product categories shows that consumers disproportionately rely on the average rating to form quality inferences and purchase intentions compared to other information such as price and the number of ratings, and that the information contained in the average rating is often not aligned with the actual product quality found by the third-party reviews.[59] Consumers' illusion of the validity of the average ratings drives the sales of the products; that is, the greater the star ratings, the better the sales of the products.[60] This, therefore, motivates businesses to fake reviews.[61] However, despite the fact that there are fake reviews, many consumers have developed their own heuristics: they rely on the star ratings for positive reviews, but focus on the number of reviews for negative reviews[62] - another piece of evidence for correspondence bias.

Customer satisfaction

Weiner's emotion and control theory has significant implications in service marketing that involves customer satisfaction and evaluation of a service failure, as it can help consumers ascribe responsibility for a service failure. For example, if a certain service failure is caused by an employee strike, which does not happen often (temporary), it does not matter whether the brand is responsible for the strike and nor does it matter whether the service failure is better or worse than expected, customer satisfaction would be likely to remain unchanged.[63] However, if the employee strikes have happened frequently (enduring) and if reasons for the strikes can be attributed to the brand's lack of response, customers' satisfaction would be more negatively impacted than if the reasons for the strikes are attributed to the employees' unreasonable requests.[64]

Repurchase intentions

Customer satisfaction is one of the key determinants of repurchase or repatronage intentions,[65] especially where service is concerned.[66] Let's use Folks, Koletsky, and Graham's field study from an airport as an example.[67]

- If Peter flew with Virgin Atlantic from London to New York and experienced an extensive delay, which was caused by a snow storm in New York, Peter would feel upset, but he would not blame the airline for this delay. This is because the controllability of weather is close to impossible. Accordingly, the possibility of his continuous patronage of the airline will not be influenced.
- However, if the delay was caused by a mechanical problem with the aircraft, then Peter would feel angry and may voice his complaint and choose other airlines in the future. This is because the maintenance of aircrafts is viewed as the airline's responsibility; that is, under its control.

3.4 COGNITIVE ILLUSION: THE FRAMING EFFECT

The psychological basis

The previous two sections have generally shown how consumers logically infer and evaluate their decisions by using available information. However, consumer inference and evaluation is often based on heuristics as also mentioned earlier, and heuristics are easily influenced by biases resulting from cognitive illusions. There are many types of cognitive illusions, but we will only focus on the framing effect, by way of introducing the prospect theory.

The framing effect: prospect theory

The framing effect suggests that people's inference, evaluation, and decision-making depends on how the information is presented. Why different presentations of the information influence people's inference, evaluation, and decision-making can be explained by the prospect theory developed by Kahneman and Tversky.[68] The key tenet of the prospect theory is that people are risk averse when gains are involved, but risk-taking when losses are possible. Under this tenet, three major principles are developed to govern the prospect theory: the principles of internal reference points, subjective value, and diminishing sensitivity.

─Box 3.3─

Prospect theory: a little history

Daniel Kahneman was awarded the Nobel Prize in 2002 for his prospect theory. Sadly, Amos Tversky passed away in 1996 before the Nobel recognition; otherwise, he would have shared the laureate title with Kahneman.[69]

The principle of internal reference points

The first, and the foremost, principle is that people form their evaluations or make their decisions based on their internal reference points. Although the internal reference points can be learned from experience (for example, most students see a pair of jeans of £300 as expensive but a pair that costs £3 as cheap), the prospect theory suggests that they can be framed via how the information is described. Consider these two examples:

A. If you buy your airline ticket in advance prior to going to the airport, you will be charged with regular prices, but if you buy your airline ticket at the airport counter, you will need to pay £50 more.
B. If you buy your airline ticket at the airport counter, you will be charged with regular prices, but if you buy your airline ticket in advance, you will be given a £50 discount.

Which sounds more attractive to you? A or B? At the first glance, most people would believe that B is a better option; however, if you consider carefully, the pricing structures of these two examples are exactly the same. The only difference is one focuses on how much more you need to pay (loss) and the other on the discount (gain). This way of framing potentially changes the reference point against which people make their relative judgements and decisions, and this shift in the reference point leads consumers to see gains involved more easily in Example B and to see losses involved more easily in Example A, thereby leading B to be the preferred option.

The principle of subjective value

The second principle is that people evaluate their prospects based on subjective value rather than absolute value, and this basis is rooted in the psychophysics of quantity,[70] indicating, for example, the difference in subjective value between £10 and £20 is greater than the subjective difference between £110 and £120.[71] How does this subjective value influence consumer decisions? Transferring the psychophysics of quantity to consumer decisions is the psychophysics of spending, suggesting that, for example, adding a £500 satellite navigation system in your brand new £50,000 BMW seems to be cheaper than adding the same satellite navigation system in your brand new £10,000 Vauxhall Corsa, and therefore consumers tend to add additional equipment when purchasing a relatively more expensive car. The psychophysics of spending holds true regardless of the wealth of consumers as well as the types of purchases, ranging from book supplies and their respective extras to expensive stereo systems and their respective extras.[72]

The principle of diminishing sensitivity

The final principle is the principle of diminishing sensitivity, suggesting that even though the internal reference points can be framed, the effects of framing diminish as the frequency of framing increases. Imagine you go to a local coffee shop and buy a cup of coffee and expect to pay £2 for the coffee. £2 is your internal reference point from your patron experience at the coffee shop, but when you get there, the coffee sells at £1 as part of their promotional scheme. Because of the £1 difference between your internal reference point and the actual price, you are happy about this positive surprise. However, because of this experience, your internal reference point starts to decrease from £2. The next day when you go back to the coffee shop, if the promotional scheme stays, you still pay £1 for the cup of coffee, but you would be less happily surprised than how you felt the previous day. As the promotional scheme stays longer, the level of the positive surprise of paying £1 for a cup of coffee will diminish and eventually disappear altogether. Diminished sensitivity implies that if a brand promotes the price too often, it risks shifting its consumers' reference point downward, and over time the promotional price will be seen as the normal price, hence reducing the effect of promotions.[73]

Implications for consumer behaviour

The framing of product attributes

The inclusion of product attributes that focus on "benefits"

Framing to shift the internal reference points leads people to perceive different realities. For example, in a beef tasting study Levin found that people could be positively framed and consequently evaluated the beef as more lean and as having better quality when a label of "75% lean" was shown, compared with a label of "25% fat".[74] This framing effect was extended and influenced consumers' tasting evaluation in the same direction.[75] That is to say, the differences in labelling (75% lean versus 25% fat) led the respondents to perceive differences in the taste of the beef, even though it was the same beef. Given that the gains are positive framing and losses are negative framing, that is why a lot of marketing information has been framed as positive when discussing their own products or brands and negative when talking about their competitors'.

The inclusion of product attributes that do not contribute to product quality

The framing of product attributes is abundant in marketing practices. For example, Procter & Gamble's Folger's coffee has used "flaked coffee crystals" to imply the shape of its coffee granules improves its taste when, in fact, the shape of instant coffee has nothing to do with its taste.[76] Alberto Natural Silk Shampoo's "We put silk in a bottle" slogan suggests that silk in shampoo makes hair silky, but, in fact, silk does not have such a function.[77] These two examples may have led you to think that the reason for the irrelevant information to work is because of the consumers' lack of knowledge in such a context or situation, but Carpenter, Glazer, and Nakamoto tell us otherwise.[78] They show that when consumers are given necessary product information to make an accurate judgement, consumers' evaluation for the product that contains the attributes that albeit sound better, but do not contribute to the quality of the product, is better than for the product that does not.

The framing of prices

The nine-ending effect

The nine-ending effect suggests that the price that ends with a nine, such as £1.99 or £59, is able to increase demand and generate more sales.[79] For example, in a field experiment, Anderson and Simester compared the sales of the same four dresses with different price endings, and found that the sales of the dresses with nine as price endings increased by about 40%, even when the prices were US$5 more than those in the nine-ending prices (i.e. US$34, 54, 64 and 74 versus US$39, 59, 69 and 79).[80]

The nine-ending effect may derive from the fact that most items on sale have a nine-price ending; therefore, consumers perceive such a price format to be a bargain.[81] Because of the deal perception from the nine-ending prices, the effect is context dependent, indicating that not all brands can increase sales by using prices with nine-endings. In fact, the nine-ending prices can sometimes lead to negative sales. That is, premium brands that adopted nine-ending prices lost 11% of sales on average.[82] Therefore, although the nine-ending price format is perceived to be a good bargain, the quality-image effect for such a price format might signal lower quality, thereby making a product less attractive. This price format should therefore be used with caution.

The left digit effect

Another explanation for the nine-ending effect is the left digit effect. The left digit effect can be explained by the following two reasons:

1. *the left-to-right digit processing* and consumers' information-processing limitations: consumers tend to truncate prices.[83] For example, a price of £25.00 or £29.99 are both usually encoded at a £20.00 level;
2. *the analogue model of numerical cognition*: the leftmost digit in a price exerts disproportionate influence on the encoding of prices because we tend to infer the quantitative meaning of the numbers by spontaneously mapping them onto an internal analogue magnitude scale.[84] For example, consider the following two pairs of prices:

    -   $2.99 and $4.00
    -   $3.00 and $4.00

Although the actual difference between $2.99 and $3.00 is one cent, consumers perceive $2.99 to be much less expensive than $3.00 when they are compared with $4.00.[85] Similarly, when comparing the pair of $1.99 and $3.00 versus $2.00 and $2.99, $1.99 is perceived as much less expensive than $2.00 when they are compared with $3.00 and $2.99 respectively.[86]

The right digit effect

The right digit effect suggests that when consumers view two prices with identical left digits, they spontaneously discount the left digits and pay more attention to the right digits.[87] In this case, the influence of the right digits is disproportionate, as opposed to the left-digit effect. Therefore, the right-digit effect is usually applied in a sale situation where the regular and sale prices are listed together.[88]

Price-off promotions: % off versus £s off

The subjective value can be framed in terms of percentage versus actual amount of money (i.e. % versus £). This % versus £ framing effect changes according to high- versus low-priced products. For a high-priced product (£1,500), a price reduction in pound terms (£150 off) is seen more significant than the same price reduction in percentage terms (10% off), but for a low-priced product (£15), the opposite (£1.50 off versus 10% off) generates higher saving perceptions.[89] Therefore, different promotional framing could be more effectively used in different situations, depending on the sizes of the purchases as well as the sizes of price-off discounts.

The framing of brand stories

Story framing is the most complex form of framing, as it involves selecting suitable themes and techniques.[90] A successful framing of brand stories relies on creating an internal reference point for the audience to anchor on in order to draw inferences.[91] For example, many years ago when the German beer Beck's entered the US market, its launching to the market message was:

> You've tasted the German beer that's the most popular in America. Now taste the German beer that's the most popular in Germany.

Before Beck's arrival, Lowenbrau occupied the first German beer position in the United States as well as the positive association of German beer. In order to turnaround this situation, Beck's created the impression of the best German beer from Germany, and their message successfully attracted the attention they wanted.[92] This story tells us that framing brand stories does not necessarily mean creating something new, but more importantly manipulating what's already up there in the mind of consumers.[93]

Story framing can be used in advertising campaigns,[94] brand biographies,[95] and brand positioning.[96] It is usually related to the business contexts or its history. For example:

> Thanks to a never-ending campaign by Apple's powerful public relations machine to protect the myths surrounding the company's origin, almost everyone believes Apple was started in a garage. . . . Actually the operation began in a bedroom . . . when the bedroom became too crowded, the operation did indeed move to the garage.[97]

Telling a story of how the brand started, struggled, and then succeeded adds to a sense of authenticity,[98] which makes the brand more human[99] and somehow more relevant to its consumers.[100] One key theme of this type of brand story is to frame the brand as an underdog, facing environmental and resources disadvantages with a passion to excel.[101] The classic advertising campaign for this type of framing is Avis's "We try harder" campaign. In 1962, Avis was a struggling market no. 2 in the car rental business, far behind the market leader, Hertz, and suffered a loss.[102] Avis decided to use a series of advertisements not to show consumers how good Avis was, but to show why consumers should go with a mere market no. 2.[103] The campaign was based on a cruel fact, but a true story, that if Avis did not try harder, it would be gone from the market forever. Avis's "We try harder" campaign reversed the company's fortunes from losing US$3.2 million to a profit of £1.2 million within a year and boosted its market share from 11% to 35% within four years.[104]

Brands do not have to be small to benefit from an underdog narrative because what drives the underdog effect is not a firm's absolute size but consumers' perceptions of the firm being small[105]. For example, despite the reality that Sam Adams is now a sizable brand, Sam Adams has used its advertising campaign entitled "Growing Up Small" to remind consumers of its diminutive competitive position, and Jim Koch, the founder and chairman of the Boston Beer Company, maker of Sam Adams beer, constantly compares his independent brewery to the Anheuser-Busch Companies, LLC with claims such as "Anheuser-Busch spills more beer than we make".[106] Instead of comparing to those small independent breweries, they choose to use the largest beer maker, Anheuser-Busch, to highlight their "small" size of brewery.

3.5 SUMMARY

1. Category-based inferences indicate people use category representations, which are classifications of objects or ideas, to conceptualise their knowledge in their cognitive system. There are three ways that people form category representations: (1) the prototype view (using abstract features to determine category membership), (2) the exemplar view (using concrete examples to determine category membership), and (3) the contingency-based view (using a mixed method, either prototype or exemplar, depending on contexts). Using category representations, consumers are then able to form category-based inferences.
2. The most common category used in consumption contexts is brand categories, which help us predict consumers' reactions to brand extensions (far versus near extensions) and modes of brand competitions (typicality versus differentiation). The prediction is based on consumers' inferences using similarities between the parent and extended brand and between the new and the existing brand; this is also known as similarity-based inferences, suggesting characteristics or qualities can be transferred between category members.
3. Causal inferences are people's if–then linkages, and can be explained by attribution theories. Jones's correspondent inference theory, a key attribution theory used in consumption contexts, suggests that there is a correspondence between dispositions (or characteristics) and behaviour. For example, consumers infer, and transfer, the personalities, attitudes and preferences from the endorsers to the brands they endorse or use, but this effect is weakened if the endorsers do so for compensation or if the endorsers endorse many brands in various product categories. Similar inferences would be drawn for influencers and online reviews. That is, consumers draw inferences about the trustworthiness of influencers based on their popularity and the product characteristics they promote, and of the reviews based on average star ratings. However, these kinds of inferences are based on heuristics, and subject to correspondence bias, thereby making for inaccurate judgements.
4. Another key attribution theory used in consumption contexts is Weiner's affect and control theory, which is particularly useful to examine customer satisfaction in service marketing. That is, in order to assign the responsibility of a service failure, Weiner's attribution theory examines causal locus (internal versus external causes), stability (enduring versus temporary) and controllability (controllable versus non-controllable). Once consumers decide who is responsible for the service failure, their satisfaction and associated emotions would drive their later behaviour. For example, if a flight is delayed

due to bad weather (an non-controllable event), passengers would be upset, but not blame the airlines, unless they handle rescheduling badly (a controllable event).

5. The framing effect, one of the cognitive illusions, can be explained via prospect theory. To put it simply, prospect theory suggests that people make inferences based on the presentation of the information. That is to say, if the same information is presented differently, people would react to different presentations of the information in different ways. This is because people prefer gains, but avoid losses, so the prospect theory is based on three elements: internal reference points, subjective value, and diminishing sensitivity. These principles can be applied to frame product attributes, prices, and brand stories in order to make the product or brand more attractive to consumers.

DISCUSSION QUESTIONS

1. What are category-based inferences? How are they applied in a consumption context? Discuss.
2. What is correspondent inference theory? How is it applied in a consumption context? Discuss.
3. What is affect and control theory? How is it applied in a consumption context? Discuss.
4. What is prospect theory? How is it applied in a consumption context? Discuss.

FURTHER READING

- Cohen, J. B., & Basu, K. (1987). Alternative Models of Categorization: Toward a Cotingent Processing Framework. *Journal of Consumer Research, 13*(4), 455–472.
- Hallahan, K. (1999). Seven Models of Framing: Implications for Public Relations. *Journal of Public Relations Research, 11*(3), 205–242.
- Kahneman, D. (2011). *Thinking, Fast and Slow.* London: Penguin Books.
- Tversky, A., & Kahneman, D. (1981). The Framing of Decisions and the Psychology of Choice. *Science, 211*(4481), 453–458.
- Weiner, B. (2000). Attributional Thoughts about Consumer Behavior. *Journal of Consumer Research, 27*(3), 382–387.

NOTES

1. Page 657 from Hastie, R. (2001). Problems for Judgement and Decision Making. *Annual Review of Psychology, 52*, 653–683.
2. Kellogg, R. T. (2012). *Fundamentals of Cognitive Psychology* (second edn). Los Angeles: Sage.
3. Loken, B., Barsalou, L. W., & Joiner, C. (2008). Categorization Theory and Research in Consumer Psychology. In C. P. Haugtvedt, P. M. Herr, & F. R. Kardes (eds), *Handbook of Consumer Psychology* (pp. 133–164). New York: Psychology Press.

4. Ibid.
5. Medin, D. L., & Smith, E. E. (1984). Concepts and Concept Formation. *Annual Review of Psychology, 35,* 113–138.
6. Galotti, K. M. (2014). *Cognitive Psychology: In and Out of the Laboratory* (fifth edn). Los Angeles: Sage.
7. Ibid.
8. Medin, D. L., & Schaffer, M. M. (1978). Context Theory of Classification Learning. *Psychological Review, 85*(3), 207–238.
9. Cohen, J. B., & Basu, K. (1987). Alternative Models of Categorization: Toward a Cotingent Processing Framework. *Journal of Consumer Research, 13*(4), 455–472.
10. Loken, B. (2006). Consumer Psychology: Categorization, Inferences, Affect, and Persuasion. *Annual Review of Psychology, 57,* 453–485.
11. Bless, H., & Schwarz, N. (2010). Mental Construal and the Emergence of Assimilation and Contrast Effects. *Advances in Experimental Social Psychology, 42,* 317–373.
12. Fong, M. C., Goto, S. G., Moore, C., Zhao, T., Schudson, Z., & Lewis, R. S. (2014). Switching Between Mii and Wii: The Effects of Cultural Priming on the Social Affective N400. *Culture and Brain, 2*(1), 52–71.
13. Mattila, A. S., & Patterson, P. G. (2004). The Impact of Culture on Consumers' Perceptions of Service Recovery Efforts. *Journal of Retailing, 80*(3), 196–206.
14. Briley, D. A., & Aaker, J. L. (2006). When Does Culture Matter? Effects of Personal Knowledge on the Correction of Culture-Based Judgments. *Journal of Marketing Research, 43*(3), 395–408.
15. Fiske, S. T., & Pavelchak, M. A. (1986). Category-Based versus Piecemeal-Based Affective Responses: Developments in Schema-Triggered Affect. In R. M. Sorrentino & E. T. Higgins (eds), *Handbook of Motivation and Cognition: Foundations of Social Behavior* (pp. 167–203). New York: Guilford Press.
16. Sujan, M. (1985). Consumer Knowledge: Effects on Evaluation Strategies Mediating Consumer Judgments. *Journal of Consumer Research, 12*(1), 31–46.
17. Meyers-Levy, J., & Tybout, A. M. (1989). Schema Congruity as a Basis for Product Evaluation. *Journal of Consumer Research, 16*(June), 39–54.
18. Redden, J. P. (2008). Reducing Satiation: The Role of Categorization Level. *Journal of Consumer Research, 34*(February), 624–634.
19. Aaker, D. A., & Keller, K. L. (1990). Consumer Evaluations of Brand Extensions. *Journal of Marketing, 54*(January), 27–41.
20. Ibid.
21. Ibid; Boush, D. M., & Loken, B. (1991). A Process-Tracing Study of Brand Extension Evaluation. *Journal of Marketing Research, 28*(February), 16–28; Bottomley, P. A., & Holden, S. J. S. (2001). Do We Really Know How Consumers Evaluate Brand Extensions? Empirical Generalizations Based on Secondary Analysis of Eight Studies. *Journal of Marketing Research, 38*(4), 494–500; Sichtmann, C., & Diamantopoulos, A. (2013). The Impact of Perceived Brand Globalness, Brand Origin Image, and Brand Origin-Extension Fit on Brand Extension Success. *Journal of the Academy of Marketing Science, 41*(5), 567–585; Völckner, F., &

Sattler, H. (2006). Drivers of Brand Extension Success. *Journal of Marketing, 70*(April), 18–34; DelVecchio, D., & Smith, D. C. (2005). Brand-Extension Price Premiums: The Effects of Perceived Fit and Extension Product Category Risk. *Journal of the Academy of Marketing Science, 33*(2), 184–196; Mao, H., & Krishnan, H. S. (2006). Effects of Prototype and Exemplar Fit on Brand Extension Evaluations: A Two-Process Contingency Model. *Journal of Consumer Research, 33*(June), 41–49.

22. Völckner, F., Sattler, H., Hennig-Thurau, T., & Ringle, C. M. (2010). The Role of Parent Brand Quality for Service Brand Extension Success. *Journal of Service Research, 13*(4), 379–396; Song, P., Zhang, C., Xu, Y. C., & Huang, L. (2010). Brand Extension of Online Technology Products: Evidence from Search Engine to Virtual Communities and Online News. *Decision Support Systems, 49*(1), 91–99.

23. Loken, Consumer Psychology.

24. Klink, R. R., & Smith, D. C. (2001). Treats to the External Validity of Brand Extension Research. *Journal of Marketing Research, 38*(3), 326–335; Dens, N., & De Pelsmacker, P. (2010). Advertising for Extensions: Moderating Effects of Extension Type, Advertising Strategy, and Product Category Involvement on Extension Evaluation. *Marketing Letters, 21*(2), 175–189.

25. Pham, M. T., & Muthukrishnan, A. V. (2002). Search and Alignment in Judgment Revision: Implications for Brand Positioning. *Journal of Marketing Research, 39*(1), 18–30.

26. Sood, S., & Drèze, X. (2006). Brand Extensions of Experiential Goods: Movie Sequel Evaluations. *Journal of Consumer Research, 33*(December), 352–360.

27. Carpenter, G. S., & Nakamoto, K. (1996). Impact of Consumer Preference Formation on Marketing Objectives and Competitive Second Mover Strategies. *Journal of Consumer Psychology, 5*(4), 325–358; Fischer, E., & Reuber, R. (2007). The Good, the Bad, and the Unfamiliar: The Challenges of Reputation Formation Facing New Firms. *Entrepreneurship Theory and Practice, 31*(1), 53–75; Veryzer, R. W., Jr., & Hutchinson, J. W. (1998). The Influence of Unity and Prototypicality on Aesthetic Response to New Product Designs. *Journal of Consumer Research, 24*(March), 374–394.

28. Carpenter & Nakamoto, Impact of Consumer Preference Formation on Marketing Objectives and Competitive Second Mover Strategies.

29. Babin, B. J., & Babin, L. (2001). Seeking Something Different? A Model of Schema Typicality, Consumer Affect, Purchase Intentions and Perceived Shopping Value. *Journal of Business Research, 54*(2), 89–96.

30. Pham & Muthukrishnan, Search and Alignment in Judgment Revision.

31. van Horen, F., & Pieters, R. (2012). When High-Similarity Copycats Lose and Moderate-Similarity Copycats Gain: The Impact of Comparative Evaluation. *Journal of Marketing Research, 49*(1), 83–91.

32. Carpenter & Nakamoto, Impact of Consumer Preference Formation on Marketing Objectives and Competitive Second Mover Strategies; Moreau, C. P., Lehmann, D. R., & Markman, A. B. (2001). Entrenched Knowledge Structures and Consumer Response to New Products. *Journal of Marketing Research, 38*(1), 14–29; Zhang, S., & Markman,

A. B. (1998). Overcoming the Early Entrant Advantage: The Role of Alignable and Nonalignable Differences. *Journal of Marketing Research, 35*(4), 413–426.

33. Kardes, F. R., & Kalyanaram, G. (1992). Order-of-Entry Effects on Consumer Memory and Judgment: An Information Integration Perspective. *Journal of Marketing Research, 29*(3), 343–357.

34. Zhang & Markman, Overcoming the Early Entrant Advantage.

35. Zhang, S., Kardes, F. R., & Cronley, M. L. (2002). Comparative Advertising: Effects of Structural Alignability on Target Brand Evaluation. *Journal of Consumer Psychology, 12*(4), 303–311.

36. Zhang & Markman, Overcoming the Early Entrant Advantage.

37. Kruglanski, A. W., & Webster, D. M. (1996). Motivated Closing of the Mind: "Seizing" and "Freezing". *Psychological Review, 103*(2), 263–283.

38. Kardes, F. R., Posavac, S. S., Cronley, M. L., & Herr, P. M. (2008). Consumer Inference. In C. P. Haugtvedt, P. M. Herr, & F. R. Kardes (eds), *Handbook of Consumer Psychology* (pp. 165–191). New York: Lawrence Erlbaum Associates.

39. Kelley, H. H. (1973). The Processes of Causal Attribution. *American Psychologist, 28*(2), 107–128.

40. Jones, E. E. (1979). The Rocky Road From Acts to Dispositions. *American Psychologist, 34*(2), 107–117.

41. Ibid; Jones, E. E., & Davis, K. E. (1965). From Acts to Dispositions: The Attribution Process in Person Perception. *Advances in Experimental Social Psychology, 2*, 219–266; Jones, E. E., & Harris, V. A. (1967). The Attribution of Attitudes. *Journal of Experimental Social Psychology, 3*(1), 1–24; Jones, E. E. (1990). *Interpersonal Perception.* New York: W. H. Freeman; Jones, E. E., & McGillis, D. (1976). Correspondent Inferences and the Attribution Cube: A Comparative Reappraisal. In J. H. Harvey, W. J. Ickes, & R. F. Kidd (eds), *New Directions in Attribution Research* (Vol. 1, pp. 389–420). Hillsdale, NJ: Erlbaum.

42. Gilbert, D. T., & Malone, P. S. (1995). The Correspondence Bias. *Psychological Bulletin, 117*(1), 21–38.

43. Weiner, B. (1985). An Attributional Theory of Achievement Motivation and Emotion. *Psychological Review, 92*(4), 548–573.

44. Ibid.

45. McCracken, G. (1989). Who Is the Celebrity Endorser? Cultural Foundations of the Endorsement Process. *Journal of Consumer Research, 16*(December), 310–321.

46. Silvera, D. H., & Austad, B. (2004). Factors Predicting the Effectiveness of Celebrity Endorsement Advertisements. *European Journal of Marketing, 38*(11/12), 1509–1526.

47. Arsena, A., Silvera, D. H., & Pandelaere, M. (2014). Brand Trait Transference: When Celebrity Endorsers Acquire Brand Personality Traits. *Journal of Business Research, 67*(7), 1537–1543.

48. Cronley, M. L., Kardes, F. R., Goddard, P., & Houghton, D. C. (1999). Endorsing Products for the Money: The Role of the Correspondence Bias in Celebrity Advertising. In E. J. Arnould & L. M. Scott (eds), *NA – Advances in Consumer Research* (Vol. 25, pp. 627–631). Provo, UT: Association for Consumer Research.

49. Cronley et al., Endorsing Products for the Money.

50. Campbell, C., & Farrell, J. R. (2020). More than Meets the Eye: The Functional Components Underlying Influencer Marketing. *Business Horizons, 63*(4), 469–479.

51. De Veirman, M., Cauberghe, V., & Hudders, L. (2017). Marketing through Instagram Influencers: The Impact of Number of Followers and Product Divergence on Brand Attitude. *International Journal of Advertising, 36*(5), 798–828.

52. Ibid.

53. Kay, S., Mulcahy, R., & Parkinson, J. (2020). When Less Is More: The Impact of Macro and Micro Social Media Influencers' Disclosure. *Journal of Marketing Management, 36*(3–4), 248–278.

54. De Veirman et al., Marketing through Instagram Influencers.

55. Machleit, K. A., Eroglu, S. A., & Mantel, S. P. (2000). Perceived Retail Crowding and Shopping Satisfaction: What Modifies This Relationship? *Journal of Consumer Psychology, 9*(1), 29–42.

56. Kay et al., When Less Is More.

57. Kim, T. (2012). *Consumers' Correspondence Inference on Celebrity Endorsers: The Role of Correspondence Bias and Suspicion* (PhD Unpublished doctoral thesis). University of Tennessee, Knoxville.

58. Laczniak, R. N., DeCarlo, T. E., & Ramaswami, S. N. (2001). Consumers' Responses to Negative Word-of-Mouth Communication: An Attribution Theory Perspective. *Journal of Consumer Psychology, 11*(1), 57–73.

59. De Langhe, B., Fernbach, P. M., & Lichtenstein, D. R. (2016). Navigating by the Stars: Investigating the Actual and Perceived Validity of Online User Ratings. *Journal of Consumer Research, 42*(6), 817–833.

60. Chevalier, J. A., & Mayzlin, D. (2006). The Effect of Word of Mouth on Sales: Online Book Reviews. *Journal of Marketing Research, 43*(August), 345–354.

61. Luca, M., & Zervas, G. (2016). Fake It Till You Make It: Reputation, Competition, and Yelp Review Fraud. *Management Science, 62*(12), 3412–3427; Mayzlin, D., Dover, Y., & Chevalier, J. (2014). Promotional Reviews: An Empirical Investigation of Online Review Manipulation. *American Economic Review, 104*(8), 2421–2455.

62. Hong, S., & Pittman, M. (2020). eWOM Anatomy of Online Product Reviews: Interaction Effects of Review Number, Valence, and Star Ratings on Perceived Credibility. *International Journal of Advertising, 39*(7), 892–920.

63. Tsiros, M., Mittal, V., & Ross, W. T., Jr. (2004). The Role of Attributions in Customer Satisfaction: A Reexamination. *Journal of Consumer Research, 31*(September), 476–483.

64. Ibid.

65. Mittal, V., & Kamakura, W. A. (2001). Satisfaction, Repurchase Intent, and Repurchase Behavior: Investigating the Moderating Effect of Customer Characteristics. *Journal of Marketing Research, 38*(1), 131–142.

66. Hellier, P. K., Geursen, G. M., Carr, R. A., & Rickard, J. A. (2003). Customer Repurchase Intention: A General Structural Equation Model. *European Journal of Marketing, 37*(11/12), 1762–1800.

67. Folkes, V. S., Koletsky, S., & Graham, J. L. (1987). A Field Study of Causal Inferences and Consumer Reaction: The View from the Airport. *Journal of Consumer Research, 13*(4), 534–539.

68. Kahneman, D., & Tversky, A. (1979). Prospect Theory: An Analysis of Decision under Risk. *Econometrica, 47*(2), 263–291; Tversky, A., & Kahneman, D. (1992). Advances in Prospect Theory: Cumulative Representation of Uncertainty. *Journal of Risk and Uncertainty, 5*(4), 297–323.

69. Kahneman, D. (2011). *Thinking, Fast and Slow*. London: Penguin Books.

70. Thaler, R. (1985). Mental Account and Consumer Choice. *Marketing Science, 4*(3), 199–214.

71. Tversky, A., & Kahneman, D. (1981). The Framing of Decisions and the Psychology of Choice. *Science, 211*(4481), 453–458.

72. Christensen, C. (1987). The Psychophysics of Spending. *Journal of Behavioral Decision Making, 2*(2), 69–80.

73. DelVecchio, D., Henard, D. H., & Freling, T. H. (2006). The Effect of Sales Promotion on Post-Promotion Brand Choice: A Meta Analysis. *Journal of Retailing, 82*(3), 203–213; DelVecchio, D., Krishnan, H. S., & Smith, D. C. (2007). Cents or Percent? The Effects of Promotion Framing on Price Expectations and Choice. *Journal of Marketing, 71*(July), 158–170.

74. Levin, I. P. (1987). Associative Effects of Information Framing. *Bulletin of the Psychonomics Society, 25*(March), 85–86.

75. Levin, I. P., & Gaeth, G. J. (1988). How Consumers Are Affected by the Framing of Attribute Information Before and After Consuming Product. *Journal of Consumer Research, 15*(December), 374–378.

76. Riezebos, R., Kist, B., & Kootstra, G. (2002). *Brand Management: A Theoretical and Practical Approach*. Harlow: Pearson.

77. *Adweek*. (1986, 19 May). Silk in a Bottle, p. 18.

78. Carpenter, G. S., Glazer, R., & Nakamoto, K. (1994). Meaningful Brands from Meaningless Differentiation: The Dependence on Irrelevant Attributes. *Journal of Marketing Research, 31*(August), 339–350.

79. Anderson, E., & Simester, D. (2003). Mind Your Pricing Cues. *Harvard Business Review, 81*(September), 96–103; Gendall, P., Holdershaw, J., & Garland, R. (1997). The Effect of Odd Pricing on Demand. *European Journal of Marketing, 31*(11/12), 799–813; Stiving, M., & Winer, R. S. (1997). An Empirical Analysis of Price Endings with Scanner Data. *Journal of Consumer Research, 24*(June), 57–68; Schindler, R. M., & Kibarian, T. M. (1996). Increased Consumer Sales Response through Use of 99-Ending Prices. *Journal of Retailing, 72*(Summer), 187–200.

80. Anderson, E., & Simester, D. (2003). Effects of $9 Price Endings on Retail Sales: Evidence from Field Experiments. *Quantitative Marketing and Economics, 1*(1), 93–110.

81. Schindler, R. M., & Kirby, P. N. (1997). Patterns of Rightmost Digits Used in Advertised Prices: Implications for Nine-Ending Effects. *Journal of Consumer Research, 24*(September), 192–201.

82. Macé, S. (2012). The Impact and Determinants of Nine-Ending Pricing in Grocery Retailing. *Journal of Retailing, 88*(1), 115–130.

83. Schindler & Kibarian, Increased Consumer Sales Response through Use of 99-Ending Prices.

84. Dehaene, S. (1997). *The Number Sense: How the Mind Creates Mathematics.* New York: Oxford University Press; Hinrichs, J. V., Yurko, D. S., & Hu, J.-M. (1981). Two-Digit Number Comparison: Use of Place Information. *Journal of Experimental Psychology: Human Perception and Performance, 7*(4), 890–901.

85. Thomas, M., & Morwitz, V. (2005). Penny Wise and Pound Foolish: The Left-Digit Effect in Price Cognition. *Journal of Consumer Research, 32*(June), 54–64.

86. Manning, K. C., & Sprott, D. E. (2009). Price Endings, Left-Digit Effects, and Choice. *Journal of Consumer Research, 36*(August), 328–335.

87. Poltrock, S. E., & Schwartz, D. R. (1984). Comparative Judgments of Multidigit Numbers. *Journal of Experimental Psychology: Learning, Memory, and Cognition, 10*(1), 32–45.

88. Coulter, K. S., & Coulter, R. A. (2007). Distortion of Price Discount Perceptions: The Right Digit Effect. *Journal of Consumer Research, 34*(August), 162–173.

89. DelVecchio, D., Krishnan, H. S., & Smith, D. C. (2007). Cents or Percent? The Effects of Promotion Framing on Price Expectations and Choice. *Journal of Marketing, 71*(July), 158–170; Chen, S.-F. S., Monroe, K. B., & Lou, Y.-C. (1998). The Effects of Framing Price Promotion Messages on Consumers' Perceptions and Purchase Intentions. *Journal of Retailing, 74*(3), 353–372.

90. Hallahan, K. (1999). Seven Models of Framing: Implications for Public Relations. *Journal of Public Relations Research, 11*(3), 205–242.

91. Maheswaran, D., & Meyers-Levy, J. (1990). The Influence of Message Framing and Issue Involvement. *Journal of Marketing Research, 27*(August), 361–367.

92. Ries, A., & Trout, J. (2001). *Positioning: The Battle for Your Mind.* New York: McGraw-Hill.

93. Ibid.

94. Stern, B. B. (1994). Classical and Vignette Television Advertising Dramas: Structural Models, Formal Analysis, and Consumer Effects. *Journal of Consumer Research, 20*(March), 601–615.

95. Paharia, N., Keinan, A., Avery, J., & Schor, J. B. (2011). The Underdog Effect: The Marketing of Disadvantage and Determination through Brand Biography. *Journal of Consumer Research, 37*(February), 775–790.

96. Ries & Trout, *Positioning: The Battle for Your Mind.*

97. Page 1 from Linzmayer, O. (1999). *Apple Confidential: The Real Story of Apple Computer Inc.* San Francisco: No Starch.

98. Beverland, M. (2009). *Building Brand Authenticity: 7 Habits of Iconic Brands.* Basingstoke: Palgrave Macmillan.

99. Beverland, M., Lindgreen, A., & Vink, M. W. (2008). Projecting Authenticity through Advertising. *Journal of Advertising, 37*(1), 5–15.

100. Paharia, N., Keinan, A., Avery, J., & Schor, J. B. (2011). The Underdog Effect: The Marketing of Disadvantage and Determination through Brand Biography. *Journal of Consumer Research, 37*(February), 775–790; Parmentier, M.-A. (2011). When David Met Victoria: Forging A Strong Family Brand. *Family Business Review, 24*(3), 217–232; Leigh, T. W., Peters, C., & Shelton, J. (2006). The Consumer Quest for Authenticity: The Multiplicity of Meanings within the MG Subculture of Consumption. *Journal of the Academy of Marketing Science, 34*(4), 481–493.

101. Paharia et al., The Underdog Effect.

102. Parekh, R. (2012, 27 August). After 50 Years, Avis Drops Iconic "We Try Harder" Tagline. *AdvertisingAge.* Retrieved from http://adage.com/article/news/50–years-avis-drops-iconic-harder-tagline/236887/

103. Avis. (2012). Classic Avis "We Try Harder". Retrieved from http://blog.avis.co.uk/blog/category/we-try-harder-slogan/

104. Parekh, After 50 Years, Avis Drops Iconic "We Try Harder".

105. Paharia, N., Avery, J., & Keinan, A. (2014). Positioning Brands against Large Competitors to Increase Sales. *Journal of Marketing Research, 51*(6), 647–656.

106. Paharia, N., Keinan, A., & Avery, J. (2014). The Upside to Large Competitors. *MIT Sloan Management Review, 56*(1), 10–11.

4

CONSUMER IMPLICIT COGNITION

┌─Learning objectives─┐

To explore, understand, and explain:

- the distinction between implicit and explicit cognition
- the psychological basis of implicit cognition
- the concept of implicit knowledge and its applications in a consumption context
- the concept of implicit learning, its applications in consumer behaviour, and its associated limitations in marketing practices

4.1 INTRODUCTION

Implicit cognition involves little or no cognitive (or conscious) effort, in contrast to explicit cognition where cognitive effort is needed. Chapter 2 focuses on explicit cognition, discussing the role of memory and knowledge in the formation of our perceptions as rational beings, and Chapter 3 emphasises how we form our opinions and attitudes *efficiently* through categories, causal relationships, and framing effects; most of which bridge between explicit and implicit cognition. As people tend to reserve efforts for necessary and more important tasks, we greatly rely on implicit cognition, even for high-level thinking activities,[1] in our day-to-day lives; research shows that we rely for about 95% of the time on implicit cognition,[2] suggesting that persuasion needs no or little consciousness.[3] This chapter will therefore focus on the conceptualisation of implicit cognition (Section 4.2) and the role of implicit cognition in consumer behaviour (Sections 4.3 and 4.4).

4.2 THE BASICS: THE IMPLICIT-EXPLICIT DISTINCTION

Implicit and explicit cognition is notably known as the dual process proposed by Evans in 1984. Implicit cognition has been discussed under various names in psychology, including System 1 (versus System 2)[4] and heuristic/intuitive/holistic (versus analytic or systematic).[5] Simply speaking, the distinction between implicit and explicit cognition is determined by whether or not consciousness is used to account for the generation of perception, evaluation, and behaviour.[6] When consciousness is used, explicit cognition is at work; and when explicit cognition is at work, it is usually cognitively effortful. On the other hand, when consciousness is not involved or little involved, it is the implicit cognition that dominates our perception, evaluation, and behaviour.

Implicit cognition works like an intuition, which comes quickly and with little effort. For example, look at the problem: $1 + 1 = ?$ For most readers of this book, the answer to this problem almost comes immediately without much effort. By contrast, look at the problem: $4 \times 8 + 11 \times 22 = ?$ Most of us will need to stop what we are doing and concentrate on the problem (maybe by using pen and paper, or a calculator) to calculate the correct answer (which is 274), except perhaps for someone who is good or trained at mental arithmetic. In the circumstances where we take time to make a decision, such as the decision for the answer to the previous maths problem, we are conscious of what we are doing and it is cognitively effortful – this is where we rely on our explicit cognition.

Using the state of consciousness and memory stores to explain implicit–explicit distinction is, though easily understood, overly simplified. Psychologists have reminded us that the state of consciousness is on a continuum, not a none-or-all state.[7] Moreover, although the implicit and explicit memory stores have been shown to be based on neuro-anatomically distinct structures,[8] they interact closely.[9] As a result, it is almost impossible to find functionally pure instantiations of them.[10] Therefore, recent studies have focused more on the functions of implicit–explicit cognition. According to Bargh,[11] implicit cognition is able to initiate automatic processes and reflects one or a combination of the below characteristics:

1.   lack of awareness
2.   lack of intentionality
3.   lack of controllability
4.   high efficiency (non-reliance on cognitive resources)

In order to reflect the focus on functions, Stanovich and West[12] coined the generic terms System 1 and System 2 to indicate implicit and explicit cognition. These generic terms have been popularly used in businesses since the publication of Kahneman's *Thinking, Fast and Slow* in 2011. According to Kahneman:[13]

System 1 operates automatically and quickly, with little or no effort and no sense of voluntary control. System 2 allocates attention to the effortful mental activities that demand it, including complex computations. The operations of System 2 are often associated with the subjective experience of agency, choice, and concentration. . . . When we think of ourselves, we identify with System 2, the conscious, reasoning self that has beliefs, makes choices, and decides what to think about and what to do. Although System 2 believes itself to be where the action is, the automatic System 1 . . . as effortlessly originating impressions and feelings that are the main sources of the explicit beliefs and deliberate choices of System 2.

See Table 4.1 for a range of examples of activities generated by System 1 and System 2.

Table 4.1 Examples of the activities that are attributed to System 1 and System 2[14]

	System 1	System 2
Activities	• Detect that one object is more distant than another. • Orient to the source of a sudden sound. • Make a "disgust face" when shown a horrible picture. • Detect hostility in a voice. • Answer to 2 + 2 = ? • Drive a car on an empty road. • Find a strong move in chess (if you are a chess master). • Understand simple sentences.	• Look for a woman with white hair. • Search memory to identify a surprising sound. • Monitor the appropriateness of your behaviour in a social situation. • Count the occurrences of the letter *a* in a page of text. • Park in a narrow space. • Compare two washing machines for overall value. • Fill out a tax form. • Check the validity of a complex logical argument.

In a nutshell, the distinction between implicit and explicit cognition lies in the distinction between mental process and mental experience: *mental process* is the operation of the mind (i.e. our conscious, cognitive thinking process), whereas *mental experience* is the subjective life that emerges from that operation.[15] As Carlston puts it, mental experience is the residue of a lifetime of observation and thought.[16]

4.3 IMPLICIT KNOWLEDGE

The psychological basis

As implicit cognition is a result of a lifetime of learning, observation, and thought,[17] how people extract and combine information to understand the world can be seen as people's knowledge (or perception) of the world and is usually in a tacit form.[18] That is, what you have learned is hidden in your subconsciousness or dropped below your consciousness level into nonconsciousness even if you were once very conscious about it when you were learning it. Because of this, implicit knowledge usually includes knowledge about language, traits, categorisation, acculturation, and aesthetic preferences,[19] which are commonly known as intuition, incubation, or insight.[20]

With implicit knowledge, we are able to make judgements based on *thin-slice information*; that is, limited information.[21] For example, people are able to form an impression of a person based on less than five minutes of observation[22] or of a brand based on static cues, such as a print advertisement.[23] Though information is limited, the accuracy of judgements can be high,[24] and thin-slice information judgements demonstrate three main characteristics:

1. Lack of the ability to articulate the criteria we use to make judgements[25] – what we sometimes refer to as "just a hunch". If we are asked to explain our criteria[26] or given more information than thin sliced,[27] poor performance will be likely to increase.
2. Adding a cognitive load, which tends to disrupt explicit memory in information processing, does not influence the accuracy of judgements based on thin-slice information.[28]
3. Increased cognitive effort aiming to improve accuracy of the judgement outcome does not improve its accuracy.[29]

Implications for consumer behaviour

Product/brand evaluation

The application of thin-slice information (or implicit knowledge) in consumer judgement is abundant. For example, price[30] and warranty[31] have been used by consumers to determine product quality or brand superiority or model attractiveness linked to how effective advertisements are in certain product categories.[32]

─Box 4.1─

Thin-slice information and Internet advertising

The use of thin-slice information appears in the more modern marketing tools, such as Internet advertising. More than 80% of web surfers spend only a few seconds on web banner advertisements to decide whether they will click through the advertisement.[33] Besides, their judgements of a website's usefulness, effectiveness, and trustworthiness are not only accurate[34] but also prompt.[35]

─Box 4.2─

The role of social impact

As consumer judgement is a type of social judgement, the influence of the same thin-slice information on our evaluation may change in time and space. For example, as modern consumers have become savvier, the effect of price on quality perception has weakened in recent years.[36] Similarly, as the definition of model attractiveness has changed – thanks to Dove's Real Beauty campaign and modern awareness of related health issues regarding traditional thin-beauty – and as the emphasis on appearance to judge people has decreased (or at least has become politically incorrect), the effectiveness of using highly attractive models as endorsers in advertisements has declined.[37]

Recognition

When consumers are able to recognise brand information, this recognition can sometimes lead to positive preference of a piece of the information (including brand elements, such as brand names, logos, and packaging).[38] This is because recognition helps reduce consumers' information processing time.[39] As a result, common marketing practices do not change a brand's element, such as logo or packaging, too much at a time. If companies do not recognise such importance, they should consider Tropicana's packaging fiasco in 2009, when they spent millions of dollars to launch a brand new packaging of Tropicana orange juice, they had to return to the old packaging because of a close to $33 million plummet in sales (that is, 20% decrease) within a two-month period.[40]

The recognition effect does not only work on well-known brands. A *mere recognition* of a brand can lead consumers to believe the product to be of better quality.[41] That is, when shoppers have only two options to choose from, they would go for something that they have heard of, not something that they do not know about, because the latter suggests higher risks than the former. This effect is a long-term effect that encourages repeated purchase of merely recognisable brands.[42] However, the mere recognition effect disappears when people are motivated to process further information.[43]

─Box 4.3─

Brand halo effect: a potentially biased (inaccurate) judgement

The *brand halo effect* (or the *brand transformational effect*) suggests that if a brand is reputable or favourable, perceivers tend to evaluate most attributes of the brand positively. On the other hand, if a brand has a bad reputation, perceivers tend to discredit the brand on most dimensions

(Continued)

of what the brand does. However, a reputable brand does not necessarily guarantee its superior quality on every dimension, and similarly a problematic brand does not necessarily suggest its inferior quality on every dimension. This effect is an example of the biased or inaccurate judgement that a consumer is likely to make based on thin-slice information.

Box 4.4

The impact of misleading information in judgements based on thin-slice information

Although we are able to make reasonably good judgements based on thin-slice information, if the information we are exposed to is misleading, this information can significantly influence our subsequent judgements. How much are we influenced by misleading information? The experiments of Hall, Johansson, Tärning, Sikström, and Deutgen can give us some idea.[44] They set up a tasting table at a supermarket and invited passerby shoppers to sample two different varieties of jam (including blackcurrant versus blueberry, ginger versus lime, or cinnamon-apple versus grapefruit) and tea (including apple pie versus honey, caramel and cream versus cinnamon, or Pernod versus mango). Immediately afterwards the participants decided which alternative they preferred, they were asked again to sample the chosen alternative, and to verbally explain why they preferred the flavour they chose. However, unknown to the participants, they sampled the chosen alternative from the containers in which the contents were switched to the opposite of what the participants intended. For such different tastes between the experimental pairs, the results showed that less than 34% of the participants detected the mismatch between the intended and the actual sample of jam or tea. These results suggest how much we can be influenced just by the labels of the containers, let alone the potential bias from a brand name (see Box 4.3). Because the potentially "misleading" information comes from brand itself, in order to avoid any bias (positive or negative), practitioners engage in a type of market research called blind-testing in the hope that they can obtain information that is not distorted by brand information.

Sound symbolism

Sound symbolism includes phonetic speech sounds, tones, and other parameters of musical expression,[45] and is considered as a specific area of thin-slice information as it suggests that we make our judgements or evaluations based on what we hear, usually a word or a brand name. Studies have shown that human beings are able to distinguish between utterances spoken in their native language and those spoken in foreign tongues when they are as young as two months old.[46] This is because, despite not understanding at the age of two months old, infants have become attuned to the natural flow (i.e. rhythm) of language.[47] This section introduces two areas in sound symbolism with regards to brand names: phonetic effects and sound repetition (musical expression) effects.

Phonetic effects

Extensive studies have shown that a match-up between sound symbolism and brand positioning can produce a favourable impact[48]– see Box 4.5 for how sound conveys meaning. For example, Klink[49] examined sound symbolism effect across three product categories: shampoo, pain reliever, and laptop computer. In his experiments, he positioned the shampoo as "leaving hair soft", the pain reliever as "fast-working", and the laptop computer as "light-weight", and created two sets of fictitious brand names: one set embedded sound symbolism (Silbee shampoo, Zindin pain reliever, Vextrill laptop computer), but the other did not (Polbee shampoo, Bondin pain reliever, Goxtrill laptop computer). The results demonstrated that the participants believed more the products' marketing communication of product positioning when these products were under the brand names with sound symbolism, and therefore liked the products more.

─Box 4.5─

Sound and meaning

Linguists suggest that sound and meaning in human language are linked.[50] Sounds generate different acoustic frequencies, which are based on the position and curvature of the tongue in the mouth, ranging from a high-front to low-back position;[51] for example, beat, bit, bet, bait, bat, boat, bought, posh, but, put, and boot in a rough order from high-front to low-back position.[52] Compared with consonants, vowels are better able to convey meanings.[53] High-front vowels convey meanings associated with smaller size than low-back vowels; for example, "teeny" in English, "chico" in Spanish, "petit" in French, "mikros" in Greek, and "shiisai" in Japanese are words composed of high-front vowels, whereas "humongous" in English, "gordo" in Spanish, "grand" in French, "macros" in Greek, and "ookii" in Japanese are words composed of low-back vowels.[54] In addition to smallness, front vowels (versus back vowels) in brand names convey attribute qualities of lightness, mildness, thinness, fastness, coldness, bitterness, femininity, weakness, and prettiness.[55]

Sound repetition

Sounds do not merely convey meanings, but also connote emotions.[56] Take music as an example. The repetitive rhythm frequently appears in energetic music,[57] which is able to trigger stimulation and produces hedonic value leading to positive or improved product evaluation.[58] However, it is not just the sound of music that demonstrates this property. The sound of a word has a similar effect, such that sound repetition in a brand name leads to a positive brand evaluation.[59] Examples of sound repetition in brand names include well-known brands such as Coca-Cola and Kit Kat.

4.4 IMPLICIT LEARNING

The influence at cognitive level

The psychological basis

Implicit learning is learning that occurs without intention, or without conscious awareness of what has been learned.[60] It is learning that does not only take place when our attention is elsewhere;[61] it also takes place when we are asleep[62] or under anaesthesia.[63] Implicit learning has been shown to influence our cognition. Research finds that a semantically related prime can speed word–non-word judgements; for example, priming bread facilitates recognition of butter.[64] This priming effect still holds when the semantically related prime is presented subliminally.[65]

Implications for consumer behaviour

Homophones can be used to influence consumer behaviour when cognitive resources are limited. For example, Davis and Herr used "bye" and "so long" in a travel blog talking about the blogger's last day in Canada and recommending places and things to do in Canada and mentioning the things that he was going to miss.[66] At the end of the blog, they used either "bye bye" or "so long" to conclude this entry. In the first stage, the participants read this blog entry and evaluated how informative they found it was. In the second stage, the participants carried out an unrelated task: they were informed of a restaurant that was opening locally. The restaurant was promoting a "name your own price" dinner-for-two package, and the participants indicated how much they were willing to pay for this specific package. The results indicated that the participants engaging in a cognitive load task (i.e. memorising a seven-digit number) while reading the blog showed their willingness to pay the highest value if the blog entry ended with "bye bye". In other words, the participants who read "bye" while under cognitive load gave higher willingness-to-pay amounts to "buy" a restaurant package. Reading "bye" appears to have primed "buy" under cognitive load. Priming did not occur in the absence of load, suggesting sufficient cognitive resources were able to suppress alternative meanings.

Perception without awareness

The psychological basis

The influence of implicit learning at the cognitive level has been extended and referred to as perception without awareness, suggesting that we are able to generate perception (or make judgements) without conscious awareness.[67] Bargh and Piertromonaco's experiments are best to explain this phenomenon.[68] That is, in their experiments, they subliminally presented 100 words randomly selected from lists of controlled words (e.g. water, long, or number) and hostility-related words (e.g. hate, hurt, and insult) to the subjects while they were occupied with a "vigilance task". Either 0%, 20%, or 80% of words were hostility-related. Following the vigilance task, the subjects were asked to carry out an unrelated task, in which the subjects read a behavioural description of a fictional character named Donald, and rated Donald on several trait dimensions. While the description about Donald was ambiguous regarding how hostile he was, the subjects rated Donald on the hostility dimension in accordance to their exposure to the hostility-related words. In other words, the subjects with higher exposure to hostility-related words rated Donald as more hostile in his personality trait. Moreover, as the level of Donald's hostility increased, the subjects liked Donald less and less.

Implications for consumer behaviour

Brand exposure

Brand exposure is able to elicit automatic behavioural effects. For example, Fitzsimons et al.[69] demonstrated that the participants subliminally primed with Apple logos (versus IBM logos) behaved more creatively, and that those subliminally primed with Disney logos (versus E! logos) behaved more honestly.

Incidental consumer brand encounters: social influence on the choice of brand

We are not exposed to brands only through advertisements. In fact, we encounter brands all the time, including seeing other people use brands. In these circumstances, we may or may not notice this type of exposure. Ferraro et al. term this type of exposure as "incidental consumer brand encounters",[70] and in psychology it is known as *mere exposure*. The mere exposure effect suggests a positive relationship between positive attitudes of a stimulus and the frequency of its exposure,[71] and it can also be observed in implicit learning.[72]

Ferraro et al. simulated mere brand exposure to examine how people respond to such exposures with limited awareness.[73] Their simulation included 20 photos, each featuring a focal person engaging in various everyday activities, such as waiting for the bus, eating lunch, and so on. The photos contained the focal people either with or without the focal brand, Dasani water, and the frequency of brand exposure varied across three levels: zero, four, or 12 exposures. The participants were instructed to focus on the facial expressions of the people in the photos, and after viewing the photos, they were thanked for participating in the study by being given a bottled water of a brand of their choice from Dasani, Aquafina, Deer Park, and Poland Spring. The results showed that, for the participants not aware of the brand exposure, 17% of the participants in the zero exposure group selected Dasani, as compared to 22% in the four-exposure and 40% in the 12-exposure groups. If the focal people were seen as a member from the participants' social groups (in-group versus out-group), the percentage choosing Dasani increased even further.

The limitations

What has been discussed in this section so far seems to have suggested that subliminal messages are effective in influencing our cognition, evaluation, and behaviour. However, if presenting subliminal messages could be this effective, the marketplace would be flooded with this manner of communication, if, of course, the policy makers had no problem with consumers being unconsciously manipulated. The reality is actually more complicated than what we have learned in the labs where the experiments were carried out.

The popularity of subliminal advertising started in 1957 when James M. Vicary and Francis Thayer conducted an experiment, in which they flashed messages "Eat popcorn" and "Drink Coca-Cola" for 3 milliseconds, a duration that is well below conscious perception threshold, throughout a movie, and they claimed that popcorn sales increased by 58% and Coca-Cola sales by 18% as a result of the experiment. However, many other studies afterwards were unable to replicate the findings.[74] Even when studies did show some effects of subliminal advertising, the effect size was small.[75] This stream of studies became quiet after many failed attempts to replicate Vicary's claim and in particular after 1962 when Vicary admitted that his results were in fact fraudulent.

More recently, some scholars have started to refocus on how non-consciousness influences consumer choices,[76] and a stream of these studies have appeared (and is discussed in this section). However, the applications of implicit learning in the marketplace are still limited because of three main constraints:

1. *The constraint of the methods studying implicit learning*: Early studies have shown that the design and presentation of subliminal messages can be so difficult that they become a barrier to achieving reliable results in early studies.[77] Although the methods for presenting subliminal messages have been improved significantly in the last half a century, it is still difficult to avoid the mere-measurement effect, which suggests that simply asking consumers about their purchase intentions can increase the likelihood of purchase.[78] Because of this, any slight contamination in the experiments may lead to unreliable results. Moreover, because of implicit cognition, participants in experiments are unable to pin down the reasons underlying their decisions. Even if they could, the chances are that they would do so because of post-decision rationalisation,[79] rather than the actual mechanism of implicit learning.

2. *The constraint of the fact that consciousness is on a continuum; it is not a none-or-all state*: Even if we claim that we are not aware of something, it does not necessarily mean that we are unaware of it. The experiments are able to manipulate the target messages to ensure they are presented in a subliminal manner, but where do we draw a line on the consciousness continuum in practice? Studies of product or brand placement suggest that in order to be effective, attention is important,[80] but studies in implicit cognition demonstrate that the effect of implicit learning is significant only when it is truly implicit.[81] When participants are aware of the manipulation, the effect decreases to non-significant. But how subliminal can a message be in a normal day-to-day encounter? Even if we can obtain results from

carefully executed experiments, how much of what we learn from the experiments can translate into the marketplace is another question.

3. *The constraint of the interaction between implicit learning and our already developed perceptions and behaviours*: Verwijmeren et al. suggest that the effect of implicit learning on what has already developed and is strongly entrenched in our minds and life, such as habits, is minimal.[82] Similarly, Vargas reviewed recent studies and concluded that the effect of implicit learning in persuasion is weak at best.[83] He said:

> The evidence collected to date suggests that subliminal stimuli can be used to evoke abstract concepts and affect, and can influence related judgments and behaviours where the primed concepts can reasonably be availed (e.g., increase hostility in an already frustrating situation, walk more slowly when asked to walk down a hall, drink more of a beverage when thirsty). But subliminal stimuli cannot be used to directly persuade or dictate behaviour (i.e., cause hostile outbursts without provocation, get up and walk down the hallway, go to the soda machine and buy a beverage). Increasing accessibility via subliminal priming is possible, and it can affect behaviour to the extent that the newly accessible primes are applicable to the current situation.[84]

It is a long way from liking to persuasion in implicit learning. Practitioners should be cautious about being too optimistic of the effects from implicit learning.

4.5 SUMMARY

1. The basic distinction between implicit and explicit cognition lies in whether or not consciousness is involved in information processing. If consciousness is involved, it is explicit cognition; otherwise, it is implicit cognition. Therefore, implicit cognition is known to be automatic without much cognitive effort. Although implicit memory is stored in a different brain region than explicit memory, it is critical to know that the interaction between implicit and explicit cognition is so close that it is impossible to separate their functions in our general information processing.

2. Implicit knowledge is developed over a lifetime of learning, observation, and thought, and it usually includes knowledge about language, traits, categorization, acculturation, and aesthetic preferences. Two main applications of implicit knowledge are discussed, namely, making judgements based on thin-slice information and sound symbolism.

3. People have been found to make reasonably good judgements based on thin-slice information, but it is also easy for people to make biased judgements; for example, the brand halo effect. Sound symbolism is a specific area in thin-slice information, because it suggests that we make our judgements based on what we hear, usually just a word or a brand name. Research in sound symbolism is usually based on studies in linguistics. Two topics of sound symbolism are discussed in relation to consumer perceptions: phonetic effects and sound repetition.

4. Implicit learning is learning that occurs without intention, or without conscious awareness of what has been learned. To put it simply, it is learning without knowing. Research studying implicit learning relies on subliminally priming subjects; that is, subjects are primed without their awareness. Implicit learning has been found to influence our cognition and our subsequent behaviour; for example, the mere exposure effect, generated from brand logos, advertisements, or brand users, is observed even if the mere exposure occurs subliminally.

5. Practitioners should be cautious of using implicit learning in the marketplace because it bears key limitations, including the reliability of experimental results, the translation of experimental results to reality, and the interaction between continuous implicit learning and our already developed perceptions and behaviours. More importantly, manipulating consumers without their knowledge (especially for commercial purposes!) is considered unethical.

DISCUSSION QUESTIONS

1. What are the functions of implicit and explicit cognition? Use consumer-relevant examples to illustrate your discussion.
2. What is sound symbolism? Discuss how sound symbolism can influence consumer perception.
3. How does implicit learning influence consumer cognition?
4. Discuss the limitations of implicit learning in consumer behaviour.

FURTHER READING

- Fitzsimons, G. J., Hutchinson, J. W., Williams, P., Alba, J. W., Chartrand, T. L., Huber, J., . . . Tavassoli, N. (2002). Non-Conscious Influences on Consumer Choice. *Marketing Letters, 13*(3), 269–279.
- Moore, T. E. (1982). Subliminal Advertising: What You See Is What You Get. *Journal of Marketing, 46*(2), 38–47.
- Peracchio, L., & Luna, D. (2006). The Role of Thin-Slice Judgments in Consumer Psychology. *Journal of Consumer Psychology, 16*(1), 25–32.
- Spence, C. (2012). Managing Sensory Expectations Concerning Products and Brands: Capitalizing on the Potential of Sound and Shape Symbolism. *Journal of Consumer Psychology, 22*(1), 37–54.
- Yang, L. W., Cutright, K. M., Chartrand, T. L., & Fitzsimons, G. J. (2014). Distinctively Different: Exposure to Multiple Brands in Low-Elaboration Settings. *Journal of Consumer Research, 40*(5), 973–992.

NOTES

1. Bargh, J. A., & Ferguson, M. J. (2000). Beyond Behaviorism: On the Automaticity of Higher Mental Processes. *Psychological Bulletin, 126*(6), 925–945.
2. Bargh, J. A., & Chartrand, T. L. (1999). The Unbearable Automaticity of Being. *American Psychologist, 54*(7), 462–479.
3. Chartrand, T. L., Maddux, W. W., & Lakin, J. L. (2005). Beyond the Perception–Behavior Link: The Ubiquitous Utility and Motivational Moderators of Nonconscious Mimicry. In R. R. Hassin, J. S. Uleman, & J. A. Bargh (eds), *The New Unconscious* (pp. 334–361). Oxford: Oxford University Press.
4. Stanovich, K. E., & West, R. F. (2000). Individual Differences in Reasoning: Implications for the Rationality Debate. *Behavioral and Brain Sciences, 23*(5), 645–665.
5. Chaiken, S. (1980). Heuristic Versus Systematic Information Processing and the Use of Source Versus Message Cues in Persuasion. *Journal of Personality and Social Psychology, 39*(5), 752–766; Evans, J. S. B. T. (1984). Heuristic and Analytic Processes in Reasoning. *British Journal of Psychology, 75*(4), 451–468; Hammond, K. R. (1996). *Human Judgment and Social Policy: Irreducible Uncertainty, Inevitable Error, Unavoidable Injustice.* Oxford: Oxford University Press; Nisbett, R. E., Peng, K., Choi, I., & Norenzayan, A. (2001). Culture and Systems of Thought: Holistic Versus Analytic Cognition. *Psychological Review, 108*(2), 291–310.
6. Eysenck, M. W., & Keane, M. T. (2010). *Cognitive Psychology: A Student's Handbook* (sixth edn). Hove: Psychology Press; Kellogg, R. T. (2012). *Fundamentals of Cognitive Psychology* (second edn). Los Angeles: Sage; Coxon, M. (2012). *Cognitive Psychology.* London: Sage.
7. Carlston, D. (2010). Models of Implicit and Explicit Mental Representation. In B. Gawronski & B. K. Payne (eds), *Handbook of Implicit Social Cognition* (pp. 38–61). New York: Guilford Press; Litman, L., & Reber, A. S. (2005). Implicit Cognition and Thought. In K. J. Holyoak & R. G. Morrison (eds), *The Cambridge Handbook of Thinking and Reasoning* (pp. 431–453). Cambridge: Cambridge University Press.
8. Cabeza, R., & Nyberg, L. (2000). Imaging Cognition II: An Empirical Review of 275 PET and fMRI Studies. *Journal of Cognitive Neuroscience, 12*(1), 1–47.
9. Dienes, Z., & Perner, J. (1999). A Theory of Implicit and Explicit Knowledge. *Behavioral and Brain Science, 22*(5), 735–808.
10. Reber, A. S. (1993). *Implicit Learning and Tacit Knowledge: An Essay on the Cognitive Unconscious.* New York: Oxford University Press.
11. Bargh, J. A. (1994). The Four Horsemen of Automaticity: Awareness, Intention, Efficiency and Control in Social Cognition. In R. S. Wyer & T. K. Srull (eds), *The Handbook of Social Cognition* (Vol. 1, pp. 1–40). Hillsdale, NJ: Lawrence Erlbaum Associates.
12. Stanovich, K. E., & West, R. F. (2000). Individual Differences in Reasoning: Implications for the Rationality Debate. *Behavioral and Brain Sciences, 23*(5), 645–665.
13. Pages 20-21 in Kahneman, D. (2011). *Thinking, Fast and Slow.* London: Penguin Books.
14. Examples extracted from ibid.

15. Nosek, B. A. (2007). Implicit–Explicit Relations. *Current Directions in Psychological Science, 16*(2), 65–69.
16. Carlston, Models of Implicit and Explicit Mental Representation.
17. Ibid.
18. Reber, A. S., Reber, E., & Allen, R. (2009). *The Penguin Dictionary of Psychology*. London: Penguin Books.
19. Litman & Reber, Implicit Cognition and Thought.
20. Wertheimer, M. (1961). *Productive Thinking*. London: Tavistock Publications; Köhler, W. (1947). *Gestalt Psychology: An Introduction to New Concepts in Modern Psychology*. New York: Liveright; Koffka, K. (1935). *Principles of Gestalt Psychology*. London: Routledge.
21. Ambady, N., Bernieri, F. J., & Richeson, J. A. (2000). Toward a Histology of Social Behavior: Judgmental Accuracy from Thin Slices of the Behavioral Stream. In M. P. Zanna (ed.), *Advances in Experimental Social Psychology* (Vol. 32, pp. 201–271). San Diego: Academic Press.
22. Ibid.
23. Alba, J. W. (2006). Let the Clips Fall Where They May. *Journal of Consumer Psychology, 16*(1), 14–19.
24. Vargas, P. T. (2008). Implicit Consumer Cognition. In C. P. Haugtvedt, P. M. Herr, & F. R. Kardes (eds), *Handbook of Consumer Psychology* (pp. 477–504). New York: Psychology Press.
25. Smith, H. J., Archer, D., & Costanzo, M. (1991). "Just a Hunch": Accuracy and Awareness in Person Perception. *Journal of Nonverbal Behavior, 15*(1), 3–18.
26. Ambady, N., & Gray, H. M. (2002). On Being Sad and Mistaken: Mood Effects on the Accuracy of Thin-Slice Judgments. *Journal of Personality and Social Psychology, 83*(4), 947–961.
27. Ambady, N., Krabbenhoft, M. A., & Hogan, D. (2006). The 30–Sec Sale: Using Thin-Slice Judgments to Evaluate Sales Effectiveness. *Journal of Consumer Psychology, 16*(1), 4–13.
28. Ambady & Gray, On Being Sad and Mistaken.
29. Bernieri, F. J., & Gillis, J. S. (1995). Personality Correlates of Accuracy in a Social Perception Task. *Perceptual and Motor Skills, 81*(1), 168–170.
30. Yan, D., & Sengupta, J. (2011). Effects of Construal Level on the Price–Quality Relationship. *Journal of Consumer Research, 38*(2), 376–389.
31. Purohit, D., & Srivastava, J. (2001). Effect of Manufacturer Reputation, Retailer Reputation, and Product Warranty on Consumer Judgments of Product Quality: A Cue Diagnosticity Framework. *Journal of Consumer Psychology, 10*(3), 123–134.
32. Baker, M. J., & Churchill, G. A. Jr. (1977). The Impact of Physically Attractive Models on Advertising Evaluations. *Journal of Marketing Research, 14*(4), 538–555; Kahle, L. R., & Homer, P. M. (1985). Physical Attractiveness of the Celebrity Endorser: A Social Adaptation Perspective. *Journal of Consumer Research, 11*(March), 954–961.
33. Peracchio, L., & Luna, D. (2006). The Role of Thin-Slice Judgments in Consumer Psychology. *Journal of Consumer Psychology, 16*(1), 25–32.
34. McKnight, D. H., Choudhury, V., & Kacmar, C. (2002). The Impact of Initial Consumer Trust on Intentions of Transact with a Web Site: A Trust Building Model. *Journal of Strategic Information Systems, 11*(3), 297–323.

35. Haried, P., & Zahedi, M. (2006). *Understanding Online Consumer Trust Using Thin Slices of Web Sites*. Paper presented at the 12th Americas Conference on Information Systems AMCIS.

36. Völckner, F., & Hofmann, J. (2007). The Price-Perceived Quality Relationship: A Meta-Analytic Review and Assessment of Its Determinants. *Marketing Letters, 18*(3), 181–196.

37. Bower, A. B., & Landreth, S. (2001). Is Beauty Best? Highly Versus Normally Attractive Models in Advertising. *Journal of Advertising, 30*(1), 1–12.

38. Janiszewski, C., & Meyvis, T. (2001). Effects of Brand Logo Complexity, Repetition, and Spacing on Processing Fluency and Judgment. *Journal of Consumer Research, 28*(1), 18–32; Lee, A. Y., & Labroo, A. A. (2004). The Effect of Conceptual and Perceptual Fluency on Brand Evaluation. *Journal of Marketing Research, 41*(2), 151–165.

39. Jacoby, L. L., & Dallas, M. (1981). On the Relationship between Autobiographical Memory and Perceptual Learning. *Journal of Experimental Psychology: General, 110*(3), 306–340.

40. Zmuda, N. (2009, 2 April 2009). Tropicana Line's Sales Post-Rebranding. *Ad Age*. Retrieved from http://adage.com/article/news/tropicana-line-s-sales-plunge-20-post-rebranding/135735/

41. Hoyer, W. D., & Brown, S. P. (1990). Effects of Brand Awareness on Choice for a Common, Repeat-Purchase Product. *Journal of Consumer Research, 17*(September), 141–148.

42. Macdonald, E. K., & Sharp, B. M. (2000). Brand Awareness Effects on Consumer Decision Making for a Common, Repeat Purchase Product: A Replication. *Journal of Business Research, 48*(1), 5–15.

43. Chaiken, Heuristic Versus Systematic Information Processing and the Use of Source Versus Message Cues in Persuasion; Petty, R. E., Cacioppo, J. T., & Schumann, D. (1983). Central and Peripheral Routes to Advertising Effectiveness: The Moderating Role of Involvement. *Journal of Consumer Research, 10*(September), 135–146.

44. Hall, L., Johansson, P., Tärning, B., Sikström, S., & Deutgen, T. (2010). Magic at the Marketplace: Choice Blindness for the Taste of Jam and the Smell of Tea. *Cognition, 117*(1), 54–61.

45. Spence, C. (2012). Managing Sensory Expectations Concerning Products and Brands: Capitalizing on the Potential of Sound and Shape Symbolism. *Journal of Consumer Psychology, 22*(1), 37–54.

46. Dehaene-Lambertz, G., & Houston, D. (1998). Faster Orientation Latencies toward Native Language in Two-Month-Old Infants. *Language and Speech, 41*(1), 21–43; Mehler, J., Jusczyk, P., Lambertz, G., Halsted, N., Bertoncini, J., & Amiel-Tison, C. (1988). A Precursor of Language Acquisition in Young Infants. *Cognition, 29*(2), 143–178; Gervain, J., & Mehler, J. (2010). Speech Perception and Language Acquisition in the First Year of Life. *Annual Review of Psychology, 61*, 191–218.

47. Ramus, F., Nespor, M., & Mehler, J. (1999). Correlates of Linguistic Rhythm in the Speech Signal. *Cognition, 73*(3), 265–292.

48. Lowrey, T. M., & Shrum, L. J. (2007). Phonetic Symbolism and Brand Name Preference. *Journal of Consumer Research, 34*(October), 406–414; Shrum, L. J., Lowrey, T. M., Luna, D.,

Lerman, D. B., & Liu, M. (2012). Sound Symbolism Effects across Languages: Implications for Global Brand Names. *International Journal of Research in Marketing, 29*(3), 275–279; Klink, R. R. (2000). Creating Brand Names and Meaning: The Use of Sound Symbolism. *Marketing Letters, 11*(1), 5–20; Klink, R. R. (2001). Creating Meaningful New Brand Names: A Study of Semantics and Sound Symbolism. *Journal of Marketing Theory & Practice, 9*(2), 27–34; Klink, R. R., & Wu, L. (2014). The Role of Position, Type, and Combination of Sound Symbolism Imbeds in Brand Names. *Marketing Letters, 25*(1), 13–24; Kuehnl, C., & Mantau, A. (2013). Same Sound, Same Preference? Investigating Sound Symbolism Effects in International Brand Names. *International Journal of Research in Marketing, 30*(4), 417–420; Yorkston, E., & Menon, G. (2004). A Sound Idea: Phonetic Effects of Brand Names on Consumer Judgments. *Journal of Consumer Research, 31*(June), 43–51.

49. Klink, Creating Meaningful New Brand Names.
50. Hinton, L., Nichols, H., & Ohala, J. (1994). Introduction: Sound Symbolic Processes. In L. Hinton, H. Nichols, & J. Ohala (eds), *Sound Symbolism* (pp. 1–14). Cambridge: Cambridge University Press.
51. Klink, Creating Brand Names and Meaning.
52. Yorkston, E., & Menon, G. (2004). A Sound Idea: Phonetic Effects of Brand Names on Consumer Judgments. *Journal of Consumer Research, 31*(June), 43–51.
53. Klink & Wu, The Role of Position, Type, and Combination of Sound Symbolism Imbeds in Brand Names.
54. Ohala, J. (1984). An Ethological Perspective on Common Cross-Language Utilization of FO of Voice. *Phonetica, 41*(1), 1–16.
55. Klink, Creating Brand Names and Meaning; Yorkston & Menon, A Sound Idea.
56. Whissell, C. (2006). Historical and Socioeconomic Predictors of the Emotional Associations of Sounds in Popular Names. *Perceptual and Motor Skills, 103*(2), 451–456.
57. Gaston, E. T. (1968). Man and Music. In E. T. Gaston (ed.), *Music in Therapy* (pp. 7–21). New York: Macmillan.
58. Zhu, R. J., & Meyers-Levy, J. (2005). Distinguishing between the Meanings of Music: When Background Music Affects Product Perceptions. *Journal of Marketing Research, 42*(August), 333–345.
59. Argo, J. J., Popa, M., & Smith, M. C. (2010). The Sound of Brands. *Journal of Marketing, 74*(July), 97–109.
60. Dienes, Z., & Berry, D. (1997). Implicit Learning: Below the Subjective Threshold. *Psychonomic Bulletin & Review, 4*(1), 3–23; Litman & Reber, Implicit Cognition and Thought; Seger, C. A. (1994). Implicit Learning. *Psychological Bulletin, 115*(2), 162–196; Shanks, D. R. (2005). Implicit Learning. In K. Lamberts & R. Goldstone (eds), *Handbook of Cognition* (pp. 202–220). London: Sage.
61. Mulligan, N. W. (1998). The Role of Attention during Encoding in Implicit and Explicit Memory. *Journal of Experimental Psychology: Learning, Memory, and Cognition, 24*(1), 27–47.
62. Cheour, M., Martynova, O., Näätänen, R., Erkkola, R., Sillanpää, M., Kero, P., . . . Hämäläinen, H. (2002). Speech Sounds Learned by Sleeping Newborns. *Nature, 415*(6872), 599–600.

63. Merikle, P. M., & Daneman, M. (1996). Memory for Unconsciously Perceived Events: Evidence from Anesthetized Patients. *Consciousness and Cognition, 5*(4), 525–541.

64. Meyer, D. E., & Schvaneveldt, R. W. (1971). Facilitation in Recognizing Pairs of Words: Evidence of a Dependence between Retrieval Operations. *Journal of Experimental Psychology, 90*(2), 227–234; Neely, J. H. (1991). Semantic Priming Effects in Visual Word Recognition: A Selective Review of Current Findings and Theories. In D. Besner & G. W. Humphreys (eds), *Basic Processes in Reading: Visual Word Recognition* (pp. 264–336). Hillsdale, NJ: Lawrence Erlbaum Associates.

65. Balota, D. A. (1983). Automatic Semantic Activation and Episodic Memory Encoding. *Journal of Verbal Learning and Verbal Behavior, 22*(1), 88–104; Eich, E. (1984). Memory for Unattended Events: Remembering with and without Awareness. *Memory & Cognition, 12*(2), 105–111.

66. Davis, D. F., & Herr, P. M. (2014). From Bye to Buy: Homophones as a Phonological Route to Priming. *Journal of Consumer Research, 40*(April), 1063–1077.

67. Merikle, P. M., Smilek, D., & Eastwood, J. D. (2001). Perception without Awareness: Perspectives from Cognitive Psychology. *Cognition, 79*(1–2), 115–134.

68. Bargh, J. A., & Piertromonaco, P. (1982). Automatic Information Processing and Social Perception: The Influence of Trait Information Presented Outside of Conscious Awareness on Impression Formation. *Journal of Personality and Social Psychology, 43*(3), 437–449.

69. Fitzsimons, G., Chartrand, T. L., & Fitzsimons, G. J. (2008). Automatic Effects of Brand Exposure on Motivated Behavior: How Apple Makes You "Think Different". *Journal of Consumer Research, 35*(June), 21–35.

70. Ferraro, R., Bettman, J. R., & Chartrand, T. L. (2009). The Power of Strangers: The Effect of Incidental Consumer Brand Encounters on Brand Choice. *Journal of Consumer Research, 35*(February), 729–741.

71. Zajonc, R. B. (1968). Attitudinal Effects of Mere Exposure. *Journal of Personality and Social Psychology, 9*(2), 1–27.

72. Bornstein, R. F. (1992). Subliminal Mere Exposure Effects. In R. F. Bornstein & T. S. Pittman (eds), *Perception without Awareness: Cognitive, Clinical, and Social Perspectives* (pp. 191–210). New York: Guilford Press.

73. Ferraro et al., The Power of Strangers.

74. Champion, J. M., & Turner, W. W. (1959). An Experimental Investigation of Subliminal Perception. *Journal of Applied Psychology, 43*(6), 382–384; DeFleur, M. L., & Petranoff, R. M. (1959). A Televised Test of Subliminal Persuasion. *Public Opinion Quarterly, 23*(2), 168–180; Beatty, S. E., & Hawkins, D. I. (1989). Subliminal Stimulation: Some New Data and Interpretation. *Journal of Advertising, 18*(3), 4–8; George, S. G., & Jennings, L. B. (1975). Effect of Subliminal Stimuli on Consumer Behavior: Negative Evidence. *Perceptual and Motor Skills, 41*(3), 847–854; Smith, K. H., & Rogers, M. (1994). Effectiveness of Subliminal Messages in Television Commercials: Two Experiments. *Journal of Applied Psychology, 79*(6), 866–874.

75. Theus, K. T. (1994). Subliminal Advertising and the Psychology of Processing Unconscious Stimuli: A Review of Research. *Psychology & Marketing, 11*(3), 271–290; Trappey, C.

(1996). A Meta-Analysis of Consumer Choice and Subliminal Advertising. *Psychology & Marketing, 13*(5), 517–530.

76. Fitzsimons, G. J., Hutchinson, J. W., Williams, P., Alba, J. W., Chartrand, T. L., Huber, J., . . . Tavassoli, N. (2002). Non-Conscious Influences on Consumer Choice. *Marketing Letters, 13*(3), 269–279.

77. Moore, T. E. (1988). The Case Aginst Subliminal Manipulation. *Psychology & Marketing, 5*(4), 297–316; Vokey, J. R., & Read, J. D. (1985). Subliminal Messages. *American Psychologist, 40*(11), 1231–1239.

78. Morwitz, V. G., Johnson, E., & Schmittlein, D. (1993). Does Measuring Intent Change Behavior? *Journal of Consumer Research, 20*(June), 46–61; Fitzsimons, G. J., & Williams, P. (2000). Asking Questions Can Change Choice Behavior: Does It Do So Automatically or Effortfully? *Journal of Experimental Psychology: Applied, 6*(3), 195–206; Morwitz, V. G., & Fitzsimons, G. J. (2004). The Mere-Measurement Effect: Why Does Measuring Intentions Change Actual Behavior? *Journal of Consumer Psychology, 14*(1&2), 64–73.

79. Elliott, R. (1998). A Model of Emotion-Driven Choice. *Journal of Marketing Management, 14*(1/3), 95–108.

80. Lee, M., & Faber, R. J. (2007). Effects of Product Placement in On-Line Games on Brand Memory: A Perspective of the Limited-Capacity Model of Attention. *Journal of Advertising, 36*(4), 75–90; Brennan, I., Dubas, K. M., & Babin, L. A. (1999). The Influence of Product-Placement Type & Exposure Time on Product-Placement Recognition. *International Journal of Advertising, 18*(3), 323–337.

81. Ferraro et al., The Power of Strangers; Vargas, Implicit Consumer Cognition; Yang, L. W., Cutright, K. M., Chartrand, T. L., & Fitzsimons, G. J. (2014). Distinctively Different: Exposure to Multiple Brands in Low-Elaboration Settings. *Journal of Consumer Research, 40*(February), 973–992.

82. Verwijmeren, T., Karremans, J. C., Stroebe, W., & Wigboldus, D. H. J. (2011). The Workings and Limits of Subliminal Advertising: The Role of Habits. *Journal of Consumer Psychology, 21*(2), 206–213.

83. Vargas, Implicit Consumer Cognition.

84. Ibid., p. 492.

5

CONSUMER DEVELOPMENT AND SOCIALISATION

─Learning objectives─

To explore, understand, and explain:

- Piaget's theory in relation to children's development of cognitive and social skills between 0 and 16 years of age
- children at different stages (perceptual, analytical, and reflective) develop as consumers
- physiological changes in ageing consumers and associated marketing implications
- the influence of physiological, social, and psychological ageing in their decision-making

5.1 INTRODUCTION

Consumer development and socialisation is defined as the process by which people acquire the skills, knowledge, and attitudes necessary to function as consumers.[1] This process is shaped by a combination of physiological, sociocultural, and psychological forces. Although consumer development and socialisation is a life-long process, the discussion of this chapter will focus on children consumers (Section 5.2), whose cognitive and social skills are underdeveloped, and ageing consumers (Section 5.3), whose focus in life has shifted.

The discussion of children consumers uses Piaget's theory to examine the stages children go through in their cognitive and social development. The main age groups include the perceptual stage (3–7 years old), analytical stage (7–11 years old), and reflective stage (11–16 years old), and we will explore how these groups of children differ in their understanding of brands and advertising and in the role of social influences (family and peers) on their decision-making.

The discussion of ageing consumers first looks at how physiological changes influence the elderly in their daily life and what implications can be derived from these changes. More importantly, how ageing consumers make decisions will be explored, and these decision-making strategies include their tendency to reduce information search and to rely on emotional processing. Both children and ageing consumers can be seen as vulnerable, and associated ethical issues will be raised.

5.2 CHILDREN CONSUMERS: FROM CHILDHOOD TO ADOLESCENCE

The psychological basis

Developmental psychologists tend to associate an age range with each stage of development, but children may exhibit some degree of variance in their speed of development. Therefore, the ages indicated in the below stages are approximations.

Cognitive skills

Piaget's theory of cognitive development is the most influential theory in developmental psychology in the 20th century. There are two central ideas in Piaget's theory:

- *The process of coming to know;* that is, maturation determining cognitive development and therefore ability.[2] For example, some neurological structures become mature at a particular age, so before reaching a certain age, young children are unable to rely on the structures as older children are to produce their perception or cognition.[3]

- *The stages we move through as we come to know are fixed.* In other words, we will be only able to move to the next stage when the current stage of cognitive development is complete.[4] Piaget's theory suggests that the developments in cognitive abilities involve four main stages, and the key development in each stage can be found in Table 5.1.

Social skills

Social development covers a wide range of topics, but the most critical to consumer socialisation are social perspective taking and impression formation:[5]

- *Social perspective taking* refers to the ability to see the perspectives of others,[6] thus it is related to how children develop this skill to influence and negotiate with their parents about, for example, their purchase requests.[7]
- *Impression formation* is the ability to form impressions about objects, situations, events, and people.[8] Since these impressions are used as a basis to perceive one's role in a group or make subsequent social comparisons, they are related to understanding the social aspects of the consumption of products or brands.[9]

Three stages are involved in the development of social skills with the stages of sensorimotor and preoperational in the cognitive development combined – see Table 5.1 for the key social abilities developed for each stage.

Table 5.1 Stages of cognitive and social development

Stage	Age	Main Cognitive Skills Developed	Main Social Skills Developed
Sensorimotor stage	0-2 years old	• Ability to coordinate their sensory and sensorimotor; for example, ○ Grasping ○ Sucking • Ability to develop habits and internalise schemas	For both sensorimotor and preoperational stages (aged 0-7). *Social perspective taking:* • Egocentric – unaware of other people's perspectives *Impression formation:* • Ability to form impressions based on concrete elements; for example,
Preoperational stage	2-7 years old	• Ability to form stable concepts • Ability to reason using one concrete feature	○ Physical appearances (e.g. "Mary is tall") ○ Overt behaviours (e.g. "Peter likes to play")

(Continued)

Table 5.1   (Continued)

Stage	Age	Main Cognitive Skills Developed	Main Social Skills Developed
Concrete operational stage	7-11 years old	• Ability to reason using more than one concrete feature • Ability to solve problems using concrete events or objects	*Social perspective taking:* Early stage: • Ability to be aware of other people's opinions • Ability to see information influence opinion formation Later stage: • Ability to consider another person's position *Impression formation:* Early stage: • Ability to make comparisons based on concrete features Later stage: • Ability to form impressions using abstract attributes (e.g. "Uncle Bob is nice")
Adulthood-like (or formal) operational stage	11+ years old	• Ability to abstract thinking and hypothetical reasoning • Ability to mimic the way adults would think and behave	*Social perspective taking:* • Ability to compare their own opinions with those of others • Ability to understand social systems (such as family and friendship groups) *Impression formation:* • Ability to make comparisons using abstract attributes (e.g. "Michael is smarter than Tony") • Ability to mimic adult-like impression formation

Source: Summary based on Harris and Butterworth[10] and Santrock[11]

Implications for consumer behaviour

Children start to exhibit their role as consumers from around the age of two to three, so the discussion of consumer socialisation usually skips the sensorimotor stage. The below sections will use John's categorization of the stages in consumer socialisation; namely, perceptual stage (3–7 years old), analytical stage (7–11 years old), and reflective stage (11–16 years old).[12]

Figure 5.1 shows what abilities children at various stages develop at cognitive and social levels and how persuasion in the marketplace takes place.

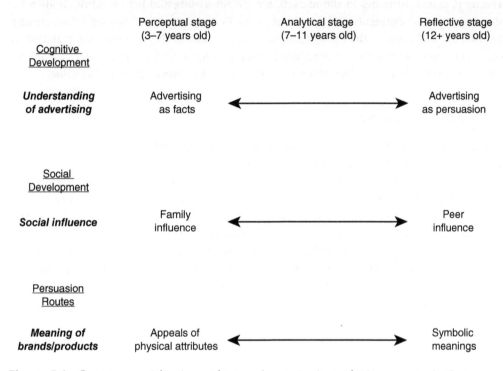

Figure 5.1   Consumer socialisation and persuasion routes in marketing communication

Perceptual stage: 3-7 years old

Children at the perceptual stage value physical, tangible goods, as opposed to intangible services or socially oriented products.[13] Their desire for physical goods is driven by simple considerations, such as novelty or quantity.[14] They have yet to develop as complicated beings.

Cognitive skills

Product evaluations

Children at this stage usually form their preferences by using such concrete attributes as colours, shapes, or sizes.[15] For example, young children prefer blue, yellow, and red,[16] and prefer colours that are bright, rather than dark.[17] The positive emotions stimulated by colours are tied with colour preferences in young children, but this effect decreases with age.[18] This emotion–colour relationship explains why toys or products targeted at young children are generally colourful and brightly coloured.

Perceptions of advertising

The most salient attributes in the marketplace are advertising and brands. Most children by about age five can distinguish TV advertising from TV programmes.[19] They see TV advertising as "shorter" or "funnier" than programmes.[20] To them, advertising is entertaining and often conveys correct information. In other words, they are unable to completely detect the selling intent of advertising at this stage and therefore tend to take advertising at its face value.

Developing brand preferences

Children are able to recognize and recall brand names at an early age. As brands are advertised on television, displayed in stores, and used at home, children, even before they acquire reading ability, are able to recognise familiar product packages[21] and familiar characters (e.g. Mickey Mouse, Peppa Pig, Winnie-the-Pooh, et cetera) on products, such as toys and clothing.[22] They rely on highly visible attributes, including colour patterns, design patterns, and cartoon characters, to categorise products and discriminate brands.[23]

Another important factor to influence young children's brand preferences is the parental or family influence. That is, parents explaining to children about their brand preferences influences the formation of children's brand preferences as a consequence.[24] During this time, children not only develop a preference for particular brands, but also begin to express a preference for familiar branded items over generic offerings.[25]

Social skills

Purchase influence and negotiation strategies

At this stage, children's goal is to get what they want instead of persuading parents.[26] For example, before children are able to express themselves well enough, they tend to grab wanted items off store shelves and put them inside their parents' shopping trolley.[27] As for more verbal children, they ask directly, and if their purchase requests are denied, they would use such techniques as begging, screaming, and whining to get what they want.[28]

Analytical stage: 7–11 years old

As children enter the analytical stage, they are able to deal with more complicated information, accumulate more market experience and knowledge, and learn to negotiate to get what they want. Though they approach matters in more detailed and analytical ways, they have not yet developed adult-like capabilities.[29]

Cognitive skills

Product evaluations

One of the most important developments is that they start to process information at an abstract level.[30] Their ability to process abstract information enables their reliance on functional dimensions to think about products.[31] By 6–8 years old, children are able to group objects according to taxonomic relationships indicated by attributes or core concepts.[32] For example, they are able to differentiate fruit juices as healthy drinks and soft drinks as unhealthy ones, and to classify belts and socks to the same product category – clothing.

Perception and understanding of advertising

At the beginning of the analytical stage (ages 7–8), children evaluate advertisements based on their liking of the advertised product, but as they grow older (ages 10–11) they will have learned to view advertisements in a more analytical manner and to focus on the creative content and execution.[33] Research suggests that the entertainment value, especially humour, elicited from advertising can be an important factor for children at this age to rate the advertisements favourably. For example, almost all children are able to identify their favourite advertisements, which are the ones that make them laugh.[34]

However, children's advocates, policy makers, and the like are worried about children's vulnerability to advertisements,[35] especially the ones children particularly enjoy, because children's cognitive skills may not be able to resist specific selling efforts in advertising.[36] During the analytical stage, children start to comprehend the purpose of business is to make profits. This understanding leads them to recognise bias and deception in advertising and to realise that commercials do not always tell the truth,[37] and thereby helping them develop *cognitive defence* against advertising, which may shield them from being persuaded unfairly. However, cognitive defence is not absolute, and children can still be vulnerable to commercial manipulation.[38] This is because children at this stage need a reminder to use their cognitive defence,[39] and without a reminder they would not use it even though they have the ability.[40]

However, the advertising environment has changed very fast in the last two decades, and some new advertising techniques may make it even more difficult to evoke cognitive defence;[41] for example, in-game brand placement.[42] This may be because the influence is more implicit than explicit. In-game advertisements, therefore, influence children from two perspectives: brand prominence (explicit influence) leads to increased brand recall and recognition, while game involvement (implicit influence) leads to increased positive brand attitudes.[43] In this case, children's vulnerability to susceptibility to advertising is doubled.

Developing brand knowledge and preferences

Children at the perceptual stage are able to name popular brands in most child-oriented product categories, such as cereal, snacks, and toys.[44] Moreover, they also start to demonstrate their familiarity or knowledge of at least one brand in an adult-oriented product category, such as cameras and petrol stations.[45] The sources of their brand knowledge and preference come from family,[46] peer,[47] advertising,[48] and more importantly product experience.[49] Later in this stage, children start to rely on product experience to determine their brand preferences, as their product experience weakens the emotional influence from advertising, and is able to generate higher levels of confidence than advertising in brands.[50]

Social skills

Negotiation strategies

Children at the analytical stage start to see other people's positions, and they merge that understanding into their influence to their parents. Therefore, they start to use bargaining, compromising, and persuasion as their negotiation strategies to influence their purchase request.[51] These reasoning techniques have matured through years of listening to their parents describing why some of their requests can or cannot be honoured.[52] They understand that they do not have absolute decision power in purchases, but know that parents are more likely to honour their requests if they exhibit sufficient product knowledge with regards to the item requested for purchase, use good behaviour in exchange for parents' granting their purchase request, and select a reasonable item to request.[53]

Understanding of symbolic meanings

Children at the analytical stage also begin to understand social meanings and status attached to possessions. They are able to analyse products or brands from their own experiences,[54] and this way of analysis fuels their understanding of the symbolic meanings and status accorded to products. For example, analytical stage children see the new house owners as happier, with more friends, and more desirable to visit[55] and see the large car owners as people with a lot of money and a lot of new things.[56]

Influence from peers

Fitting into a social group or making friends is one of the main social motivations for children's decisions about their behaviour,[57] and this tendency becomes obvious after children spend most of their awake time at school.[58] Research has shown that peer pressure contributes to children's materialism and, therefore, consumer behaviour.[59] For example, peers can strongly influence children's buying certain clothes, liking certain music, having (or maintaining) a certain body shape, eating certain foods, watching certain TV, et cetera.[60]

Reflective stage: 11-16 years old

As children enter the reflective stage, their cognitive abilities start to demonstrate adult-like ways of reasoning and making decisions.[61] They mimic adults in their flexibility of choosing different decision-making strategies to suit the decision situations and different negotiation strategies to achieve their purchase requests. As they are still in the process of shaping their identity, especially an identity that separates them from their family, the influence from their peers starts to be dominant in their decision-making.

Cognitive skills

Product evaluations - value perception

The differences of value perception in different ages are perhaps best explained by what Fox and Kehret-Ward observed:[62]

> Young children see pricing through the seller's eyes, older children see pricing through the eyes of a seller who is keeping his eye on the consumer, and adults see pricing through the eyes of a seller who is keeping his eye on other sellers as well as on buyers.

This explains the increased sophistication of how children perceive value as they grow up. By the time children enter pre-adolescence, they have learned to associate the price they pay with the value they receive.[63] Though children before the age of 12 have developed a solid understanding of money, not until early adolescence do they start to appreciate the concept of transactions in an integrated economic system, for example, from raw materials to manufacturers and from manufacturers to wholesalers and retailers.[64] Similarly, according to Fox and Kehret-Ward's[65] naïve theories of price (Box 5.1), 13-year-olds are able to display a more abstract level of reasoning of pricing; that is, viewing prices as a function of the quality of the product's inputs and preferences of potential buyers. In other words, at the reflective stage, children have adult-like ways of thinking about prices and values.

─Box 5.1─

Naïve theories of price: a developmental model

Naïve theories of price suggest how children perceive value in the marketplace (Table 5.2). The perception is formed based on two components: (1) the criterion children believe should be used in determining a market price and (2) the sources of the criterion. The sources include buyer preferences, product features, product quality, product size (as it matters according to the raw

(Continued)

material input and the technology it involves to make it small or big; the former is termed as input quantity and the latter is termed as input quality).

Table 5.2 Naïve theories of price[66]

Age	Theory of Price/Value
5	Unable to use a source of value to explain how prices are determined
10	Able to use input quantity as a source of value
13	Able to use input quality and buyer preference as a source of value
Adult	Able to make substantial use of relative scarcity as a source of value

Decision-making strategies

Pre-adolescents start to exhibit their ability to consider different and complex attributes in making a decision,[67] to seek out additional information to make a decision,[68] and to discriminate the importance and relevance of different information and focus on the more important and relevant information for making a decision.[69] In other words, they exhibit higher efficiency in information search (i.e. search less exhaustively) and greater use of various strategies, compared to when they were younger.[70] This is referred to as the adaptive decision-making strategies. Adaptive decision-making suggests a flexibility in decision-making that is used to simplify, but optimise, decision tasks.[71] In order to obtain this adaptability and flexibility in decision-making, sufficient prior knowledge is essential,[72] and that is why adaptive decision-making does not appear until the reflective stage.[73]

Advertising knowledge

When children are at the analytical stage, they have developed the understanding that advertising can be deceptive, but they are unable to pinpoint specific instances of deception in advertising. Not until the reflective stage do their abilities to pinpoint specific deceptions in advertising mature.[74] They are able to use the subtle differences in voice, manner, and language to determine the manipulative (or misleading) extent in advertising. For example, they are able to understand overstatements via the way the endorsers talk, the use of visual tricks (e.g. fake things), the high frequency of showing the same or similar advertisements, or the great detail given in a commercial.[75] This understanding shows that children have gained sufficient knowledge of advertising tactics. Children at this age demonstrate adult-like reasoning,[76] and view advertising in a more sceptical, analytical, and discerning fashion.[77]

Social skills

Negotiation strategies

By the time children reach early adolescence, a repertoire of negotiation strategies will be available at their disposal[78] and their practice of these rational negotiation strategies will have become more sophisticated.[79] These strategies are appealing to parents because of their seemingly rational approach and children, by this time, are able to use them in a flexible manner to match the situation. The most favoured and used strategies by this group of children are bargaining and persuasion strategies:[80]

- *Bargaining strategies*: Children use bargaining strategies to create agreement based on mutual gain and mutual satisfactory outcomes between themselves and their parents.[81] These strategies usually take the form of "If you do this, I'll do that".[82] For example, they can offer to pay for part of the requested item or to do what their parents wish them to do (e.g. additional housework or schoolwork) to encourage their parents' willingness to support. Alternatively, they can take the form of reasoning and the aim of reasoning also involves achieving a mutually satisfying outcome for parents and children.[83] For example, an upgraded version of the requested item may be a little more expensive, but it will last longer.
- *Persuasion strategies*: Persuasion strategies are children's attempt to convince their parents to make a decision of their desire.[84] Like bargaining strategies, persuasion strategies involve mutual agreement between children and their parents. But unlike bargaining strategies, persuasion strategies focus on unilateral gain for the children, rather than mutual gain for both children and parents. There are four persuasion strategies: expressions of opinions (likes or dislikes), persistence, begging, and whining.[85]

These two strategies are children's preferred strategies because they are, in part, perceived to be the most effective in getting their parents to say yes.

Understanding and use of symbolic meanings

Older children start to understand more sophisticated symbolic meanings attached to brands, such as the meaning of status, prestige, or trendiness conveyed by brands. For example, when showing advertisements featuring wearers of Levi's and Kmart's jeans to 8-year-olds and 12-year-olds, 8-year-olds do not see much difference in the owners of different brands, whereas the 12-year-olds believe Levi's owners to be more attractive and popular than Kmart owners.[86]

The main reason that older children are able to understand symbolic meaning of brands is their heightened awareness of other people's perspectives at this stage.[87] As a result, they become more focused on the social meanings in order to shape their own identity and to symbolise their group identity.[88] The main means for them to shape their own identity and to symbolise their group identity is through material possessions. Among all products, cloth-ing is particularly notable as it is a means of fitting in and as a way to identify membership in a particular subgroup, such as the "preppies" and "hip-hops".[89] As material possessions are strongly associated with their social motivation for self and social identity, children at this stage show the strongest materialistic tendencies.[90]

Influence from peers

Children at the reflective stage prefer information from peers to information from parents or mass media.[91] In fact, peers are the most important social agent from which older children learn symbolic meaning of goods.[92] For example, peers are able to help their friends evaluate prod-ucts, brands, and stores. Shopping with peers (friends) may ensure that they make purchases that create favourable images among their friends, and thereby strengthen their belongingness of group membership.[93] At the same time, they also want to avoid circumstances where they buy the "wrong" product or brand and therefore have to endure social consequences of non-conformity, such as being ridiculed.[94] Adolescents welcome this type of information when they shop, so when they are accompanied by their peers who are good at providing such informa-tion, they enjoy shopping more and therefore spend more[95] or end up buying impulsively.[96]

Peer influence is not always positive. For example, research has demonstrated a strong link between peer influence and adolescents' materialism,[97] or peer influence can be used as a form of peer pressure[98] in which children who violate consumption norms would have to endure embarrassment and their peers' ridicule.[99] However, if peer influence can be shown in a posi-tive light, supportive peers, in fact, boost adolescents' self-esteem, which decreases their need to turn to material goods to develop positive self-concept.[100]

Table 5.3 summarises previous discussions by outlining the consumer behaviour for chil-dren at perceptual, analytic, and reflective stage.

Table 5.3　The development and socialisation of children consumer

	Perceptual Stage: 3-7 years old	Analytic Stage: 7-11 years old	Reflective Stage 11-16 years old
Product evaluation	Relying on concrete attributes: • Colour • Shapes • Sizes	Relying on abstract attributes: • Functional attributes	Relying on • adaptive decision-making strategies • value, an abstract level of reasoning of pricing
Perception of advertising	Taking information in advertising as facts	• Ability to recognise selling intent in advertising • Ability to activate cognitive defence when reminded	• Ability to pinpoint specific deceptions in advertising • Ability to view advertising in a more sceptical, analytical, and discerning fashion

	Perceptual Stage: 3-7 years old	Analytic Stage: 7-11 years old	Reflective Stage 11-16 years old
Brand preferences	Sources of brand preferences: • Familiar product packages and characters • Parental influences	Sources of brand preferences: • Parents/family • Peers • Advertising • Product experience	Sources of brand preferences: • Peers
Negotiation strategies	• Grab wanted items off store shelves • Begging, screaming, and whining	• Bargaining • Compromising • Persuasion	• Ability to use various strategies in a flexible manner to match the situation

Symbolic meanings of possessions and brands	Not yet developed	• Ability to understand social meanings and status attached to possessions and brands	• Ability to understand more sophisticated symbolic meanings attached to brands
			  o Status
			  o Prestige
			  o Trendiness

5.3 AGEING CONSUMERS

The increasing importance of ageing consumers

According to the developmental psychologists, people aged between 65 and 75 are categorized as "young-old", aged between 75 and 85 as "old-old", and aged 85+ as "oldest-old".[101] Using this categorization, as of 2021, for example, there are over 11 million people aged 65 and above in the UK, about 19% of the UK population, and 1.7 million people aged 85 and above, 2.5% of the population.[102] These figures are projected to grow, and by 2042 about 25% of the UK population will be aged 65+ with 4.3% in the 85+ category.[103] The ageing population is not unique to the UK; it is a global phenomenon: 9% of the world population are aged 65+ in 2019, and by 2050 this figure is predicted to grow to 16%.[104] Similarly, because of the increase of life expectancy, the number of people aged 80+ worldwide will triple from 143 million in 2019 to 425 million in 2050.[105] Therefore, businesses are encouraged by government or insurance company funding to develop products that will assist the elderly to remain functionally healthy and independent (e.g. medical monitoring devices).[106]

—Box 5.2—

Research in ageing consumers

Research into ageing consumers is limited, compared with that of child, adolescent, and adult consumers. Three main reasons contribute to limited ageing consumer research (both from businesses and from academics):

- The ageing population has in the past been negligible in size, compared to other segments.
- The stereotypical image of ageing consumers decreases motivation and funding for research into this demographic group:
  o Ageing consumers spend less because of lack of regular income or financial means.[107]
- Increased difficulty in accessing ageing consumers, especially for the old-old and oldest-old segments:
  o Difficult to reach
  o Difficult to converse with (because of their declined health or memory)

—Box 5.3—

How old are ageing consumers?

There is no consensus in consumer literature on the age range for senior consumers.[108] Some researchers see people aged 50+ as senior while others believe the retirement age, 65, to be an appropriate benchmark as the starting age for senior citizens. In order to broaden the discussion of senior consumers, this section does not strictly follow developmental psychologists' definition to discuss the old, but relies on studies that self-categorise as studying senior consumers.

Physiological changes

The physiological basis

As people age, they experience physiological changes which, in turn, can influence the way they interact with the environment.[109] Therefore, the design of equipment and facilities to suit the senior is seen as necessary not only from a humanitarian point of view for the senior's safety and comfort[110] but also from a business point of view for the increased market opportunities.[111] In general, the main physiological changes include increased vision impairment, reduced hearing, declined motor functions (e.g. muscle strength), and reduced cognitive ability (e.g. memory and learning). For example, in terms of food packaging, the old encounter such problems as tight lids (too weak in their hands or wrists to open tight lids with ease or without spillage during opening) or small printing (impaired vision makes reading labels difficult); therefore, larger ring pulls on aluminium cans, more sliding resealable closures on packaging, or larger print are welcomed.[112]

Implications for consumer behaviour

Most of these operational problems can be resolved through good product design. It is essential for marketers and product managers to appreciate difficulties that the old encounter in their daily life and integrate this thinking when they target the ageing market. This integration, however, can be challenging as most marketers and product managers are below the age of 50. Although a 65-year-old knows what it was like to be 30, a 30-year-old, in most cases, cannot empathise with what it is like to be 65.[113] Table 5.4 can be used as a starting point for youngsters to understand the most frequent physiological changes in the elderly and their associated marketing implications.[114]

Table 5.4 Physiological changes in ageing people and their implications in marketing

Key problematic areas	Summary of Physiological Changes and Functional Capabilities	Guidelines for Marketing
Vision	1. loss of acuity 2. less sensitivity to light 3. declined ability to distinguish colours 4. declined ability to judge depth and distances	• increase illumination • increase contrasts • minimise glare • use larger font sizes • present key message in the centre
Hearing	1. high frequency hearing loss (pitches) 2. declined ability to detect low-intensity (dB) sounds 3. declined ability to filter out background noise 4. increased risks of having age-related hearing illness (e.g. tinnitus)	• use pitches in the range of 500-1,000 Hz with an intensity of at least 60 dB
Motor functions	1. loss in fine motor control (i.e. increased difficulty in tasks that would require selecting small objects) 2. slower reaction times 3. weakened muscle strength	• ensure product development for user friendly interface for senior adults, especially the design of smaller gadgets (such as hearing aids and cell phones) for the senior.

(Continued)

Table 5.4   (Continued)

Key problematic areas	Summary of Physiological Changes and Functional Capabilities	Guidelines for Marketing
Memory	1. deterioration in working memory 2. diminished inhibitory mechanisms (declined ability to process *only* relevant information) 3. declined ability in encoding operations	• minimise the number of cognitive operations • minimise the time to carry out an activity with the product • minimise the probability of error across the chain of steps

Sources: summary based on the reviews by Yoon and Cole [115] and Charness et al.[116]

Changes in decision-making

Tendency to reduce information search

The psychological basis

There are two factors contributing to the elderly's tendency to reduce information search:

- Their declined cognitive abilities prevent them from searching and processing as much information as the young would do.[117]
- Their years of experience lead to the decreased need to search information[118] – see more details in the next section on their reliance on implicit processing.

Implications for consumer behaviour

Most research suggests that senior consumers tend to search less information to inform their decision-making.[119] Their reduced information search is especially obvious for the decisions that may require elaborative processing (i.e. a process that involves more cognitive efforts), such as making unfamiliar (e.g. buying a new product) or complex decisions (e.g. buying a car).[120]

Tendency to rely on implicit processing

The psychological basis

Implicit processing (also known as experiential/emotional processing), introduced in Section 4.2, suggests "preconscious, rapid, automatic, holistic, primarily nonverbal, intimately associated with affect".[121] The reason that the implicit decision-making style can be successful for the elderly is because of their years of experience, which has internalised as crystallised intelligence,[122] referring to the ability to use the skills, knowledge, and experience one has acquired through one's lifetime. Research has suggested that crystallised intelligence increases with age[123] and therefore requires little or no cognitive effort in order to achieve the same goal as the youngsters using elaborative processing[124] or aided emotional processing.[125] In fact, unless their cognitive abilities are significantly compromised, the decision quality with reduced cognitive effort is usually good enough,[126] if not better.[127]

Another key explanation for the elderly's reliance on implicit processing comes from Socioemotional Selectivity Theory (SST). According to SST,[128] "the perception of time plays a fundamental role in the selection and pursuit of social goals. . . . When time is perceived as open-ended, knowledge-related goals are prioritized. In contrast, when time is perceived limited, emotional goals assume primacy."[129] Therefore, growing old suggests "increasing motivation to derive emotional meaning from life and decreasing motivation to expand one's horizons",[130] for example, balancing emotional states and sensing that one is needed by others.[131] This theory also explains why older consumers are more attached to familiar brands[132] and shops[133] and place great importance on brand trust and partnership in their brand choice.[134]

Implications for consumer behaviour

Relying on emotional processing makes senior consumers more susceptible to framing effects,[135] especially when the frames involve an emotional component, as older adults have extensive schema networks with strong ties with emotional components.[136] For example, adding an emotional category label (poor, fair, good, excellent) alters age differences in decision-making when participants are making choices about health plans.[137] This susceptibility, if abused, may lead to deceptive business practices targeted at the elderly consumers.[138] Ageing consumers can be vulnerable and ethical concerns of inappropriate business practices should be considered; see Table 5.5 for a summary of what could be seen as inappropriate business practices.

Table 5.5 Main ethical issues concerning ageing consumers

Ageing consumers: Main ethical issues
1. Deceptive business practices from the abuse of emotional communication.
2. How can ageing consumers maintain their self-esteem when they perceive that others want to put them "out to pasture"?
3. How can ageing consumers feel valued when media images exclude them in favour of the 18-49 demographic?
4. How can they cope with negative portrayals such as physical and mental decline, unattractiveness and loss of independence when they encounter images of their own demographic group?

Sources: Summarised from the studies by Moschis et al.[139] and Perry and Wolburg[140]

The limitations

So far ageing consumers have been discussed as if they were homogeneous. In fact, they are far from homogeneous. The common characteristics of ageing consumers are outlined so that it is easier for us to understand what goes through ageing consumers' mind in general. However, as ageing consumers have had different life experiences, they have gone through different extents of physiological, social, and psychological ageing.[141] This diversity suggests ageing consumers can be classified as healthy hermits, ailing outgoers, healthy indulgers, and frail recluses;[142] see Table 5.6. Different groups of ageing consumers may be susceptible to different marketing activities.

Table 5.6 Definition and classification of ageing consumers

Classification	Definition
Healthy indulgers	They have experienced the fewest life-changing events because of ageing. They are the group that differs the least from the younger generation.
Healthy hermits	They have experienced life events that have worsened their psychological ageing. For example, they start to doubt their self-worth, so they react by becoming psychologically withdrawn
Ailing outgoers	Although this group of people encounter health problems, they maintain positive self-esteem. They accept their "old age" status and acknowledge their limitations, but are still interested in getting the most out of life.
Frail recluses	They have experienced the largest number of life changing events because of physiological, social, and psychological ageing.

Source: Summary based on Moschis [143]

5.4 SUMMARY

1. Children at the perceptual stage (3–7 years old) demonstrate limited cognitive and social abilities. They rely on single physical and tangible elements (such as colours or size) to evaluate products. They see advertising as entertaining, but shorter, programmes, and usually take advertising at its face value. They do not yet know how to negotiate their purchase requests, so the most frequently applied method is egocentric-oriented, such as grabbing wanted items off store shelves and putting them inside their parents' shopping cart or screaming or whining to get what they desire.

2. Children at the analytical stage (7–11 years old) are able to deal with more complicated information and negotiate to get what they want. They are able to consider more attributes at the same time and understand intangible elements for product evaluation. Their understanding of advertising becomes more sophisticated, and they are able to

view advertising not only based on their liking of the advertisement, but also based on the creativity in the advertisement. Their negotiation skills have also evolved from an egocentric approach to a social approach, using such techniques as bargaining, compromising, and persuasion. As they start to understand symbolic meanings, the influence from peers starts to be obvious, especially in the areas of clothes and entertainment (e.g. books, music, and TV programmes).

3. Children at the analytical stage start to develop cognitive defence against susceptibility to advertising, because they start to understand the concept of business and profits and advertising's selling intent. However, research has shown that having cognitive defence is different from using it, as although children have cognitive defence, they still need reminders to use their cognitive defence in order to make it effective. Although children these days know more about advertising, compared with those two decades ago, because of the rapidly changing advertising environment, their more evolved knowledge does not exempt them from their vulnerability to susceptibility to advertising. In fact, their vulnerability is doubled, especially when they encounter modern advertising techniques, such as in-game advertisements.

4. Children at the reflective stage (11–16 years old) exhibit adult-like ways of reasoning and behaviour. They are able to use various decision-making and negotiation strategies towards their advantage in different situations in a systematic manner. Their understanding of symbolic meanings has become more sophisticated and they start to use symbolic meanings to identify their group membership. At this stage, peer influence is important, and more important than family or media influence. However, peer influence is not always positive as peer influence directly influences adolescents' materialism and can sometimes be seen as peer pressure.

5. The segment of ageing consumers has been growing over the years, and its importance started to show with its growth. The main focus of ageing consumers is to understand how their physiological changes, including impaired vision, reduced hearing, and declined motor functions and memory, influence their decision-making. This understanding can then be fed back to the guidelines for marketing implications in product development or marketing communication.

6. There are different types of ageing processes, including physiological, social, and psychological. Thus, ageing consumers are heterogeneous depending on which experiences they have encountered during their physiological, social, and psychological changes because of ageing. Four main groups are identified: healthy indulgers, healthy hermits, ailing outgoers, and frail recluses. Despite the fact that they are different, their general decision-making tendency is to reduce information search and to rely on experiential/emotional processes. This is because, according to socioemotional selectivity theory, as time is perceived limited, they prefer to focus on emotional goals. It also explains why ageing consumers are more attached to familiar brands and place more importance on brand trust.

DISCUSSION QUESTIONS

1. Describe Piaget's theory of development and the extent to which it applies to children consumers.
2. How old are children at the reflective stage? What are their cognitive and social abilities like? How are their cognitive and social abilities reflected in their role as a consumer?
3. Discuss how socioemotional selectivity theory influences ageing consumers' decision-making.
4. Discuss what ethical issues businesses face with ageing consumers and how businesses deal with those issues.

FURTHER READING

- Buijzen, M., Van Reijmersdal, E. A., & Owen, L. H. (2010). Introducing the PCMC Model: An Investigative Framework for Young People's Processing of Commercialized Media Content. *Communication Theory*, *20*(4), 427–450.
- Charles, S. T., & Carstensen, L. L. (2009). Social and Emotional Aging. *Annual Review of Psychology*, *61*, 383–409.
- John, D. R. (1999). Consumer Socialization of Children: A Retrospective Look at Twenty-Five Years of Research. *Journal of Consumer Research*, *26*(December), 183–213.
- Moschis, G. P. (2012). Consumer Behavior in Later Life: Current Knowledge, Issues, and New Directions for Research. *Psychology & Marketing*, *29*(2), 57–75.
- Wright, P., Friestad, M., & Boush, D. M. (2005). The Development of Marketplace Persuasion Knowledge in Children, Adolescents, and Young Adults. *Journal of Public Policy & Marketing*, *24*(2), 222–233.

NOTES

1. Gunter, B., & Furnham, A. (1998). *Children as Consumers: A Psychological Analysis of the Young People's Market*. London: Routledge.
2. Piaget, J., & Inhelder, B. (2000). *The Psychology of the Child*. New York: Basic Books.
3. Welsh, M. C., & Pennington, B. F. (1988). Assessing Frontal Lobe Functioning in Children: Views from Developmental Psychology. *Developmental Neuropsychology*, *4*(3), 199–230; Paus, T., Zijdenbos, A., Worsley, K., Collins, D. L., Blumenthal, J., Giedd, J. N., . . . Evans, A. C. (1999). Structural Maturation of Neural Pathways in Children and Adolescents: In Vivo Study. *Nature*, *283*(5409), 1908–1911.
4. Lourenço, O., & Machado, A. (1996). In Defense of Piaget's Theory: A Reply to 10 Common Criticisms. *Psychological Review*, *103*(1), 143–164; Huitt, W., & Hummel, J. (2003). Piaget's Theory of Cognitive Development. *Educational Psychology Interactive*. Retrieved from www.edpsycinteractive.org/topics/cognition/piaget.html

5. John, D. R. (2008). Stages of Consumer Socialization: The Development of Consumer Knowledge, Skills, and Values from Childhood to Adolescence. In C. P. Haugtvedt, P. M. Herr, & F. R. Kardes (eds), *Handbook of Consumer Psychology* (pp. 221–246). New York: Psychology Press.

6. Selman, R. L. (1980). *The Growth of Interpersonal Understanding: Developmental and Clinical Analyses*. New York: Academic Press.

7. John, Stages of Consumer Socialization.

8. Barenboim, C. (1981). The Development of Person Perception in Childhood and Adolescence: From Behavioural Comparisons to Psychological Constructs to Psychological Comparisons. *Child Development, 52*(1), 129–144.

9. John, Stages of Consumer Socialization.

10. Harris, M., & Butterworth, G. (2002). *Developmental Psychology: A Student's Handbook.* Sussex: Psychology Press.

11. Santrock, J. W. (2004). *Child Development.* New York: McGraw-Hill.

12. John, Stages of Consumer Socialization.

13. Goldberg, M. E., & Gorn, G. J. (1978). Some Unintended Consequences of TV Advertising to Children. *Journal of Consumer Research, 5*(June), 22–29.

14. Baker, S. M., & Gentry, J. W. (1996). Kids as Collectors: A Phenomenological Study of First and Fifth Graders. In K. P. Corfman & J. G. Lynch Jr. (eds), *Advances in Consumer Research* (Vol. 23, pp. 132–137). Provo, UT: Association for Consumer Research.

15. Melkman, R., Koriat, A., & Pardo, K. (1976). Preference for Color and Form in Preschoolers as Related to Color and Form Differentiation. *Child Development, 47*(4), 1045–1105; Suchman, R. G., & Trabasso, T. (1966). Color and Form Preference in Young Children. *Journal of Experimental Child Psychology, 3*(2), 177–187.

16. Terwogt, M. M., & Hoeksma, J. B. (1995). Colors and Emotions: Preferences and Combinations. *Journal of General Psychology, 122*(1), 5–17.

17. Boyatzis, C. J., & Varghese, R. (1994). Children's Emotional Associations with Colors. *Journal of Genetic Psychology: Research and Theory on Human Development, 155*(1), 77–85; Zentner, M. R. (2001). Preferences for Colours and Colour-Emotion Combinations in Early Childhood. *Developmental Science, 4*(4), 389–398; Read, M. A., & Upington, D. (2009). Young Children's Colour Preferences in the Interior Environment. *Early Childhood Education Journal, 36*(6), 491–496.

18. Terwogt & Hoeksma, Colors and Emotions.

19. Blosser, B. J., & Roberts, D. F. (1985). Age Differences in Children's Perceptions of Message Intent Responses to TV News, Commercials, Educational Spots, and Public Service Announcements. *Communication Research, 12*(4), 455–484; Mallalieu, L., Palan, K. M., & Laczniak, R. N. (2005). Understanding Children's Knowledge and Beliefs about Advertising: A Global Issue that Spans Generations. *Journal of Current Issues & Research in Advertising, 27*(53–64).

20. Butter, E. J., Popovich, P. M., Stackhouse, R. H., & Garner, R. K. (1981). Discrimination of Television Programs and Commercials by Preschool Children. *Journal of Advertising Research, 21*(2), 53–56; Palmer, E. L., & McDowell, C. N. (1979). Program/Commercial Separators in Children's Television Programming. *Journal of Communication, 29*(3), 197–201.

21. McNeal, J. U., & Ji, M. F. (2003). Children's Visual Memory of Packaging. *Journal of Consumer Marketing, 20*(5), 400–427.

22. Haynes, J. L., Burts, D. C., Dukes, A., & Cloud, R. (1993). Consumer Socialization of Preschoolers and Kindergartners as Related to Clothing Consumption. *Psychology & Marketing, 10*(2), 151–166; Mizerski, R. (1995). The Relationship between Cartoon Trade Character Recognition and Attitude Toward Product Category in Young Children. *Journal of Marketing, 59*(October), 58–70.

23. John, D. R., & Lakshmi-Ratan, R. (1992). Age Differences in Children's Choice Behavior: The Impact of Available Alternatives. *Journal of Marketing Research, 29*(May), 216–226; Macklin, M. C. (1996). Preschooler's Learning of Brand Names from Visual Cues. *Journal of Consumer Research, 23*(December), 251–261.

24. Bahn, K. D. (1987). How and When Do Brand Perceptions and Preferences First Form? A Cognitive Developmental Investigation. *Journal of Consumer Research, 13*(December), 382–393.

25. Otnes, C., Kim, Y. C., & Kim, K. (1994). All I Want for Christmas: An Analysis of Children's Brand Requests to Santa Claus. *Journal of Popular Culture, 27*(4), 183–194.

26. John, Stages of Consumer Socialization.

27. Rust, L. (1993). Parents and Children Shopping Together: A New Approach to the Qualitative Analysis of Observational Data. *Journal of Advertising Research, 33*(4), 65–70.

28. McNeal, J. U. (1992). *Kids as Customers: A Handbook of Marketing to Children*. New York: Lexington Books.

29. John, Stages of Consumer Socialization.

30. Ibid.

31. John & Lakshmi-Ratan, Age Differences in Children's Choice Behavior; John, D. R., & Sujan, M. (1990). Age Differences in Product Categorization. *Journal of Consumer Research, 16*(4), 452–460; Klees, D. M., Olson, J., & Wilson, R. D. (1988). An Analysis of the Content and Organization of Children's Knowledge Structures. In M. J. Houston (ed.), *Advances in Consumer Research* (Vol. 15, pp. 153–157). Provo, UT: Association for Consumer Research.

32. John, Stages of Consumer Socialization.

33. Moore, E. S., & Lutz, R. J. (2000). Children, Advertising, and Product Experiences: A Multimethod Inquiry. *Journal of Consumer Research, 27*(June), 31–48.

34. Lawlor, M.-A., & Prothero, A. (2008). Exploring Children's Understanding of Television Advertising – Beyond the Advertiser's Perspective. *European Journal of Marketing, 42*(11/12), 1203–1223; Lawlor, M.-A., & Prothero, A. (2003). Children's Understanding of Television Advertising Intent. *Journal of Marketing Management, 19*(3–4), 411–431.

35. Moore, E. S. (2004). Children and the Changing World of Advertising. *Journal of Business Ethics, 52*(2), 161–167.

36. Macklin, M. C. (2003). Children: Targets of Advertising. In J. McDonough & K. Egolf (eds), *Encyclopedia of Advertising* (Vol. 1, pp. 294–298). New York: Fitzroy Dearborn.

37. Bever, T. G., Smith, M. L., Bengen, B., & Johnson, T. G. (1975). Young Viewers' Troubling Response to TV Ads. *Harvard Business Review, 53*(November–December), 109–118/;

Robertson, T. S., & Rossiter, J. R. (1974). Children and Commercial Persuasion: An Attribution Theory Analysis. *Journal of Consumer Research, 1*(June), 13–20; Ward, S. (1972). Children's Reactions to Commercials. *Journal of Advertising Research, 12*(2), 37–45; Ward, S., Wackman, D. B., & Wartella, E. (1977). *How Children Learn to Buy: The Development of Consumer Information-Processing Skills.* Beverly Hills: Sage.

38. Rozendaal, E., Buijzen, M., & Valkenburg, P. (2009). Do Children's Cognitive Advertising Defenses Reduce Their Desire for Advertised Products. *Communications, 34*(3), 287–303.

39. Brucks, M., Armstrong, G. M., & Goldberg, M. E. (1988). Children's Use of Cognitive Defenses Against Television Advertising: A Cognitive Response Approach. *Journal of Consumer Research, 14*(March), 471–482.

40. Moore, Children and the Changing World of Advertising.

41. An, S., & Stern, S. (2011). Mitigating the Effects of Advergames on Children: Do Advertising Breaks Work. *Journal of Advertising, 40*(1), 43–56.

42. Owen, L., Lewis, C., Auty, S., & Buijzen, M. (2013). Is Children's Understanding of Non-traditional Advertising Comparable to Their Understanding of Television Advertising? *Journal of Public Policy & Marketing, 32*(2), 195–206.

43. van Reijmersdal, E. A., Rozendaal, E., & Buijzen, M. (2012). Effects of Prominence, Involvement, and Persuasion Knowledge on Children's Cognitive and Affective Responses to Advergames. *Journal of Interactive Marketing, 26*(1), 33–42.

44. McNeal, *Kids as Customers.*

45. Ward et al., *How Children Learn to Buy.*

46. Hsieh, Y.-C., Chiu, H.-C., & Lin, C.-C. (2006). Family Communication and Parental Influence on Children's Brand Attitudes. *Journal of Business Research, 59*(10–11), 1079–1086.

47. Valkenburg, P., & Cantor, J. (2001). The Development of a Child into a Consumer. *Journal of Applied Developmental Psychology, 22*(1), 61–72.

48. Gunter, B., & Furnham, A. (1998). *Children as Consumers: A Psychological Analysis of the Young People's Market.* London: Routledge.

49. Moore & Lutz, Children, Advertising, and Product Experiences

50. Ibid.

51. Rust, Parents and Children Shopping Together.

52. John, Stages of Consumer Socialization.

53. Flurry, L. A., & Burns, A. C. (2005). Children's Influence in Purchase Decisions: A Social Power Theory Approach. *Journal of Business Research, 58*(5), 593–601.

54. Belk, R. W., Mayer, R. N., & Driscoll, A. (1984). Children's Recognition of Consumption Symbolism in Children's Products. *Journal of Consumer Research, 10*(March), 386–397.

55. Belk, R. W., Bahn, K. D., & Mayer, R. N. (1982). Developmental Recognition of Consumption Symbolism. *Journal of Consumer Research, 9*(June), 4–17.

56. Mayer, R. N., & Belk, R. W. (1982). Acquisition of Consumption Stereotypes by Children. *Journal of Consumer Affairs, 16*(2), 307–321.

57. Shaffer, D. R., & Kipp, K. (2014). *Developmental Psychology: Childhood and Adolescence* (ninth edn). Cengage Learning.

58. Berndt, T. J. (1996). Friendship Quality Affects Adolescents' Self-Esteem and Social Behavior. In W. M. Bukowski, A. F. Newcomb, & W. W. Hartup (eds), *The Company They Keep: Friendship in Childhood and Adolescence* (pp. 346–365). New York: Cambridge University Press.

59. Banerjee, R., & Dittmar, H. (2008). Individual Differences in Children's Materialism: The Role of Peer Relations. *Personality and Social Psychology Bulletin, 34*(1), 17–31.

60. Ibid.

61. John, D. R. (1999) Consumer Socialization of Children: a Retrospective Look at Twenty-Five Years of Research, *Journal of Consumer Research, 26*(December), 183–213; Valkenburg, P. (2004). *Children's Responses to the Screen: A Media Psychological Approach.* Mahwah, NJ: Lawrence Erlbaum.

62. Fox, K. F. A., & Kehret-Ward, T. (1985). Theories of Value and Understanding of Price: A Developmental Perspective. In E. Hirschman & M. B. Holbrook (eds), *Advances in Consumer Research* (Vol. 12, pp. 79–84). Provo, UT: Association for Consumer Research.

63. Berti, A. E., & Bombi, A. S. (1981). The Development of the Concept of Money and Its Value: A Longitudinal Study. *Child Development, 52*(4), 1179–1182.

64. Webley, P. (2005). Children's Understanding of Economics. In M. Barrett & E. Buchanan-Barrow (eds), *Children's Understanding of Society* (pp. 43–67). Hove: Psychology Press.

65. Fox, K. F. A., & Kehret-Ward, T. (1990). Naïve Theories of Price: A Developmental Model. *Psychology & Marketing, 7*(4), 311–329.

66. Ibid.

67. Capon, N., & Kuhn, D. (1980). A Developmental Study of Consumer Information-Processing Strategies. *Journal of Consumer Research, 7*(December), 225–233; Klayman, J. (1985). Children's Decision Strategies and Their Adaptation to Task Characteristics. *Organizational Behavior and Human Decision Processes, 35*(2), 179–201; Nakajima, Y., & Hotta, M. (1989). A Developmental Study of Cognitive Processes in Decision Making: Information Searching as a Function of Task Complexity. *Psychological Reports, 64*(1), 67–79.

68. Moore, R. L., & Stephens, L. F. (1975). Some Communication and Demographic Determinants of Adolescent Consumer Learning. *Journal of Consumer Research, 2*(September), 80–92.

69. Davidson, D. (1991). Developmental Differences in Children's Search of Predecisional Information. *Journal of Experimental Child Psychology, 52*(2), 239–255; Mata, R., von Helversen, B., & Rieskamp, J. (2011). When Easy Comes Hard: The Development of Adaptive Strategy Selection. *Child Development, 82*(2), 687–700.

70. Davidson, Developmental Differences in Children's Search of Predecisional Information; Klayman, Children's Decision Strategies and Their Adaptation to Task Characteristics.

71. Payne, J. W., Bettman, J. R., & Johnson, E. J. (1993). *The Adaptive Decision Maker.* Cambridge: Cambridge University Press.

72. Ibid.

73. Gregan-Paxton, J., & John, D. R. (1997). The Emergence of Adaptive Decision Making in Children. *Journal of Consumer Research, 24*(1), 43–56.

74. John, Stages of Consumer Socialization; Robertson & Rossiter, Children and Commercial Persuasion; Ward, Children's Reactions to Commercials.

75. Bever, T. G., Smith, M. L., Bengen, B., & Johnson, T. G. (1975). Young Viewers' Troubling Response to TV Ads. *Harvard Business Review, 53*(November-December), 109–118.
76. Boush, D. M., Friestad, M., & Rose, G. M. (1994). Adolescent Skepticism toward TV Advertising and Knowledge of Advertiser Tactics. *Journal of Consumer Research, 21*(June), 165–175.
77. John, Stages of Consumer Socialization.
78. Kim, C., Lee, H., & Hall, K. (1991). A Study of Adolescents' Power, Influence Strategy, and Influence on Family Purchase Decisions. In T. L. Childers (ed.), *AMA Winter Marketing Educator's Conference Proceedings* (pp. 37–45). Chicago: American Marketing Association; Manchanda, R. V., & Moore-Shay, E. S. (1996). Mom, I Want That! The Effects of Parental Style, Gender and Materialism on Children's Choice of Influence Strategy. In E. A. Blair & W. A. Kamakura (eds), *AMA Winter Marketing Educator's Conference Proceedings* (pp. 81–90). Chicago: American Marketing Association; Palan, K. M., & Wilkes, R. E. (1997). Adolescent–Parent Interaction in Family Decision Making. *Journal of Consumer Research, 24*(September), 159–169.
79. John, Stages of Consumer Socialization.
80. Kim et al., A Study of Adolescents' Power; Palan & Wilkes, Adolescent–Parent Interaction in Family Decision Making.
81. Davis, H. L. (1976). Decision Making within the Household. *Journal of Consumer Research, 2*(March), 241–260.
82. Spiro, R. L. (1983). Persuasion in Family Decision-Making. *Journal of Consumer Research, 9*(March), 393–402.
83. Palan & Wilkes, Adolescent–Parent Interaction in Family Decision Making.
84. Davis, Decision Making within the Household.
85. Palan & Wilkes, Adolescent–Parent Interaction in Family Decision Making.
86. Achenreiner, G. B., & John, D. R. (2003). The Meaning of Brand Names to Children: A Developmental Investigation. *Journal of Consumer Psychology, 13*(3), 205–219.
87. John, Stages of Consumer Socialization.
88. Chaplin, L. N., & John, D. R. (2005). The Development of Self-Brand Connections in Children and Adolescents. *Journal of Consumer Research, 32*(June), 119–129.
89. Jamison, D. J. (2006). Idols of the Tribe: Brand Veneration, Group Identity, and the Impact of School Uniform Policies. *Academy of Marketing Studies Journal, 10*(1), 19–41.
90. Chaplin, L. N., & John, D. R. (2007). Growing up in a Material World: Age Differences in Materialism in Children and Adolescents. *Journal of Consumer Research, 34*(December), 480–493.
91. Moore & Stephens, Some Communication and Demographic Determinants of Adolescent Consumer Learning; Moschis, G. P., & Moore, R. L. (1979). Decision Making among the Young: A Socialization Perspective. *Journal of Consumer Research, 6*(September), 101–112; Tootelian, D. H., & Gaedeke, R. M. (1992). The Teen Market: An Exploratory Analysis of Income, Spending and Shopping Patterns. *Journal of Consumer Marketing, 9*(4), 35–44.
92. Churchill, G. A., Jr., & Moschis, G. P. (1979). Television and Interpersonal Influences on Adolescent Consumer Learning. *Journal of Consumer Research, 6*(June), 23.

93. Mangleburg, T. F., Doney, P. M., & Bristol, T. (2004). Shopping with Friends and Teens' Susceptibility to Peer Influence. *Journal of Retailing, 80*(2), 101–116.

94. Wooten, D. B. (2006). From Labeling Possessions to Possessing Labels: Ridicule and Socialization Among Adolescents. *Journal of Consumer Research, 33*(September), 188–198.

95. Mangleburg et al., Shopping with Friends and Teens' Susceptibility to Peer Influence.

96. Shim, S. (1996). Adolescent Consumer Decision-Making Styles: The Consumer Socialization Perspective. *Psychology & Marketing, 13*(6), 547–569.

97. Goldberg, M. E., Gorn, G. J., Peracchio, L. A., & Bamossy, G. (2003). Understanding Materialism among Youth. *Journal of Consumer Psychology, 13*(3), 278–288; Achenreiner, G. B. (1997). Materialistic Values and Susceptibility to Influence in Children. In M. Brucks & D. J. MacInnes (eds), *Advances in Consumer Research* (Vol. 24, pp. 82–88). Provo, UT: Association for Consumer Research; Jiang, J., Zhang, Y., Ke, Y., Hawk, S. T., & Qiu, Y. (2015). Can't Buy Me Friendship? Peer Rejection and Adolescent Materialism: Implicit Self-Esteem as a Mediator. *Journal of Experimental Social Psychology, 58*(May), 48–55.

98. Banerjee, R., & Dittmar, H. (2008). Individual Differences in Children's Materialism: The Role of Peer Relations. *Personality and Social Psychology Bulletin, 34*(1), 17–31.

99. Wooten, From Labeling Possessions to Possessing Labels.

100. Chaplin, L. N., & John, D. R. (2010). Interpersonal Influences on Adolescent Materialism: A New Look at the Role of Parents and Peers. *Journal of Consumer Psychology, 20*(2), 176–184.

101. Smith, J., & Baltes, P. B. (1997). Profiles of Psychological Functioning in the Old and Oldest Old. *Psychology and Aging, 12*(3), 455–472.

102. UK's Office for National Statistics. (2022). *National Population Projections: 2020-Based Interim*. Retrieved from www.ons.gov.uk/peoplepopulationandcommunity/populationandmigration/populationprojections/bulletins/nationalpopulationprojections/2020basedinterim#changing-age-structure

103. UK's Office for National Statistics, *National Population Projections*.

104. UN's Department of Economic and Social Affairs. (2019). *World Population Prospects 2019*. Retrieved from population.un.org/wpp/Publications/Files/WPP2019_Highlights.pdf

105. UK's Office for National Statistics, *National Population Projections*.

106. Goldberg, M. E. (2009). Consumer Decision Making and Aging: A Commentary from a Public Policy/Marketing Perspective. *Journal of Consumer Psychology, 19*(1), 28–34.

107. Sudbury, L., & Simcock, P. (2009). A Multivariate Segmentation Model of Senior Consumers. *Journal of Consumer Marketing, 26*(4), 251–262.

108. Yoon, C., & Cole, C. A. (2008). Aging and Consumer Behavior. In C. P. Haugtvedt, P. M. Herr, & F. R. Kardes (eds), *Handbook of Consumer Psychology* (pp. 247–270). New York: Psychology Press.

109. Ibid

110. Salvendy, G. (ed.) (2012). *Handbook of Human Factors and Ergonomics* (fourth edn). New York: John Wiley & Sons.

111. Thompson, N. J., & Thompson, K. E. (2009). Commentary: Can Marketing Practice Keep Up With Europe's Ageing Population? *European Journal of Marketing, 43*(11/12), 1281–1288.

112. Duizer, L. M., Robertson, T., & Han, J. (2009). Requirements for Packaging from an Age-ing Consumer's Perspective. *Packaging Technology and Science*, *22*(4), 187–197.
113. Thompson & Thompson, Commentary.
114. Charness, N., Champion, M., & Yordon, R. (2010). Designing Products for Older Consumers: A Human Factors Perspective. In A. Drolet, N. Schwarz, & C. Yoon (eds), *The Aging Consumer: Perspectives from Psychology and Economics* (pp. 249–268). New York: Routledge; Yoon & Cole, Aging and Consumer Behavior.
115. Yoon & Cole, Aging and Consumer Behavior.
116. Charness et al., Designing Products for Older Consumers.
117. Besedeš, T., Deck, C., Sarangi, S., & Shor, M. (2012). Decision-Making Strategies and Perfor-mance among Seniors. *Journal of Economic Behavior and Organization*, *81*(2), 524–533; Den-burg, N. L., Tranel, D., & Bechara, A. (2005). The Ability to Decide Advantageously Declines Prematurely in Some Normal Older Persons. *Neuropsychologia*, *43*(7), 1099–1106.
118. Peters, E., Dieckmann, N. F., & Weller, J. (2011). Age Differences in Complex Decision Making. In K. W. Schaie & S. L. Willis (eds), *Handbook of the Psychology of Aging* (Vol. 7). London: Academic Press.
119. Cole, C. A., & Balasubramanian, S. K. (1993). Age Differences in Consumers' Search for Information: Public Policy Implications. *Journal of Consumer Research*, *20*(June), 157–169; Ende, J., Kazis, L., Ash, A., & Moskowitz, M. A. (1989). Measuring Patients' Desire for Autonomy: Decision Making and Information-Seeking Preferences among Medical Patients. *Journal of General Internal Medicine*, *4*(1), 23–30; Lambert-Pandraud, R., Laurent, G., & Laper-sonne, E. (2005). Repeat Purchasing of New Automobiles by Older Consumers: Empirical Evidence and Interpretations. *Journal of Marketing*, *69*(April), 97–113; Mata, R., & Nunes, L. (2010). When Less Is Enough: Cognitive Aging, Information Search, and Decision Quality in Consumer Choice. *Psychology & Aging*, *25*(2), 289–298.
120. Yoon & Cole, Aging and Consumer Behavior.
121. Page 972 from Pacini, R., & Epstein, S. (1999). The Relation of Rational and Experiential Information Processing Styles to Personality, Basic Beliefs, and the Ratio-Bias Phenomenon. *Journal of Personality and Social Psychology*, *76*(6), 972–987.
122. Horn, J. L., & Cattell, R. B. (1967). Age Differences in Fluid and Crystallized Intelligence. *Acta Psychologica*, *26*, 107–129.
123. Ibid; Baltes, P. B., & Lindenberger, U. (1997). Emergence of a Powerful Connection between Sensory and Cognitive Functions across the Adult Life Span: A New Window to the Study of Cognitive Aging. *Psychology & Aging*, *12*(1), 12–21; Baltes, P. B., Corne-lius, S. W., Sprio, A., Nesselroade, J. R., & Willis, S. L. (1980). Integration versus Differ-entation of Fluid/Crystallized Intelligence in Old Age. *Developmental Psychology*, *16*(6), 625–635.
124. Peters, E. (2010). Aging-Related Changes in Decision Making. In A. Drolet, N. Schwarz, & C. Yoon (eds), *The Aging Consumer: Perspectives from Psychology and Economics* (pp. 75–101). New York: Routledge.
125. Hibbard, J. H., & Peters, E. (2003). Supporting Informed Consumer Health Care Deci-sions: Data Presentation Approaches that Facilitate the Use of Information in Choice. *Annual Review of Public Health*, *24*, 413–433.

126 Besedeš et al., Decision-Making Strategies and Performance Among Seniors; Mata & Nunes, When Less Is Enough.

127. Peters, Aging-Related Changes in Decision Making.

128. Carstensen, L. L. (1995). Evidence for a Life-Span Theory of Socioemotional Selectivity. *Current Directions in Psychological Science, 4*(5), 151–156; Carstensen, L. L. (2006). The Influence of a Sense of Time on Human Development. *Science, 312*(5782), 1913–1915; Charles, S. T., & Carstensen, L. L. (2009). Social and Emotional Aging. *Annual Review of Psychology, 61*, 383–409.

129. Page 165 from Carstensen, L. L., Isaacowitz, D. M., & Charles, S. T. (1999). Taking Time Seriously: A Theory of Socioemotional Selectivity. *American Psychologist, 54*(3), 165–181.

130. Page 103 from Carstensen, L. L., Fung, H. H., & Charles, S. T. (2003). Socioemotional Selectivity Theory and the Regulation of Emotion in the Second Half of Life. *Motivation and Emotion, 27*(2), 103–123.

131. Charles & Carstensen, Social and Emotional Aging.

132. Lambert-Pandraud, R., & Laurent, G. (2010). Why Do Older Consumers Buy Older Brands? The Role of Attachment and Declining Innovativess. *Journal of Marketing, 74*(September), 104–121.

133. Kim, D., & Jang, S. S. (2015). Cognitive Decline and Emotional Regulation of Senior Consumers. *International Journal of Hospitality Management, 44*, 111–119.

134. Jahn, S., Gaus, H., & Kiessling, T. (2012). Trust, Commitment, and Older Women: Exploring Brand Attacment Differences in the Elderly Segment. *Psychology & Marketing, 29*(6), 445–457.

135. Kim, S., Goldstein, D., Hasher, L., & Zacks, R. T. (2005). Framing Effects in Younger and Older Adults. *Journal of Gerontology: Psychological Sciences, 60B*(4), P216–P218.

136. Reyna, V. F. (2004). How People Make Decisions that Involve Risk: A Dual Processes Approach. *Current Directions in Psychological Science, 13*(2), 60–66; Myles-Worsley, M., Johnston, W. A., & Simons, M. A. (1988). The Influence of Expertise on X-Ray Image Processing. *Journal of Experimental Psychology: Learning, Memory, and Cognition, 14*(3), 553–557.

137. Finucane, M. L., Slovic, P., Hibbard, J. H., Peters, E., Mertz, C. K., & MacGregor, D. G. (2002). Aging and Decision-Making Competence: An Analysis of Comprehension and Consistency Skills in Older versus Younger Adults Considering Health-Plan Options. *Journal of Behavioral Decision Making, 15*(2), 141–164.

138. Moschis, G. P., Mosteller, J., & Fatt, C. K. (2011). Research Frontiers on Older Consumers' Vulnerability. *Journal of Consumer Affairs, 45*(3), 467–491.

139. Ibid.

140. Perry, V. G., & Wolburg, J. M. (2011). Aging Gracefully: Emerging Issues for Public Policy and Consumer Welfare. *Journal of Consumer Affairs, 45*(3), 365–371.

141. Charles & Carstensen, Social and Emotional Aging; Charness et al., Designing Products for Older Consumers: A Human Factors Perspective; Carstensen, Evidence for a Life-Span Theory of Socioemotional Selectivity; Moschis, G. P. (2012). Consumer Behavior

in Later Life: Current Knowledge, Issues, and New Directions for Research. *Psychology & Marketing, 29*(2), 57–75; Yoon & Cole, Aging and Consumer Behavior.

142. Moschis, G. P. (2003). Marketing to Older Adults: An Updated Overview of Present Knowledge and Practice. *Journal of Consumer Marketing, 20*(6), 516–525.

143. Ibid.

6

EMOTIONS IN CONSUMER BEHAVIOUR

To explore, understand, and explain:

- the role of emotions in our judgement, decisions, and behaviour
- the psychological bases and implications for consumer behaviour of positive emotions:
    - happiness
    - pride
- psychological bases and implications for consumer behaviour of negative emotions
    - fear
    - anger
    - regret

6.1 INTRODUCTION

The effects of emotions can surpass those of reasoning. Emotions are a subjective experience and can be positive or negative. They are able to activate bodily arousal, which can be an automatic reflex (such as fear) or depend on a thought process (such as guilt). The effects of emotions are immediate to our judgement, decisions, and behaviour, as they are able to activate specific mental processes and memory by interrupting ongoing cognition. That is why emotions sometimes override cognition. This chapter will introduce the psychological bases of specific emotions and discuss their implications in consumer behaviour. Two positive emotions (happiness and pride) and three negative emotions (fear, anger, and regret) will be introduced, discussed, and examined. The chapter begins with an introduction of what emotions are and how they influence our judgement, decisions, and behaviour.

6.2 THE BASICS OF EMOTIONS
A brief introduction of emotion

There are six basic (or prototypical) emotions: surprise, happiness, anger, fear, disgust, and sadness.[1] Of course, there are more emotions than these, but these six emotions are raw emotions that encompass most other emotions. For example, a combination of surprise and fear is tenseness, and a combination of surprise and happiness is excitement. Box 6.1 shows the emotions that are frequently used in consumer research.

─Box 6.1─

Emotions used in consumer psychology

There are many different emotion inventories used in consumer psychology. Early consumer psychologists used the PANAS scale developed by D. Watson, Clark, and Tellegen[2] or the PAD (pleasure-arousal-dominance) scale developed by Mehrabian and Russell.[3] In 1997 Richins[4] devised the consumption emotion set (CES), which has become the most commonly used inventory in consumption context, as it is a comprehensive scale that focuses on all emotions that can happen in a consumption context. CES identifies 16 types of emotions, plus four emotions in the "others" category.

Negative emotions

1.   *Anger*: frustrated, angry, irritated
2.   *Discontent*: unfulfilled, discontented
3.   *Worry*: nervous, worried, tense

4. *Sadness*: depressed, sad, miserable
5. *Fear*: scared, afraid, panicky
6. *Shame*: embarrassed, ashamed, humiliated
7. *Envy*: envious, jealous
8. *Loneliness*: lonely, homesick

Positive emotions

1. *Romantic love*: sexy, romantic, passionate
2. *Love*: loving, sentimental, warm hearted
3. *Peacefulness*: calm, peaceful
4. *Contentment*: contented, fulfilled
5. *Optimism*: optimistic, encouraged, hopeful
6. *Joy*: happy, pleased, joyful
7. *Excitement*: excited, thrilled, enthusiastic
8. *Surprise*: surprised, amazed, astonished

Other emotions

Guilty, proud, eager, relieved

Emotion-related terminologies

Emotions are sometimes confused with or used interchangeably with such terms as affect, mood, or feelings.[5] However, they mean slightly different aspects of emotions (Figure 6.1):

- Affect, similar to feelings, is usually used as an overarching term to describe all types of feeling states.[6] Moods and emotions are specific examples of such states.
- Mood is a subjective and internal feeling state but with *low* intensity. The source of mood can be internal (e.g. hormonal activity) or external (e.g. music), but the influence of the sources is not always clear to us. Mood, therefore, suggests our experience of a vague sense of feeling happy or sad without necessarily knowing why. The use of mood in marketing is usually related to shopper (or retail) marketing (see Chapter 9).
- Emotion is also a subjective and internal feeling state, but with *high* intensity. For example, Procter & Gamble's "Thank You, Mum" advertisement, aired in 2012 during the Olympics in London, is able to stir intensive emotions about family love, support, and pride.

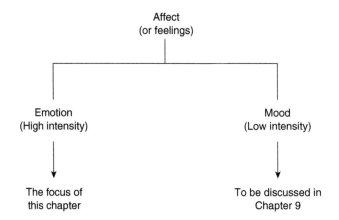

Figure 6.1   The distinction between affect, emotion, and mood

This chapter will focus on emotion, an intensive, subjective, and internal psychological feeling state. See Chapter 9 for the discussion of mood.

How do emotions influence?

The *appraisal-tendency framework*, used to explain how specific emotions influence our judgement, decisions, and behaviour, suggests that different emotions are able to activate different specific cognitive and motivational processes that are then manifested in different biological and behavioural reactions.[7] This activation is speedy because it interrupts ongoing cognitive processes and releases our cognitive capacity (such as attention, memory, and judgement).[8] That is why some psychologists argue that emotions serve as information to influence our judgement and decisions,[9] and why we are able to respond to what happens without thinking a lot.[10] The purpose of the speedy reactions is to quickly deal with encountered opportunities or problems,[11] so that we can maintain positive emotions[12] or repair negative emotions.[13] For this reason, emotional cues in advertising can be more effective than cognitive cues.[14]

Research has shown that emotions influence our memory, evaluations, judgement, and decisions.[15] In particular, emotions influence evaluations and judgement via our attitude.[16] For example, people or objects that elicit pleasant feelings are evaluated more favourably; nicely decorated desserts are preferred; attractive actors or actresses are liked. Because of the strong association between emotions and our attitude and evaluation, these emotions are often mistakenly taken as attitude or evaluation.[17] In fact, emotions and evaluation form attitudes of the target object, but emotions are emotional responses generated by the object, while evaluation refers to cognitive responses (i.e. thoughts and beliefs) about the object. Compared with evaluation (or cognition), emotions can better predict attitude,[18] judgement,[19] and behaviour.[20]

Emotion-congruence effect

Emotions are able to activate specific mental processes and stored information. That is, we are more likely to recall information from memory that is congruent with our current emotions,[21]

or we are more likely to give an evaluation that is associated with our current emotions.[22] This is called emotion-congruence effect.

6.3 POSITIVE EMOTIONS

Happiness

The psychological basis

Happiness is an important aspect in subjective well-being, but this section will not deal with subjective well-being, which will be introduced in Chapter 11. This section only focuses on the role of happiness in consumer behaviour. Happiness is a complicated concept, as it can mean different things to different people (Table 6.1).

Table 6.1 Types of happiness

Dimensions of happiness	Types of happiness		
Arousal level[23]	High: excitement	versus	Low: tranquillity
Pleasure seeking[24]	Purely at the sensation level	versus	Governed by doing what is worth doing
Duration of happiness	Short-term, momentary happiness (an activation of the pleasure centre of the brain[25])	versus	Chronic state of happiness

Although there are different types of happiness, these types are positive emotions.[26] Research has shown that happiness leads us to broaden the scope of attention and action (e.g. open to novelty), [27] to be creative in our problem-solving,[28] to engage in heuristic processing,[29] to be optimistic about favourable events occurring,[30] and to be able to focus on the big picture and think abstractly.[31] However, happiness is likely to induce false memory[32] that overestimates the intensity of the emotion[33] and that imagines events to reinforce their happiness.[34]

Implications for consumer behaviour

Inducing happiness

Happiness can be induced by pleasant things, including:

- a pleasant product, such as an iced tea (versus water)[35] and a trusted brand[36]
- a pleasant experience, such as shopping (Box 6.2), watching a happy advertisement, and the sufficient variety of options for consumers to choose from[37]

—Box 6.2—

The effect of shopping on happiness

Retail therapy (or shopping therapy) is seen as strategic behaviour, as a pick-me-up and to in-crease our happiness.[38] Research has shown that buying for experiences (e.g. a holiday) is happier compared with a cost-comparable material possession (e.g. a designer's bag).[39] This is because experience purchase is more likely to involve social interaction,[40] and because it takes more time to adapt (or appreciate) for experience purchase than for material purchase. Taking time makes the enjoyment so much better, but this effect only applies for positive outcomes of the purchase, not for negative outcomes.[41] However, for negative outcomes, the misery in experiential purchase magnifies as time goes by to adapt (or to accumulate the negative emotions) the purchase.

Dunn et al. said "if money doesn't make you happy,[42] then you probably aren't spending it right" and proposed eight principles of purchase to make one happy:

1. buy more experiences and fewer material goods
2. use your money to benefit others (donation)
3. buy many small pleasures rather than fewer large ones
4. eschew extended warranties and other forms of overpriced insurance
5. delay consumption
6. consider how peripheral features of their purchases may affect their day-to-day lives
7. beware of comparison shopping
8. pay close attention to the happiness of others

However, as previously discussed, happiness can mean different things to different people, and the trigger of happiness needs to match with how happiness is viewed. For example, young people are happier with extraordinary experiences (e.g. going to Hawaii for a holiday) than with ordinary ones (e.g. went out to my garden to a bright sun shining), whereas old people are equally happy with either extraordinary or ordinary experiences.[43]

Evaluation of advertisements

The emotion-congruence effect suggests that we tend to evaluate advertisements more favour-ably when the advertisements contain emotional appeals that are consistent with our emotion at the time of evaluation. Our evaluation influenced by happiness is associated with how we see happiness (Table 6.1). Therefore, if happiness means excitement to us and if we feel excited, our evaluation for products with adventurous appeals will be more favourable.[44] By the same token, if we experience peacefulness as happiness, our evaluation for those with serene appeals will be more positive.[45]

The influence of temporal foci on happiness

There are two main temporal foci: present versus future, and our temporal foci influence our evaluation and behaviour. A focus on the present makes us seek comfort and tranquillity, whereas a focus on the future makes us desire novelty and adventure.[46] Therefore, when we focus on the present (versus future), we tend to choose products containing calmness (versus excitement) appeals.[47]

Information processing

Happiness reduces our cognitive elaboration[48] and encourages us to use heuristic process for the task at hand.[49] In short, happiness in a way gives us a perception of having sufficient time to do what we wish.[50] Consequently, when we feel happy, we prefer advertisements focusing on the benefits that lack immediacy, for example about future or an abstract benefit, as opposed to the benefits with immediacy, for example, about now or a concrete benefit.[51]

Memory

Our memory is not always correct regarding emotions. That is, our remembered happy experience is usually greater than the actual happy experience.[52] Although the remembered happy experience is not a true representation of the actual experience, the remembered happy experience is better able to predict our future choices than the actual experience.[53]

In addition, our remembered happy experience may not have happened at all as advertisements are able to encode and then create that happy experience in our memory. For example, advertisements using an autobiographical approach to portray an experience (e.g. Disneyland, shaking hands with Mickey Mouse) can create false memory that leads us to believe how enjoyable our experience (in Disneyland) was, when, in fact, we did not have a happy experience.[54]

Pride

The psychological basis

There are two types of pride: authentic and hubristic pride[55] (Table 6.2). Both authentic and hubristic pride convey a sense of accomplishment or superiority.[56] *Authentic pride* is positively viewed and associated with either one's own accomplishment or an accomplishment from one's associations,[57] whereas *hubristic pride* is usually negatively appraised because, unlike authentic pride, it is not founded on a solid foundation, such as accomplishments. Without a solid foundation, hubristic pride implies, in some cases, narcissism.[58] Therefore, authentic pride is usually pro-social,[59] whereas hubristic pride is anti-social.[60] Whilst hubristic pride is negatively evaluated, the emotion that people with this pride experience is still positive.

Table 6.2 Types of pride

Types of Pride	Sources of Pride	Exemplar Emotions in Pride

Authentic pride	• One's own accomplishment (e.g. I got a job promotion)[61]
	• An accomplishment from one's associations:
	  ○ people who are related to us (e.g. My daughter has been admitted to the best university in the world)
	  ○ nations that we belong to[62]
	  ○ possessions we have (e.g. I have the best car)[63]
		• Accomplished
		• Confident

Hubristic pride	• Exaggerated self-confidence[64] • Inflated positive self-image[65]	• Arrogant • Conceited

Pride influences information processing, memory, and behaviour through seeking positive distinctiveness or enhanced self-evaluation. For example, pride makes us:

- want to associate with people who are strong[66]
- remember details of those events involving positive self-evaluation[67]

Because of pride, we are willing to sacrifice the short-term benefit in order to achieve the long-term goal which involves greater accomplishment that enhances positive self-image. Therefore, pride motivates us to persevere on tasks despite initial costs,[68] even if the initial costs may make decisions appear somewhat unreasonable for the short term.[69]

Implications for consumer behaviour

Consumption goals

Pride is closely associated with our goals, outcomes of our goals, and how the outcomes come about. In other words, we feel proud when we are able to achieve our goals.[70] There are mainly three ways where consumers take pride:

- through what we consume or have, as the outcomes are socially valued[71] – see more details in the next section, luxury consumption
- through what we do, including healthy (e.g. eating healthily), ethical (e.g. fair-trade), and sustainable (e.g. organic) consumption,[72] as the outcomes are related to the efforts we put in
- through how well we do what we do, as, for example, reflected from the "I designed it myself effect" in the products that offer the opportunity for consumers to customise[73]

Luxury consumption

Consumers' pride

Luxury brands are able to communicate a sense of status, wealth, and achievement.[74] However, whether or not pride is positively associated with luxury consumption depends on what kind of pride: authentic or hubristic pride. People with authentic pride do not necessarily purchase luxury brands, but people with hubristic pride do.[75] This is perhaps because people with authentic pride tie their achievement to their hard work, not what they buy/have; they do not have the urgency to use consumption to present themselves. By contrast, people with hubristic pride do not experience genuine achievement; therefore, they need luxury brands as a way of maintaining their inflated self-representations.[76]

Brands' pride

Research has shown that though luxury brands can be snobbish, their snobbery in fact increases consumers' aspiration and desire for the brand.[77] However, this effect does not apply to everyone. Consumers who are already experiencing prior self-threat that hurts their pride or confidence tend to avoid those snobbish brands in favour of a competing, less-arrogant alternative.[78] Whilst consumers admire arrogant brands as reflecting high status and quality, arrogance can also make consumers feel inferior.

Consumer ethnocentrism

Another pride that will influence consumer behaviour is national pride, and this specific pride in consumption is called consumer ethnocentrism, which is rooted in patriotism.[79] Because of patriotism, morality dictates consumers to buy things made in their own country since this purchase can help the domestic economy. National pride may make people or even companies pay more for the same purchase, if that purchase involves characteristics of their national pride.[80] When domestically produced products are not available, consumers will choose products from countries with cultures similar to their own.[81]

6.4 NEGATIVE EMOTIONS

Fear

The psychological basis

Fear is an unpleasant emotion caused by the threat of danger, pain, or harm. It is an evolutionary emotion that helps us identify and avoid threats to survival.[82] Therefore, fear can act like an "emotional reflex" [83] without conscious awareness.[84] These reflexes trigger both involuntary and voluntary changes in our physical conditions or behaviour:

- involuntary changes: changes in the autonomic nervous system, such as increasing heart rate and decreasing skin temperature (i.e. low enough to make us shiver)[85]
- voluntary changes: changes in the somatic nervous system, such as running away from a spider if you are afraid of it

There are two mechanisms that produce fear. The first mechanism is via classical conditioning. If fear is learned through classical conditioning, it is difficult to completely remove the association once it is established.[86] Whilst extinction may suppress your expression or memory of fear, the association is never fully lost. Because of this, it is very easy to reinstate conditioned fear. The second mechanism is via mental processes. For example, visualising yourself in a scary situation can trigger fear reflex responses.[87] This visualising can also be applied to mere observation; observing others conditioned to fear a specific stimulus can make one acquire the same fear association.[88]

Implications for consumer behaviour

Message induced fear: fear appeal advertisements

Fear appeal advertisements are a technique often used by social marketing to encourage people to engage in safe behaviour; for example, using condoms to avoid HIV/AIDS, quitting smoking to avoid health issues, driving safely (no speeding or drink-driving) to avoid accidents, or exercising regularly to avoid health problems. Although fear appeals are effective in influencing attitudes, intentions, and behaviour,[89] their influence is not static. The influence differs from people to people in terms of demographic characteristics; for example, better-educated people are subjected to greater influence from fear appeals with regard to health concerns.[90]

The pattern of the effectiveness of fear presents an inverse U curve (Figure 6.2); that is, too strong or too weak levels of fear are not effective. This is because a fear appeal that is too weak cannot stimulate sufficient elaboration of the harmful consequences.[91] On the other hand, an overly strong degree of fear motivates maladaptive fear control actions, such as avoiding the messages,[92] which renders the messages contained in the fear appeal ineffective. Fear appeals with neither too weak nor too strong fear degrees encourage adaptive danger control actions, such as message acceptance, thereby activating the wanted behaviour.[93]

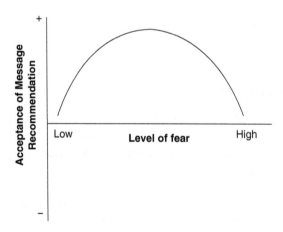

Figure 6.2   The effectiveness of fear appeal and the level of fear

Source: Ray and Wilkie[94]

Reprinted from *Journal of Marketing*, 34(January), Ray and Wilkie. Fear: The Potential of an Appeal Neglected by Marketing, 54-62, Copyright (1970), with permission from SAGE.

Fear does not act alone. Fear interacts with self-efficacy and familiarity with the threat to influence the effectiveness of fear appeal:

Self-efficacy

Whether or not fear changes our behaviour depends on the level of self-efficacy, indicating the degree to which we think we have control to act in order to resolve our fear.[95] Fear, therefore, enables us to calculate and act rationally. Only when we have sufficient self-efficacy do we determine to engage in behavioural change to avoid a fearful outcome.[96] As a result, fear appeal advertisements with messages strengthening self-efficacy can be more effective than just the fearful content.

Familiarity with the threat

Familiarity with the threat determines how we perceive the severity of the threat. When we are familiar with the threat, sufficient information about the threat is more important and effective than the fearful, graphic content.[97] On the other hand, when we are unfamiliar with the threat, the fearful, graphic content is more effective to attract our attention and process the information regarding the threat.[98]

Incidental fear

Incidental negative emotions have been found to associate with negative evaluations of the product, brand, or advertisements. Because of this, marketers, in general, try to avoid associating their brands with fearful content, such as product placement in horror films. In addition, incidental fear triggers behaviours that emphasise:

1. risk averse: For example, incidental fear makes people prone to an earlier sell-off of their stocks in the financial market should there be a risk.[99] This is because they tend to be more pessimistic about risks.[100]
2. social conformity: People who are afraid for whatever reason tend to conform to their surroundings as part of a self-protection mechanism.[101] In the case of consumption, they tend to choose products that are popular, rather than limited editions,[102] and become more attached to their brands.[103]

Anger

The psychological basis

We feel angry when we are harmed or endure injustices because of others' actions. Anger is a unique negative emotion in two ways. First, unlike people with other negative emotions who tend to use systematic (analytic) information processing, angry people tend to use heuristic information processing,[104] which enables anger to serve as information, leading a perception of a gloomy future. Therefore, with heuristics information processing, angry people become pessimistic,[105] and inclined to avoiding risks.[106]

However, angry people do sometimes use systematic information processing. When they do, another characteristic that differentiates anger from other negative emotions appears: unlike other negative emotions that avoid the problems at hand, anger approaches the problems.[107] Anger activates the left frontal hemisphere[108] and peripheral physiology, such as blood flow to the hand.[109] These activations suggest that angry people are prepared to fight[110] and willing to take risks.[111] This is a defensive optimism that anger activates, as anger can be intimidating enough to force the counterpart into submission. Consequently, angry people can be effectively calculating.[112]

Implications for consumer behaviour

Integral anger

Anger as a result of service failure

Angry customers are highly dissatisfied and more likely to complain and to spread negative word-of-mouth.[113] There are three main sources of service failure, which lead to different degrees of anger, from irritation and frustration to anger:[114]

- Service failure as a result of uncontrollable events (e.g. bad weather delays flights), we experience irritation.
- Service failure as a result of incompetent personnel, we experience frustration.
- Service failure as a result of the company's controllable, deliberate, and unjustified action, we experience anger.

Anger, compared with irritation and frustration, has the greatest effects in spreading negative word-of-mouth and decreasing re-patronage intentions.

The coping strategies angry customers adopt can be broadly categorised into two types: *conciliatory* and *retaliatory coping*.[115] Conciliatory coping adopts an active behaviour focusing on problem-solving through a confrontational approach.[116] Whilst it is confrontational in nature, customers' anger can be most effectively managed if their helplessness can be reduced,[117] their problems resolved,[118] and their emotions understood and supported.[119] Success in dealing with customers' anger, especially for those who are originally loyal to the company, can further enhance their loyalty.[120] However, if conciliatory coping is not successful, customers then turn to retaliatory coping, which involves such behaviour as stopping patronage and spreading vindictive word-of-mouth, and this behaviour in turn increases customer rumination, which further increases customer anger.[121]

Anger as a result of observation and interaction at the service space

Anger is a highly contagious emotion; if you observe anger, you are highly likely to become angry.[122] Imagine that you are waiting at the airport for a flight from New York to London for

Christmas holidays, but the flight is delayed because of severe winter weather. Some angry passengers start to yell at the airline employees for not knowing when they will be able to fly, and their anger can spread very quickly to other passengers, despite the fact that weather is an uncontrollable condition. Now imagine that you are one of the airline employees that is being shouted at. You feel their anger is not justified since neither you nor your company can control the weather. Their anger makes you angry and makes you want to counter-attack.[123] This conflict between the front-line employee and customer is referred to as the *incivility spiral*.[124] Therefore, it is essential that the front-line employees are conscious of this effect in their prior training and prevent it from spreading to other present customers and to themselves.

Incidental anger

One of the most researched areas of incidental anger is anger as a result of self-control. For example, people on a diet tend to be aggressive.[125] As self-control is associated with anger, companies might do well advertising anger-themed movies and videogames (e.g. "Angry Birds") next to healthy food aisles, for example, since anger makes people prefer anger-themed content.[126] Self-control to maintain or improve subjective well-being can exert pride (see Section 6.3), but a strict self-control may result in conflicts with our basic psychological need: pleasure-seeking. Too much of a good thing can be bad. Everything in moderation, including self-control, may be a modern way of living a healthy life.

Regret

The psychological basis

There are two important elements in regret: counterfactual thinking and self-blame.[127] Counterfactual thinking is about comparing what happened and what could have happened,[128] and as a result, regret is a cognitive emotion,[129] and it is an emotion that we can experience after about the age of seven when we are cognitively capable of such comparisons.[130] Counterfactual thinking often leads us to believe that the "could have happened" outcome is more attractive than "what happened".[131]

However, mere counterfactual thinking does not necessarily lead to regret. It could be disappointment. To differentiate regret from disappointment, we need the second element: self-blame.[132] Self-blame suggests that we take responsibility for the decision that led to the actual outcome. In other words, when one experiences regret, the regret involves feeling that "one should have known better, thinking about what a mistake one has made, feeling a tendency to kick oneself and to correct one's mistake, and wanting to undo the event and to get a second chance".[133] Whilst the "kicking oneself" in regret can potentially decrease subjective well-being,[134] the wanting to get a second chance in regret motivates people to reflect on their mistakes, thereby striving for a better life.[135] Therefore, regret has important implications in our behaviour and decision-making by, for example, changing our expectations of the decision outcomes, justifying our decisions, or changing our decisions in the future.[136]

Implications for consumer behaviour

Types of consumption regret

There are four main types of consumption regret – see Table 6.3. The majority of research focuses on retrospective and anticipated regret, which will be discussed in the below sections.

Table 6.3 Types of consumption regret

Types of Regret	Sources of Regret	Example
Retrospective regret[137]	Regret about past decisions	I regret that I missed the opportunity to purchase the product on sale.
Anticipated regret[138]	Regret about future decisions	I might regret if I miss the opportunity to purchase the product on sale.

Outcome regret[139]	Regret about decision outcomes:
	• Regret of not buying the alternatives
	• Regret of buying the current product
	  o Wrong perception of needing the current product
	  o Needs of the current product changed
		I regret that I bought the Mac computer as most of my existing software is incompatible.

Process regret[140]	Regret about inappropriate degrees of consideration: • Under-consideration • Over-consideration	*Under-consideration*: If I had done more, I would have been able to make a better decision. *Over-consideration*: I could have made the same decision without spending so much time on researching the products/brands.

Retrospective regret in consumption

Retrospective regret reduces consumer satisfaction,[141] increases switching behaviour (switching to a different brand),[142] spreads negative word-of-mouth,[143] and defers purchase.[144] The most important determinant of retrospective regret is the performance of the purchase not meeting expectations.[145] However, even when the expectations are met and consumers are satisfied, consumers may still experience regret. This is because the post-purchase information, such as product reviews and price comparisons, could have changed our purchase decision. In this case, the information we could have received but did not leads to consumers feeling regret over post-purchase comparisons.[146]

Anticipated regret in consumption

Short-term anticipated regret

Short-term anticipated regret happens immediately, or not too long, prior to the purchase. Unlike retrospective regret deferring purchase, anticipated regret brings purchase forward. For example, if we anticipate that we would regret if we do not buy home insurance should an accident happen, this anticipation makes us purchase insurance.[147] If we anticipate that the sale will end soon and we will regret it if we do not purchase during the sale, this anticipation makes us buy at the current sale, as opposed to waiting for a better (or another) sale.[148]

When consumers are asked to anticipate how they would feel if they made the wrong decision, they tend to choose a more expensive and well-known brand[149] or a status quo brand.[150] This is because a cheaper and lesser-known brand is more likely to go wrong. That is why a repeat purchase of the status quo makes consumers feel less regret than switching to a different brand, and this repeat purchase is called the *status quo effect*.

Long-term anticipated regret

Long-term anticipated regret is about us focusing on what we would regret in 10 or 20 years time. Research shows that long-term anticipated regret is able to relax self-control, which leads us to choose indulgence, rather than functional products.[151] This is because when we think about life over the next 30 years, we are able to escape the influence of indulgence guilt.[152] When we think long term, we are more aware of our tendency to miss out on the fun experiences in life, as life is full of emphasis on the need to work hard.[153]

6.5 SUMMARY

1. Different from mood which is a low-intensity feeling state, emotions are a high-intensity feeling state. Similar to mood, emotions are a subjective experience. As emotions can activate an automatic (reflex) response (such as fear) or depend on a thought process (such as regret), emotions influence our judgement, decisions, and behaviour. In addition, as their influence can interrupt ongoing cognitive processes, the emotional reactions are usually very strong and fast. The strong response implies that emotions are better than cognition to predict our attitude, judgement, and behaviour, and the fast response allows us to quickly deal with the encountered opportunities or problems so that we are able to maintain positive emotions or repair negative ones.

2. When we are happy, we tend to think less and elaborate less on information at hand. Our thinking less allows us to step back and focus on the big picture. For this reason, when we are happy, we prefer advertisements focusing on the benefits that lack immediacy, for example, about future or an abstract benefit. However, as the definition of happiness differs from people to people, our definition of happiness influences what

cognitive and motivational process is activated. For example, if we believe happiness is about excitement (peacefulness), we prefer excitement (peacefulness) in advertisements, and therefore are able to better recall that advertisement when, at the time of our viewing of the advertisement, we are happy. Similarly, our definition also determines how our happiness is induced.

3. Pride influences information processing, memory, and behaviour through seeking positive distinctiveness or enhanced self-evaluation. There are two different types of pride: authentic pride and hubristic pride. Authentic pride is associated with our accomplishment or the accomplishment by association. Our consumption accomplishment can come from healthy (e.g. eating healthily), ethical (e.g. supporting fair trade), and sustainable (e.g. supporting organic farming) consumption. Our accomplishment requires a level of self-control, which gives us permission to indulge later when our goal is achieved. On the other hand, hubristic pride is associated with exaggerated self-confidence, and sometimes, narcissism. Because people with hubristic pride do not really have a true accomplishment to anchor for their pride, they would need, for example, luxury consumption to maintain their inflated self-presentations.

4. Fear is an evolutionary emotion that acts as an emotional reflex without conscious awareness. To merely think about fearful objects can arouse the feeling of fear. Fear appeals in advertisements are quite common. The effectiveness of fear appeals presents an inverse U curve – it means that an advertisement that is too fearful activates people's defensive avoidance or reactance to avoid the advertisement, whilst too weak it cannot stimulate sufficient elaboration of the harmful consequences. The main reason that the fear appeals are effective is because we would like to control our actions in order to resolve fear. For this reason, successful fear appeals in advertisements focus on arousing people's motivation to change their behaviour (e.g. by buying a certain product).

5. Incidental fear encourages risk adverse behaviour and conforming to their social surroundings. As a result, people feeling fear tend to choose popular products, as opposed to limited editions products. They might even increase brand attachment to a brand in the presence of fear.

6. Anger makes consumers complain, spread negative (sometimes vindictive) word-of-mouth, and decrease future purchases. Unlike other negative emotions that avoid the problems at hand, anger confronts them. Unlike other negative emotions that use systematic processing to process information, anger uses heuristics. In addition, anger is a highly contagious emotion. We experience anger when anger is around us, so it is important for companies to manage their service space by not allowing customers' anger to become uncontrollable. For example, anger can spread to other customers and across to their first-line service employees.

7. Regret is a cognitive emotion that is generated when we compare what happened with what could have happened, and we blame ourselves for the outcome of what happened. Though regret can potentially decrease subjective well-being, regret motivates people

to reflect on their mistakes, thereby striving for a better life. Regret can be experienced about past (retrospective regret) and future (anticipated regret) decisions. Retrospective regret reduces consumer satisfaction, increases switching behaviour, spreads negative word-of-mouth, and defers purchase, whilst anticipated regret makes consumers choose a more expensive and well-known brand or a status quo brand.

DISCUSSION QUESTIONS

1. Discuss the effects of happiness and their implications for marketers.
2. Discuss the effects of pride and their implications for marketers.
3. Discuss the effects of fear and their implications for marketers.
4. Discuss the effects of anger and their implications for marketers.

FURTHER READING

- Bagozzi, R. P., Gopinath, M., & Nyer, P. U. (1999). The Role of Emotions in Marketing. *Journal of the Academy of Marketing Science, 27*(2), 184–206.
- Elliott, R. (1998). A Model of Emotion-Driven Choice. *Journal of Marketing Management, 14*(1/3), 95–108.
- Lerner, J. S., Li, Y., Valdesolo, P., & Kassam, K. S. (2015). Emotion and Decision Making. *Annual Review of Psychology, 66*, 799–823.
- So, J., Achar, C., Han, D., Agrawal, N., Duhachek, A., & Masheswaran, D. (2015). The Psychology of Appraisal: Specific Emotions and Decision-Making. *Journal of Consumer Psychology, 25*(3), 359–371.
- Watson, L., & Spence, M. T. (2007). Causes and Consequences of Emotions on Consumer Behaviour. *European Journal of Marketing, 41*(5/6), 487–511.

NOTES

1. Ekman, P. (1984). Expression and the Nature of Emotion. In K. R. Scherer & P. Ekman (eds), *Approaches to Emotion* (pp. 319–343). Hillsdale, NJ: Erlbaum; Russell, J. A., & Barrett, L. F. (1999). Core Effect, Prototypical Emotional Episodes, and Other Things Called Emotion: Distracting the Elephant. *Journal of Personality and Social Psychology, 76*(5), 805–819.
2. Watson, D., Clark, L. A., & Tellegen, A. (1988). Development and Validation of Brief Measures of Positive and Negative Affect: The PANAS Scales. *Journal of Personality and Social Psychology, 54*(6), 1063–1070.
3. Mehrabian, A., & Russell, J. A. (1974). *An Approach to Environmental Psychology.* Cambridge, MA: MIT Press.

4. Richins, M. L. (1997). Measuring Emotions in the Consumption Experience. *Journal of Consumer Research, 24*(September), 127–146.

5. Cohen, J. B., Pham, M. T., & Andrade, E. B. (2008). The Nature and Role of Affect in Consumer Behavior. In C. P. Haugtvedt, P. M. Herr, & F. R. Kardes (eds), *Handbook of Consumer Psychology* (pp. 297–348). New York: Psychology Press.

6. Cohen, J. B., & Areni, C. S. (1991). Affect and Consumer Behavior. In T. S. Robertson & H. H. Kassarjian (eds), *Handbook of Consumer Behavior* (pp. 188–240). Englewood Cliffs, NJ: Prentice-Hall.

7. Lerner, J. S., & Keltner, D. (2000). Beyond Valence: Toward a Model of Emotion-Specific Influences on Judgement and Choices. *Cognition and Emotion, 14*(4), 473–493; Lerner, J. S., & Keltner, D. (2001). Fear, Anger, and Risk. *Journal of Personality and Social Psychology, 81*(1), 146–159.

8. Lazarus, R. S. (1991). Progress on a Cognitive-Motivational-Relational Theory of Emotion. *American Psychologist, 46*(8), 819–834.

9. Reading, A. (2011). Feelings as Information. In A. Reading (ed.), *Meaningful Information: The Bridge between Biology, Brain, and Behavior* (pp. 111–122). New York: Springer; Schwarz, N. (1990). Feelings as Information: Informational and Motivational Functions of Affective States. In R. M. Sorrentino & E. T. Higgins (eds), *The Handbook of Motivation and Cognition: Foundations of Social Behavior* (Vol. 2, pp. 527–561). New York: Guilford Press; Schwarz, N., & Clore, G. L. (1983). Mood, Misattribution, and Judgments of Well-Being: Informative and Directive Functions of Affective States. *Journal of Personality and Social Psychology, 45*(3), 512–523.

10. Clore, G. L., & Centerbar, D. B. (2004). Analyzing Anger: How to Make People Mad. *Emotion, 4*(2), 139–144.

11. Oatley, K., & Johnson-Laird, P. N. (1996). The Communicative Theory of Emotions: Empirical Tests, Mental Models, and Implications for Social Interactions. In L. L. Martin & A. Tesser (eds), *Striving and Feeling: Interactions Among Goals, Affect, and Self-Regulation* (pp. 363–393). Mahwah, NJ: Lawrence Erlbaum Associates.

12. Isen, A. M., Nygren, T. E., & Ashby, F. G. (1988). Influence of Positive Affect on the Subjective Utility of Gains and Losses: It is Just Not Worth the Risk. *Journal of Personality and Social Psychology, 55*(5), 710–717.

13. Gross, J. J. (1998). The Emerging Field of Emotion Regulation: An Integrative Review. *Review of General Psychology, 2*(3), 271–299.

14. Shiv, B., & Fedorikhin, A. (1999). Heart and Mind in Conflict: The Interplay of Affect and Cognition in Consumer Decision Making. *Journal of Consumer Research, 26*(December), 278–292.

15. Cohen & Areni, Affect and Consumer Behavior.

16. Cohen, J. B., Pham, M. T., & Andrade, E. B. (2008). The Nature and Role of Affect in Consumer Behavior. In C. P. Haugtvedt, P. M. Herr, & F. R. Kardes (eds), *Handbook of Consumer Psychology* (pp. 297–348). New York: Psychology Press.

17. Fishbein, M., & Ajzen, I. (1975). *Belief, Attitude, Intention and Behavior: An Introduction to Theory and Research*. Reading, MA: Addison-Wesley Publishing.

18. Bodur, H. O., Brinberg, D., & Coupey, E. (2000). Believe, Affect, and Attitude: Alternative Models of the Determinants of Attitude. *Journal of Consumer Psychology, 9*(1), 17–28.

19. Oliver, R. L. (1993). Cognitive, Affective, and Attribute Bases of the Satisfaction Response. *Journal of Consumer Research, 20*(December), 418–430.

20. Allen, C. T., Machleit, K. A., & Kleine, S. S. (1992). A Comparison of Attitudes and Emotions as Predictors of Behaviour at the Diverse Levels of Behavioural Experience. *Journal of Consumer Research, 18*(4), 493–504.

21. Bower, G. H. (1981). Mood and Memory. *American Psychologist, 36*(2), 129–148.

22. Bower, G., H., & Cohen, P. R. (1982). Emotional Influences in Memory and Thinking: Data and Theory. In M. S. Clark & S. T. Fiske (eds), *Affect and Cognition: The Seventeeth Annual Carnegie Symposium on Cognition* (pp. 291–331). Hillsdale, NJ: Lawrence Erlbaum Associates.

23. Averill, J. R., & More, T. A. (2000). Happiness. In M. Lewis & J. M. Haviland-Johnes (eds), *Handbook of Emotions* (second edn, pp. 663–676). New York: The Guilford Press.

24. Ryan, R. M., & Deci, E. L. (2001). On Happiness and Human Potentials: A Review of Research on Hedonic and Eudaimonic Well-Being. *Annual Review of Psychology, 52,* 141–166.

25. Wise, R. A., & Bozarth, M. A. (1984). Brain Reward Circuit: Four Circuit Elements "Wired" in Apparent Series. *Brain Research Bulletin, 12*(2), 203–208.

26. Barrett, L. F. (1998). Discrete Emotions or Dimensions? The Role of Valence Focus and Arousal Focus. *Cognition and Emotion, 12*(4), 579–599; Tsai, J., Knutson, B., & Fung, H. (2007). Cultural Variation in Affect Valuation. *Journal of Personality and Social Psychology, 90*(2), 288–307.

27. Biswas-Diener, R., Diener, E., & Tamir, M. (2004). The Psychology of Subjective Well-Being. *Daedalus, 133*(2), 18–25.

28. Isen, A. M. (1999). On the Relationship between Affect and Creative Problem Solving. In S. Russ (ed.), *Affect, Creative Experience, and Psychological Adjustment* (pp. 3–17). Philadelphia: Taylor & Francis.

29. Schwarz, N., & Clore, G. L. (1983). Mood, Misattribution, and Judgments of Well-Being: Informative and Directive Functions of Affective States. *Journal of Personality and Social Psychology, 45*(3), 512–523.

30. Wright, W. F., & Bower, G. H. (1992). Mood Effects on Subjective Probability Assessment. *Organizational Behavior and Human Decision Processes, 52*(July), 276–291.

31. Labroo, A. A., & Patrick, V. M. (2009). Psychological Distancing: Why a Positive Mood Helps Seeing the Big Picture. *Journal of Consumer Research, 35*(February), 800–809.

32. Storbeck, J., & Clore, G. L. (2005). With Sadness Comes Accuracy; With Happiness, False Memory. *Psychological Science, 16*(10), 785–791.

33. Thomas, D., & Diener, E. (1990). Memory Accuracy in the Recall of Emotions. *Journal of Personality and Social Psychology, 59*(2), 291–297.

34. Levine, L. J., & Bluck, S. (2004). Painting with Broad Strokes: Happiness and the Malleability of Event Memory. *Cognition and Emotion, 18*(4), 559–574.

35. Isen, A. M., Labroo, A. A., & Durlach, P. (2004). An Influence of Product and Brand Name on Positive Affect: Implicit and Explicit Measures. *Motivation and Emotion, 28*(1), 43–63.

36. Ibid.

37. Desmeules, R. (2002). The Impact of Variety on Consumer Happiness: Marketing and the Tyranny of Freedom. *Academy of Marketing Science Review, 12*, 1–18.

38. Atalay, A. S., & Meloy, M. G. (2011). Retail Therapy: A Strategic Effort to Improve Mood. *Psychology & Marketing, 28*(6), 638–660.

39. van Boven, L., & Gilovich, T. (2003). To Do or To Have? That Is the Question. *Journal of Personality and Social Psychology, 85*(6), 1193–1202.

40. Caprariello, P. A., & Reis, H. T. (2013). To Do, To Have, or To Share? Valuing Experiences over Material Possessions Depends on the Involvement of Others. *Journal of Personality and Social Psychology, 104*(2), 199–215.

41. Nicolao, L., Irwin, J. R., & Goodman, J. K. (2009). Happiness for Sale: Do Experiential Purchases Make Consumer Happier than Material Purchases. *Journal of Consumer Research, 36*(August), 188–198.

42. Dunn, E. W., Gilbert, D. T., & Wilson, T. D. (2011). If Money Does't Make You Happy, Then You Probably Aren't Spending It Right. *Journal of Consumer Psychology, 21*(2), 115–125.

43. Bhattacharjee, A., & Mogilner, C. (2014). Happiness from Ordinary and Extrordinary Experiences. *Journal of Consumer Research, 41*(June), 1–17.

44. Kim, H., Park, K., & Schwarz, N. (2010). Will This Trip Really Be Exciting? The Role of Incidental Emotions in Product Evaluation. *Journal of Consumer Research, 36*(April), 983–990.

45. Ibid.

46. Carstensen, L. L., Isaacowitz, D. M., & Charles, S. T. (1999). Taking Time Seriously: A Theory of Socioemotional Selectivity. *American Psychologist, 54*(3), 165–181.

47. Mogilner, C., Aaker, J., & Kamvar, S. D. (2012). How Happiness Affects Choice. *Journal of Consumer Research, 39*(August), 429–443.

48. Bless, H., Bohner, G., Schwarz, N., & Strach, F. (1990). Mood and Persuasion: A Cognitive Response Analysis. *Personality and Social Psychology Bulletin, 16*(2), 331–345.

49. Schwarz & Clore, Mood, Misattribution, and Judgments of Well-Being

50. Labroo & Patrick, Psychological Distancing.

51. Ibid.

52. Thomas & Diener, Memory Accuracy in the Recall of Emotions.

53. Wirtz, D., Kruger, J., Scollon, C. N., & Diener, E. (2003). What to Do on Spring Break? The Role of Predicted, On-line, and Remembered Experience in Future Choice. *Psychological Science, 14*(5), 520–524.

54. Ibid.

55. Braun, K. A., Ellis, R., & Loftus, E. F. (2002). Make My Memory: How Advertising Can Change Our Memories of the Past. *Psychology & Marketing, 19*(1), 1–23.

56. Lazarus, R. S. (1991). *Emotion and Adaptation*. Oxford: Oxford University Press; Tracy, J. L., & Robins, R. W. (2007). The Psychological Structure of Pride: A Tale of Two Facets. *Journal of Personality and Social Psychology, 92*(3), 506–525.

57. Lewis, M. (2000). Self-Conscious Emotions: Embarrassment, Pride, Shame, and Guilt. In M. Lewis & J. M. Haviland-Johnes (eds), *Handbook of Emotions* (second edn, pp. 623–636). New York: Guilford Press.

58. Tracy, J. L., Chen, J. T., Robins, R. W., & Trzesniewski, K. H. (2009). Authentic and Hubristic Pride: The Affective Core of Self-Esteem and Narcissism. *Self and Identity, 8*(2–3), 196–213; Morrison, A. P. (1989). *Shame: The Underside of Narcissism*. Hillsdale, NJ: Analytic Press.

59. Tracy & Robins, The Psychological Structure of Pride.

60. Ibid.

61. Lewis, M. (2000). Self-Conscious Emotions: Embarrassment, Pride, Shame, and Guilt. In M. Lewis & J. M. Haviland-Johnes (eds), *Handbook of Emotions* (Second ed., pp. 623–636). New York: The Guilford Press.

62. Hope, O.-K., Thomas, W., & Vyas, D. (2011). The Cost of Pride: Why Do Firms From Developing Countries Bid Higher? *Journal of International Business Studies, 42*(1), 128–151.

63. Lazarus, R. S. (1991). *Emotion and Adaptation*. Oxford: Oxford University Press.

64. Lewis, Self-Conscious Emotions

65. McGregor, I., Nail, P. R., Marigold, D. C., & Kang, S.-J. (2005). Defensive Pride and Consensus: Strength in Imaginary Numbers. *Journal of Personality and Social Psychology, 89*(6), 978–996.

66. Oveis, C., Horberg, E. J., & Keltner, D. (2010). Compassion, Pride, and Social Intuitions of Self-Other Similarity. *Journal of Personality and Social Psychology, 98*(4), 618–630.

67. D'Argembeau, A., & Van der Linden, M. (2008). Remembering Pride and Shame: Self-Enhancement and the Phenomenology of Autobiographical Memory. *Memory, 16*(5), 538–547.

68. Williams, L. A., & DeSteno, D. (2008). Pride and Perseverance: The Motivational Role of Pride. *Journal of Personality and Social Psychology, 94*(6), 1007–1017.

69. Lea, S. E. G., & Webley, P. (1997). Pride in Economic Psychology. *Journal of Economica Psychology, 18*(2), 323–340.

70. Soscia, I. (2007). Gratitude, Delight, or Guilt: The Role of Consumers' Emotions in Predicting Postconsumption Behaviors. *Psychology & Marketing, 24*(10), 871–894.

71. Sredl, K. (2010). Consumer Pride: Emotion as a Social Phenomenon. In M. C. Campbell, J. Inman, & R. Pieters (eds), *NA – Advances in Consumer Research* (Vol. 37, pp. 907–909). Duluth, MN: Association for Consumer Research.

72. Onwezen, M. C., Bartels, J., & Antonides, G. (2014). The Self-Regulatory Function of Anticipated Pride and Guilt in a Sustainable and Healthy Consumption Context. *European Journal of Social Psychology, 44*(1), 53–68; Antonetti, P., & Maklan, S. (2014). Exploring Postconsumption Guilt and Pride in the Context of Sustainability. *Psychology & Marketing, 31*(9), 717–735.

73. Kirk, C. P., Swain, S. D., & Gaskin, J. E. (2015). I'm Proud of It: Consumer Tehcnology Appropriation and Psychological Ownership. *Journal of Marketing Theory and Practice, 23*(2), 166–184; Franke, N., Schreier, M., & Kaiser, U. (2010). The "I Designed It Myself" Effect in Mass Customization. *Management Science, 56*(1), 125–140.

74. Han, Y. J., Nunes, J. C., & Drèze, X. (2010). Signaling Status with Luxury Goods: The Role of Brand Prominence. *Journal of Marketing, 74*(July), 15–30.

75. McFerran, B., Aquino, K., & Tracy, J. L. (2014). Evidence for Two Faces of Pride in Consumption: Findings from Luxury Brands. *Journal of Consumer Psychology, 24*(4), 455–471.

76. McFerran, B., Aquino, K., & Tracy, J. L. (2011). Evidence for Two Faces of Pride in Consumption: Findings from Luxury Brands. In D. W. Dahl, G. V. Johar, & S. M. J. van Osselaer (eds), *NA – Advances in Consumer Research* (Vol. 38, pp. 479–480). Duluth, MN: Association for Consumer Research.

77. Ward, M. K., & Dahl, D. W. (2014). Should the Devil Sell Prada? Retail Rejection Increases Aspiring Consumers' Desire for the Brand. *Journal of Consumer Research, 41*(October), 590–609.

78. Munichor, N., & Steinhart, Y. (2016). Saying No to the Glow: When Consumers Avoid Arrogant Brands. *Journal of Consumer Psychology, 26*(2), 179–192.

79. Shimp, T. A., & Sharma, S. (1987). Consumer Ethnocentrism: Construction and Validation of the CETSCALE. *Journal of Marketing Research, 24*(August), 280–289.

80. Hope et al., The Cost of Pride.

81. Watson, J. J., & Wright, K. (2000). Consumer Ethnocentrism and Attitudes toward Domestic and Foreign Products. *European Journal of Marketing, 34*(9/10), 1149–1166.

82. Cosmides, L., & Tooby, J. (2000). Evolutionary Psychology and the Emotions. In M. Lewis & J. M. Haviland-Johnes (eds), *Handbook of Emotions* (pp. 91–115). New York: Guilford Press.

83. LeDoux, J. E. (1998). *The Emotional Brain: The Mysterious Underpinnings of Emotional Life*. London: Weidenfeld & Nicolson.

84. Öhman, A. (2002). Automaticity and the Amygdala: Nonconscious Responses to Emotional Faces. *Current Directions in Psychological Science, 11*(2), 62–66.

85. Ekman, P., Levenson, R. W., & Friesen, W. V. (1983). Autonomic Nervous System Activity Distinguishes Among Emotions. *Science, 221*(4616), 1208–1210.

86. LeDoux, *The Emotional Brain*.

87. Cook, E. W., Hawk, L. W., Davis, T. L., & Stevenson, V. E. (1991). Affective Individual Differences and Startle Reflex Modulation. *Journal of Abnormal Psychology, 100*(1), 5–13.

88. Olsson, A., & Phelps, E. A. (2004). Learned Fear of "Unseen" Faces after Pavlovian, Observational, and Instructed Fear. *Psychological Science, 15*(12), 822–828.

89. Tannenbaum, M. B., Hepler, J., Zimmerman, R. S., Saul, L., & Jacobs, S. (2015). Appealing to Fear: A Meta-Analysis of Fear Appeal Effectiveness and Theories. *Psychological Bulletin, 141*(6), 1178–1204.

90. Burnett, J. J., & Oliver, R. L. (1979). Fear Appeal Effects in the Field: A Segmentation Approach. *Journal of Marketing Research, 16*(May), 181–190.

91. Keller, P. A., & Block, L. G. (1996). Increasing the Persuasiveness of Fear Appeals: The Effect of Arousal and Elaboration. *Journal of Consumer Research, 22*(March), 448–459.

92. Henthorne, T. L., LaTour, M., & Nataraajan, R. (1993). Fear Appeals in Print Advertising: An Analysis of Arousal and Ad Response. *Journal of Advertising, 22*(2), 59–69; Witte, K., & Allen, M. (2000). A Meta-Analysis of Fear Appeals: Implications for Effective Public Health Campaigns. *Health Education & Behavior, 27*(5), 591–615.

93. Leshner, G., Bolls, P., & Wise, K. (2011). Motivated Processing of Fear Appeal and Disgust Images in Televised Anti-Tobacco Ads. *Journal of Media Psychology, 23*(2), 77–89; Witte & Allen, A Meta-Analysis of Fear Appeals.

94. Ray, M. L., & Wilkie, W. (1970). Fear: The Potential of an Appeal Neglected by Marketing. *Journal of Marketing, 34*(January), 54–62.

95. Rogers, R. W. (1983). Cognitive and Physiological Processes in Fear Appeals and Attitude Change: A Revised Theory of Protection Motvation. In J. T. Cacioppo & R. E. Petty (eds), *Social Psychophysiology* (pp. 153–176). New York: Guilford.

96. Manyiwa, S., & Brennan, R. (2012). Fear Appeals in Anti-Smoking Advertising: How Important is Self-Efficacy? *Journal of Marketing Management, 28*(11–12), 1419–1437; Arthur, D., & Quester, P. (2004). Who's Afraid of That Ad? Applying Segmentation to the Protection Motivation Model. *Psychology & Marketing, 21*(9), 671–696.

97. De Pelsmacker, P., Cauberghe, V., & Dens, N. (2011). Fear Appeal Effectiveness for Familiar and Unfamiliar Issues. *Journal of Social Marketing, 1*(3), 171–191.

98. Ibid.

99. Lee, C. J., & Andrade, E. B. (2011). Fear, Social Projection, and Financial Decision Making. *Journal of Marketing Research, 68*(Special Issue), S121–S129.

100. Lerner, J. S., & Keltner, D. (2001). Fear, Anger, and Risk. *Journal of Personality and Social Psychology, 81*(1), 146–159.

101. Öhman, A., & Mineka, S. (2001). Fears, Phobias, and Preparedness: Toward an Evolved Module of Fear and Fear Learning. *Psychological Review, 108*(3), 483–522.

102. Griskevicius, V., Goldstein, N. J., Mortensen, C. R., Sundie, J. M., Cialdini, R. B., & Kenrick, D. T. (2009). Fear and Loving in Las Vegas: Evolution, Emotion, and Persuasion. *Journal of Marketing Research, 46*(3), 384–395.

103. Dunn, L., & Hoegg, J. (2014). The Impact of Fear on Emotional Brand Attachment. *Journal of Consumer Research, 41*(June), 152–168.

104. Bodenhausen, G. V., Sheppard, L. A., & Kramer, G. P. (1994). Negative Affect and Social Judgment: The Differential Impact of Anger and Sadness. *European Journal of Social Psychology, 24*(1), 45–62; Lerner, J. S., Goldberg, J. H., & Tetlock, P. E. (1998). Sober Second Thought: The Effects of Accountability, Anger, and Authoritarianism on Attributions of Responsibility. *Personality and Social Psychology Bulletin, 24*(6), 563–574.

105. DeSteno, D., Petty, R. E., Wegener, D. T., & Rucker, D. D. (2000). Beyond Valence in the Perception of Likelihood: The Role of Emotion Specificty. *Journal of Personality and Social Psychology, 78*(3), 397–416.

106. Baumann, J., & DeSteno, D. (2012). Context Explains Divergent Effects of Anger on Risk Taking. *Emotion, 12*(6), 1196–1199.

107. Carver, C. S., & Harmon-Jones, E. (2009). Anger Is an Approach-Related Affect: Evidence and Implications. *Psychological Bulletin, 135*(2), 183–204.

108. Harmon-Jones, E. (2003). Clarifying the Emotive Functions of Asymmetrical Frontal Cortical Activity. *Psychophysiology, 40*(6), 838–848.

109. Ekman, P., Levenson, R. W., & Friesen, W. V. (1983). Autonomic Nervous System Activity Distinguishes Among Emotions. *Science, 221*(4616), 1208–1210.

110. Frijda, N. H., Kuipers, P., & ter Schure, E. (1989). Relations among Emotion, Appraisal, and Emotional Action Readiness. *Journal of Personality and Social Psychology, 57*(2), 212–228.

111. Lerner & Keltner, Fear, Anger, and Risk.

112. Baumann & DeSteno, Context Explains Divergent Effects of Anger on Risk Taking.

113. Kalamas, M., Laroche, M., & Makdessian, L. (2008). Reaching the Boiling Point: Consumers' Negative Affective Reactions to Firm-Attributed Service Failures. *Journal of Business Research, 61*(8), 813–824.

114. Walker-Harrison, L. J. (2012). The Role of Cause and Effect in Service Failure. *Journal of Services Marketing, 26*(2), 115–123.

115. Bonifield, C., & Cole, C. (2007). Affective Responses to Service Failure: Anger, Regret, and Retaliatory Versus Conciliatory Responses. *Marketing Letters, 18*(1–2), 85–99.

116. Yi, S., & Baumgartner, H. (2004). Coping with Negative Emotions in Purchase-Related Situations. *Journal of Consumer Psychology, 14*(3), 303–317.

117. Gelbrich, K. (2010). Anger, Frustration, and Helplessness after Service Failure: Coping Strategies and Effective Informational Support. *Journal of the Academy of Marketing Science, 38*(5), 567–585.

118. Strizhakova, Y., Tsarenko, Y., & Ruth, J. A. (2012). "I'm Mad and I Can't Get That Service Failure off My Mind": Coping and Rumination as Mediators of Anger Effects on Customer Intentions. *Journal of Service Research, 15*(4), 414–429.

119. Menon, K., & Dubé, L. (2007). The Effect of Emotional Provider Support on Angry Versus Anxious Consumers. *International Journal of Research in Marketing, 24*(3), 268–275.

120. Grégoire, Y., Tripp, T. M., & Legoux, R. (2009). When Customer Love Turns into Lasting Hate: The Effects of Relationship Strength and Time on Customer Revenge and Avoidance. *Journal of Marketing, 73*(November), 18–32.

121. Strizhakova et al., "I'm Mad and I Can't Get That Service Failure off My Mind".

122. Menon, K., & Dubé, L. (2004). Service Provider Responses to Anxious and Angry Customers: Different Challenges, Different Payoffs. *Journal of Retailing, 80*(3), 229–237.

123. Dallimore, K. S., Sparks, B. A., & Butcher, K. (2007). The Influence of Angry Customer Outbursts on Service Providers' Facial Displays and Affective States. *Journal of Service Research, 10*(1), 78–92.

124. Andersson, L., & Pearson, C. M. (1999). "Tit for Tat?" The Spiraling Effect of Incivility in the Work Place. *Academy of Management Review, 24*(3), 452–471.

125. Denson, T. F., von Hippel, W., Kemp, R. I., & Teo, L. S. (2010). Glucose Consumption Decreases Impulsive Aggression in Response to Provocation in Aggressive Individuals. *Journal of Experimental Social Psychology, 46*(6), 1023–1028; DeWall, C. N., Baumeister, R. F., Stillman, T. F., & Gailliot, M. T. (2007). Violence Restrained: Effects of Self-Regulation and Its Depletion on Aggression. *Journal of Experimental Social Psychology, 43*(1), 62–76; Polivy, J. (1996). Psychological Consequences of Food Restriction. *Journal of the American Dietetic Association, 96*(6), 589–592.

126. Gal, D., & Liu, W. (2011). Grapes with Wrath: the Angry Effects of Self-Control. *Journal of Consumer Research, 38*(October), 445–458.

127. Lee, S. H., & Cotte, J. (2009). Post-Purchase Consumer Regret: Conceptualization and Development of the PPCR Scale. In A. L. McGill & S. Shavitt (eds), *NA – Advances in Consumer Research* (Vol. 32, pp. 456–462). Duluth, MN: Association for Consumer Research.

128. Roese, N. J. (1997). Counterfactual Thinking. *Psychological Bulletin, 121*(1), 133–148.

129. Zeelenberg, M., & Pieters, R. (2007). A Theory of Regret Regulation 1.0. *Journal of Consumer Psychology, 17*(1), 3–18.

130. Guttentag, R., & Ferrell, J. (2004). Reality Compared with Its Alternatives: Age Differences in Judgments of Regret and Relief. *Developmental Psychology, 40*(5), 764–775.

131. Roese, Counterfactual Thinking.

132. van Dijk, W. W., van der Pligt, J., & Zeelenberg, M. (1999). Effort Invested in Vain: The Impact of Effort on the Intensity of Disappointment and Regret. *Motivation and Emotion, 23*(3), 203–220; Zeelenberg, M., van Dijk, W. W., Manstead, A. S. R., & van der Pligt, J. (1998). The Experience of Regret and Disappointment. *Cognition and Emotion, 12*(2), 221–230.

133. Landman, J. (1993). *Regret: The Persistence of the Possible.* New York: Oxford University Press; Zeelenberg et al., The Experience of Regret and Disappointment.

134. Jokisaari, M. (2003). Regret Appraisals, Age, and Subjective Well-Being. *Journal of Research in Personality, 37*(6), 487–503.

135. Landman, *Regret* ; Zeelenberg & Pieters, A Theory of Regret Regulation 1.0.

136. Pieters, R., & Zeelenberg, M. (2007). A Theory of Regret Regulation 1.1. *Journal of Consumer Psychology, 17*(1), 29–35.

137. Zeelenberg & Pieters, A Theory of Regret Regulation 1.0.

138. Ibid.

139. Lee, S. H., & Cotte, J. (2009). Post-Purchase Consumer Regret: Conceptualization and Development of th PPCR Scale. In A. L. McGill & S. Shavitt (eds), *NA - Advances in Consumer Research* (Vol. 32, pp. 456–462). Duluth, MN: Association for Consumer Research.

140. Ibid.

141. Bui, M., Krishen, A. S., & Bates, K. (2011). Modeling Regret Effects on Consumer Post-Purchase Decisions. *European Journal of Marketing, 45*(7/8), 1068–109; Tsiros, M., & Mittal, V. (2000). Regret: A Model of Its Antecedents and Consequences in Consumer Decision Making. *Journal of Consumer Research, 26*(March), 401–417; Voorhees, C. M., Baker, J., Bourdeau, B. L., Brocato, E. D., & Cronin Jr., J. J. (2009). It Depends: Moderating the Relationships among Perceived Waiting Time, Anger, and Regret. *Journal of Service Research, 12*(2), 138–155.

142. Bui et al., Modeling Regret Effects of Consumer Post-Purchase Decisions; Inman, J. J., & Zeelenberg, M. (2002). Regret in Repeat Purchase Versus Switching Decisions: The Attenuating Role of Decision Justifiability. *Journal of Consumer Research, 29*(June), 116–128; Zeelenberg, M., & Pieters, R. (1999). Comparing Service Delivery to What Might Have Been: Behavioral Responses to Regret and Disappointment. *Journal of Service Research, 2*(1), 86–97.

143. Sánchez-García, I., & Currás-Pérez, R. (2011). Effects of Dissatisfaction in Tourist Services: The Role of Anger and Regret. *Tourism Management, 32*(6), 1397–1406; Zeelenberg, M., & Pieters, R. (2004). Beyond Valence in Customer Dissatisfaction: A Review and New Findings on Behavioral Responses. *Journal of Business Research, 57*(4), 445–455.

144. Tsiros, M. (2009). Releasing the Regret Lock: Consumer Response to New Alternatives after a Sale. *Journal of Consumer Research, 35*(April), 1039–1059.

145. Taylor, K. (1997). A Regret Theory Approach to Assessing Consumer Satisfaction. *Marketing Letters, 8*(2), 229–238.

146. Cooke, A. D. J., Meyvis, T., & Schwartz, A. (2001). Avoiding Future Regret in Purchase-Timing Decisions. *Journal of Consumer Research, 27*(March), 447–459.

147. Hetts, J. J., Boninger, D. S., Armor, D. A., Gleicher, F., & Nathanson, A. (2000). The Influence of Anticipated Counterfactual Regret on Behavior. *Psychology & Marketing, 17*(4), 345–368.

148. Simonson, I. (1992). The Influence of Anticipating Regret and Responsibility on Purchase Decisions. *Journal of Consumer Research, 19*(June), 105–118.

149. Ibid.

150. Inman & Zeelenberg, Regret in Repeat Purchase Versus Switching Decisions.

151. Keinan, A., & Kivetz, R. (2008). Remedying Hyperopia: The Effects of Self-Control Regret on Consumer Behavior. *Journal of Marketing Research, 45*(December), 676–689.

152. Kivetz, R., & Keinan, A. (2006). Repenting Hyperopia: An Analysis of Self-Control Regrets. *Journal of Consumer Research, 33*(September), 373–382.

153. Ibid.

7

CONSUMER MOTIVATION

Learning objectives

To explore, understand, and explain:

- the two motivation perspectives: top-down and bottom-up motivation, and their applications in consumer behaviour
    - expectancy-value theory
    - Maslow's hierarchy of needs
- the psychological bases of self-regulation and self-regulation failure and their applications in consumer behaviour
- the psychological basis of regulatory focus theory and its applications in consumer behaviour

7.1 INTRODUCTION

Motivation is a critical determinant in human behaviour. Motivation is closely related to our goals: goals are the results of our motivational behaviour, and motivation is the reason that drives our willingness and behaviour to achieve our goals. The importance of motivation is reflected in a number of theories focusing on motivation, including content (needs) theories such as Herzberg's two-factor theory, biological theories such as arousal theory, behaviourist theories such as operant conditioning, and cognitive theories such as attribution theories. From these theories, this chapter will discuss two theories: cognitive theory's expectancy theory (Section 7.2) and needs theory's Maslow's hierarchy of needs (Section 7.3). These two theories are most important and relevant in explaining various consumption situations, including loyalty programmes, weight control, and financial savings. Following two main motivation theories, we will focus on whether or not we can persist in our behaviour towards our goals depending on our self-regulation (i.e. self-control), which will be explained in Section 7.4. Understanding consumer motivation can help marketers develop appropriate marketing programmes to encourage purchases, and can help us enhance wanted behaviour and avoid unwanted behaviour. Now let's begin with the top-down motivation perspective: expectancy theory.

7.2 MOTIVATION: A TOP-DOWN PERSPECTIVE

The psychological basis

Psychologists have relied on a hierarchical structure to understand human motivations.[1] That is, motivations have different levels; namely, the superordinate goal, focal goal, and subordinate goal.[2] The superordinate goal refers to an individual's ultimate goal, for example self-esteem, and the focal goal refers to the specific goal that, when once achieved, the individual is closer to achieving his superordinate goal. In order to achieve the focal goal, subordinate goals are set. Suppose having a healthy life and being attractive are one's superordinate goals, then losing weight is the focal goal which can help achieve the desired superordinate goals. In order to lose weight successfully, one has to follow a diet and exercise regime, and following this regime is the subordinate goal (Figure 7.1). A superordinate goal is a concept from the top-down process of motivation,[3] which suggests that a superordinate goal is identified first and then other focal or subordinate goals are determined in order to achieve the superordinate goal. A key theory that can illustrate the top-down motivation is the expectancy-value theory of motivation.

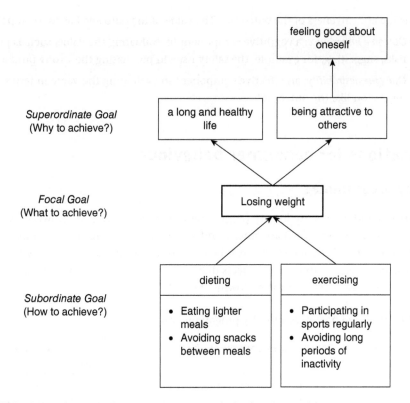

Figure 7.1 A top-down goal structure: an example for losing weight

Source: Pieters et al.[4]

Reprinted from *International Journal of Research in Marketing*, 12(3), Pieters et al. A Means-End Chain Approach to Consumer's Goal Structure, 227–244, Copyright (1995), with permission from Elsevier.

Expectancy-value theory of motivation

The expectancy-value theory of motivation, proposed by Vroom, focuses on the outcome (e.g. rewards) of achieving the goal, as it is these rewards that drive our behaviour.[5] The rewards can be seen as superordinate goals (Figure 7.1). The theory has two elements: expectancy and value:

- *Expectancy*: our expectations of how realistic it is to achieve the goal determined by external efficacy and internal efficacy:[6]
    - External efficacy (aka response efficacy): our beliefs in the external environment responding to our actions toward achieving our goal
    - Internal efficacy (aka self-efficacy): our beliefs in our ability to achieve that goal

- *Value*: the attractiveness of the outcome.[7] The value of the outcome has two components:
  - o *Outcome importance*: a cognitive component in evaluating the value, such as purchase risks, suggesting, for example, the safety issue in purchasing the wrong product[8]
  - o *Outcome desirability*: an affective component in evaluating the value in terms of how much you like the outcome[9]

Implications for consumer behaviour

Loyalty programmes

Many retailers and brands use loyalty programmes to attract customers. However, some programmes are more successful than others, and some customers are more willing to collect loyalty points. Why? External efficacy can be used to understand why and how loyalty programmes work. There are three main effects drawing from external efficacy: the goal gradient effect, the small area effect, and the endowment effect (Table 7.1).

Table 7.1   Why and how does a loyalty programme work?

Effects of Loyalty Programmes	Psychologies underlying the Effects	Examples of Designing a Loyalty Programme
The goal gradient effect *Definition*: The closer we are to our goal, the more effort we demonstrate to achieve the goal.[10]	As we approach our goal, it becomes easier to visualise the goal, and it is this visualisation that increases our goal pursuit efforts.[11]	People in a café reward programme purchase coffee more frequently the closer they are to earning a free coffee.[12]
The small area effect *Definition*: People striving toward a goal show greater motivation when their attention is directed to whichever is smaller in size: their accumulated or remaining progress required to achieve their goal.[13]	High motivation towards the end is because of the goal gradient effect,[14] whereas high motivation at the beginning of goal pursuit is because of the greater perceived marginal impact of their action.[15] The focus on small areas increases motivation by creating an illusion of fast progress.[16]	At the beginning of goal pursuit, people demonstrate more goal pursuit efforts if their attention focuses on the accumulated progress, whereas, with closeness to the goal, people show more goal pursuit efforts if their attention focuses on the remaining progress.[17]

Effects of Loyalty Programmes	Psychologies underlying the Effects	Examples of Designing a Loyalty Programme
The endowment effect *Definition*: Loyalty programmes with initial give-away points are more likely to motivate consumers to collect points.[18]	The endowment effect is effective because the goal gradient effect is at work (i.e. consumers' perception of easiness of task completion), not because they do not want to waste the endowed stamps.[19]	Collect 12 points to get 1 drink free (with 2 points give-away) versus collect 10 points to get 1 drink free (without initial give-away points): consumers with the former loyalty card are more motivated to collect points and therefore get their free drinks faster.[20]

The impact of internal efficacy on consumer behaviour

Health behaviour

Internal efficacy can be enhanced by the health-care providers' expertise, as their expertise is able to make it clear to us what we should do in becoming healthy.[21] When people are clear of what they should do and how they could do it (i.e. the subordinate goals), they focus on problem-focused coping strategies, such as eating healthily and exercise regularly.[22]

However, the use of drugs decreases self-efficacy. This is because the effectiveness of drugs actually decreases people's belief in their ability to engage and, therefore, compromises their intentions to engage in a healthy lifestyle.[23] In order to activate our motivations to engage in a healthy lifestyle, especially when we fall ill, it is critical to not just increase external efficacy (i.e. the effectiveness of drugs), but also to enhance self-efficacy.[24] In other words, we would engage in a healthier lifestyle if we are told the drugs would work only if we live more healthily.

Environmental behaviour

Advertising messages to encourage us to engage in environmental behaviour can be framed as loss or gain (see the regulatory focus theory in Section 7.4). The loss-frame focuses on the negative outcomes of inactions (e.g. waste destroys the environment), whilst the gain-frame emphasises the positive outcomes of actions (e.g, recycling saves the world).[25] Research shows that loss frames are more effective when the advertising message depicts subordinate goals (i.e. specific actions people should do or avoid), whereas gain frames are more effective when the advertisement message highlights superordinate goals (i.e. the ultimate outcomes of the actions) in people's environmental behaviour.[26] The main reason for this pairing of messages (loss-frame with subordinate goals and gain-frame with superordinate goals) to work is that the pairing increases *processing fluency*,[27] suggesting how easily we can appreciate what is said in the advertisement. It is the increased processing fluency that leads to enhanced self-efficacy,[28] and it is the enhanced self-efficacy that amplifies our environment-friendly behaviour.[29]

Innovation adoption behaviour

Self-efficacy in handling relevant technology determines consumers' adoption or resistance of innovation.[30] For example, at the beginning of a social networking site in 2004 when Facebook started, whether or not users chose to join the site depended on their self-efficacy in the Internet technology.[31] Therefore, for radically new product development, one of the important stages in product launch is to increase the target users' self-efficacy.[32]

Value: involvement

When people are certain of the attainability of their goal, the influence of expectancy disappears. They then shift to focus on the value of the reward.[33] The impact of value is straightforward – the higher the value of the outcome reward, the higher the motivation we have to pursue the goal. The value of the outcome is operationalised as involvement in consumer behaviour.[34]

Involvement directly influences our motivation to search for information[35] and to process the information (e.g. advertisement) we find.[36] That is, the more we are involved in our purchase, the more we are motivated to search for information and the more we are motivated to put effort in to processing the information we find. In other words, the level of involvement with products, advertisements or purchases suggests the level of motivations for activating our cognitive efforts.

7.3 MOTIVATION: A BOTTOM-UP PERSPECTIVE

The psychological basis

In contrast to the top-down perspective of motivation people with the ability to identify clear superordinate goals, the bottom-up perspective suggests that superordinate goals are unclear to us.[37] The bottom-up perspective explains situations where we are only able to identify the next stage of goal in the hierarchical structure after we achieve the current stage of goal. The most famous motivation theory that uses a bottom-up perspective to explain motivation is Maslow's[38] hierarchy of needs.

Maslow's hierarchy of needs

Maslow's hierarchy of needs is one of the most well-known and popular motivation theories in psychology. The hierarchy suggests that our motivation to behave focuses on satisfying our needs. Maslow outlines five main human needs for motivation: physiological needs, safety needs, belongingness and love needs, esteem needs, and self-actualisation needs (Figure 7.2).[39] We are unable to move up the hierarchy unless the lower levels of needs are sufficiently satisfied.[40]

Figure 7.2   Maslow's hierarchy of needs

The popularity of Maslow's hierarchy of needs also exposes the theory to being extensively scrutinised.[41] The main criticism is Maslow's conceptualisation itself. That is, do human motivations strictly follow the hierarchy as a bottom-up approach? Plenty of examples contradict Maslow's assumption. For example, Nelson Mandela pursued self-actualisation needs despite the fact that he was physically in danger, or Vincent van Gogh pursued self-actualisation despite the fact that he lived in poverty. This obvious contradiction may be attributed to Maslow's overly subjective methodology, in addition to his limited, and somewhat biased, samples. Recent research conducted by Tay and Diener[42] with more than 60,000 participants across 123 countries demonstrates that the ordering of Maslow's hierarchy on psychological needs holds, but that psychological needs operate independent of basic needs. In other words, it is possible for people to move up the hierarchy to the psychological needs without them first satisfying their basic needs, but the psychological needs follow a bottom-up hierarchy: the lower levels of needs are satisfied before moving up the hierarchy.

Implications for consumer behaviour

Vague superordinate goals

The use of Maslow's exact hierarchy of needs in consumer behaviour is limited, but Maslow's theorisation offers consumer psychologists an alternative approach from which to examine consumer motivation, as we do not always clearly know our superordinate goals. Rather, superordinate goals emerge only after we achieve our focal goals. In addition, the level of clarity in our goals influences our motivation: specific goals enhance our motivation when we are closer to achieving those goals, but by contrast vague goals enhance motivation when we are at the initial stage.[43]

Most consumer-relevant goals are focal, not superordinate, and they are specific; for example, to lose 10 kilos in weight control programmes, to spend £10,000 to gain 1% cash back rewards, or to fly 200,000 miles to receive a class upgrade. This section will use two examples where consumers do not usually have a clear goal to illustrate: participation in brand community and collection behaviour.

Participation in a brand community

Consumers join a brand community for various reasons, including functional needs, entertaining needs, and social needs.[44] Research has found that as there is no specific superordinate goal when consumers join a brand community, their moving up the motivation hierarchy depends on whether or not their lower levels of needs are satisfied.[45] Tseng et al. classify knowledge and entertainment needs as the basic needs, which are the initial motivations for consumers to join or participate in a community or discussion forum.[46] Social needs become their main motivator only when their basic needs are sufficiently satisfied. As consumers have higher initial motivations when their goal specification is vague,[47] speeding up consumers' transition from their basic needs to social needs can be critical in strengthening consumers' commitment to the brand community.

─Box 7.1─

What is a brand community?

A brand community is a community with activities surrounding a specific brand that the community members love. These communities are organised both offline[48] and online.[49] Traditional brand communities are limited by geographic constraints, but thanks to the Internet and social media technologies, it has become easier for consumers to join a brand community; for example, following a branded fan page on Facebook or a branded YouTube channel.

Collection behaviour

As collection can encourage customer retention, loyalty, and commitment, many brands develop collectible products,[50] which range from vintage branded products (e.g. Coca-Cola collectable cans or Starbucks mugs), promotion-related collection (e.g. McDonald's Happy Meal toys), to digital collection (e.g. the heat of Pokémon Go in 2016). What is the tipping point for consumers to decide that they want to actively collect these objects? The tipping point occurs after owning two or three of the collectable items.[51] At this point, it is more likely for consumers to be motivated to henceforth actively collect the collectables. It is because owning two or three collectable items is difficult for the owners to justify owning them as it is neither here nor there.[52] If brands wish to encourage consumers' collection behaviour, they could weight the costs of endowing consumers with the first two to three items against the benefits of increased consumers' active collection.

Box 7.2

Types of collection behaviour and motivation to collect

There are two broad types of collection behaviour:

1. Collection focuses on collectables' aesthetic, emotional, or monetary value[53] for reasons such as self-identity expressions, nostalgic reasons, or monetary purposes.[54] The motivation for this type of collection follows a top-down motivation.
2. Collection happens by accident. That is, our liking for our collectible items happens later, after we own the items, not before. For example, you may be given several collectible model trains as birthday gifts. This kind of collection is initially unintended or only loosely planned.[55] Without a clear goal, this type of collection follows a bottom-up motivation.[56]

7.4 SELF-REGULATION

Self-regulation

The psychological basis

Self-regulation, also known as self-control, is a mechanism which regulates (or controls) our behaviour so that we are able to attain our goals. No pain, no gain. Gain brings pleasure, but in order to taste that pleasure, we need to be painstakingly disciplined. For example, if we wish to achieve high grades in the next exams, we will need to work hard, including preparing for class discussion and doing further research after class. Self-regulation has been related to self-efficacy discussed in Section 7.2,[57] as successful self-regulation can increase our confidence,[58] and therefore our performance.[59]

There are three elements in self-regulation: (1) standards, (2) goal commitment, and (3) monitoring and feedback.[60]

1. Standards are our goals. Two requirements in setting the standards can help us achieve our goals:

    •   A specific and clear goal: the more specific our goals are, the easier we can monitor our progress.[61] The easier we can monitor our progress, the more likely it is that we achieve our goals.

    •   A reasonable (i.e. consistent, achievable goals, but not conflicting with personal beliefs) but challenging enough goal can help us succeed in self-regulation.[62]

2. Goal commitment: necessary actions involved to move ourselves from the current state to our desired state.

3. Monitoring our process and providing feedback for our actions: the monitoring and feedback loop is able to provide substantial and immediate improvement to our goal attaining process.[63]

Implications for consumer behaviour

Impulsive buying

Have you bought anything impulsively? Most people have. Impulsive buying occurs when we experience a sudden and powerful urge to buy something immediately,[64] and it is a result of an acute loss of impulse control.[65] However, self-regulation can be trained and strengthened, just like we strengthen our muscles.[66] To engage in self-regulation activities, such as regular exercises or regular reading, we are able to reduce the impulse buying tendency.[67] In addition to training our self-regulation capacity, if we really want to, we are able to avoid all kinds of impulses, as research has suggested.[68] Our commitment gives power to self-regulation,[69] even for people, such as Alzheimer's patients, whose self-regulation is significantly impaired.[70]

Other consumer behaviour

The influence of self-regulation on other consumer behaviour, including engaging in financial savings, a healthy lifestyle, and a sustainable lifestyle, is similar to that of self-regulation on impulse buying. In other words, self-regulation can lead to high probability of successful financial savings,[71] maintaining a healthy lifestyle,[72] and participating in sustainable activities.[73]

Self-regulation failure

Self-regulation failure leads to failure to achieving our goals. There are two types of self-regulation failure: under-regulation and mis-regulation.[74] *Under-regulation* suggests that we do not put enough efforts into pursuing our goals, whereas *mis-regulation* indicates that, although we do put in effort towards our goal, our efforts are *mis-guided*, resulting in a counterproductive approach where we misdirect efforts. Mis-regulation is not relevant to consumer behaviour (it is more relevant to education and work performance), so our focus will be on under-regulation. There are three theories that explain under-regulation: (1) resource-depletion theory, (2) self-determination theory, and (3) the licensing effect. These theories can be used to understand consumer behaviour of impulsive buying, saving money, maintaining a healthy lifestyle, participating in environmental activities, and controlling body weight, to name a few. To avoid repetition, we will use weight control as an example to illustrate these three theories, and we will begin by highlighting how serious the overeating issue is.

Overeating

Overweight and obesity has become a common problem in modern society. One of the reasons that modern society has a high overweight and obesity rate is that self-regulation in dieting is challenging. To put this challenge into context, a longitudinal study finds that less than 3% of its research subjects were able to maintain their post-treatment weight.[75] More specifically, within five years of the final treatment in diet training, 97% of the subjects had, in fact, gained more weight than when they began the experiment. All three theories explaining self-regulation failure can account for our overeating behaviour, so we will use these theories to explain overeating behaviour.

Resource-depletion theory

The psychological basis

Resource-depletion theory, proposed by Baumeister, Bratslavsky, Muraven, and Tiee, suggests that self-regulation requires cognitive resources to curb our impulse[76] and, if we do not have sufficient resources, our ability to self-regulate reduces.[77] However, resource-depletion can be only our perception, rather than real depletion.[78] In these cases, changing the mind-set can increase willpower which leads to better self-regulation.

Implications for consumer behaviour

Resource-depletion theory is evidenced by Ward and Mann, who find that when people are on a diet, and when their cognitive tasks are taxing, their cognitive resources of monitoring their diet reduces.[79] It is this reduction that makes people increase their consumption of food. In Ward and Mann's study, they instructed their participants to undertake a memory task as a way to increase the participants' cognitive load.[80] However, the increase of cognitive load can come from many areas, such as making an important decision[81] or regulating one's emotion (e.g. cheering oneself up).[82] Resource-depletion theory suggests that resisting temptation requires cognitive resources; therefore, the effect of increasing cognitive load on overeating mainly occurs with dieters, not non-dieters.

Self-determination theory

The psychological basis

Self-determination theory, devised by Deci and Ryan, is a theory of motivation focusing on the distinction of *intrinsic* versus *extrinsic* motivations.[83] The theory suggests that human beings are motivated to satisfied their innate psychological needs, such as self-esteem,[84] which are intrinsic motivations. (By contrast, extrinsic motivations are people's motivations to receive external rewards.) The basic premise of the theory indicates that if outcomes of the goal cannot increase self-esteem, the attractiveness of pursuing the goal decreases. Self-regulation failure is attributed to a lack of self-determination, resulting in low or no commitment to pursue the goal.[85] A lack of self-determination decreases the possibility that we internalise our goal,[86] and internalisation plays a significant role in motivating our self-regulation behaviour.[87]

Implications for consumer behaviour

Self-regulation failure in dieting results from the fact that people cannot accept they have to tolerate reduction in comfort, which leads to reduced commitment.[88] Failure to self-regulate is a result of a lack of determination, hence providing the support for self-determination theory. Research has shown that if we have the will, then we are able to resist temptation, as the food-rich environment, instead of being a temptation to indulge, can serve as our goal representation of weight control.[89]

   A lack of determination is also related to the fact that people have yet to internalise their decision.[90] Internalisation of their decision can bring about the reasonability and responsibility to self-regulate, which results in autonomy. That is to say, because "I want" to control my diet, therefore "I will".

The licensing effect

The psychological basis

The licensing effect, put forward by Khan and Dhar, is another reason that may result in self-regulation failure.[91] The licensing effect suggests that an earlier good behaviour serves as a license for people to indulge without guilt.[92] This effect is closely related to the emotion pride, as discussed in the previous chapter (Section 6.3), as being good gives us a sense of pride, and that pride implies that "being good gives us permission to be a little bad".[93] For example, Khan and Dhar's[94] experiments demonstrate that after their research participants volunteered doing community services or made a donation to a charity, nearly 60% of the participants chose a hedonic (as opposed to utilitarian) product to purchase, compared with less than 30% of the participants who did not involve themselves in these "being good" activities.

The progress bias

Related to the licensing effect is the progress bias. People tend to magnify the impact of behaviours that help them attain their goals, but underestimate that of behaviours that drive them further away from their goals.[95] This asymmetry is referred to as the progress bias. However, the progress bias occurs only when we believe we can easily achieve our goals.[96] Ironically, therefore, our high hope of achieving our goal may end up driving away from the goal.

Implications for consumer behaviour

The compensation effect

Research has shown that there is compensation between people's efforts and food consumption, and these efforts can be physical (e.g. exercising[97]), mental (e.g. writing an assignment[98]), or even imagined.[99] In other words, after these increased efforts, we would feel that we are allowed to indulge ourselves by eating more and more indulgent food (e.g. chocolate cake). However, the energy intake can offset the energy consumption of these efforts, easily resulting in self-regulation failure of weight control.[100] This is also a manifestation of the progress bias.

To overcome the compensation effect, we should focus on the fun of pursuing our efforts, rather than concentrating on the efforts themselves.[101] For example, compared with people focusing on walking itself while walking in the park, people who focus on the scenic view of the park during their walking in the park eat less and consume on average 200+ calories less.[102] Similarly, compared with people freely choosing healthy foods, people concentrating on choosing to eat healthily want to eat more (indulgently) later on.[103]

▬Box 7.3 ▬

Are activity trackers effective in weight control?

Brands of activity trackers have promoted their devices by linking the use of the devices with health benefits, including increased physical activities and better weight control. The brands are able to claim these health benefits because many studies have found that wearing an activity tracker helps the wearer increase physical activities and reduce weight.[104] However, most of these studies are limited by small sample sizes (e.g. 11 participants in Washington et al.'s study[105]) or short study durations (e.g. a two-week observation period in Yingling et al.'s study[106]), which casts doubt on the effectiveness of activity trackers.[107] Below are two studies with longitudinal data researching a large sample size: one focuses on healthy individuals' usage of activity trackers, and one focuses on overweight/obese individuals' usage.

(Continued)

Research of healthy individual's usage of activity trackers by Finkelstein et al.[108]

800 people doing office jobs aged 21–65 years participated in the study for 12 months. These people were randomly assigned to one of four groups: (i) wearing activity trackers (Fitbit) plus cash incentive; (ii) wearing activity trackers plus charity/donation incentive; (iii) wearing activity trackers without any incentives (Fitbit only group); and (iv) not wearing activity trackers (the control group). The incentive, if there was, was tied to their moderate-to-vigorous physical activity level, and these interventions continued for six months. Interventions stopped at the seventh month, but the follow-up measures were taken for another six months to see whether the interventions had a lasting effect. The tracking period lasted for 12 months in total.

The results demonstrated that cash incentive was the strongest motivator to increase the research participants' moderate-to-vigorous physical activities, but its effectiveness ceased after intervention stopped; that is, its effectiveness decreased after six months when the intervention stopped, and disappeared at the 12th-month check. There was no difference in the moderate-to-vigorous physical activities levels between the Fitbit-only group and the control group. No evidence of improvements in health outcomes was found across all groups. As a result, the researchers called into question the value of these devices for health promotion.

Research of overweight/obese individual's usage of activity trackers by Jakicic et al.[109]

417 participants, aged 18–35 years with a BMI 25–40 on weight control programmes with counselling sessions, participated in the study for two years, and weight and health measures were taken at six-month intervals over the two-year period. As these participants were on weight control programmes, they were on a low-calorie diet, prescribed increases in physical activities, and group counselling sessions as part of the programmes. After six months of the programme activities, the participants were randomly assigned to one of two groups: the standard intervention and the enhanced intervention groups. Those in the standard intervention groups went to group-initiated self-monitoring of diet and physical activity using a website, and those in the enhanced intervention group, in addition to the standard intervention activities, were wearing activity trackers, which were accompanied by web interface to monitor diet and physical activity.

The results were interesting – the addition of an activity tracker device to a standard behavioural intervention resulted in less weight loss over two years. At the end of the two-year period, those in the standard intervention group lost on average more than 2.4kg than those in the enhanced intervention group. In addition, although both groups had significant improvements in body composition, fitness, physical activity, and diet, the improvements between both groups were similar. The less weight loss in the enhanced intervention group may be attributed to the licensing effect. An activity tracker can tell us how active we are on a daily basis, and it is possible that when we are particularly active, we may want to give ourselves additional treats.

The health-halo effect

The health-halo effect suggests an overestimation of the food's healthiness and an underestimation of its energy content. For example, people tend to underestimate the energy level of the main dishes, and thereby choose higher-calorie side dishes, drinks, or desserts.[110] This effect is in particular evident in the influence of nutrition labels. Nutrition labels can be misleading (and most *are* misleading), as they only stress a particular health benefit without providing overall health information. For example, a yogurt can be low fat but containing a high level of sugar or a soda contains no sugar but with artificial sweetener, and such biased nutrition labels are able to stimulate sales.[111] Another example of nutrition labels is the calories-per-serving for indulgent or less healthy food. Most calories-per-serving information is lower than our expectation, and providing calories-per-serving information makes those people who pay close attention to calorie information or watch their weight ironically eat more.[112]

The regulatory focus theory

The psychological basis

The regulatory focus, also known as goal orientation, is our guide for our motivation, and our regulatory focus can be induced by self-intentions, situations, or as a chronic tendency as a result of socialization.[113] Higgins specifies two different foci in self-regulation: promotion focus and prevention focus.[114]

- A *promotion regulatory focus* inspires us to pursue accomplishments and aspirations. People with a promotion focus pursue their goals with eagerness and favour the presence of positive behavioural outcomes (gains[115]). They follow an approach strategy for decision-making.[116]
- A *prevention regulatory focus* motivates us in working towards duties and responsibilities. People with a prevention focus strive to fulfil their goals with vigilance and prefer the absence of negative outcomes (loss[117]). They follow an avoidance strategy for their decision-making.[118]

The effects of the regulatory fit

We experience a "regulatory fit" when our goal pursuit strategy fits with our regulatory orientation;[119] that is, the strategy we use (approach versus avoidance) to pursue our goals fits with our regulatory orientation (promotion- versus prevention-focus). When there is a regulatory fit, our motivation to act towards our goal increases, so as the likelihood of succeeding in attaining the goal.[120] This is because a regulatory fit leads us to think more positively about our decisions for action, to believe what we do is valuable, and to derive more enjoyment from our actions.[121]

In addition, regulatory focus fit also occurs when our regulatory orientation fits with how, for example, information is presented to us.[122] In this case, our processing fluency for the information fit with our regulatory focus increases,[123] thereby enhancing our positive evaluation for that specific information.[124]

Implications for consumer behaviour

Design of marketing communications

"Get £100 off" is promotion-focused whereas "Save £100" is prevention-focused. Similar promotion strategies can be seen in many retailers online or offline. Table 7.2 shows what promotion- versus prevention-focused people prefer in various aspects of marketing communications. These preferences can be summarised by how promotion- versus prevention-focused people process information; that is promotion-focused people listen to their feelings, whereas prevention-focused people obey their reasoning.[125]

Table 7.2   Preferences of promotion- versus prevention-focused people

	Promotion-focused	Prevention-focused
Preferred information is ...[126]	1. Framed as gain pursuit 2. Abstract 3. Hedonic 4. With a focus on independent self-view 5. With a focus on future	1. Framed as loss avoidance 2. Concrete 3. Utilitarian 4. With a focus on interdependent self-view 5. With a focus on now
Preferred information search approach is ...[127]	1. More and at global level 2. Large size of consideration set	1. Less and at local level 2. Small size of consideration set
Immunity to marketers' manipulation is ...[128]	More immune	Less immune
Preferred brand is ...[129]	Less popular products or less known brands	Status Quo products or well-known brands
New product adoption approach ...[130]	High-tech goods and very new products	More established/mature products
Preferred financial products are ...[131]	Stocks and trading	Mutual funds, retirement funds
Preferred pricing display[132]	Combined pricing	Partition pricing
Online privacy concerns ...[133]	Less	More
Online review approach is ...[134]	When there is a positive experience	When there is a negative experience

In addition, situations or external stimuli are able to shape our regulatory focus, so marketing communications need to match their intended orientation to create regulatory focus fit. For example, appeals presented in gain frames are more persuasive when the message is promotion-focused, whereas loss-framed appeals are more persuasive when the message is prevention-focused.[135]

Information processing

The amount of information promotion-focused and prevention-focused people process is similar,[136] but the promotion- and prevention-focused people prefer different types of information (Table 7.2). In general, promotion-focused people look at the big picture, whilst prevention-focused people pay attention to details. As a result, promotion-focused (versus prevention-focused) people tend to have a large consideration set.[137]

In addition, prevention-focused people are more influenced by what others think, whereas promotion-focused people are not.[138] This may be because prevention-focused people hold interdependent self-views[139] and they do not want to make social mistakes. By contrast, promotion-focused people hold independent self-views,[140] and hedonic experiences are more important to them.[141] Therefore, prevention-focused people tend to choose status quo products[142] or well-known brands,[143] compared with promotion-focused people.

Participating in an online environment

Prevention-focused people are more cautious, so they tend to be concerned more about online privacy issues. Therefore, they become more hesitant to share much, especially personal information, on social media, whereas promotion-focused do not mind much sharing personal information on social media.[144]

In addition, the reasons prevention- and promotion-focused people share a product review online are different. That is, prevention-focused people are more inclined to post a review when they undergo a negative experience, whilst promotion-focused people are more likely to share a review when their experience is positive.[145]

7.5 SUMMARY

1. Motivation to engage in goal pursuit behaviour can be examined by external (response) efficacy in terms of the goal pursuit progress; that is, how close are we to achieve our goals: in the beginning, in the middle, or towards the end? *The goal gradient effect* suggests that consumers' purchase frequencies increase the closer they approach their goal in a loyalty programme. However, *the small area effect* suggests that consumers' purchase frequencies in a loyalty programme increase when their attention focuses on the accumulating or remaining progress, whichever is smaller as the small area is able

to create an illusion of either enlarged marginal effect (accumulating progress) or goal gradient effect (the remaining progress). Finally, consumers' purchase frequencies can be enhanced if the loyalty programme gives bonus points. For example, instead of giving consumers the regular ten-stamp reward cards, the loyalty programme can use 12-stamp rewards with two pre-existing "bonus" stamps. Although both contains ten purchases in exchange for a reward, consumers with the card with the pre-existing bonus stamps complete the ten purchases faster, and this is called *the endowment effect*.

2. Value in the expectancy-value theory is translated to consumer involvement. There are three broad types of consumer involvement: involvement with products, with advertisements, and with purchase situations. The more we are involved in products, advertisements and purchase situations, the more we are motivated to search information and to process the information we find. Involvement has a positive association with our cognitive efforts.

3. Maslow's hierarchy of needs is the representative theory for a bottom-up perspective of motivation, suggesting that we do not have clear superordinate goals. Despite the criticisms of Maslow's hierarchy of needs, this theory provides a way to examine most of consumer behaviour, which usually follows a bottom-up approach; for example, to lose 10 kilos in weight control programmes, to spend £10,000 to gain 1% cash back rewards, or to fly 20,000 miles to receive class upgrade. These are focal, and clear, goals. In addition, the bottom-up perspective can also be used to explain consumers' participation in a brand community and unplanned collection behaviour.

4. In order to achieve our goals, we rely on self-regulation (self-control). Self-regulation can lead to a high probability of successful financial savings, maintaining a healthy lifestyle, and participating in sustainable activities (e.g. recycling). Self-regulation failure can be caused by limited cognitive resources, insufficient commitment, and the licensing effect. In other words, self-regulation failure occurs when our cognitive resources are occupied elsewhere (for example, making an important decision), when we do not have the determination to commit to self-regulation, and when we feel our good behaviour should allow us to slack in our goal pursuit.

5. Our goal orientation is our guide for our motivation, and there are two orientations: promotion versus prevention regulatory focus. The former focuses on pursuing accomplishments and aspirations, whereas the latter stresses duties and responsibilities. People with different regulatory foci would prefer marketing communications that fit with their regulatory foci. For example, people with promotion regulatory focus prefer abstract and hedonic-focused messages, whereas those with prevention regulatory focus prefer concrete and utilitarian-focused messages.

DISCUSSION QUESTIONS

1. Explain expectancy-value theory of motivation and how it applies to consumer behaviour.
2. Explain Maslow's hierarchy of needs and how it applies to consumer behaviour.

3. Discuss the reasons for self-regulation failure.
4. Explain the regulatory focus theory and how it influences the design of marketing communications.

FURTHER READING

- Drèze, X., & Nunes, J. C. (2011). Recurring Goals and Learning: The Impact of Successful Reward Attainment on Purchase Behavior. *Journal of Marketing Research, 48*(April), 268–281.
- Kopetz, C. E., Kruglanski, A. W., Arens, Z. G., Etkin, J., & Johnson, H. M. (2012). The Dynamics of Consumer Behavior: A Goal Systemic Perspective. *Journal of Consumer Psychology, 22*(2), 208–223.
- Touré-Tillery, M., & Fishbach, A. (2018). Three Sources of Motivation. *Consumer Psychology Review, 1*, 123–134.
- van Osselaer, S. M. J., & Janiszewski, C. (2012). A Goal-Based Model of Product Evaluation and Choice. *Journal of Consumer Research, 39*(August), 260–292.
- Vohs, K. D., Baumeister, R. F., & Tice, D. M. (2008). Self-Regulation: Goals, Consumption, and Choices. In C. P. Haugtvedt, P. M. Herr & F. R. Kardes (eds), *Handbook of Consumer Psychology* (pp. 349–366). New York: Psychology Press.

NOTES

1. Austin, J. T., & Vancouver, J. B. (1996). Goal Constructs in Psychology: Structure, Process, and Content. *Psychological Bulletin, 120*(3), 338–375; Chulef, A. S., Read, S. J., & Walsh, D. A. (2001). A Hierarchcial Taxonomy of Human Goals. *Motivation and Emotion, 25*(3), 191–232; Brett, J. F., & WalleVande, D. (1999). Goal Orientation and Goal Content as Predictors in a Training Program. *Journal of Applied Psychology, 84*(6), 863–873; Maslow, A. H. (1943). A Theory of Human Motivation. *Psychological Review, 50*(4), 370–396; Wagner, T., & Rudolph, T. (2010). Towards a Hierarchical Theory of Shopping Motivation. *Journal of Retailing and Consumer Services, 17*(5), 415–429; Unsworth, K., Yeo, G., & Beck, J. (2014). Multiple Goals: A Review and Derivation of General Principles. *Journal of Organizational Behavior, 35*(8), 1064–1078.
2. Hyland, M. E. (1988). Motivational Control Theory: An Integrative Framework. *Journal of Personality and Social Psychology, 55*(4), 642–651; Bagozzi, R. P., & Dholakia, U. M. (1999). Goal Setting and Goal Striving in Consumer Behavior. *Journal of Marketing, 63*(Special Issue), 19–32; Pieters, R., Baumgartner, H., & Allen, D. (1995). A Means–End Chain Approach to Consumer's Goal Structure. *International Journal of Research in Marketing, 12*(3), 227–244.
3. Austin & Vancouver, Goal Constructs in Psychology.
4. Pieters et al., A Means–End Chain Approach to Consumers' Goal Structure.
5. Vroom, V. H. (1964). *Work and Motivation*. Oxford: Wiley.

6.   Bandura, A. (1982). Self-Efficacy Mechanism in Human Agency. *American Psychologist, 37*(2), 122–147; Rogers, R. W. (1983). Cognitive and Physiological Processes in Fear Appeals and Attitude Change: A Revised Theory of Protection Motivation. In J. T. Cacioppo & R. E. Petty (eds), *Social Psychophysiology* (pp. 153–176). New York: Guilford.

7.   Brehm, J. W., & Self, E. A. (1989). The Intensity of Motivation. *Annual Review of Psychology, 40*, 109–131; Eccles, J. S., & Wigfield, A. (2002). Motivational Beliefs, Values, and Goals. *Annual Review of Psychology, 53*, 109–132; Vroom, *Work and Motivation.*

8.   Dholakia, U. M. (2001). A Motivational Process Model of Product Involvement and Consumer Risk Perception. *European Journal of Marketing, 35*(11/12), 1340–1362; Laurent, G., & Kapferer, J.-N. (1985). Measuring Consumer Involvement Profiles. *Journal of Marketing Research, XXII*(February), 41–53.

9.   Klein, J. G., Smith, N. C., & John, A. (2004). Why We Boycott: Consumer Motivations for Boycott Participation. *Journal of Marketing, 68*(July), 92–109.

10. Hull, C. L. (1932). The Goal-Gradient Hypothesis and Maze Learning. *Psychological Review, 39*(1), 25–43; Hull, C. L. (1934). The Rats' Speed of Locomotion Gradient in the Approach to Food. *Journal of Comparative Psychology, 17*(3), 393–422.

11. Cheema, A., & Bagchi, R. (2011). The Effect of Goal Visualization on Goal Pursuit: Implications for Consumers and Managers. *Journal of Marketing, 75*(March), 109–123.

12. Kivetz, R., Urminsky, O., & Zheng, Y. (2006). The Goal-Gradient Hypothesis Resurrected: Purchase Acceleration, Illusionary Goal Progress, and Customer Retention. *Journal of Marketing Research*(February), 39–58.

13. Koo, M., & Fishbach, A. (2012). The Small-Area Hypothesis: Effects of Progress Monitoring on Goal Adherence. *Journal of Consumer Research, 39*(October), 493–509.

14. Touré-Tillery, M., & Fishbach, A. (2018). Three Sources of Motivation. *Consumer Psychology Review, 1*, 123–134.

15. Huang, S.-C., & Zhang, Y. (2011). Motivational Consequences of Perceived Velocity in Consumer Goal Pursuit. *Journal of Marketing Research, 48*(December), 1045–1056.

16. Koo & Fishbach, The Small-Area Hypothesis.

17. Ibid.

18. Kivetz et al., The Goal-Gradient Hypothesis Resurrected.

19. Nunes, J. C., & Drèze, X. (2006). The Endowed Progress Effect: How Artificial Advancement Increases Effort. *Journal of Consumer Research, 32*(4), 504–512.

20. Kivetz et al., The Goal-Gradient Hypothesis Resurrected.

21. Dellande, S., Gilly, M. C., & Graham, J. L. (2004). Gaining Compliance and Losing Weight: The Role of the Service Provider in Health Care Services. *Journal of Marketing, 68*(July), 78–91.

22. Han, D., Duhachek, A., & Agrawal, N. (2016). Coping and Construal Level Matching Drives Health Message Effectiveness via Response Efficacy or Self-Efficacy Enhancement. *Journal of Consumer Research, 43*(October), 429–447.

23. Bolton, L. E., Reed II, A., Volpp, K. G., & Armstrong, K. (2008). How Does Drug and Supplement Marketing Affect a Healthy Lifestyle? *Journal of Consumer Research, 34*(February), 713–726.

24. Ibid.

25. Maheswaran, D., & Meyers-Levy, J. (1990). The Influence of Message Framing and Issue Involvement. *Journal of Marketing Research, 27*(August), 361–367; Shiv, B., Edell, J. A., & Payne, J. W. (2004). Does Elaboration Increase or Decrease the Effectiveness of Negatively Versus Positvely Framed Messages. *Journal of Consumer Research, 31*(1), 199–208.

26. White, K., MacDonnell, R., & Dahl, D. W. (2011). It's the Mind-Set That Matters: The Role of Construal Level and Message Framing in Influencing Consumer Efficacy and Conservation Behavior. *Journal of Marketing Research, 48*(June), 472–485.

27. Lee, A. Y., & Aaker, J. L. (2004). Bringing the Frame into Focus: The Influence of Regulatory Fit on Processing Fluencing and Persuasion. *Journal of Personality and Social Psychology, 86*(2), 205–218.

28. White et al., It's the Mind-Set That Matters.

29. Lee & Aaker, Bringing the Frame into Focus; Song, H., & Schwarz, N. (2008). If It's Hard to Read, It's Hard to Do: Processing Fluency Affects Effort Prediction and Motivation. *Psychological Science, 19*(10), 986–988.

30. Bagozzi, R. P., & Lee, K.-H. (1999). Consumer Resistance to, and Acceptance of, Innovations. In E. J. Arnould & L. M. Scott (eds), *NA – Advances in Consumer Research* (Vol. 26, pp. 218–225). Provo, UT: Association for Consumer Research.

31. Gangadhardbatla, H. (2008). Facebook Me: Collective Self-Esteem, Need to Belong, and Internet Self-Efficacy as Predictors of the IGeneration's Attitudes towards Social Networking Sites. *Journal of Interactive Marketing, 8*(2), 5–15.

32. Schreier, M., & Prügl, R. (2008). Extending Lead-User Theory: Antecedents and Consequences of Consumers' Lead Userness. *Journal of Product Innovation Management, 25*(4), 331–346.

33. Zhang, Y., & Huang, S.-C. (2010). How Endowed Versus Earned Progress Affects Consumer Goal Commitment and Motivation. *Journal of Consumer Research, 37*(December), 641–654.

34. Zaichkowsky, J. L. (1985). Measuring the Involvement Construct. *Journal of Consumer Research, 12*(3), 341–352; Zaichkowsky, J. L. (1994). The Personal Involvement Inventory: Reduction, Revision, and Application to Advertising. *Journal of Advertising, 23*(4), 59–70.

35. Schmidt, J. B., & Spreng, R. A. (1996). A Proposed Model of External Consumer Information Search. *Journal of the Academy of Marketing Science, 24*(3), 246–256; Bloch, P. H., Sherrell, D. L., & Ridgway, N. M. (1986). Consumer Search: An Extended Framework. *Journal of Consumer Research, 13*(June), 119–126.

36. Petty, R. E., Cacioppo, J. T., & Schumann, D. (1983). Central and Peripheral Routes to Advertising Effectiveness: The Moderating Role of Involvement. *Journal of Consumer Research, 10*(September), 135–146; MacKenzie, S. B., & Spreng, R. A. (1992). How Does Motivation Moderate the Impact of Central and Peripheral Processing on Brand Attitudes and Intentions? *Journal of Consumer Research, 18*(March), 519–529.

37. Austin & Vancouver, Goal Constructs in Psychology.

38. Maslow, A Theory of Human Motivation; Maslow, A. H. (1968). *Toward a Psychology of Being*. New York: Van Nostrand Reinhold; Maslow, A. H. (1970). *Motivation and Personality* (second edn). New York: Harper & Row.

39. Maslow, A Theory of Human Motivation; Maslow, A. H. (1954). *Motivation and Personality*. New York: Harper & Row.

40. Maslow, A. H. (1987). *Motivation and Personality* (third edn). New York: HarperCollins.

41. Neher, A. (1991). Maslow's Theory of Motivation. *Journal of Humanistic Psychology, 31*(3), 89–112; McLeod, S. A. (2018). Maslow's Hierarchy of Needs. Retrieved from www. simplypsychology.org/maslow.html; Soper, B., Miliford, G. E., & Rosenthal, G. T. (1995). Belief When Evidence Does Not Support Theory. *Psychology & Marketing, 12*(5), 415–422.

42. Tay, L., & Diener, E. (2011). Needs and Subjective Well-Being around the World. *Journal of Personality and Social Psychology, 101*(2), 354–365.

43. Wallace, S. G., & Etkin, J. (2018). How Goal Specificity Shapes Motivation: A Reference Points Perspective. *Journal of Consumer Research, 44*(February), 1033–1051.

44. Dholakia, U. M., & Bagozzi, R. P. (2004). Motivational Antecedents, Constituents, and Consequents of Virtual Community Identity. In S. H. Godar & S. P. Ferris (eds), *Virtual and Collaborative Teams: Process, Technologies, and Practice* (pp. 253–268). London: Idea Group.

45. Tseng, T.-H., Huang, H. H., & Setiawan, A. (2017). How Do Motivations for Commitment in Online Brand Communities Evolve? The Distinction between Knowledge- and Entertainment-Seeking Motivations. *Computers in Human Behavior, 77*, 326–335.

46. Ibid.

47. Wallace & Etkin, How Goal Specificity Shapes Motivation.

48. Muñiz, A. M., Jr., & O'Guinn, T. C. (2001). Brand Community. *Journal of Consumer Research, 27*(4), 412–432; McAlexander, J. H., Schouten, J. W., & Koenig, H. F. (2002). Building Brand Community. *Journal of Marketing, 66*(1), 38–54.

49. Zhou, Z., Wu, P., Zhang, Q., & Xu, S. (2013). Transforming Visitors into Members in Online Brand Communities: Evidence from China. *Journal of Business Research, 66*(12), 2438–2443; Jones, L., & Huang, H. H. (2011). Building Online Brand Community: A Social Media Perspective. Paper presented at the Second International Colloquium on Consumer Brand Relationship, Orlando, Florida; Schau, H. J., Muñiz, A. M. J., & Arnould, E. J. (2009). How Brand Community Practices Create Value. *Journal of Marketing, 73*(5), 30–51.

50. Slater, J. S. (2000). Collecting the Real Thing: A Case Study Exploration of Brand Loyalty Enhancement among Coca-Cola Brand Collectors. In S. J. Hoch & R. J. Meyer (eds), *NA – Advances in Consumer Research* (Vol. 27, pp. 202–208). Provo, UT: Association for Consumer Research.

51. Gao, L., Huang, Y., & Simonson, I. (2014). The Influence of Initial Possession Level on Consumers' Adoption of a Collection Goal: A Tipping Point Effect. *Journal of Marketing, 78*(November), 143–156.

52. Ibid.

53. Belk, R. W. (1995). *Collecting in a Consumer Society*. New York: Routledge.

54. Pearce, S. M. (1992). *Museums, Objects, and Collections: A Cultural Study*. Leicester: Leicester University Press.

55. Belk, *Collecting in a Consumer Society*.

56. Gao et al., The Influence of Initial Possession Level on Consumers' Adoption of a Collection Goal.

57. White, K., MacDonnell, R., & Dahl, D. W. (2011). It's the Mind-Set That Matters: The Role of Construal Level and Message Framing in Influencing Consumer Efficacy and Conservation Behavior. *Journal of Marketing Research, 48*(June), 472–485.

58. Avnet, T., & Higgins, E. T. (2006). How Regulatory Fit Affects Value in Consumer Choices and Opinions. *Journal of Marketing Research, 43*(February), 1–10.

59. Hong, J., & Lee, A. Y. (2008). Be Fit and Be Strong: Mastering Self-Regulation through Regulatory Fit. *Journal of Consumer Research, 34*(February), 682–695.

60. Vohs, K. D., Baumeister, R. F., & Tice, D. M. (2008). Self-Regulation: Goals, Consumption, and Choices. In C. P. Haugtvedt, P. M. Herr, & F. R. Kardes (eds), *Handbook of Consumer Psychology* (pp. 349–366). New York: Psychology Press.

61. Baumeister, R. F., Heatherton, T. F., & Tice, D. M. (1994). *Losing Control: How and Why People Fail at Self-Regulation.* San Diego, CA: Academic Press; Gollwitzer, P. M., & Sheeran, P. (2006). Implementation Intentions and Goal Achievement: A Meta-Analysis of Effects and Processes. *Advances in Experimental Social Psychology, 38,* 69–119.

62. Latham, G. P., & Locke, E. A. (1991). Self-Regulation through Goal Setting. *Organizational Behavior and Human Decision Processes, 50*(2), 212–247.

63. Baumeister et al., *Losing Control.*

64. Rook, D. W. (1987). The Buying Impulse. *Journal of Consumer Research, 14*(September), 189–199.

65. Ibid.

66. Baumeister, R. D., Vohs, K. D., & Tice, D. M. (2007). The Strength Model of Self-Control. *Current Directions in Psychological Science, 16*(6), 351–355.

67. Sultan, A. J., Joireman, J., & Sprott, D. E. (2012). Building Consumer Self-Control: The Effect of Self-Control Excercises on Impulse Buying Urges. *Marketing Letters, 23*(1), 61–72.

68. Baumeister, R. F., & Heatherton, T. F. (1996). Self-Regulation Failure: An Overview. *Psychological Inquiry, 7*(1), 1–15.

69. Vohs et al., Self-Regulation.

70. Muraven, M., & Slessareva, E. (2003). Mechanisms of Self-Control Failure: Motivation and Limited Resources. *Personality and Social Psychology Bulletin, 29*(7), 894–906.

71. Howlett, E., Kees, J., & Kemp, E. (2008). The Role of Self-Regulation, Future Orientation, and Financial Knowledge in Long-Term Financial Decisions. *Journal of Consumer Affairs, 42*(2), 223–242.

72. Abraham, C., Sheeran, P., & Johnston, M. (1998). From Health Beliefs to Self-Regulation: Theoretical Advances in the Psychology of Action Control. *Psychology & Health, 13*(4), 569–591.

73. Kollmuss, A., & Agyeman, J. (2002). Mind the Gap: Why Do People Act Environmentally and What Are the Barriers to Pro-Environmental Behavior? *Environmental Education Research, 8*(3), 239–260.

74. Baumeister & Heatherton, Self-Regulation Failure.

75. Kramer, F. M., Jeffery, R. W., Forster, J. L., & Snell, M. K. (1989). Long-Term Follow-up of Behavioral Treatment for Obesity: Patterns of Weight Regain Among Men and Women. *International Journal of Obesity, 13*(2), 123–136.

76. Baumeister, R. F., Bratslavsky, E., Muraven, M., & Tiee, D. M. (1998). Ego Depletion: Is the Active Self a Limited Resource? *Journal of Personality and Social Psychology, 74*(5), 1252–1265.

77. Muraven, M., Tice, D. M., & Baumeister, R. F. (1998). Self-Control as a Limited Resource: Regulatory Depletion Patterns. *Journal of Personality and Social Psychology, 74*(3), 774–789.

78. Job, V., Dweck, C. S., & Walton, G. M. (2010). Ego Depletion – Is It in Your Head? Implicit Theories about Willpower Affect Self-Regulation. *Psychological Science, 21*(11), 1686–1693; Burnette, J. L., O'Boyle, E. H., VanEpps, E. M., Pollack, J. M., & Finkel, E. J. (2013). Mind-Sets Matter: A Meta-Analytic Review of Implicit Theories and Self-Regulation. *Psychological Bulletin, 139*(3), 655–701.

79. Ward, A., & Mann, T. (2000). Don't Mind if I Do: Disinhibited Eating Under Cognitive Load. *Journal of Personality and Social Psychology, 78*(4), 753–763.

80. Ibid.

81. Kahan, D., Polivy, J., & Herman, C. P. (2003). Conformity and Dietary Disinhibition: A Test of the Ego-Strength Model of Self-Regulation. *International Journal of Eating Disorders, 33*(2), 165–171.

82. Svaldi, J., Tuschen-Caffier, B., Lackner, H. K., Zimmermann, S., & Naumann, E. (2012). The Effects of Emotion Regulation on the Desire to Overeat in Restrained Eaters. *Appetite, 59*(2), 256–263.

83. Deci, E. L., & Ryan, R. M. (1980). The Empirical Exploration of Intrinsic Motvational Processes. *Advances in Experimental Social Psychology, 13*, 39–80; Deci, E. L., & Ryan, R. M. (1985). *Intrinsic Motivation and Self-Determination in Human Behavior*. New York: Plenum Press.

84. Deci, E. L., & Ryan, R. M. (2000). The "What" and "Why" of Goal Pursuits: Human Needs and the Self-Determination of Behavior. *Psychological Inquiry, 11*(4), 227–268.

85. Gagné, M., & Deci, E. L. (2006). Self-Determination Theory and Work Motivation. *Journal of Organizational Behavior, 25*(4), 331–362.

86. Ryan & Deci, Self-Determination.

87. Bellg, A. J. (2003). Maintenance of Health Behavior Change in Preventive Cardiology: Internalization and Self-Regulation of New Behaviors. *Behavior Modification, 27*(1), 103–131.

88. Forman, E. M., & Butryn, M. L. (2015). A New Look at the Science of Weight Control: How Acceptance and Commitment Strategies and Address the Challenge of Self-Regulation. *Appetite, 84*(1), 171–180.

89. Stroebe, W., van Koningsbruggen, G. M., Papies, E. K., & Aarts, H. (2013). Why Most Dieters Fail but Some Succeed: A Goal Conflict Model of Eating Behavior. *Psychological Review, 120*(1), 110–138.

90. Bellg, Maintenance of Health Behavior Change in Preventive Cardiology.

91. Khan, U., & Dhar, R. (2006). Licensing Effect in Consumer Choice. *Journal of Marketing Research, 43*(2), 259–266.

92. Kivetz, R., & Simonson, I. (2002). Earning the Right to Indulge: Effort as a Determinant of Consumer Preferences toward Frequency Program Rewards. *Journal of Marketing Research, 39*(May), 155–170.

93. Jiao, J. (2015). *Pride and Licensing Effects: When Being Good Gives Us Permission to Be a Little Bad.* (PhD). University of Iowa.

94. Khan & Dhar, Licensing Effect in Consumer Choice.

95. Campbell, M. C., & Warren, C. (2015). The Progress Bias in Goal Pursuit: When One Step Forward Seems Larger Than One Step Back. *Journal of Consumer Research, 41*(February), 1316–1331.

96. Ibid.

97. Chang, C.-C. A., & Lin, Y.-C. (2015). Physical Activity and Food Consumption. *Journal of Health Psychology, 20*(5), 490–499; Martins, C., Morgan, L. M., Bloom, S. R., & Robertson, M. D. (2007). Effects of Exercise on Gut Peptides, Energy Intake and Appetite. *Journal of Endocrinology, 193*(2), 251–258.

98. Chaput, J.-P., Drapeau, V., Poirier, P., Teasdale, N., & Tremblay, A. (2009). Glycemic Instability and Spontaneous Energy Intake: Association with Knowledge-Based Work. *Psychosomatic Medicine, 70*(7), 797–804.

99. Werle, C. O. C., Wansink, B., & Payne, C. R. (2011). Why Exercise Makes Us Fat: Compensation between Physical Activity and Food Consumption. In R. Ahluwalia, T. L. Chartrand, & R. K. Ratner (eds), *NA – Advances in Consumer Research* (Vol. 39, pp. 506–508). Duluth, MN: Association for Consumer Research.

100. Chang & Lin, Physical Activity and Food Consumption.

101. Werle, C. O. C., Wansink, B., & Payne, C. R. (2015). Is It Fun or Exercise? The Framing of Physical Activity Biases Subsequent Snacking. *Marketing Letters, 26*(4), 691–702; Woolley, K., & Fishbach, A. (2016). For the Fun of It: Harnessing Immediate Rewards to Increase Persistence in Long-Term Goals. *Journal of Consumer Research, 42*(April), 952–966.

102. Werle et al., Is It Fun or Exercise?

103. Finkelstein, S. R., & Fishbach, A. (2010). When Healthy Food Makes You Hungry. *Journal of Consumer Research, 37*(October), 357–367.

104. Coughlin, S. S., & Stewart, J. (2016). Use of Consumer Wearable Devices to Promote Physical Activity: A Review of Health Intervention Studies. *Journal of Environment and Health Sciences, 2*(6), 1–6.

105. Washington, W. D., Banna, K. M., & Gibson, A. L. (2014). Preliminary Efficacy of Prize-Based Contingency Management to Increase Activity Levels in Healthy Adults. *Journal of Applied Behavior Analysis, 47*(2), 231–245.

106. Yingling, L. R., Brooks, A. T., Wallen, G. R., Peters-Lawrence, M., McClurkin, M., Cooper-McCann, R., . . . Powell-Wiley, T. M. (2016). Community Engagement to Optimize the Use of Web-Based and Wearable Technology in a Cardiovascular Health and Needs Assessment Study: A Mixed Methods Approach. *JMIR mHealth and uHealth, 4*(2), e38.

107. Coughlin, S. S., & Stewart, J. (2016). Use of Consumer Wearable Devices to Promote Physical Activity: A Review of Health Intervention Studies. *Journal of Environment and Health Sciences, 2*(6), 1–6.

108. Finkelstein, E. A., Haaland, B. A., Bilger, M., Sahasranaman, A., Sloan, R. A., Nang, E. E. K., & Evenson, K. R. (2016). Effectiveness of Activity Trackers with and without Incentives to Increase Physical Activity (TRIPPA): A Randomised Controlled Trial. *The Lancet Diabetes & Endocrinology, 4*(12), 983–995.

109. Jakicic, J. M., Davis, K. K., Rogers, R., King, W. C., Marcus, M. D., Helsel, D., . . . Belle, S. H. (2016). Effect of Wearable Technology Combined With a Lifestyle Intervention on Long-Term Weight Loss: The IDEA Randomized Clinical Trial. *Journal of the American Medical Association, 316*(11), 1161–1171.

110. Chandon, P., & Wansink, B. (2007). The Biasing Health Halos of Fast-Food Restaurant Health Claims: Lower Calorie Estimates and Higher Side-Dish Consumption Intentions. *Journal of Consumer Research, 34*(3), 301–314.

111. Elshiewy, O., Jahn, S., & Boztug, Y. (2016). Seduced by the Label: How the Recommended Serving Size on Nutrition Labels Affects Food Sales. *Journal of the Association for Consumer Research, 1*(1), 104–114.

112. Tangari, A. H., Bui, M., Haws, K. L., & Liu, P. J. (2019). That's Not So Bad, I'll Eat More! Backfire Effects of Calories-Per-Serving Information on Snack Consumption. *Journal of Marketing, 83*(1), 133–150.

113. Motyka, S., Grewal, D., Puccinelli, N. M., Roggeveen, A. L., Avnet, T., Daryanto, A., . . . Wetzels, M. (2014). Regulatory Fit: A Meta-Analytic Synthesis. *Journal of Consumer Psychology, 24*(3), 394–410.

114. Higgins, E. T. (1997). Beyond Pleasure and Pain. *American Psychologist, 52*(12), 1280–1300; Higgins, E. T. (1998). Promotion and Prevention: Regulatory Focus as a Motivational Principle. *Advances in Experimental Social Psychology, 30*, 1–46.

115. Kahneman, D., & Tversky, A. (1979). Prospect Theory: An Analysis of Decision under Risk. *Econometrica, 47*(2), 263–291.

116. Idson, L. C., Liberman, N., & Higgins, E. T. (2000). Distinguishing Gains from Nonlosses and Losses from Nongains: A Regulatory Focus Perspective on Hedonic Intensity. *Journal of Experimental Social Psychology, 36*(3), 252–274.

117. Kahneman & Tversky, Prospect Theory.

118. Idson et al., Distinguishing Gains from Nonlosses and Losses from Nongains.

119. Higgins, E. T. (2000). Make a Good Decision: Value from Fit. *American Psychologist, 55*(November), 1217–1230.

120. Hong, J., & Lee, A. Y. (2008). Be Fit and Be Strong: Mastering Self-Regulation through Regulatory Fit. *Journal of Consumer Research, 34*(February), 682–695.

121. Higgins, Make a Good Decision; Freitas, A., & Higgins, E. T. (2002). Enjoying Goal-Directed Action: The Role of Regulatory Fit. *Psychological Science, 13*(1), 1–6.

122. Motyka et al., Regulatory Fit.

123. Lee, A. Y., Keller, P. A., & Sternthal, B. (2010). Value from Regulatory Construal Fit: The Persuasive Impact of Fit between Consumer Goals and Message Concreteness. *Journal of Consumer Research, 36*(February), 735–747.

124. Lee, A. Y., & Labroo, A. A. (2004). The Effect of Conceptual and Perceptual Fluency on Brand Evaluation. *Journal of Marketing Research, 41*(2), 151–165.

125. Avnet & Higgins, How Regulatory Fit Affects Value in Consumer Choices and Opinions.

126. White et al., It's the Mind-Set That Matters; Lee et al., Value from Regulatory Construal Fit; Ramanathan, S., & Dhar, S. K. (2010). The Effect of Sales Promotions on the Size and Composition of the Shopping Basket: Regulatory Compatibility from Framing and Temporal Restrictions. *Journal of Marketing Research, 47*(3), 542–552; Roy, R., & Ng, S. (2012). Regulatory Focus and Preference Reversal Between Hedonic and Utilitarian Consumption. *Journal of Consumer Behaviour, 11*(1), 81–88; Kareklas, I., Carlson, J. R., & Muehling, D. D. (2012). The Role of Regulatory Focus and Self-View in "Green" Advertising Message Framing. *Journal of Advertising, 41*(4), 25–39; Kees, J., Burton, S., & Tangari, A. H. (2010). The Impact of Regulatory Focus, Temporal Orientation, and Fit on Consumer Responses to Health-Related Advertising. *Journal of Advertising, 39*(1), 19–34; Khajehzadeh, S., Oppewal, H., & Tojib, D. (2014). Consumer Responses to Mobile Coupons: The Roles of Shopping Motivation and Regulatory Fit. *Journal of Business Research, 67*(11), 2447–2455; Aaker, J., & Lee, A. Y. (2001). "I" Seek Pleasures and "We" Avoid Pains: The Role of Self-Regulatory Goals in Information Processing and Persuasion. *Journal of Consumer Research, 28*(June), 33–49.

127. Pham, M. T., & Chang, H. H. (2010). Regulatory Focus, Regulatory Fit, and the Search and Consideration of Choice Alternative. *Journal of Consumer Research, 37*(December), 626–640.

128. Kirmani, A., & Zhu, R. J. (2007). Vigilant Against Manipulation: The Effect of Regulatory Focus on the Use of Persuasion Knowledge. *Journal of Marketing Research, 44*(4), 688–701.

129. Ramanathan & Dhar, The Effect of Sales Promotions on the Size and Composition of the Shopping Basket; Chernev, A. (2004). Goal Orientation and Consumer Preference for the Status Quo. *Journal of Consumer Research, 31*(December), 557–565.

130. Herzenstein, M., Posavac, S. S., & Brakus, J. J. (2007). Adoption of New and Really New Products: The Effects of Self-Regulation Systems. *Journal of Marketing Research, 44*(May), 251–260.

131. Zhou, R., & Pham, M. T. (2004). Promotion and Prevention across Mental Accounts: When Financial Products Dictate Consumers' Investment Goals. *Journal of Consumer Research, 31*(June), 125–135.

132. Lee, K., Choi, J., & Li, Y. J. (2014). Regulatory Focus as a Predictor of Attitudes toward Partitioned and Combined Pricing. *Journal of Consumer Psychology, 24*(3), 355–362.

133. Mosteller, J., & Poddar, A. (2017). To Share and Protect: Using Regulatory Focus Theory to Examine the Privacy Paradox of Consumers' Social Media Engagement and Online Privacy Protection Behaviors. *Journal of Interactive Marketing, 39*, 27–38.

134. Shin, D., Song, J. H., & Biswas, A. (2014). Electronic Word-Of-Mouth (eWOM) Generation in New Media Platforms: The Role of Regulatory Focus and Collective Dissonance. *Marketing Letters, 25*(2), 153–165.

135. Aaker & Lee, "I" Seek Pleasures and "We" Avoid Pains.

136. Pham & Chang, Regulatory Focus, Regulatory Fit, and the Search and Consideration of Choice Alternative.

137. Ibid.

138. Bagozzi, R. P., Baumgartner, H., & Yi, Y. (1992). State versus Action Orientation and the Theory of Reasoned Action: An Application to Coupon Usage. *Journal of Consumer Research*, *18*(March), 505–518.

139. Aaker & Lee, "I" Seek Pleasures and "We" Avoid Pains.

140. Ibid.

141. Khajehzadeh, S., Oppewal, H., & Tojib, D. (2014). Consumer Responses to Mobile Coupons: The Roles of Shopping Motivation and Regulatory Fit. *Journal of Business Research*, *67*(11), 2447–2455.

142. Chernev, A. (2004). Goal Orientation and Consumer Preference for the Status Quo. *Journal of Consumer Research*, *31*(December), 557–565.

143. Ramanathan & Dhar, The Effect of Sales Promotions on the Size and Composition of the Shopping Basket.

144. Mosteller, J., & Poddar, A. (2017). To Share and Protect: Using Regulatory Focus Theory to Examine the Privacy Paradox of Consumers' Social Media Engagement and Online Privacy Protection Behaviors. *Journal of Interactive Marketing*, *39*, 27–38.

145. Shin, D., Song, J. H., & Biswas, A. (2014). Electronic Word-of-Mouth (eWOM) Generation in New Media Platforms: The Role of Regulatory Focus and Collective Dissonance. *Marketing Letters*, *25*(2), 153–165.

8

CONSUMER IDENTITY – I SHOP; THEREFORE, I AM

┤Learning objectives├

To explore, understand, and explain:

*   the psychological bases of self and social identity
*   how individuals use consumption to form self and social identity
*   the role of the brand-as-person metaphor in consumer identity
*   the role of self-construal in consumer behaviour

8.1 INTRODUCTION

Identity is another key motivator for people's behaviour. As what we have represents who we are,[1] brands have relied on identity-marketing to appeal to consumers.[2] In addition, identity is related to subjective well-being; that is, self-esteem is the main reason that drives people to maintain, verify, and enhance their positive identities (see Table 8.1 for the main terms used in identity research). Consumption is usually used as a way to maintain or enhance our self-esteem, and understanding identity has become a critical subject in understanding not just consumer behaviour but also human behaviour at large. This chapter will first start with the influence of William James's empirical self on identity-consistent consumption, such as self-brand congruence and self-brand connection.[3] This stream of research contributes to the development of the metaphor, brand-as-person: brand personality and brand relationship, which will be discussed next (Section 8.2). Following the discussion of the influence of self-identity on consumer behaviour, the role of social identity will be introduced in terms of social identification, reference groups, and social defaults (Section 8.3). Finally, Section 8.4 will discuss the influence of culture by focusing on self-construal.

Table 8.1   Definitions of frequently used motivations and actions in identity research

Motivations and Actions	Definition	Implications
Self-esteem	Self-esteem is self-respect, and reflects one's satisfaction and confidence in one's own abilities and situations via subjective self-evaluation. Self-esteem is the second highest level on Maslow's hierarchy of needs (just below need for self-actualisation) discussed in Chapter 7 (Figure 7.2).	Identity clarity both at personal[4] and social/cultural level[5] improves self-esteem.
Self-maintenance	Self-maintenance suggests identity-consistent motivation or behaviour in order to maintain one's identity.	Being able to maintain identity continuity increases self-esteem, whereas lack of identity continuity increases confusion, [6] thereby decreasing self-esteem and increasing risks of depression. [7]
Self-enhancement	Self-enhancement suggests motivation or behaviour focusing on enhancing and strengthening one's positive identity.	Self-enhancement drives people to behave towards their ideal selves.[8]
Self-verification	Self-verification suggests motivation or behaviour focusing on verifying both positive and negative self-perceived identity.	Self-verification leads people to strive to behave towards their actual selves[9] by seeking both favourable and unfavourable feedback about their self.[10] Success through the self-verification process can increase people's trust towards their interpersonal relationship partners.[11]

8.2 SELF-IDENTITY
William James's empirical self
The psychological basis

Self-identity is a term that has been used loosely and interchangeably with the "self", "identity", or "self-concept" in psychology.[12] The first proper account of self-identity can be traced back to William James's *Principles of Psychology*.[13] According to James, self-identity, also known as the empirical self, is organised by memories, habits, and a sense of the self-owned identity, and can be classified into the material self, social self, and the spiritual self (Table 8.2). James's self-identity focuses on consciousness in self-identity; that is, only the identities that we are consciously aware of or recognise can be classified as self-identity. However, recent research has included implicit identity to enrich our understanding of self-identity.[14] Today, self-identity is defined as the totality of an individual's both conscious and unconscious thoughts and feelings that represent the individual.

Table 8.2   Classification of empirical self

Classification of empirical self	Definition	Examples
Material self	• Also known as the extended self • Containing an individual's possessions	Possessions include bodily and material possessions: • Body parts • Branded and non-branded possessions *Relevance to consumer behaviour*: to be covered in self-identity (this section)
Social self	• The views others hold of an individual	Social roles, including: • Personal relationships • Ethnic backgrounds • Religious beliefs • Political affiliations • Occupations *Relevance to consumer behaviour*: to be covered in social identity (Section 8.3)
Spiritual self	• An individual's inner being	Examples of inner being include: • Attitudes • Emotions • Interests • Motives • Desires *Relevance to consumer behaviour*: covered in consumer emotions (Chapter 6) and motivation (Chapter 7)

Implications for consumer behaviour

Identity-consistent consumption: self-brand congruence

James's material self is consistent with Belk's extended self in consumer research. Belk has argued that "we are what we have".[15] What we have is a repertoire of brands. As brands have meanings,[16] user-imagery,[17] or personality,[18] consumers are able to use the underlying meanings, user-imagery, or personality of these brands to reflect and enhance their self-identity.[19] The brands we buy signal our self-identity and indicate the "I shop; therefore, I am" phenomenon.[20]

Self-brand congruence is also termed as self-congruence, self-brand congruity, and self-congruity (Box 8.1). It suggests that consumers' self-image is consistent with the image of the brands they use. Research has shown that we like to buy brands with an image that is consistent with our own,[21] as self-brand congruence generates positive influences on our brand evaluation,[22] brand preference,[23] brand experience,[24] brand loyalty,[25] brand attachment,[26] and enjoyment in using the brand.[27]

—Box 8.1—

Difference between self-brand congruence and product congruence

Self-brand congruence suggests that our self-image is congruent (or consistent) with the image of the brand we use, whereas *product congruence* suggests product functionality congruence between actual and ideal product functionality. Product congruence (or congruity) has nothing to do with self-image or identity; rather, it focuses on the functional side of the brand.

Self-brand connection

Self-brand connection, also known as consumer-brand identification[28] or self-concept connection,[29] suggests the extent to which individuals have incorporated a brand into their self-concept,[30] that is, a connection between a consumer and his brand is formed when he uses the associations of his brand to construct his self-identity and, as a result, he is able to identify with the brand. Consumers with a stronger connection with their brands prefer stories focusing on brands' experiential value, and they tend to access such stories from interactive media, whereas those with weaker connection focus on brand's functional value and tend to use traditional media.[31] As consumers, we started to use brands to construct our identities as early as around 12 years old.[32]

Self-brand connection implies that the brand image reflected from brand associations is attractive to the consumer, and it is attractive because of identity similarity (i.e. self-brand congruence), brand prestige, and brand distinctiveness[33] (Figure 8.1). Similar to the consequences of self-brand congruence discussed in the previous section, self-brand connection results in positive brand evaluation,[34] strong brand commitment,[35] enhanced brand loyalty,[36] and increased brand advocacy (positive WOM[37]) and brand-purchase/usage intentions[38] (Figure 8.1). Self-brand connection is able to make consumers resistant to switching brands even when the competing brand is attractive, such as a radically new and good product introduced to the market.[39]

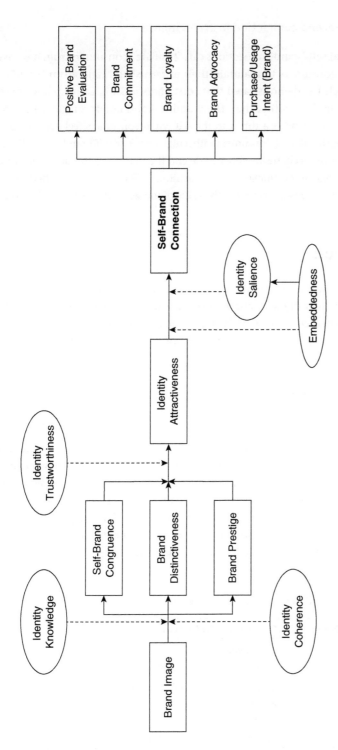

Figure 8.1 The antecedents and consequences of self-brand connection

Adapted from Bhattacharya and Sen [40]

Reprinted from *Journal of Marketing*, 67(April), Bhattacharya and Sen. Consumer-Company Identification: A Framework for Understanding Consumers' Relationships with Companies, 76-88, Copyright (2003), with permission from SAGE.

The influence of self-brand connection in brand failure

Research has shown that self-brand connections can "insulate" consumers from negative brand information, allowing consumers to maintain their untarnished brand attitude and loyalty.[41] However, recent research has demonstrated that consumers resist negative brand information in order to protect themselves, rather than the brand.[42] Brand failure suggests a threat to the brand, and a threat to the brand is a threat to the self when consumers feel connected with the brand. When the brand is threatened, consumers with a high degree of self-brand connection, but low self-esteem, activate defence mechanisms either to defend the brand[43] or to bury their heads in the sand maintaining their original favourable brand evaluations.[44] This "insulation" effect of self-brand connection disappears when consumers restore the value of the self and raise their self-esteem.[45]

Brand-as-person

The brand-as-person metaphor has significant implications in consumers' self-identity, as we, as consumers, are able to identify with our brands and want to connect with this brand-person. Two important and related concepts that facilitate consumers' identification and connection with the brand-person will be introduced: brand personality and brand relationship.

The psychological basis

Brand personality

Brand personality originates in the personality research and heavily relies on the trait perspective of personality. The trait perspective sees a direct connection between overt behaviour and under-lying traits, and as a result personality traits are the "consistent patterns in the way individuals behave, feel, and think".[46] This view has encouraged a lexical approach to study traits; that is, gathering the possible terms of personality attributes from natural language and using statistics to classify these attributes.[47] Table 8.3 shows the common personality factor models in psychology, and the contemporary Big Five (the five-factor) model is the most popular model used in psychology.[48]

Table 8.3 Commonly used personality factor models

Models of Personality Factors	Factors and Definition
Eysenck's two-factor model[49]	1. Extraversion
	2. Neuroticism → Emotional stability
Eysenck's three-factor model[50]	1. Psychoticism → Anti-sociability
	2. Extraversion
	3. Neuroticism
	Also dubbed as the P-E-N model

Models of Personality Factors	Factors and Definition	
Cattell's 16 PF (Personality Factors)[51]	1. Abstractedness	→ Imagination
	2. Apprehension	→ Confidence
	3. Dominance	→ Powerfulness
	4. Emotional stability	
	5. Liveliness	→ Spontaneity
	6. Openness to change	→ Flexibility
	7. Perfectionism	
	8. Privateness	
	9. Reasoning	→ Abstract versus concrete
	10. Rule-consciousness	→ Conforming versus non-conforming
	11. Self-reliance	→ Independence
	12. Sensitivity	
	13. Social boldness	→ Uninhibited versus shy
	14. Tension	→ Patience
	15. Vigilance	→ Trusting
	16. Warmth	→ Extraversion
The Big Five[52]	1. Extraversion	
	2. Neuroticism	→ Emotional stability
	3. Agreeableness	→ Social harmony
	4. Conscientiousness	→ Self-discipline and diligence
	5. Openness to new experience	→ Imagination and curiosity

Using the idea of personality traits from psychology, Aaker developed the first, and most rigorous, conceptualisation of brand personality.[53] Aaker's brand personality also identifies five dimensions: sincerity, excitement, competence, sophistication, and ruggedness. Among these dimensions, sincerity, excitement, and competence capture similar concepts of agreeableness, extraversion, and conscientiousness of the Big Five personality dimensions respectively (Table 8.4). However, while the same factors generated from the Big Five largely show a cross-cultural consistency,[54] brand personality has been found to lack this consistency across culture.[55]

Table 8.4 A comparison between Big Five personality in psychology and Aaker's brand personality

Human Personality The Big Five[b][56]		Brand Personality[57]	
Dimension Label	**Measures**	**Dimension Label**	**Measures**
Extraversion	• Extraverted	**Excitement**[c]	• Daring
	• Enthusiastic		• Spirited
	• Reserved[a]		• Imaginative
	• Quiet[a]		• Up-to-date

(Continued)

Table 8.4   (Continued)

Human Personality The Big Five[b] [56]		Brand Personality[57]	
Dimension Label	**Measures**	**Dimension Label**	**Measures**
Agreeableness	• Sympathetic • Warm • Critical[a] • Quarrelsome[a]	**Sincerity**[c]	• Down-to-earth • Honest • Wholesome • Cheerful
Conscientiousness	• Dependable • Self-disciplined • Disorganised[a] • Careless[a]	**Competence**[c]	• Reliable • Intelligent • successful
Emotional stability	• Calm • Emotionally stable • Anxious[a] • Easily upset[a]		
Openness to new experiences	• Open to new experiences • Complex • Conventional[a] • Uncreative[a]		
		Sophistication	• Upper class • Charming
		Ruggedness	• Outdoorsy • Tough

[a] reverse-coded items

[b] This Big Five personality instrument in the table is developed by Gosling et al.,[58] and it is only one of the instruments available, but the shortest one.

[c] According to Aaker, the dimension of excitement in brand personality is similar to that of extraversion in human personality, sincerity to agreeableness, and competence to conscientiousness.[59] The distinctive dimensions of brand personality are sophistication and ruggedness.

Brand relationships

Brand relationship is an extension of brand personality: brand relationship implies a consumer's ability to interact with a brand-person in order to form a relationship. Borrowing the inter-personal relationship literature, Fournier extended earlier work on brand relationships and identified different types of brand relationship, including close friendships (e.g. Apple), flings (e.g. Starbucks), parent–child (e.g. Disney), master–slave (e.g. Marlboro), and so on based on the intensity of the relationships and the social versus functional rewards from the relationships.[60]

Brand relationships can help consumers in a way similar to how close interpersonal relation-ships can help us. Research shows that the social support from close interpersonal relationships is able to shelter relationship partners from pain.[61] So can brand relationships: strong and close brand relationships are able to reduce physical pain[62] or to not feel lonely.[63]

However, the concept of brand relationships suffers from one key limitation: brands are unable to reciprocate like relationship partners do in interpersonal relationships. Therefore, it can be difficult, at least for some consumers, to describe their brands as active relationship partners,[64] unless they have sufficient imagination to personify brands.[65]

Implications for consumer behaviour

Brand evaluation and purchase intentions

The effects of brand personality are conclusive: strong and favourable brand personality leads to positive brand evaluation,[66] trust,[67] attachment,[68] loyalty,[69] and purchase intentions.[70] These positive effects are generated because brand personality provides consumers with emotional fulfilment,[71] such that they are able to enhance their self-perceptions after using brands with appealing personalities.[72]

—Box 8.2—

Criticisms of the use of brand personality in consumer research

There are two issues with the use of brand personality. First, some studies accumulate the average ratings on each dimension to represent the general perception of the *existence* of brand personality. In other words, studies saying brand personality leads to strong loyalty beg the question of *what* brand personality. Surely, cold brand-people (low on the warmth dimension score) have the opposite personality to warm brand-people, rather than those with no personality. In addition, introvert brand-people with an openness to experiences and closed-minded extroverts are not the same, but can be reflected as the same through this over-simplified method. Despite the fact that there are correlations between some dimensions of the Big Five, personality researchers have been careful not to use the accumulated scores across dimensions.

The second issue then lies in the fact that some studies seem to suggest that the more sincere, excited, competent, sophisticated, and rugged the brand is, the stronger the effects of brand personality. While one may not question the positive correlation between brand competence and brand evaluation, it is a wonder why all consumers prefer excited, sophisticated, or rugged brands, when consumers with a different personality are supposed to use brands with a different brand personality to reflect their own identity. To rectify these issues, we should either focus on specific dimensions of brand personality[73] or on brand personality favourability[74] to study the outcomes of brand personality we wish to examine.

Sincere versus exciting brands

A good brand strategy dictates a consistency in its marketing communication; however, consistency may not be necessary for exciting brands. For example, negative sensory disconfirmation (e.g. where touch reveals worse quality than expected by sight) results in negative consumer evaluation in general, but not for exciting brands, whereas positive sensory confirmation (e.g. where touch reveals better quality than expected by sight) results in positive evaluation, but not for sincere brands.[75] This occurs because consumers view disconfirmation as more authentic for an exciting brand, and view confirmation as more authentic for a sincere brand. Aaker et al. demonstrate similar findings that brand transgression can excite, and therefore is viewed positively for exciting brands.[76]

Box 8.3

The effects of different dimensions of brand personality

The effects of the specific brand personality dimensions are not conclusive. For example, sincerity has been found to be positive by some researchers,[77] but negative by others.[78] For example, competence has been found to be positive by some,[79] but negative by others.[80] One of the reasons for these seemingly contradictory results is because of individual differences in their preferences for brand personality - see the discussion in the next section.

Individual differences

As brand personality is a personal construct (i.e. different people may infer different personalities from the same brand), the effects of brand personality may vary from individual to individual. Some people prefer exciting brands, others prefer sincere brands,[81] and still others prefer negative or dark brand personalities.[82] For example, the lack of fit of brand extension can be positive, as brand personality is enhanced for those people who focus on process, rather than on outcome[83] (Box 8.4). This is because, if we focus on process, whatever happens in-between counts, and can strengthen our perception of brand personality by updating it gradually. If, however, we focus on outcome, whatever happens in-between does not count, and when we only focus on the outcome, the lack of fit becomes abrupt and unfavourable.

Box 8.4

Process- versus outcome-focused orientation

The theoretical term for process- versus outcome-focused is called implicit self-theories. That is, individuals maintain different implicit theories about the world around them:[84]

- entity theory orientation (aka entity theorists), focusing on the outcome with a belief that personality is fixed; or
- incremental theory orientation (aka incremental theorists), focusing on the process with a belief that personality is malleable.

The development of brand relationships over time

Brand relationships are not static. They evolve with time and experience. For example, relationships with sincere brands deepen over time, while relationships with exciting brands weaken over time.[85] This may be because emotional arousal decreases over the brand relationship span, while inclusion of the brand into our self-identity increases over time.[86] As the emotional element is important at the start of a brand relationship, marketing communications cultivating the emotional side of brands increase the likelihood of building strong brand relationships, whereas communications focusing on reasoning or cognitive attention reduces the strength of the brand relationships.[87]

Box 8.5

The development of brand relationships in the digital age

Technology advancement has made two-way communication possible. Brands are able to communicate with consumers on social media, and this two-way communication can enhance our brand relationships.[88] Although brands can communicate with their consumers on social media and encourage their consumers to share positive word-of-mouth through this channel, this encouragement needs to be used with caution. This is because oral communicators, focusing on social interaction, are more likely to express self-related thoughts, thereby boosting the strength of brand relationships, than written communicators.[89]

Brand transgressions

Brand transgressions are the violations of a brand's promise to its consumers. Strong brand relationships have been seen as having powers to shelter consumers from brand transgressions, allowing consumers to maintain their brand loyalty.[90] However, based on the interpersonal relationship literature, research has demonstrated the likely negative effects of strong brand relationships. This is because consumers have psychological contracts with brands, which dictate the terms of the relationship.[91] Brand transgressions represent perceived betrayal,[92] and those beloved brands represent consumers' identities.[93] Imagine if your other half cheated on you! Thus, consumers in strong brand relationships react negatively to brand transgressions violating the psychological contracts, but not if there is no violation, whereas consumers in weak brand relationships react negatively to all brand transgressions.[94]

Higgins's self-discrepancy theory

The psychological basis

Self-discrepancy theory, proposed by Higgins, suggests that individuals experience negative emotions if discrepancies exist between actual and ideal self and between actual and ought self, and that we are motivated to remove negative emotions by minimising our self-discrepancies.[95] Self-discrepancies can manifest in different areas, including intellect, achievement, wealth, and appearances, and discrepancies here connote a negative, worse actual self than ideal or ought self:

- Actual self: true representations of who you are
- Ideal self: ideal representations of who you are, including your hopes and aspirations of who you want to be
- Ought self: "should be" representations, indicating your responsibilities of who you should be

Implications for consumer behaviour

Actual versus ideal self: which is more important in consumer behaviour?

Self-brand congruence suggests consumers tend to involve in identity-consistent consumption; that is, consumers buy brands with images that are consistent with their own self-images (see p.184). But it raises the question of which self-image we refer to: the actual or ideal self? Based on the self-discrepancy theory, we endeavour to reduce the gap between the actual and ideal self, and thus using a brand consistent with our ideal self may close the gap. However, the majority of the existing research finds otherwise: actual self is a better predictor than ideal self, of consumer behaviour,[96] and this also holds true in their evaluation of the online shopping environment[97] and in their social media behaviour.[98] The reason that actual self outweighs ideal self may be because of authenticity that can be reflected from the actual self.[99] However, as actual and ideal self are highly correlated, some studies combine actual and ideal self into a single self-brand congruence index.[100]

In addition, research has shown that consumption situations,[101] consumer involvement,[102] and brand personality[103] can influence the relative importance of actual and ideal self. For example, actual self is more important for sincere brands, whereas ideal self is more important for sophisticated brands.[104] Another example is that actual self is more important for functional consumption, whereas ideal self is more important for symbolic consumption.[105] These examples provide marketers with the direction of whether to target their consumers' actual self or their ideal self in their marketing communications. If targeting actual self, consumers prefer more concrete messages than abstract ones, whereas if targeting ideal self, consumers prefer more abstract messages than concrete ones.[106]

Self-threat: compensatory consumption

Self-discrepancies between actual and ideal self suggest that critical identity threats exist,[107] and the discrepancies usually occur when the actual self is dented, such as in an occasion (e.g. performance review) where we are made conscious of our self-deficits. The dent in actual self implies an increase in the discrepancies between actual and ideal self. Self-discrepancy theory suggests that people are motivated to repair their dented self-identity (self-repair), and as consumption is able to provide meanings, consumption is a means for self-repair. For example, when our intelligence is threatened, we would choose intelligence-related products, such as fountain pens, as a way to repair our threatened identity.[108] This type of consumption is called compensatory consumption, and more details of this type of consumption can be found in Chapter 11.

8.3 SOCIAL IDENTITY

The psychological basis

Social identity is the social self in James's empirical self[109] (Table 8.2), and refers to individuals' identification of social groups, including interpersonal relationships, gender groups, ethnic backgrounds, religious beliefs, political affiliations, and professions.[110] Identification of social groups involves the roles the individuals play in these social groups,[111] and, in particular, social identity suggests that individuals can derive emotional and value significance from belonging to these groups.[112] For example, people in a family usually present emotional attachment to one another and value the views of their family members in terms of moral standards, career advice, and so on. As a result, our social identity implies that members of the same social group share knowledge and emotions about the group membership,[113] and see these groups as in-groups, as opposed to out-groups, which we do not belong to. Social identity is formed through the process of self-categorisation, social categorisation, and social comparison, and these terms are often used when discussing social identity in the literature (Table 8.5).

Table 8.5 Key processes that form social identity

Processes that form Social Identity	Definition
Self-categorisation	Self-categorisation suggests that individuals are able to categorise themselves as a member of a specific group.[114] They learn and internalise the group norms to regulate their behaviour.
Social categorisation	Social categorisation suggests that people use various characteristics (e.g. race, age, and gender) and attributes (e.g. well-dressed, well-spoken, et cetera) to categorise other people into specific social groups.[115]
Social comparison	Social comparison suggests that individuals have a tendency to compare themselves with other people in order to gain accurate self-evaluation to define their identity.[116]
Self-presentation	Self-presentation refers to people's actions to present themselves in ways that create a desired impression.[117]

Box 8.6

Social identity theory

Social identity theory, proposed by Tajfel and Turner, suggests that, as the groups we belong to can represent ourselves, we strive for the success of our groups, and this endeavour results in a positive in-group (versus out-group) bias.[118] The in-group bias indicates that we like our own groups more than out-groups,[119] which can manifest in the more positive language we use for in-groups than for out-groups,[120] and in the more positive memory we recall for in-groups than for out-groups.[121]

Implications for consumer behaviour

Strength of social identification

The strength of social identification depends on social distance, which can be reflected in the strength of social ties. For example, identifying with celebrities is a distant group identification with weak social ties,[122] whereas identifying with family members is close group identification with strong social ties.[123] The influence of close group identification is stronger than that of distant group identification.[124] As social groups dictate their own group norms, these group norms may yield different behaviour. For example, shopping with peer groups makes us buy more, but shopping with family members makes us buy less.[125] Although we may be swayed by our group identification and abandon our own preferences, research indicates that compatibility between our consumption preferences and those of the group norms improves our well-being.[126]

The influence of strong versus weak social ties also appears between consumers and brand-as-person. For example, the strength of the "social" ties between consumers and brands explains how much they love their brands.[127]

Reference groups

There are three types of reference groups:

- Membership groups: the groups we belong to, which reflect an actual social self
- Aspirational groups: the groups we want to belong to, which reflect an ideal social self; positive out-groups, such as celebrities
- Dissociative groups: the groups we want to avoid; negative out-groups

Brands often used by specific reference groups imply specific brand meanings associated with those groups, and people are able to infer and appropriate these meanings to construct their identity.[128] As a result, they prefer brands used by their membership groups and aspirational groups,[129] but avoid brands used by dissociative groups.[130]

Social defaults: the power of strangers

Social defaults suggest that we tend to mimic other people's choices even those other people who are strangers to us: the observed choices become our choice defaults.[131] This mimicry significantly increases if we believe the strangers to be our in-group members,[132] and the in-group suggestion can be framed simply by situations and locations. For example, in a series of field experiments in hotels, Goldstein et al. compared the effectiveness of traditional appeal and grouping appeals in encouraging hotel guests to reuse towels.[133] The traditional appeal focused only on the environmental impact of the reuse behaviour, whilst the grouping appeals emphasised the fact that the majority of hotel guests (or people in general) reused their towels. The most effective appeal was "the majority of *the guests staying in this room* reuse their towels", followed by "the majority of *this hotel's guests* reuse their towels." The more specific grouping, the more impact, and the least effective approach was the traditional appeal which encouraged about 10% less guests to reuse their towels.

Social defaults go beyond our product choice and brand choice: people mimic each other's emotion in a social environment. For example, Ramanathan and McGill simulated a cinema environment and found that their research participants' moment-to-moment reactions changed to be more in line with those of the other person with whom they watched the movie.[134]

Specifically, when the research participants looked at each other at the same time, they appeared to note whether the other person's face expressed the same or different emotion than their own. Congruity of expressions increased their emotional expression for a few more seconds and incongruity moderated, also for a few more seconds, their subsequent expressions to be more in line with the observed than those moments when they did not share a look.

Social threats

Discrepancies between actual and ideal social selves

The reason that people engage in identity-consistent purchases (i.e. self-brand congruence discussed in the previous section) is because of their social motives for seeking self-enhancement,[135] which is manifested in choosing identity-consistent brands with their aspirational groups.[136] However, if people face threats of not being accepted by their membership groups, their behaviour, including consumer behaviour, focuses on identity-consistency with their membership groups for self-verification purposes.[137]

Social rejections

Social rejections can also result in the discrepancies between actual and ideal social selves. For example, we think we are knowledgeable, but our knowledge is rejected by our membership groups. Knowledge seeking is a common behaviour before we determine what to purchase. If our knowledge of products is rejected, we would become less open to external information[138] but, at the same time, be more willing to display our knowledge.[139] In addition, the rejection can come from our aspirational reference groups, which, for example, can be represented by aspirational brands. For example, luxury brands' sales assistants sometimes demonstrate a snobbish demeanour towards those customers who may not be seen as belonging to the luxury market. In this case, rejections encourage conformity in such a way that we increase our efforts to affiliate with and gain approval from the rejecting.[140] As a result, we would desire the brand even more despite the snobbery.[141]

8.4 CULTURE AND THE SELF: SELF-CONSTRUAL

The psychological basis

Self-construal is referred to as independence versus interdependence of self-construal,[142] and also known as individualism versus collectivism. Individuals with independent self-construal see themselves as autonomous, having control of their own fate and motivated to achieve excellence for themselves. In contrast, individuals with interdependent self-construal view themselves as intertwined with their significant others (i.e. a highly selective in-group members, such as family). They focus on fitting in, so they have skills and willingness to adjust to their social environment by attending to the needs, desires, and goals of their significant others. For example, students with interdependent self-construal tend to study hard for others, such as their parents, whereas students with independent self-construal tend to study hard for themselves.[143]

Different self-construal influences how we think, what we feel, and why we are motivated,[144] and this influence works both at explicit and implicit levels.[145] For example, as people with interdependent self-construal focus on fitting-in with their social environment, they have learned to adapt to different identities across different social situations. Although identity-inconsistence is common in, for example, East Asian cultures, Western cultures with independent self-construal emphasise identity-consistence.[146] As a result, identity inconsistence reduces subjective wellbeing in people from cultures with independent self-construal, but does not influence those from cultures with interdependent self-construal.[147]

Implications for consumer behaviour

Identity-consistent consumption

As discussed in Section 8.2, consumers use brands to construct their identity. However, the decision whether to focus on their self-identity or social identity depends on the consumers' self-construal. People with independent self-construal have stronger self-differentiation goals, but people with interdependent self-construal have stronger social-belongingness goals. The former stresses self-identity through self-expression, and the latter emphasises social identity through self-improvement.[148] Therefore, when independent people are compared with an out-group, their heightened self-identity yields negative feelings towards a brand that has a consistent image with the out-group, but this does not happen for interdependent consumers.[149] In addition, compared with independent people, who do not differentiate the preferences of their in-groups or out-groups, interdependent people prefer a brand that shares their in-group members' preferences.[150]

Information processing

In general, the marketing messages or designs that are consistent with the characteristics of our self-construal are preferred (Table 8.6). However, these preferences occur only during the initial, automatic reactions to the given messages or in low-involvement situations, and disappears when more deliberative processing occurs.[151] This is because high-involvement situations trigger more effortful, analytic thinking.

Table 8.6 Preferences for marketing messages and designs: independent versus interdependent self-construal

	Independent Self-Construal	Interdependent Self-Construal
Thinking style	Analytic thinking style[152] → Content-independent information processing[153]	Holistic thinking style[154] → Content-dependent information processing[155]
Marketing message designs	• Individuality & autonomy[156] • Promotion-focus[157] • Information-orientation[158] o More susceptible to negative publicity info[159] o Less inclined to using price info to infer product quality[160]	• Interdependence & togetherness[161] • Prevention-focus[162] • Relationship-orientation[163] o Less susceptible to negative publicity info[164] o More inclined to using price info to infer product quality[165]
Creative designs	Confrontation: angular-shaped[166]	Compromising: round-shaped[167]
Brand extension	• Less likely to see an extension fit[168] • Less likely to accept moderate fit brand extensions[1691]	• More likely to see an extension fit[170] • More likely to accept moderate fit brand extensions[171]

Pleasure-seeking, impulsivity, and risk-taking behaviour

Independent self-construal focuses on the self, whereas interdependent self-construal focuses on the significant others.[172] Since people with interdependent self-construal pay attention to their significant others, they are under pressure to justify their decision. Consequently, they rely more on reason for their decisions, and focus on responsibilities, not pleasure-seeking from impulse or risky behaviour.[173] As a result, they tend to prefer cognitively superior options.[174] By contrast, people with independent self-construal seek pleasures from affectively superior options,[175] impulsive consumption,[176] and risky behaviour.[177]

—Box 8.7—

The cushion hypothesis

The cushion hypothesis has found the opposite results regarding risk-seeking behaviour between people with independent versus interdependent self-construal. The cushion hypothesis, proposed by Weber and Hsee, suggests that the social networks of people with interdependent self-construal are able to serve as a cushion to support them should they fall.[178]

For this reason, people with interdependent self-construal can be more likely to take risks than those with independent self-construal who do not have such a cushion, and the larger the size of their social networks, the more risk-seeking those people with interdependent self-construal are.[179] However, the risks people with interdependent self-construal are willing to take are financial risks, not social risks.[180]

8.5 SUMMARY

1. William James identifies three types of self-identities: the material self, the social self, and the spiritual self. The implications of self-identity in consumer behaviour rely on the material self, indicating an individual's possessions and interpersonal relationships are extended self representing the individual. Brands have meanings, user-imagery, and personality, and consumers use the underlying meanings, user-imagery, and personality of their brands to reflect and enhance their self-identities, engage in identity-consistent consumer behaviour (i.e. a consumer chooses a brand with an image that is consistent with his own; aka self-brand congruence), and connect with their brands (self-brand connection).

2. The main reason that consumers can identify with their brands is that they see a brand as person, and the concepts of brand personality and brand relationship are developed on the brand-as-person metaphor. Similar to the personality psychology, brand personality demonstrates five dimensions (sincerity, excitement, competence, sophistication, and ruggedness), but different from the personality psychology, these dimensions are inconsistent across cultures. The influence of which dimensions of brand personality are the strongest is inconclusive, given that different people prefer different personalities.

3. Brand relationship is an extension of brand personality, and implies consumers' ability to interact with the brand-person in order to form a relationship. The development of brand relationship is based on interpersonal relationship literature. There are different types of brand relationship, including close friendships, flings, parent–child, master–slave, and so on. Similar to close interpersonal relationships, brand relationships are able to help consumers to shelter from both physical and social pains. However, during brand transgressions, strong brand relationships do not necessarily suggest that consumers would maintain their loyalty. This is also similar to close interpersonal relationships, as brand transgressions represent betrayal, which people may find it difficult to overcome.

4. Higgins's self-discrepancy theory suggests that individuals experience negative emotions if discrepancies exist between actual and ideal self and between actual and ought self, and that they are motivated to remove negative emotions by minimising our self-discrepancies. Actual and ideal self are highly correlated, but when actual self is threatened or damaged, the gap between actual and ideal self would enlarge. When it

occurs, people would use consumption to repair their threatened/damaged identity by buying or using a brand or a product that signals their ideal self. This consumption is called compensatory consumption.

5. Social identity is the social self in James's empirical self, and formed through the process of self-categorisation, social categorisation, and social comparison. Social identity theory suggests that we usually demonstrate a positive in-group (versus out-group) bias, indicating that we like our own groups more and tend to behave in a manner to please our in-group members. For example, shopping with peer groups makes us buy more, but with family members makes us buy less.

6. There are three types of reference groups: membership groups, aspirational groups, and dissociative groups. Membership groups are the groups we belong to, which reflect an actual social self. Aspirational groups are the groups we want to belong to, which reflect an ideal social self. Dissociative groups are the groups we want to avoid being associated with. Brands often used by specific reference groups imply specific brand meanings associated with those groups, and peoples are able to infer and appropriate these meanings to construct their identity. As a result, they prefer brands used by their membership groups and aspirational groups, but avoid brands used by dissociative groups.

7. Social defaults suggest that we tend to mimic other people's choice even if those other people are strangers to us. That is, the observed choices become our choice default. This mimicry significantly increases if we believe the strangers to be our in-group members. Social defaults go beyond our product choice and brand choice: people mimic each other's emotion in a social environment. For example, in a cinema, we moderate our emotions because of the emotions demonstrated by other audience members even if we do not know them.

8. People with independent self-construal focus on self-expression, and their information process is characterised as analytic, context-independent thinking, preferring information that is promotion-focused and can separate them from others. People with interdependent self-construal focus on relationships, and their information process is characterised as holistic, context-dependent thinking, preferring information that is prevention-focused and can signify their social belongingness. However, their holistic thinking occurs for low-involvement products, brands, and situations. When involvement increases, deliberative information process is called for and, as a result, their information process mode is changed to analytic thinking.

DISCUSSION QUESTIONS

1. Discuss the role of self-identity in consumer behaviour.
2. Discuss the role of social identity in consumer behaviour.
3. Discuss how the brand-as-person metaphor influences consumer behaviour.
4. Discuss the influence of self-construal in consumer behaviour.

FURTHER READING

- Belk, R. W. (2013). Extended Self in a Digital World. *Journal of Consumer Research*, 40(October), 477–499.
- Mandel, N., Rucker, D. D., Levav, J., & Galinsky, A. D. (2017). The Compensatory Consumer Behavior Model: How Self-Discrepancies Drive Consumer Behavior. *Journal of Consumer Psychology*, 27(1), 133–146.
- MacInnis, D. J., & Folkes, V. S. (2017). Humanizing Brands: When Brands Seem to Be Like Me, Part of Me, and in a Relationship with Me. *Journal of Consumer Psychology*, 27(3), 355–374.
- Oyserman, D. (2009). Identity-Based Motivation: Implications for Action-Readiness, Procedural-Readiness, and Consumer Behavior. *Journal of Consumer Psychology*, 19(3), 250–260.
- Strizhakova, Y., & Coulter, R. (2019). Consumer Cultural Identity: Local and Global Cultural Identities and Measurement Implications. *International Marketing Review*, 36(5), 610–627.

NOTES

1. Belk, R. W. (1988). Possessions and the Extended Self. *Journal of Consumer Research*, 15(September), 139–168.
2. Chernev, A., Hamilton, R., & Gal, D. (2011). Competing for Consumer Identity: Limits to Self-Expression and the Perils of Lifestyle Branding. *Journal of Marketing*, 75(May), 66–82.
3. James, W. (1890). *The Principles of Psychology* (Vol. I). New York: Henry Folt and Company.
4. Campbell, M. C. (1990). Self-Esteem and Clarity of the Self-Concept. *Journal of Personality and Social Psychology*, 59(3), 538–549.
5. Usborne, E., & Taylor, D. M. (2010). The Role of Cultural Identity Clarity for Self-Concept Clarity, Self-Esteem, and Subjective Well-Being. *Personality and Social Psychology Bulletin*, 36(7), 883–897; Hogg, M. A. (2000). Subjective Uncertainty Reduction through Self-Categorization: A Motivational Theory of Social Identity Processes. *European Review of Social Psychology*, 11(1), 223–255.
6. Ethier, K. A., & Deaux, K. (1994). Negotiating Social Identity When Contexts Change: Maintaining Identification and Responding to Threat. *Journal of Personality and Social Psychology*, 67(2), 243–251.
7. Donahue, E. M., Robins, R. W., Roberts, B. W., & John, O. P. (1993). The Divided Self: Concurrent and Longitudinal Effects of Psychological Adjustment and Social Roles on Self-Concept Differentiation. *Journal of Personality and Social Psychology*, 64(5), 834–846.
8. Escalas, J. E., & Bettman, J. R. (2003). You Are What They Eat: The Influence of Reference Groups on Consumers' Connections to Brands. *Journal of Consumer Psychology*, 13(3), 339–348.
9. Ibid.

10. Swann, W. B., Jr., Pelham, B. W., & Krull, D. S. (1989). Agreeable Fancy or Disagreeable Truth? Reconciling Self-Enhancement and Self-Verification. *Journal of Personality and Social Psychology, 57*(5), 782–791.

11. Burke, P. J., & Stets, J. E. (1999). Trust and Commitment through Self-Verification. *Social Psychology Quarterly, 62*(4), 347–360.

12. Leary, M. R., & Tangney, J. P. (2003). The Self as an Organizing Construct in the Behavioral and Social Sciences. In M. R. Leary & J. P. Tangney (eds), *Handbook of Self and Identity* (pp. 3–14). New York: Guilford Press; Epstein, S. (1973). The Self-Concept Revisited or a Theory of a Theory. *American Psychologist, 28*(May), 404–416.

13. James, *Principles of Psychology*.

14. Devos, T., & Banaji, M. R. (2003). Implicit Self and Identity. In M. R. Leary & J. P. Tangney (eds), *Handbook of Self and Identity* (pp. 153–175). New York: Guilford Press.

15. Belk, Possessions and the Extended Self.

16. Gardner, B. B., & Levy, S. J. (1955). The Product and the Brand. *Harvard Business Review, 3*(March/April), 33–39.

17. Sirgy, M. J. (1982). Self-Concept in Consumer Behavior: A Critical Review. *Journal of Consumer Research, 9*(December), 287–300.

18. Aaker, J. L. (1997). Dimensions of Brand Personality. *Journal of Marketing Research, 34*(August), 347–356.

19. Levy, S. J. (1959). Symbols for Sale. *Harvard Business Review, 37*(July-August), 117–124.

20. Dittmar, H. (1992). *The Social Psychology of Material Possessions: To Have Is To Be*. London: Simon & Schuster.

21. Sirgy, M. J., Johar, J. S., Samli, A. C., & Claiborne, C. B. (1991). Self-Congruity versus Functional Congruity: Predictors of Consumer Behavior. *Journal of the Academy of Marketing Science, 19*(4), 363–375.

22. Graeff, T. R. (1996). Image Congruence Effects on Product Evaluations: The Role of Self-Monitoring and Public/Private Consumption. *Psychology & Marketing, 13*(5), 481–499.

23. Jamal, A. (2001). Consumers and Brands: A Study of the Impact of Self-Image Congruence on Brand Preference and Satisfaction. *Marketing Intelligence & Planning, 19*(7), 482–492.

24. Hosany, S., & Maritin, D. (2012). Self-Image Congruence in Consumer Behavior. *Journal of Business Research, 65*(5), 685–691.

25. Kressmann, F., Sirgy, M. J., Herrmann, A., Huber, F., Huber, S., & Lee, D.-J. (2006). Direct and Indirect Effects of Self-Image Congruence on Brand Loyalty. *Journal of Business Research, 59*(9), 955–964.

26. Malär, L., Krohmer, H., Hoyer, W. D., & Nyffenegger, B. (2011). Emotional Brand Attachment and Brand Personality: The Relative Importance of the Actual and Ideal Self. *Journal of Marketing, 75*(July), 35–52.

27. Chugani, S. K., Irwin, J. R., & Redden, J. P. (2015). Happily Ever After: The Effect of Identity-Consistency on Product Satiation. *Journal of Consumer Research, 42*(December), 564–577.

28. Stokburger-Sauer, N., Ratneshwar, S., & Sen, S. (2012). Drivers of Consumer-Brand Identification. *International Journal of Research in Marketing, 29*(4), 406–418.

29. Fournier, S. (1994). *A Consumer–Brand Relationship Framework for Strategic Brand Management* (PhD Unpublished doctoral thesis). University of Florida, Gainesville, FL.

30. Escalas & Bettman, You Are What They Eat.

31. Granitz, N., & Forman, H. (2015). Building Self-Brand Connections: Exploring Brand Stories Through a Transmedia Perspective. *Journal of Brand Management, 22*(1), 38–59.

32. Chaplin, L. N., & John, D. R. (2005). The Development of Self-Brand Connections in Children and Adolescents. *Journal of Consumer Research, 32*(June), 119–129.

33. Bhattacharya, C. B., & Sen, S. (2003). Consumer–Company Identification: A Framework for Understanding Consumers' Relationships with Companies. *Journal of Marketing, 67*(April), 76–88; Wolter, J. S., Brach, S., Cronin Jr., J. J., & Bonn, M. (2016). Symbolic Drivers of Consumer–Brand Identification and Disidentification. *Journal of Business Research, 69*(2), 785–793.

34. Moore, D. J., & Homer, P. M. (2008). Self-Brand Connections: The Role of Attitude Strength and Autobiographical Memory Primes. *Journal of Business Research, 61*(7), 707–714.

35. Tuškej, U., Golob, U., & Podnar, K. (2013). The Role of Consumer–Brand Identification in Building Brand Relationships. *Journal of Business Research, 66*(1), 53–59.

36. Stokburger-Sauer et al., Drivers of Consumer–Brand Identification.

37. Eelen, J., Özturan, P., & Verlegh, P. W. J. (2017). The Differential Impact of Brand Loyalty on Traditional and Online Word of Mouth: The Moderating Roles of Self-Brand Connection and the Desire to Help the Brand. *International Journal of Research in Marketing, 34*(4), 872–891.

38. Hollebeek, L. D., Glynn, M. S., & Brodie, R. J. (2014). Consumer Brand Engagement in Social Media: Conceptualization, Scale Development and Validation. *Journal of Interactive Marketing, 28*(2), 149–165.

39. Lam, S. K., Ahearne, M., Hu, Y., & Schillewaert, N. (2010). Resistance to Brand Switching When a Radically New Brand Is Introduced: A Social Identity Theory Perspective. *Journal of Marketing, 74*(November), 128–146.

40. Bhattacharya & Sen, Consumer–Company Identification.

41. Ahluwalia, R., Burnkrant, R. E., & Unnava, H. R. (2000). Consumer Response to Negative Publicity: The Moderating Role of Commitment. *Journal of Marketing, 37*(May), 203–214; Hess, J., Ronald L., Ganesan, S., & Klein, N. (2003). Service Failure and Recovery: The Impact of Relationship Factors on Customer Satisfaction. *Journal of the Academy of Marketing Science, 31*(2), 127–145.

42. Cheng, S. Y. Y., White, T. B., & Chaplin, L. N. (2012). The Effects of Self-Brand Connections on Responses to Brand Failure: A New Look at the Consumer–Brand Relationship. *Journal of Consumer Psychology, 22*(2), 280–288; Lisjak, M., Lee, A. Y., & Gardner, W. L. (2012). When a Threat to the Brand Is a Threat to the Self: The Importance of Brand Identification and Implicit Self-Esteem in Predicting Defensiveness. *Personality and Social Psychology Bulletin, 20*(10), 1–13.

43. Lisjak et al., When a Threat to the Brand Is a Threat to the Self.

44. Cheng et al., The Effects of Self-Brand Connections on Responses to Brand Failure.

45. Lisjak et al., When a Threat to the Brand Is a Threat to the Self; Cheng et al., The Effects of Self-Brand Connections on Responses to Brand Failure.

46. Pervin, L. A., Cervone, D., & John, O. P. (2005). *Personality: Theory and Research* (ninth edn). Hoboken, NJ: John Wiley & Sons, Inc.

47. John, O. P., Angleitner, A., & Ostendorf, F. (1988). The Lexical Approach to Personality: A Historical Review of Trait Taxonomic Review. *European Journal of Personality, 2*(3), 171–203.

48. Goldberg, L. R. (1981). Language and Individual Difference: The Search for Universals in Personality Lexicons. In L. Wheeler (ed.), *Review of Personality and Social Psychology* (Vol. 2, pp. 141–165). Beverly Hills: Sage; McCrae, R. R., & Costa, P. T., Jr. (1985). Updating Norman's "Adequate Taxonomy": Intelligence and Personality Dimensions in Natural Language and in Questionnaires. *Journal of Personality and Social Psychology, 1985*(49), 3.

49. Eysenck, H. J. (1947). *Dimensions of Personality*. London: Routledge.

50. Eysenck, H. J. (1969). The Biological Basis of Personality. In H. J. Eysenck & S. B. G. Eysenck (eds), *Personality Structure and Measurement* (pp. 49–62). London: Routledge & Kegan.

51. Cattell, R. B. (1965). *The Scientific Analysis of Personality*. Middlesex: Penguin Books.

52. Goldberg, Language and Individual Difference; McCrae et al., Updating Norman's "Adequate Taxonomy".

53. Aaker, Dimensions of Brand Personality.

54. Rolland, J.-P. (2002). The Cross-Cultural Generalizability of the Five-Factor Model of Personality. In R. R. McCrae & J. Allik (eds), *The Five-Factor Model of Personality Across Cultures* (pp. 7–28). New York: Klumwer Academic/Plenum Publishers.

55. Aaker, J. L., Benet-Martinez, V., & Garolera, J. (2001). Consumption Symbols as Carriers of Culture: A Study of Japanese and Spanish Brand Personality Constructs. *Journal of Personality and Social Psychology, 81*(3), 492–508.

56. Gosling, S., Rentfrow, P. J., & Swann Jr., W. B. (2003). A Very Brief Measure of the Big-Five Personality Domains. *Journal of Research in Personality, 37*(6), 504–528.

57. Aaker, J. L. (1997). Dimensions of Brand Personality. *Journal of Marketing Research, 34*(August), 347–356.

58. Gosling, S., Rentfrow, P. J., & Swann Jr., W. B. (2003). A Very Brief Measure of the Big-Five Personality Domains. *Journal of Research in Personality, 37*(6), 504–528.

59. Aaker, Dimensions of Brand Personality.

60. Fournier, S. (2009). Lessons Learned about Consumers' Relationships with Their Brands. In D. J. MacInnes, C. W. Park, & J. R. Priester (eds), *Handbook of Brand Relationships* (pp. 5–23). New York: Society for Consumer Psychology; Fournier, S. (1998). Consumer and Their Brands: Developing Relationship Theory in Consumer Research. *Journal of Consumer Research, 24*(March), 343–373.

61. Brown, J. L., Sheffield, D., Leary, M. R., & Robinson, M. E. (2003). Social Support and Experimental Pain. *Psychosomatic Medicine, 65*(2), 276–283; Montoya, P., Larbig, W., Braun, C., Preissl, H., & Birbaumer, N. (2004). Influence of Social Support and Emotional Context on Pain Processing and Magnetic Brain Responses in Fibromyalgia. *Arthritis & Rheumatology, 50*(12), 4035–4044; Younger, J., Aaron, A., Parke, S., Chatterjee, N., & Mackey, S. (2010). Viewing Pictures of a Romantic Partner Reduces Experimental Pain: Involvement of Neutral Reward Systems. *PLoS One, 5*(10), e13309.

62. Reimann, M., Nuñez, S., & Castaño, R. (2017). Brand-Aid. *Journal of Consumer Research, 44*(October), 673–691.

63. Mourey, J. A., Olson, J. G., & Yoon, C. (2017). Products As Pals: Engaging with Anthropomorphic Products Mitigates the Effects of Social Exclusion. *Journal of Consumer Research, 44*(August), 414–431.

64. Bengtsson, A. (2003). Towards a Critique of Brand Relationships. In P. A. Keller & D. W. Rook (eds), *NA – Advances in Consumer Research* (Vol. 30, pp. 154–158). Valdosta, GA: Association for Consumer Research.

65. Huang, H. H., & Mitchell, V.-W. (2014). The Role of Imagination and Brand Personification in Brand Relationships. *Psychology & Marketing, 31*(1), 38–47.

66. Valette-Florence, P., Guizani, H., & Merunka, D. (2011). The Impact of Brand Personality and Sales Promotions on Brand Equity. *Journal of Business Research, 64*(1), 24–28.

67. Krohmer, H., Lucia, M., & Bettina, N. (2006). The Interaction between a Brand's Personality and Its Consumers: Performance Implications and Implementation Issues. Paper presented at the the 35th EMAC Conference, Athens, Greece.

68. Louis, D., & Lombart, C. (2010). Impact of Brand Personality on Three Major Relational Consequences (Trust, Attachment, and Commitment to the Brand). *Journal of Product & Brand Management, 19*(2), 114–130.

69. Sung, Y., & Kim, J. (2010). Effects of Brand Personality on Brand Trust and Brand Affect. *Psychology & Marketing, 27*(7), 639–661.

70. Wang, X., & Yang, Z. (2008). Does Country-of-Origin Matter in the Relationship between Brand Personality and Purchase Intention in Emerging Economies? Evidence from China's Auto Industry. *International Marketing Review, 25*(4), 458–474.

71. Freling, T. H., & Forbes, L. P. (2005). An Examination of Brand Personality through Methodological Triangulation. *Journal of Brand Management, 13*(2), 148–162.

72. Park, J. K., & John, D. R. (2010). Got to Get You Into My Life: Do Brand Personalities Rub Off on Consumers? *Journal of Consumer Research, 37*(December), 655–669.

73. Aaker, J. L., Fournier, S., & Brasel, S. A. (2004). When Good Brands Do Bad. *Journal of Consumer Research, 31*(June), 1–16; Sundar, A., & Noseworthy, T. J. (2016). Too Exciting to Fail, Too Sincere to Succeed: The Effects of Brand Personality on Sensory Disconfirmation. *Journal of Consumer Research, 43*(June), 44–67.

74. Freling, T. H., Crosno, J. L., & Henard, D. H. (2011). Brand Personality Appeal: Conceptualization and Empirical Validation. *Journal of the Academy of Marketing Science, 39*(3), 392–406.

75. Sundar & Noseworthy, Too Exciting to Fail, Too Sincere to Succeed.

76. Aaker et al., When Good Brands Do Bad.

77. Sung & Kim, Effects of Brand Personality on Brand Trust and Brand Affect; Eisend, M., & Stokburger-Sauer, N. E. (2013). Brand Personality: A Meta-Analytic Review of Antecedents and Consequences. *Marketing Letters, 24*(3), 205–216; Maehle, N., Otnes, C., & Supphellen, M. (2011). Consumers' Perceptions of the Dimensions of Brand Personality. *Journal of Consumer Behaviour, 10*(5), 290–303.

78. Ang, S. H., & Lim, E. A. C. (2006). The Influence of Metaphors and Product Type on Brand Personality Perceptions and Attitudes. *Journal of Advertising, 35*(2), 39–53; Sundar & Noseworthy, Too Exciting to Fail, Too Sincere to Succeed.

79. Eisend & Stokburger-Sauer, Brand Personality.

80. Ang & Lim, The Influence of Metaphors.

81. Swaminathan, V., Stilley, K. M., & Ahluwalia, R. (2009). When Brand Personality Matters: The Moderating Role of Attachment Styles. *Journal of Consumer Research, 35*(April), 985–1002.

82. Sweeney, J. C., & Brand, C. (2006). Brand Personality: Exploring the Potential to Move from Factor Analytical to Circumplex Models. *Psychology & Marketing, 23*(8), 639–663.

83. Mathur, P., Jain, S., & Maheswaran, D. (2012). Consumers' Implicit Theories About Personality Influence Their Brand Personality Judgments. *Journal of Consumer Psychology, 22*(4), 545–557.

84. Dweck, C. S., & Leggett, E. L. (1988). A Social-Cognitive Approach to Motivation and Personality. *Psychological Review, 95*(2), 256–273.

85. Aaker et al., When Good Brands Do Bad.

86. Reimann, M., Castaño, R., Zaichkowsky, J., & Bechara, A. (2012). How We Relate to Brands: Psychological and Neurophysiological Insights Into Consumer-Brand Relationship. *Journal of Consumer Psychology, 22*(1), 128–142.

87. Heath, R., Brandt, D., & Nairn, A. (2006). Brand Relationships: Strengthened by Emotion, Weakened by Attention. *Journal of Advertising Research, 46*(December), 410–419.

88. Hudson, S., Huang, L., Roth, M. S., & Madden, T. J. (2016). The Influence of Social Media Interactions on Consumer-Brand Relationships: A Three-Country Study of Brand Perceptions and Marketing Behaviors. *International Journal of Research in Marketing, 33*(1), 27–41.

89. Shen, H., & Sengupta, J. (2018). Word of Mouth Versus Word of Mouse: Speaking about a Brand Connects You to It More Than Writing Does. *Journal of Consumer Research, 45*(October), 595–614.

90. Ahluwalia, R., Burnkrant, R. E., & Unnava, H. R. (2000). Consumer Response to Negative Publicity: The Moderating Role of Commitment. *Journal of Marketing, 37*(May), 203–214; Hess, J., Ronald L., Ganesan, S., & Klein, N. (2003). Service Failure and Recovery: The Impact of Relationship Factors on Customer Satisfaction. *Journal of the Academy of Marketing Science, 31*(2), 127–145.

91. Montgomery, N. V., Raju, S., Desai, K. K., & Unnava, H. R. (2018). When Good Consumers Turn Bad: Psychological Contract Breach in Committed Brand Relationships. *Journal of Consumer Psychology, 28*(3), 437–449.

92. Grégoire, Y., Tripp, T. M., & Legoux, R. (2009). When Customer Love Turns into Lasting Hate: The Effects of Relationship Strength and Time on Customer Revenge and Avoidance. *Journal of Marketing, 73*(November), 18–32.

93. Johnson, A. R., Matear, M., & Thomson, M. (2011). A Coal in the Heart: Self-Relevance as a Post-Exit Predictor of Consumer Anti-Brand Actions. *Journal of Consumer Research, 38*(June), 108–125.

94. Montgomery et al., When Good Consumers Turn Bad.

95. Higgins, E. T. (1987). Self-Discrepancy: A Theory Relating Self and Affect. *Psychological Review, 94*(3), 319–340.

96. Abel, J. I., Buff, C. L., & O'Neill, J. C. (2013). Actual Self-Concept versus Ideal Self-Concept: An Examination of Image Congruence and Consumers in the Health Club Industry. *Sport, Business and Management: An International Journal, 3*(1), 78–96; Huber, F., Eisele, A., & Myeyer, F. (2018). The Role of Actual, Ideal, and Ought Self-Congruence in the Consumption of Hedonic versus Utilitarian Brands. *Psychology & Marketing, 35*(1), 47–63; Japutra, A., Ekinci, Y., & Simkin, L. (2019). Self-Congruence, Brand Attachment and Compulsive Buying. *Journal of Business Research, 99*, 456–463; Malär, L., Krohmer, H., Hoyer, W. D., & Nyffenegger, B. (2011). Emotional Brand Attachment and Brand Personality: The Relative Importance of the Actual and Ideal Self. *Journal of Marketing, 75*(July), 35–52.

97. Koo, W., Cho, E., & Kim, Y.-K. (2014). Actual and Ideal Self-Congruity Affecting Consumers' Emotional and Behavioral Responses toward an Online Store. *Computers in Human Behavior, 36*, 147–153.

98. Back, M. D., Stopfer, J. M., Vazire, S., Gaddis, S., Schmukle, S. C., Egloff, B., & Gosling, S. D. (2010). Facebook Profiles Reflect Actual Personality, Not Self-Idealization. *Psychological Science, 21*(3), 372–374.

99. Malär et al., Emotional Brand Attachment and Brand Personality.

100. Kressmann, F., Sirgy, M. J., Herrmann, A., Huber, F., Huber, S., & Lee, D.-J. (2006). Direct and Indirect Effects of Self-Image Congruence on Brand Loyalty. *Journal of Business Research, 59*(9), 955–964; Wallace, E., Buil, I., & de Chernatony, L. (2017). Consumers' Self-Congruence with a "Liked" Brand: Cognitive Network Influence and Brand Outcomes. *European Journal of Marketing, 51*(2), 367–390.

101. Graeff, T. R. (1997). Consumption Situations and the Effects of Brand Image on Consumers' Brand Evaluations. *Psychology & Marketing, 14*(1), 49–70.

102. Sirgy, M. J., Lee, D.-J., Johar, J. S., & Tidwell, J. (2008). Effect of Self-Congruity with Sponsorship on Brand Loyalty. *Journal of Business Research, 61*(10), 1091–1097.

103. Giroux, M., & Grohmann, B. (2015). Activating Multiple Facets of the Self: How Identity Facets and Brand Personality Can Influence Self-Brand Connections. In D. Diehl & C. Yoon (eds), *NA – Advances in Consumer Research* (Vol. 43, pp. 538–539). Duluth, MN: Association for Consumer Research.

104. Ibid.

105. Zhu, X., Teng, L., Foti, L., & Yuan, Y. (2019). Using Self-Congruence Theory to Explain the Interaction Effects of Brand Type and Celebrity Type on Consumer Attitude Formation. *Journal of Business Research, 103*, 304–309.

106. Kim, D. H., Yoo, J. J., & Lee, W.-N. (2018). The Influence of Self-Concept on Ad Effectiveness: Interaction between Self-Concept and Construal Levels on Effectiveness of Advertising. *Journal of Marketing Communications, 24*(7), 734–745.

107. Mandel, N., Rucker, D. D., Levav, J., & Galinsky, A. D. (2017). The Compensatory Consumer Behavior Model: How Self-Discrepancies Drive Consumer Behavior. *Journal of Consumer Psychology, 27*(1), 133–146.

108. Gao, L., Wheeler, S. C., & Shiv, B. (2009). The 'Shaken Self': Product Choices as a Means of Restoring Self-View Confidence. *Journal of Consumer Research, 36*(June), 29–38.

109. James, *The Principles of Psychology*.

110. Deaux, K., Reid, A., Mizrahi, K., & Ethier, K. (1995). Parameters of Social Identity. *Journal of Personality and Social Psychology, 68*(2), 280–291.

111. Roberts, B. W., & Donahue, E. M. (1994). One Personality, Multiple Selves: Integrating Personality and Social Roles. *Journal of Personality, 62*(2), 199–218.

112. Tajfel, H. (1982). Social Psychology of Intergroup Relations. *Annual Review of Psychology, 33*, 1–39.

113. Smith, E. R., & Mackie, D. M. (2007). *Social Psychology* (third edn). New York: Psychology Press.

114. Turner, J. C., Oakes, P. J., Reicher, S. D., & Wetherell, M. S. (1987). *Rediscovering the Social Group: A Self-Categorization Theory*. Oxford: Basil Blackwell.

115. Turner, J. C. (1985). Social Categorization and the Self-concept: A Social Cognitive Theory of Group Behavior. *Advances in Group Processes: Theory and Research, 2*, 77–122.

116. Festinger, L. (1954). A Theory of Social Comparison Processes. *Human Relations, 7*(2), 117–140.

117. Goffman, E. (1959). *The Presentation of Self in Everyday Life*. London: The Penguin Press.

118. Tajfel, H., & Turner, J. (1979). An Integrative Theory of Intergroup Conflict. In G. A. Williams & S. Worchel (eds), *The Social Psychology of Intergroup Relations* (pp. 33–47). Belmont, CA: Wadsworth.

119. Otten, S., & Wentura, D. (2001). Self-Anchoring and in-Group Favoritism: An Individual Profiles Analysis. *Journal of Experimental Social Psychology, 37*(6), 525–532.

120. Maass, A. (1999). Linguistic Intergroup Bias: Stereotype Perpetuation through Language. *Advances in Experimental Social Psychology, 31*, 79–121.

121. Sherman, J. W., Klein, S. B., Laskey, A. & Wyer, N. A. (1998). Intergroup Bias in Group Judgment Processes: The Role of Behavioral Memories. *Journal of Experimental Social Psychology, 34*(1), 51–65.

122. Escalas, J. E., & Bettman, J. R. (2017). Connecting with Celebrities: How Consumers Appropriate Celebrity Meanings for a Sense of Belonging. *Journal of Advertising, 46*(2), 297–308.

123. Epp, A. M., & Price, L. L. (2008). Family Identity: A Framework of Identity Interplay in Consumption Practices. *Journal of Consumer Research, 35*(June), 50–70.

124. Brown, J. J., & Reingen, P. H. (1987). Social Ties and Word-of-Mouth Referral Behavior. *Journal of Consumer Research, 14*(December), 350–362.

125. Luo, X. (2005). How Does Shopping with Others Influence Impulsive Purchasing? *Journal of Consumer Psychology, 15*(4), 288–294.

126. Brick, D. J., Fitzsimons, G. M., Chartrand, T. L., & Fitzsimons, G. J. (2018). Coke vs. Pepsi: Brand Compatibility, Relationship Power, and Life Satisfaction. *Journal of Consumer Research, 44*(February), 991–1014.

127. Wallace, E., Buil, I., & de Chernatony, L. (2017). Consumers' Self-Congruence with a "Liked" Brand: Cognitive Network Influence and Brand Outcomes. *European Journal of Marketing, 51*(2), 367–390.

128. Escalas, J. E., & Bettman, J. R. (2005). Self-Construal, Reference Groups, and Brand Meaning. *Journal of Consumer Research, 32*(December), 378–389.

129. Escalas & Bettman, You Are What They Eat.

130. Berger, J., & Heath, C. (2007). Where Consumers Diverge from Others: Identity Signaling and Product Domains. *Journal of Consumer Research, 34*(August), 121–134.

131. Huh, Y. E., Vosgerau, J., & Morewedge, C. K. (2014). Social Defaults: Observed Choices Become Choice Defaults. *Journal of Consumer Research, 41*(October), 746–760.

132. Ferraro, R., Bettman, J. R., & Chartrand, T. L. (2009). The Power of Strangers: The Effect of Incidental Consumer Brand Encounters on Brand Choice. *Journal of Consumer Research, 35*(February), 729–741.

133. Goldstein, N. J., Cialdini, R. B., & Griskevicius, V. (2008). A Room with a Viewpoint: Using Social Norms to Motivate Environmental Conservation in Hotels. *Journal of Consumer Research, 35*(3), 472–482.

134. Ramanathan, S., & McGill, A. L. (2007). Consuming with Others: Social Influences on Moment-to-Moment and Retrospective Evaluations of an Experience. *Journal of Consumer Research, 34*(4), 506–524.

135. Aguirre-Rodriguez, A., Bosnjak, M., & Sirgy, M. J. (2012). Moderators of the Self-Congruity Effect on Consumer Decision-Making: A Meta-Analysis. *Journal of Business Research, 65*(8), 1179–1188.

136. Escalas & Bettman, You Are What They Eat.

137. Ibid.

138. Claus, B., Geyskens, K., Millet, K., & Dewitte, S. (2012). The Rerral Backfire Effect: The Identity-Threatening Nature of Referral Failure. *International Journal of Research in Marketing, 29*(4), 307–379.

139. Packard, G., & Wotten, D. B. (2013). Compensatory Knowledge Signaling in Consumer Word-of-Mouth. *Journal of Consumer Psychology, 23*(4), 434–450.

140. Loveland, K. E., Smmesters, D., & Mandel, N. (2010). Still Preoccupied with 1995: The Need to Belong and Preference for Nostalgic Products. *Journal of Consumer Research, 37*(October), 393–408.

141. Ward, M. K., & Dahl, D. W. (2014). Should the Devil Sell Prada? Retail Rejection Increases Aspiring Consumers' Desire for the Brand. *Journal of Consumer Research, 41*(October), 590–609.

142. Markus, H. R., & Kitayama, S. (1991). Culture and the Self: Implications for Cognition, Emotion, and Motivation. *Psychological Review, 98*(2), 224–253.

143. Ibid.

144. Ibid.

145. Cross, S. E., Morris, M. L., & Gore, J. S. (2002). Thinking about Oneself and Others: The Relational-Interdepedent Self-Construal and Social Cognition. *Journal of Personality and Social Psychology, 82*(3), 399–418.

146. Suh, E. M. (2002). Culture, Identity Consistency, and Subjective Well-Being. *Journal of Personality and Social Psychology, 83*(6), 1378–1391.

147. Ibid; Cross, S. E., Gore, J. S., & Morris, M. L. (2003). The Relational-Interdependent Self-Construal, Self-Concept Consistency, and Well-Being. *Journal of Personality and Social Psychology, 85*(5), 933–944.

148. Swaminathan, V., Page, K. L., & Gürhan-Canli, Z. (2007). "My" Brand or "Our" Brand: The Effects of Brand Relationship Dimensions and Self-Construal on Brand Evaluations. *Journal of Consumer Research, 34*(August), 248–259; Inglehart, R., & Oyserman, D. (2004). Individualism, Autonomy, Self-Expression and Human Development. In H. Vinken, J. Soeters, & P. Ester (eds), *Comparing Cultures, Dimensions of Culture in a Comparative Perspective* (pp. 74–96). Leiden: Brill; Oyserman, D., & Uskul, A. K. (2008). Individualism and Collectivisim: Societal-Level Processes with Implications for Individual-Level and Society-Level Outcomes. In F. J. R. van de Vijver, D. A. van Hermert, & Y. H. Poortinga (eds), *Multilevel Analysis of Individuals and Cultures* (pp. 145–173). Mahwah, NJ: Psychology Press.

149. Escalas & Bettman, Self-Construal, Reference Groups, and Brand Meaning.

150. Duclos, R., & Barasch, A. (2014). Prosocial Behavior in Intergroup Relations: How Donor Self-Construal and Recipient Group-Membership Shape Generosity. *Journal of Consumer Research, 41*(June), 93–108; Kramer, T., Spolter-Weisfeld, S., & Thakkar, M. (2007). The Effect of Cultural Orientation on Consumer Responses to Personalization. *Marketing Science, 26*(2), 246–258.

151. Briley, D. A., & Aaker, J. L. (2006). When Does Culture Matter? Effects of Personal Knowledge on the Correction of Culture-Based Judgments. *Journal of Marketing Research, 43*(3), 395–408; Aaker, J. L., & Maheswaran, D. (1997). The Effect of Cultural Orientation on Persuasion. *Journal of Consumer Research, 24*(December), 315–328.

152. Nisbett, R. E., Peng, K., Choi, I., & Norenzayan, A. (2001). Culture and Systems of Thought: Holistic Versus Analytic Cognition. *Psychological Review, 108*(2), 291–310.

153. de Mooij, M., & Hofstede, G. (2010). The Hofstede Model: Applications to Global Branding and Advertising Strategy and Research. *International Journal of Advertising, 29*(1), 85–110.

154. Nisbett et al., Culture and Systems of Thought.

155. de Mooij & Hofstede, The Hofstede Model.

156. Wang, C. L., Bristol, T., Mowen, J. C., & Chakraborty, G. (2000). Alternative Modes of Self-Construal: Dimensions of Connectedness-Separateness and Advertising Appeals to the Cultural and Gender-Specific Self. *Journal of Consumer Psychology, 9*(2), 107–115.

157. Aaker, J., & Lee, A. Y. (2001). "I" Seek Pleasures and "We" Avoid Pains: The Role of Self-Regulatory Goals in Information Processing and Persuasion. *Journal of Consumer Research, 28*(June), 33–49.

158. de Mooij & Hofstede, The Hofstede Model.

159. Monga, A. B., & John, D. R. (2008). When Does Negative Brand Publicity Hurt? The Moderating Influence of Analytic versus Holistic Thinking. *Journal of Consumer Psychology, 18*(4), 3210–3332.

160. Lalwani, A. K., & Shavitt, S. (2013). You Get What You Pay For? Self-Construal Influences Price-Quality Judgments. *Journal of Consumer Research, 40*(August), 255–267.
161. Wang et al., Alternative Modes of Self-Construal.
162. Aaker & Lee, "I" Seek Pleasures and "We" Avoid Pains.
163. de Mooij & Hofstede, The Hofstede Model.
164. Monga & John, When Does Negative Brand Publicity Hurt? The Moderating Influence of Analytic versus Holistic Thinking. *Journal of Consumer Psychology, 18*(4), 3210–3332.
165. Lalwani & Shavitt, You Get What You Pay For? Self-Construal Influences Price-Quality Judgments. *Journal of Consumer Research, 40*(August), 255–267.
166. Zhang, Y., Feick, L., & Price, L. J. (2006). The Impact of Self-Construal on Aesthetic Preference for Angular Versus Rounded Shapes. *Personality and Social Psychology Bulletin, 32*(6), 794–805.
167. Ibid.
168. Ahluwalia, R. (2008). How Far Can a Brand Stretch? Understanding the Role of Self-Construal. *Journal of Marketing Research, 45*(3), 337-350; Monga, A. B., & John, D. R. (2007). Cultural Differences in Brand Extension Evaluation: The Influence of Analytic versus Holistic Thinking. *Journal of Consumer Research, 33*(March), 529–536.
169. Ibid.
170. Ibid.
171. Ibid.
172 Markus & Kitayama, Culture and the Self.
173. Loewenstein, G. F. W., Elke U., Hsee, C. K., & Welch, N. (2001). Risk as Feelings. *Psychological Bulletin, 127*(2), 267–286.
174. Hong, J., & Chang, H. H. (2015). "I" Follow My Heart and "We" Rely on Reasons: The Impact of Self-Construal on Reliance on Feelings versus Reasons in Decision Making. *Journal of Consumer Research, 41*(April), 1392–1411.
175. Ibid.
176. Zhang, Y., & Shrum, L. J. (2009). The Influence of Self-Construal on Impulsive Consumption. *Journal of Consumer Research, 35*(February), 838–850; Kacen, J. J., & Lee, J. A. (2002). The Influence of Culture on Consumer Impulsive Buying Behavior. *Journal of Consumer Psychology, 12*(2), 163–176.
177. Hamilton, R. W., & Biehal, G. J. (2005). Achieving Your Goals or Protecting Their Future? The Effects of Self-View on Goals and Choices. *Journal of Consumer Research, 32*(September), 277–283.
178. Weber, E. U., & Hsee, C. K. (1998). Cross-Cultural Differences in Risk Perception, but Cross-Cultural Similarities in Attitudes towards Perceived Risk. *Management Science, 44*(9), 1205–1217.
179. Mandel, N. (2003). Shifting Selves and Decision Making: The Effects of Self-Construal Priming on Consumer Risk-Taking. *Journal of Consumer Research, 30*(June), 30–40.
180. Ibid.

9

ENVIRONMENTAL PSYCHOLOGY AND CONSUMER BEHAVIOUR

To explore, understand, and explain:

- key models of environmental psychology and their implications in consumer behaviour:
    - the Mehrabian-Russell model
    - Bitner's model of servicescape
- the psychological bases of key elements in atmospherics and their implications in consumer behaviour:
    - music
    - scents
    - lighting
    - touch

9.1 INTRODUCTION

Environmental psychology studies the relationships between individuals and their physical settings.[1] In other words, environmental psychology is concerned with people's experiences of their environment, behavioural changes as a result of the environment, and behaviours to change their environment. The implications of environmental psychology in consumer behaviour focus on consumers at the physical and virtual customer touchpoints, where there is an interaction between the environmental cues and the individual consumers. The main environmental cues that will be covered in this chapter are various atmospherics elements – music (Section 9.3), scent (Section 9.4), lighting (Section 9.5), and sense of touch (Section 9.6). Although this chapter focuses more on the customer touchpoints in a retail setting (both physical and virtual), it is noted that customer touchpoints can occur out of a store; for example, customers calling a call centre for support or being exposed to advertisements outside of a shop. Before we begin our discussion on the specific elements in consumer environmental psychology, we will first introduce two general frameworks, underpinning the influence of environmental psychology, which will now follow.

9.2 KEY MODELS OF ENVIRONMENTAL PSYCHOLOGY IN CONSUMER BEHAVIOUR

Key theories of environmental psychology

There are three main groups of theories in environmental psychology: stimulation theories, ecological psychology, and environment-centred theories (Table 9.1). Of these three groups of theories, the stimulation theories are the most extensively researched in consumer behaviour via the two most often used models, the Mehrabian–Russell model and Bitner's model of servicescapes, which will be introduced in more detail below.

Table 9.1 Key theories of environmental psychology

Key Theories	Definition
Stimulation theories	• Physical environment as a source of information[2]
	○ Types of stimulation: sensory stimulation, social stimulation, and movement[3]
	○ Dimensions of stimulation: intensity, diversity, and patterning (i.e. certainty of the stimulation)[4]
	• People have a desired level of stimulation shaped by personal characteristics and situational factors.[5]
	• *Relevance to consumer behaviour*: atmospherics in the retail setting

Key Theories	Definition
Ecological psychology	• Behaviour settings, a gestalt view of an environment, include the physical environment, the context in which the environment is situated, and the collective behavioural patterns taking place in the environment.[6]
	• With a focus on the concept that a space can be designed to facilitate the function it assumes.
	• *Relevance to consumer behaviour*: store layout
Environment-centred theories	• A branch of ecopsychology focusing on the issue of the environment's own welfare and its ability to support our own well-being. [7]
	• *Relevance to consumer behaviour*: Recycling and other sustainability-related behaviour, which will not be covered in this chapter

The Mehrabian-Russell Model

The Mehrabian–Russell model[8] has been one of the most often used models in the studies of retail environment – see Figure 9.1 for the model. This model is an extension of the stimulus–organism–response (S–O–R) paradigm (Box 9.1). It suggests that environmental input (or "stimulation" in the stimulation theories in Table 9.1) interacts with individual differences to produce the degree to which a person likes or dislikes their environment. Liking/disliking the environment has been termed as the emotional responses to the environmental input by Mehrabian and Russell, and a positive emotion (liking) produces approach behaviour such that one is inclined to stay in the environment longer, whereas a negative emotion (disliking) produces avoidance behaviour such that one intends to avoid the environment. This model has found overwhelming support for explaining consumer behaviour in the retail setting.[9]

─Box 9.1─

The Stimulus-Organism-Response (S-O-R) paradigm

The S-O-R paradigm is a revision of classical conditioning, the stimulus response theory, which suggests that a stimulus is able to produce an intended response in a subject when it is paired with something that stimulates the response. For example, Pavlov[10] paired ringing of a bell with food to stimulate a dog's production of saliva, and after a while of such pairing, the dog automatically produced saliva when hearing a bell ring even without the presence of food. The S-O-R paradigm includes "organism" in the stimulus response theory to emphasise the impact of individual

(Continued)

differences in producing a response to a stimulus.[11] Using the S–O–R paradigm, Belk[12] distinguishes situational stimuli from object stimuli in the retail environment. The object stimuli are referred to as the product stimuli, including merchandises, services, and in-store communication at the point-of-sale (e.g. buy one get one free), whereas situational stimuli, involving all other factors in the behaviour setting (using the idea from ecological psychology; see Table 9.2) of the retail environment, can be examined from five dimensions of the situation:

1. *Physical surroundings:* geographical location, décor, sounds, aromas, lighting, and visible configurations of merchandise

2. *Social surroundings:* other persons present (customers and service staff), their characteristics, their apparent roles, and interpersonal interactions

3. *Temporal perspective:* time of day, season of the year, time since last purchase, time since or until meals or payday, and time constraints to spend in the shop

4. *Task definition:* purposes for being in the retail environment, including obtaining information, shopping for self or others, shopping for hedonic reasons or functional reasons

5. *Antecedent states:* moods (e.g. anxiety, pleasantness, hostility, excitement), momentary conditions (e.g. cash on hand, fatigue, and illness)

These five dimensions are often referred to as Belk's situational taxonomy, which has laid the foundation for Baker[13] and Bitner[14] to develop the servicescape framework.

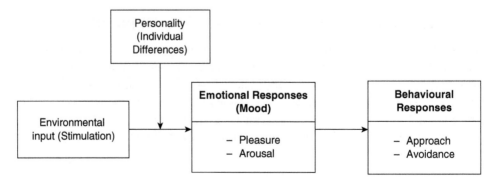

Figure 9.1   The Mehrabian–Russell Model

Adapted and revised from Mehrabian and Russell[15]

Mood - emotional responses

Mehrabian and Russell identified two dimensions of moods: pleasure and arousal (Table 9.2). Pleasure is a much more powerful predictor than arousal,[16] because the effect of arousal depends on whether the feelings of arousal are pleasant or unpleasant: if the feelings of arousal are pleasant, they are able to enhance the strength of pleasure; otherwise, pleasure would become displeasure.[17]

Table 9.2   Emotional responses in the Mehrabian–Russell model

Dimension of Emotion[a] (Mood)	Definition	Examples
Pleasure-displeasure	The degree to which one feels happy	• happy-unhappy • pleased-annoyed • satisfied-unsatisfied • contented-melancholic • hopeful-despairing • relaxed-bored
Arousal-non-arousal	The degree to which one feels stimulated and excited	• stimulated-relaxed • excited-calm • frenzied-sluggish • jittery-dull • wide-awake-sleepy • aroused-unaroused

[a.] In Mehrabian and Russell's original theorisation, another emotion, dominance (versus submissive), was included;[18] this dimension was dropped because cognition, not emotion, is involved and because the impact is deemed trivial[19]

Source: Summary based on Mehrabian & Russell[20]

Mood-based cognitive heuristic: how do I feel about it?

The inclusion of mood is the key contribution of the Mehrabian–Russell model. (In the retail environment, mood is a better term than emotion to characterise the emotional responses to the environmental input.) Mood, feelings of low intensity (see p. 127–128), is a preference for or liking of a particular environment, suggesting an experience of a vague sense of feeling good or bad without necessarily knowing why.[21] Research has shown that when people are unaware of the source of their mood, their mood biases their behaviour and evaluation of the environment.[22] For example, when a shopper is in a good mood, the servicescape would be evaluated more favourably than when in a bad mood. This is what Schwarz called the "how do I feel about it" heuristic, suggesting that people draw conclusions from their own feelings, and if they are unaware of the source of their mood, they assume the feelings are valid information to be used in evaluating the environment.[23] However, when people are aware of the source of their mood (the music), this bias disappears, and the evaluation of the environment becomes independent of mood, either a good or a bad mood.

As mood is based on a sense of familiarity, retailers are able to capitalise on the power of memory by creating a link between the brand, colour, and icon (e.g. McDonald's golden arches).[24] In other words, mood is easily manipulated through mere exposure of sensory information to form one's preferences.[25] Perhaps for this reason, most consumer research on affect deals with mood,[26] and mood is particularly relevant in the studies of atmospherics.

Bitner's model of servicescape

Whilst the Mehrabian–Russell model has been proven to be useful for examining the retail environment, it was *not* developed for the retail environment per se. Focusing on the retail environment, and extending the Mehrabian–Russell model (Figure 9.1) and Belk's situational taxonomy (Box 9.1), Bitner developed a model of servicescape (Figure 9.2).[27] Servicescape is a term coined by Boom and Bitner to combine "service" and "landscape" to refer to the environment where service is provided.[28] In this environment, physical surroundings as well as the service staff facilitate the performance of the service. As a result, primarily due to Bitner's conceptualisation, both shoppers and employees, who provide a service and may interact with shoppers, are included in the model. The interaction between shoppers and service staff constitutes social surroundings in the servicescape.

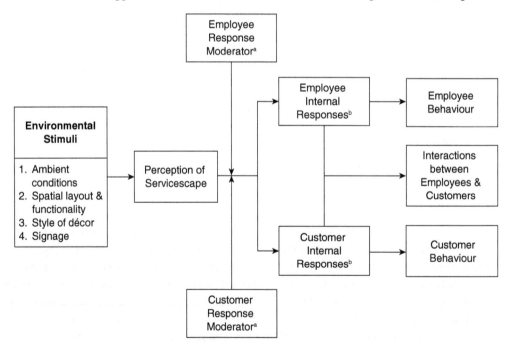

[a.] Response moderators include personal factors (e.g. personality traits and personal preferences) and situational factors (e.g. purposes for and expectations of being in the servicescape, time constraint, and momentary moods).

[b.] Internal responses include responses at levels of emotion, cognition, and physiology.

Figure 9.2   Model of servicescape

Source: Adapted and revised from Bitner[29]

The servicescape model indicates that the influence of an environment comes from the physical environment as well as the social environment. However, the research on the physical environment, especially the impact of atmospherics, is the foundation of the applications of environmental psychology in consumer behaviour, so we will only focus on atmospherics and exclude the discussion of social environment, such as the impact of service quality and crowding, from this chapter.

9.3 MUSIC

Box 9.2

Atmospherics

Atmospherics is a term coined by Kotler to describe the atmosphere elicited by the physical surroundings in a retail or commercial setting through five senses: sight, hearing, smell, touch, and taste.[30] Kotler's definition focuses on the ambient (background) elements of the design of a store, and this definition has later been extended to include socio-physical aspects of the environment.[31] This chapter will use Kotler's original definition to explore the impact of music, scent, lighting, and touch.

The psychological basis

Music has always been part of human culture. Modern research on the psychology of music can be traced back to as early as von Helmholtz[32] and Wundt.[33] Research has demonstrated that music has profound, and involuntary, influences on physiology, cognition, mood, and behaviour (Table 9.3). The impact of music on physiology, cognition, and behaviour usually works through the mood the music induces.[34] For this reason, music has been widely used for mood induction in psychological research,[35] to promote health and well-being,[36] and to improve productivity.[37] The common mood that music induces in the consumption context includes the arousal-relaxing and pleasure-sadness continua from the Mehrabian–Russell model (Table 9.2). However, the impact of music is usually subliminal; that is, consumers are unaware of the impact from music.[38]

Table 9.3 The influence of music

	Influence of Music
Physiology	Pleasant music[a] → accelerated breathing rate, heart rate, and muscular activities.[39]

(Continued)

Table 9.3   (Continued)

	Influence of Music

Cognition	• The Mozart effect,[b] a 10-minutue exposure to a Mozart sonata improved listeners' spatial IQ score by about 8 points.[40]
	• Ability to
	   o attract and to distract attention
	   o to enhance and to inhibit memory
	
	depending on how the music relates to the information that requires processing: cognitive abilities are enhanced when the type of music matches with the style of the information that is required to be processed.[41]

Mood	The influence of music on mood is the most crucial one; see Table 9.4 for more details.
Behaviour	A tendency to synchronise their motor movements with musical/sound rhythm (tempo). That is, if the tempo of the music people listen to increases, the speed of their movement during the duration of the music increases too, for example, • they cycle faster,[42] • walk faster,[43] and • eat faster.[44]

[a.] Pleasant music can be both stimulating[45] and relaxing.[46]

[b.] The Mozart effect has been called into question because of the difficulty of replicating the original study,[47] but research on the influence of music on cognition has flourished.

Music structure and mood induction

Music structure outlines the basic components that form music and includes time-, pitch-, and texture-related components.[48] Table 9.4 shows the definitions of key music components and their individual influences on mood induction. However, as a piece of music is composed of more than one component, the influences of these components are interacted, rather than independent. For example, music with fast tempo usually elicits arousal feelings,[49] but this effect of fast tempo is only pronounced for pop music, not for classical music.[50] In other words, combining the music components that have consistent effects is crucial to elicit the desire mood.

Table 9.4   Music structure and its influence on mood induction[a b]

Music Structure (and *Definition*)		Mood Induced

Time-related	**Tempo**
	The speed at which music progresses
		• In general, fast music is perceived to be more pleasant than slow music.
		   o Fast music → happiness, excitement, and liveliness
		   o Slow music → peacefulness, sadness, and gravity
		
		• Without considering the context, the preferred tempo is between 120 and 130 bpm.[c51]

Music Structure (and *Definition*)		Mood Induced
	Rhythm *The pattern of music differing in meter, sound, event density, and homogeneity*	• Firm rhythms → sacredness, dignity, robustness, and sadness • Smooth rhythms → happiness and peacefulness • Varied rhythms → joyfulness and exaltation • Irregular/rough rhythms → amusement and uneasiness
	Phrasing (or articulation) *The length of time a note sounds in comparison with the rhythmic period it occupies*	• Staccato[d] music → liveliness and energy • Legato[e] music → peacefulness, softness, and sadness.
Pitch-related	**Pitch levels**	• High pitches → gracefulness, happiness, and excitement • Low pitches → sadness and solemnity

	Melody
	The succession of notes occurring over time throughout music
		• *Pitch range:*
		  ○ Wide pitch range (more than an octave) →
		    ○ the positive feelings of brilliance and happiness
		    ○ the negative feelings of fearfulness
		  ○ Narrow pitch range (less than an octave) → delicacy, tranquillity, and sadness
		• *Melodic direction:*
		  ○ Ascending melodies → dignity and happiness
		  ○ Descending melodies → gracefulness and sadness

	Mode (or tonality) *The series of notes, arranged in a scale of ascending pitch, which provides the tonal substances of music*	• The major mode → happiness • The minor mode → sadness
	Harmony *Notes played simultaneously can be consonant or dissonant*	• Consonant harmonies → happiness and serenity • Dissonant harmonies → sadness and agitation
Texture-related	**Volume**	• Loud music → triumph and excitement • Soft music → sadness and peacefulness

(Continued)

Table 9.4   (Continued)

Music Structure (and *Definition*)	Mood Induced
Timbre *The distinctiveness in sound of the same notes played by different instruments*	• Violin sounds → sadness • Piano sounds → brilliancy, tranquillity, and sadness • Flute sounds → peacefulness
Orchestration *The sonic properties of multiple instruments weaved together*	Due to the level of complexity that is involved in orchestration, there are limited experimental studies that investigate how orchestration influences mood induction.

[a.] This table is summarised largely based on Bruner's[52] and Gabrielsson and Lindström's[53] reviews.

[b.] Moods documented in this table are the moods from the Mehrabian–Russell model; however, music is able to elicit more moods than those included in this table, including fearfulness, surprise, anger, et cetera.

[c.] This speed is similar to the speed of human natural movement.[54]

[d.] Staccato-note-filled music refers to the notes played sharply detached or separated from the others.

[e.] Legato-note-filled music refers to the notes played smoothly and connected.

Implications for consumer behaviour

Information processing

According to cognitive resource availability, music draws attention to the music itself, thereby reducing available resources for information processing.[55] For example, highly arousing music tends to draw attention to the music itself, and as a result exposure to highly arousing music, either via an advertisement[56] or in a retail setting,[57] hinders the ability to process information. However, in low-involvement conditions, it is the mood induced by the music that is more important than the ability to process information. Therefore, background music is, in fact, able to facilitate people's brand recall and enhance their positive attitudes toward the brand and advertisement in low-involvement conditions[58] where the style of music fits with the brand, product, and advertisement.[59] The fit of the music is less crucial in high-involvement conditions.

Purchase intentions: product choice and willingness to pay

The influence of music type: classic versus pop music versus . . .

Music is able to influence atmosphere in the servicescape, and consumers' purchase intentions in commercial environments, as well as their desires to socialise with other people, and this influence occurs because of the mood music elicits.[60] Different types of music elicit different moods; however, this influence does not completely depend on the types of music. There are two main factors that interact with types of music to generate the influence: (1) the fit of the music and (2) individual music preferences (Figure 9.3).

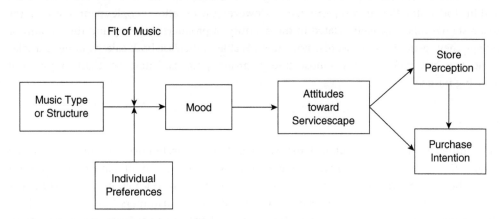

Figure 9.3 Impact of music in the servicescape

Fit of music

The fit of music can be the fit for the occasion, for the product, or for the retailer, and this fit influences how much a specific type of music is liked.[61] For example, wine shoppers tend to buy more expensive wine when exposed to classical music (versus pop music) because buying more expensive wine fits the sophisticated and upmarket stereotype of classical music.[62] Music fit does not just influence product choice, but also impacts on consumers' product evaluation and recall, as well as their willingness to pay.[63] This influence is usually implicit. For example, research showed, in a supermarket setting, French music played in the background led to French wines outselling German wines, whereas German music led to German wines outselling French wines, but the majority of the shoppers were unaware of the impact of music.[64]

Individual preferences

People who liked the music more would transfer their mood elicited from the music to the servicescape, and would then be more likely to spend more.[65] For example, the student population in North and Hargreaves's investigation in the university cafeteria may have liked both classical and pop music, and this may have reflected in their buying more expensive food when either music was played,[66] whereas pop music might be less popular with the target customers in Areni and Kim's wine cellar study, so shoppers bought more expensive wines when classical music was played in the background.[67]

The influence of music structure

Tempo

The speed of people's movements coincides with the tempo of the music (Table 9.4). That is, exposure to fast music provokes a faster pace of eating and drinking in a bar/restaurant[68] and in-store traffic flow in a supermarket.[69] However, the duration people spent in a shop (or in a restaurant) is negatively related to the quantity of products they buy and the amount of money they spend. In other words, slow music is able to increase both sales volume and sales value. This may explain why sad music leads to greater purchase intentions than happy, more arousing music.[70]

Volume

The influence of music volume depends on individual preferences or the fit of music (Figure 9.3). For example, Abercrombie & Fitch was famous in playing painfully loud music, between 85 and 90 dB, which is just below the legal limit for employees without ear protection, on purpose to drive away its unwanted (older) customers.[71] In other words, if the volume of music does not fit with the types of clientele or products the service establishment serves, the outcome may be detrimental.

Mode

Mode determines the effect of tempo. In a department store setting, the Milliman effect,[72] that slow tempo music leads to greater spending, occurs only when the music is played in minor (versus major) mode.[73] This may be because slow tempo and minor mode (or fast tempo and major mode) fit, in terms of the mood state they evoke, and therefore lead to greater enjoyment.[74]

Time perception

Music is able to shrink or expand time perception, and time perception is a critical element in service marketing. Imagine that you are waiting in a busy restaurant to be seated, reduced (or shrunk) time perception can make you more patient and wait longer whereas increased time perception may lead to impatience, which reduces the time that you would be willing to wait. Similar scenarios occur in calling centres and waiting in a queue at a bank or retail checkout. Time perception also applies to the perception of shopping duration, which determines the length a shopper spends in a shop and their purchase intentions. In general, people are willing to persist in waiting when music is played, compared with when there is no music,[75] and the impact of music structure on time perception can be found in Table 9.5.

Table 9.5 The impact of music structure on time perception

Music Structure		Impact on Time Perception
Tempo	Fast tempo (vs slow tempo)	→ time perception expanded[76]
Volume	Soft volume (vs loud volume)	→ time perception shrunk[77]
Mode	Major keys (vs minor keys)	→ time perception expanded[78]

However, increased time perception does not necessarily suggest a negative evaluation of customers' waiting or shopping experience.[79] This is because the duration of the time does not matter so much if the time is spent pleasantly, and the time would be spent pleasantly if the music played is liked by, or familiar to, the shoppers.[80] In addition to individual preferences of music, which music would be liked depends on the fit of music for the occasion. For example, in general, relaxing and soothing music decreases time perception (Table 9.5), but it increases time perception if the listener is in a state of agitation.[81] That is, for example, when consumers call service centres for support, they are usually in a state of distress or agitation, and playing more arousing/distracting music similar to their state would help decrease time perception.

9.4 SCENT

The psychological basis

Human beings are able to distinguish over 1 trillion different odours; thanks to our millions of olfactory neurons and hundreds of olfactory receptors.[82] Our sense of smell ability far outperforms the other senses in the number of different stimuli it can discriminate, and this ability implies its importance. How important is our sense of smell? We rely on our sense of smell to taste flavours. For example, without a sense of smell, Coke and Sprite would taste the same.[83] Being able to detect pleasant scents in our surroundings helps increase productivity,[84] willingness to help strangers,[85] patience for tedious tasks,[86] and problem-solving ability and creativity.[87] On the other hand, an impaired sense of smell has been linked with depression,[88] eating disorders, such as bulimia and anorexia,[89] Alzheimer's disease, and Parkinson's disease.[90]

Our sense of smell is highly connected with emotion,[91] and scents are able to evoke memories that are more emotional in nature.[92] In fact, the extent to which an odour is pleasant depends on how positive the emotions people experienced at the time were when they first smelled the odour, regardless of whether the odour is commonly considered as positive or as negative.[93] Ironically, however, the influence of scents is more impactful for cognition than for mood/emotion. Numerous studies have documented that the influence of scents on mood, though significant, is small, and that scents can be considered cognitive simulants.[94] Unlike the influence of music that follows the Mehrabian–Russell model (Figure 9.1), that of scents supports Lazarus's[95] cognitive theory of emotion, suggesting that emotion-relevant thoughts determine the type, valence, and intensity of the emotion a stimulus elicits (Figure 9.4).

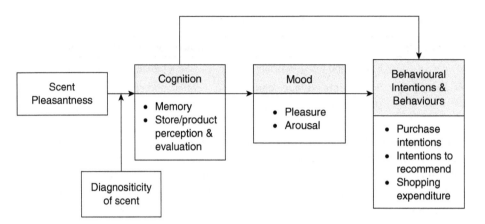

Figure 9.4   The influence of scents

Sources: Summary based on Bone and Ellen's[96] and Roschk and Hosseinpour's[97] reviews

Implications for consumer behaviour

Time perception

People in an unscented environment perceive more time elapsed than actual time passed, thereby reducing their lingering time in the shop and spending less.[98] However, in a scented environment, the degree to which the scent is pleasant (versus neutral scents) does not shrink or expand shoppers' time perception, although in the presence of pleasant ambient scents, shoppers tend to spend more time in the shop.[99]

Store/product evaluation and shopping expenditure

In the presence of a pleasant ambient scent, the store environment and products in it are evaluated more positively and favourably. The positive evaluation of the store environment and product quality is then translated into greater current[100] and future[101] spending. In particular, because of the impact of scent on cognition (Figure 9.4), pleasant ambient scents lead shoppers to spend more time evaluating product-related information,[102] which could potentially result in:

- shoppers paying more attention to and choosing unfamiliar products or brands[103]
- those who make planned, cognitive-based, purchases (as opposed to impulsive shoppers) significantly increasing their spending[104]

However, the exact effectiveness of a pleasant scent on shopping expenditure is less conclusive. In Roschk and Hosseinpour's meta-analysis of 64 articles between 1989 and 2018, they documented that shopping expenditure can be increased by 3% for an average condition of how the ambient scent is designed to emit in the shop and by an increase of as much as 23% for the most favourable scents.[105]

Diagnositicity of scent

What scent is a pleasant scent? The answer is determined by diagnositicity of scent in Figure 9.4. Diagnositicity, also known as scent congruence, is referred to as the extent to which the scent is able to help determine the quality of the object being evaluated. For example, the scent of lemon suggests cleanness, and the diagnositicity of the lemon scent for a cleaner product is high, but for furniture is low. As a result, diagnositicity of scent has a cognitive connotation.

If the scent provides helpful information that helps people to access, process, and elaborate information from their memory, their evaluation of the store, product or service would be more positive, and the evaluation influences their behaviour accordingly. For example, shoppers' evaluation of a store is more favourable when both scent and music are Christmas-y than when they are unmatched,[106] or a chocolate scent emitted in a book store leads shoppers to buy more thematically congruent books, such as food- and drink-related or romantic literature books.[107]

On the other hand, scent incongruence suggests low diagnositicity, which creates interference to our information processing, making our information processing tasks more difficult, thereby resulting in three likely outcomes:

- more imbalanced or biased information search strategy; for example, shoppers would focus more on brand information than on attribute information[108]
- more likely to make a negative evaluation[109]
- more likely to generate avoidance behaviour[110]

9.5 LIGHTING

The psychological basis

Lighting is crucial to our health and subjective well-being. That is, lighting controls circadian (day/night) sleep biorhythms through its physiological influences on the production of melatonin and cortisol, core body temperature, and heart rate.[111] As a result of these physiological changes, exposure to suitable, bright light enhances alertness,[112] leading to improved cognitive performance.[113]

The impact of bright light on alertness also affects psychological states. Exposure to bright light, on the one hand, makes one feel more energetic and happier,[114] heightens arousal and pleasure levels in the Mehrabian–Russell model (Figure 9.3), and increases the level of self-awareness and self-presentation, thereby increasing self-control and encouraging inhibition[115] and socially desirable behaviour.[116] This is because lighting conditions change visibility:

bright light leads us to perceive a greater possibility of being observed.[117] The effects of dim lighting is the opposite: dim lighting encourages risk-taking behaviour[118] and promotes self-interested or antisocial behaviour,[119] because dim light or darkness gives us the perception of anonymity, which induces a state of deindividuation.[120]

Implications for consumer behaviour

Bright- versus dim-lighting

The key benefit of bright-lighting is to increase perceptual acuity (i.e. how clearly we can see); therefore, bright-lighting is better than dim-lighting to increase pleasure and arousal levels and to stimulate purchases. Research shows that under the bright-lighting conditions, shoppers spend more time at the display, examine more products, and buy more products.[121] However, such effects do not always hold for all product categories. For example, when buying utilitarian products, such as hardware tools, bright-lighting facilitates perceptual acuity, and therefore the need to spend time at the display or to pick up tools for comparison reduces, but the reduced need does not negatively influence spending.[122] In other words, factors other than lighting, such as merchandise content, need (or lack of need) to try on merchandise, and pricing, are important factors that could potentially determine how much time consumers spend in order to choose a suitable item.

The key limitation of bright-lighting is that it could potentially be over-stimulating to the degree that increases perceived tenseness and decreases perceived cosiness.[123] This explains why, compared with fast-food restaurants, fine-dining restaurants tend to use dim-lighting, which encourages customers to stay longer and enjoy their food more.[124] In addition, the use of dim-lighting has another advantage for retail and service marketing – that is, as discussed in the psychological basis section, dim-lighting encourages disinhibition behaviour and discourages self-control behaviour. Research has shown that dim-lighting is likely to increase hedonic consumption.[125] For example, dim-lighting leads people to eat less healthily, and to eat more indulgent food.[126] In fact, dim-lighting increases food consumption by, first, making people linger in the restaurant longer and, second, by making people order an unplanned dessert or an extra drink; both of which contribute to increased food consumption.[127]

Warm- versus cool-lighting

Warm- versus cool-lighting, known as colour temperature, is another way to describe lighting, in addition to the levels of brightness. When brightness is held consistent, cool-lighting, which has a bluish colouring in the appearance of the light, would seem to be brighter than warm-lighting, which is a reddish/orange-yellowish light.[128] Research has shown that warm white lighting is evaluated more positively; that is, the servicescape, products, or brands are evaluated more positively when warm white lighting is used, as opposed to the use of cool white lighting.[129] For example, studying a bank branch space, Tantanatewin and Inkarojrit found that warm white lighting led the space to be perceived as more expressive and prestigious, whereas cool white lighting made the customers feel the bank to be more technical.[130]

9.6 TOUCH

The psychological basis

The sense of touch has attracted rapid growing research interest in recent years, particularly because of the inability to touch in an online shopping environment and because of the popularity of tactile marketing. Although touch involves any tactile information received anywhere from the surface of the human body, our hands are most often used as the primary source for tactile information. Therefore, a specific term, *haptics* or *haptic perception*, is dedicated to refer to the tactile information perceived by the hand.[131] Haptics excels at making a judgement about material properties, such as texture, softness, weight, and temperature.[132]

Touching to make a judgement about the material properties of an object is classified as *instrumental touch*.[133] However, we are not just motivated to touch only for information. The other driver for us to touch objects is fun and enjoyment that can be derived from this sense, and is classified as *autotelic touch*. Autotelic touch focuses on seeking pleasant sensory experiences through touch. The positive emotions generated through touch (e.g. feeling good leather or the warmth of feathers) can be transferred to one's positive evaluation of the object,[134] which increases motivations for hedonic or indulgent behaviour, such as impulsive buying behaviour.[135] However, the motivation to touch, or *need for touch*, differs from person to person – see Table 9.6 for the characteristics of high versus low need for touch.

Table 9.6 Characteristics for need for touch

	<u>High</u> need for touch	<u>Low</u> need for touch
Enjoyment generated from touching	High, so use **more** time exploring haptic information	Low, so use **less** time exploring haptic information
Efficiency in deducing haptic information	High, so use **less** time in touching in order to make judgement on product quality	Low, so use **more** time in touching in order to make judgement on product quality
When haptic information is unavailable (e.g. in an online shopping environment)	Written description **cannot** compensate haptic information for texture information → **reduced** confidence in making judgement	Written description **can** compensate haptic information for texture information → confidence in making judgement **unchanged**

(Continued)

Table 9.6   (Continued)

	Hi_gh_ need for touch	**Lo_w_ need for touch**
Susceptibility to the influence of diagnostically irrelevant touch elements	Low, because of the **ability** to isolate non-diagnostic elements from evaluation	High, because of the **inability** to isolate non-diagnostic elements from evaluation

Source: Summary based on the studies by Peck and Childers[136]

Implications for consumer behaviour

Product evaluation

For the products with tactile input that can easily distinguish product quality (diagnositic-ity of touch), an ability to touch increases purchase intentions.[137] For example, consumers are more motivated to touch such products as clothing, shoes, furniture, fruits/veggies, et cetera, as opposed to soda, soap, cereal, and pencils. When tactile input is diagnostic, consumers will also spend more time touching these products,[138] and the time spent is positively related to consumers' confidence in their evaluation of the product quality.[139] The increased confidence is able to enhance favourable evaluation for high-quality products as well as negative evaluation for low-quality ones.[140]

Hedonic haptic sensations

Hedonic haptic sensations are the key drivers for tactile marketing, which is to design tactile input that interacts with consumers. This design can appear on the product, product packaging, as well as advertisement. Research shows that adding a tactile element that feels good can project the positive feeling of the tactile element onto the feeling of the product, which is then translated into the evaluation of the product. For example, adding a feather on the pamphlet asking for donations to a local charity increases the positive attitudes towards the advertisement and the likelihood of donating time and money to the organisation.[141] In addition, touching also results in the feelings of psychological ownership, and it is the feelings of psychological ownership that increase product valuation and consumers' willingness to pay.[142]

There are two caveats in tactile marketing:

- *The fit of the touch element*: The fit of the touch element with tactile marketing messages does not always matter. That is, for those high in the autotelic need for touch, the presence of any touch element, even if it does not fit, is better than no touch element at all.[143]
- *Mental imagery of touching sensations*: Tactile input can be experienced via images or words, which simulate touching sensations activated by imagination.[144] In other words, tactile marketing does not require the presence of an actual tactile element.

---Box 9.3---

What happens when customers are blocked from touching products in the servicescape?

From time to time, we see signs or service staff that instruct patrons not to touch in retail environments: for example, "Do Not Touch" or "Shop by Looking Only." Touching products increases consumers' purchase intentions, impulsive purchase of, and willingness to pay for, the products,[145] so what happens when patrons are blocked from touching products? A recent study by Ringler et al. provides some useful insight.[146] The study demonstrates that when people are blocked from touching displayed products, their psychological reactance increases in order to re-establish the threatened freedom to touch, and as a result they would engage in touching more products when they are permitted to do so again. Because of the increased haptic experience from the compensatory touch, people would spend more and purchase more of the subsequently encountered products after the block of touching is stopped and their haptic freedom restored. Therefore, the store areas in which patrons are encouraged to freely touch merchandise should directly follow store areas in which patrons are restricted from touching. Interestingly, patrons who experience the active block of touching do not negatively evaluate the retailer that instates the instruction, and instead their negative evaluation targets the front-line employees who provide interpersonal instruction that blocks touching. As a result, active interpersonal haptic blocking can be used strategically to benefit the retailer.

Impression formation via hedonic tactile attributes

In the servicescape, consumers experience haptic sensations in a variety of ways, not just in order to directly evaluate products. For example, at a restaurant, customers may feel the weight of the menu, the smooth finish of a plate, or the softness of a linen napkin during the course of routine interactions with a service provider. These haptic sensations are able to influence the judgement of product quality as well as the quantity of consumption. For instance, a firm (versus flimsy) cup from which mineral water is drunk increases product quality and prices consumers perceive, despite the fact that the mineral water is the same.[147] Similarly, light (versus heavy) champagne flutes increase the quantity of alcohol consumption.[148] These influences from the service environment, product containers, or product packaging are a result of the influence of emotions – the hedonic value that can be extracted from the haptic sensations.[149]

Haptic cues in an online environment

Both diagnostic and non-diagnostic tactile information is important for consumers to evaluate and "feel" the products, so online retail environments (as well as any form of home shopping, such as TV shopping) suffer from consumers' inability to touch. Research shows that consumers' inability to touch increases perceived risk and decreases psychological ownership, thereby reducing consumers' online purchase intentions and willingness to pay.[150] So, how could e-commerce businesses decrease perceived risk and increase psychological ownership? Perceived risk is based on product evaluation relying on our cognitive efforts, and there are three main approaches to decrease perceived risk:

1. *Use clear written descriptions*: This information is particularly useful to compensate for such information as weight, size, shape, et cetera.
2. *Use consumer reviews*: This information offers user experience in fit and feel.
3. *Create cross-modal illusions*: These are perceptual illusions in which users use sensory cues in one modality to fill in the missing components of perceptual experience.[151] With appropriate synaesthetic stimulation from visual as well as auditory analogues of haptic perception, perceptual illusions are able to improve user experience.[152]

In order to increase psychological ownership, businesses could tap into their imagination of haptic perception, for as mentioned earlier the imagination is able to simulate touch sensations.[153] How could it be done? There are three main ways:

1. *Create cross-modal illusions by adding a graspable-like (such as hand action) design or product*: Research shows that a graspable-like design appealing to the viewer's dominant hand is able to enhance perceived ownership.[154] As about 90% of the world's population is right-handed,[155] the better graspable design is to position items towards shoppers' right hands.
2. *Use touch controls (as opposed to voice, gaze, or gesture control) in the virtual environment*: Research shows that using touch controls reduces mental intangibility and increases the feeling of comfort, thereby increasing consumers' purchase intentions and willingness to pay.[156]
3. *Use the cutting-edge technologies that facilitate mixed reality, a hybrid of reality and virtual reality to produce new environments and visualisations where physical and digital objects co-exist*: This can be used together with the previous two points to enhance the imagination of touching.

9.7 SUMMARY

1. Environmental psychology studies the relationships between individuals and their physical settings. The most often used theories of environmental psychology in consumer behaviour are stimulation theories. Elements in the physical environment are served as stimuli, and there are three main types of stimulation: sensory stimulation, social stimulation, and movement. Under- or over-stimulation is not desired, but what is perceived as under- or over-stimulation depends on personal preferences and situational factors.

2. Two main environmental psychology frameworks used in consumer behaviour are (1) the Mehrabian–Russell model and (2) Bitner's model of servicescape. The Mehrabian–Russell model suggests approach (e.g. spending more time in the shop) and avoidance (e.g. avoiding the shop) behaviour is a result of the responses to moods (liking versus disliking because of the degrees of pleasure and arousal emotions) towards the environmental input. The inclusion of the emotional responses is to expand the S–O–R paradigm (stimulus–organism–response) on which the model is developed. Based on the Mehrabian–Russell model, Bitner's model of servicescape is developed with a focus on the service space, which outlines detailed environmental stimuli, such as the ambient conditions, spatial layout and design, and signage, and broadens the environmental input to include the interpersonal (social) aspects between shoppers and between service staff and shoppers.

3. Music has been widely used for mood induction in psychological research, because music has profound influences on physiology, cognition, and behaviour through the mood the music induces. In a consumption context, the right music is able to facilitate consumer information processing (i.e. increase brand/advertisement recall and comprehension of advertisements), enhance positive evaluation of the product/brand/advertisement/servicescape, decrease time perception for waiting or shopping durations, improve shopping experience, and increase willingness to pay. However, what is the right music? The right music depends on the fit of the music for the occasion/product/retailer and individual preferences. For example, pop music influences younger consumers more positively, whereas classical music influences older consumers more positively. For example, relaxing music influences consumers positively in general, but arousing music may be a better fit for those consumers who are in a state of distress or agitation when they are on hold for a call at service centres for support.

4. The mood different types of music evoke can be studied via the main music properties (music structure): tempo, volume, and mode. Music with fast (versus slow) tempo, loud (versus soft) volume, and major (versus minor) keys usually sounds happier and more arousing. However, just because the background music is happy and arousing does not necessarily guarantee success for businesses. For example, fast music provokes a faster pace of eating, drinking, and traffic flow, and whilst faster pace of eating, drinking, and traffic flow may have a better turnover rate so more customers can be served, consumers usually spend less when the duration they stay in a shop/restaurant is shorter. That is why the fit of music and target customers' preferences should be taken into account in order to identify the right music.

5. Pleasant ambient scents encourage positive store and product evaluation, which increase consumer spending. The influence of scents is more impactful for cognition than for mood/emotion. That is, shoppers spend more time evaluating product-related information in a scented environment. These increased cognitive efforts are able to expand consumers' brand choices by choosing unfamiliar brands or products. In addition, our information processing, such as store or product evaluation, depends on the diagnositicity of scent, which is manifested in scent congruence. Scent congruence suggests that the scent is able to provide information that helps people to access,

process, and elaborate information from their memory with regards to the product or store. As a result, for example, household cleansers with a lemon scent (versus a coconut scent) and suntan lotions with a coconut scent (versus a lemon scent) would be evaluated more positively. However, what combination of scents would provide the best scent congruence is under-researched, and given limited research on scents properties, compared with music research.

6. Warm bright lighting (versus dim or cool white lighting) increases levels of alertness, pleasure, and arousal, and is therefore able to encourage purchases for product categories that require close examination; for example, choosing a suitable wine, selecting an appropriate outfit, or buying a hardware tool. On the other hand, bright-lighting could be over-stimulating, which results in increased tenseness and reduced cosiness. The key benefit of dim-lighting is to increase the degree of cosiness by lowering alertness. Lowered alertness decreases self-control behaviour, thereby encouraging risk-taking, self-interested, and indulgent behaviour. That's why such service environments as casinos, clubs, and fine-dining restaurants usually use dim-lighting.

7. There are two types of touch: instrumental touch and autotelic touch. Instrumental touch refers to the touch that focuses on making a judgement about the material properties. The sense of touch, or haptics, is the most useful for evaluating material properties, such as texture, softness, weight, et cetera. Autotelic touch focuses on seeking pleasant sensory experiences. The need for either instrumental or autotelic touch differs from person to person. Those high in the need for instrumental touch are efficient using haptics to make a judgement; therefore, they would spend less time touching products to make a judgement. Those high in the need for autotelic touch enjoy the hedonic sensation from touching, so they would spend more time touching products. Touching, in general, increases purchase intentions, because of the pleasant experiences and the sense of psychological ownership extracted from touching, in addition to the instrumental purposes.

8. The inability to touch for home shopping, such as online purchases, is the main barrier that prevents shoppers from shopping from home. In order to overcome this inability, retailers can use various technologies and designs to encourage the shoppers' imagination of touching, as the imagination of touching works almost as well as actual touching. For example, retailers could (1) combine the vision and haptic senses to create cross-modal illusions, (2) create graspable-like designs, and (3) utilise touch controls (as opposed to voice controls).

DISCUSSION QUESTIONS

1. Compare and contrast the implications of the Mehrabian–Russell model and of Bitner's model of servicescape in supermarkets, department stores, fast-food restaurants, and fine-dining restaurants.

2. Discuss the influences of background music and how they can be applied to different types of servicescape successfully.

3. Discuss the influences of ambient scents and how they can be applied to different types of servicescape successfully.
4. Discuss the effects of haptic information and how online retailers can mitigate the inability to touch in a virtual environment.

FURTHER READING

- De Luca, R., & Botelho, D. (2019). The Unconscious Perception of Smells as a Driver of Consumer Responses: A Framework Integrating the Emotion-Cognition Approach to Scent Marketing. *AMS Review*, 11(1), 145–161.
- Kellaris, J. J. (2008). Music and Consumers. In C. P. Haugtvedt, P. M. Herr, & F. R. Kardes (eds), *Handbook of Consumer Psychology* (pp. 837–856). New York: Psychology Press.
- Krishna, A. (2012). An Integrative Review of Sensory Marketing: Engaging the Senses to Affect Perception, Judgment and Behavior. *Journal of Consumer Psychology*, 22(3), 332–351.
- Puccinelli, N. M., Goodstein, R. C., Grewal, D., Price, R., Raghubir, P., & Stewart, D. (2009). Customer Experience Management in Retailing: Understanding the Buying Process. *Journal of Retailing*, *85*(1), 15–30.
- Wang, Y. J., Minor, M. S., & Wei, J. (2011). Aesthetics and the Online Shopping Environment: Understanding Consumer Responses. *Journal of Retailing*, *87*(1), 4658.

NOTES

1. Gifford, R. (2014). *Environmental Psychology: Principles and Practice*. Coville, WA: Optimal Books.
2. Wohlwill, J. F. (1966). The Physical Environment: A Problem for a Psychology of Stimulation. *Journal of Social Issues, 22*(4), 29–38.
3. Wohlwill, J. F. (1974). Human Adaptation to Levels of Environmental Stimulation. *Human Ecology, 2*(2), 127–147.
4. Ibid.
5. Altman, I. (1975). *The Environment and Social Behavior: Privacy, Personal Space, Territory and Crowding*. Monterey, CA: Brooks and Cole; Rapoport, A. (1975). Toward a Redefinition of Density. *Environment and Behavior, 7*(2), 133–158.
6. Barker, R. G. (1968). *Ecological Psychology: Concepts and Methods for Studying the Environment of Human Behavior*. Stanford, CA: Stanford University Press.
7. Clayton, S., & Brook, A. (2005). Can Psychology Help Save the World? A Model for Conservation Psychology. *Analyses of Social Issues and Public Policy, 5*(1), 87–102.
8. Mehrabian, A., & Russell, J. A. (1974). *An Approach to Environmental Psychology*. Cambridge, MA: MIT Press.
9. Vieira, V. A. (2013). Stimuli–Organism–Response Framework: A Meta-Analytic Review in the Store Environment. *Journal of Business Research, 66*(9), 1420–1426.

10. Pavlov, I. P. (1927). *Conditioned Reflexes*. Oxford: Oxford University Press.

11. Woodworth, R. S. (1918). *Dynamic Psychology*. New York: Columbia University Press.

12. Belk, R. W. (1975). Situational Variables and Consumer Behaviour. *Journal of Consumer Research, 2*(December), 157–167.

13. Baker, J. (1986). The Role of the Environment in Marketing Services: The Consumer Perspective. In J. A. Czpeil, C. Congram, & J. Shanaham (eds), *The Services Challenge: Integrating for Competitive Advantage* (pp. 79–84). Chicago, IL: American Marketing Association.

14. Bitner, M. J. (1992). Servicescapes: The Impact of Physical Surroundings on Customers and Employees. *Journal of Marketing, 56*(2), 57–71.

15. Mehrabian & Russell, *An Approach to Environmental Psychology*.

16. Donovan, R. J., & Rossiter, J. R. (1982). Store Atmosphere: An Environmental Psychology Approach. *Journal of Retailing, 58*(1), 34–57.

17. Mehrabian & Russell, *An Approach to Environmental Psychology*; Vieira, Stimuli–Organism–Response Framework.

18. Mehrabian & Russell, *An Approach to Environmental Psychology*.

19. Russell, J. A., & Pratt, G. (1980). A Description of the Affective Quality Attributed to Environments. *Journal of Personality and Social Psychology, 38*(2), 22.

20. Mehrabian & Russell, *An Approach to Environmental Psychology*.

21. Beedie, C., Terry, P., & Lane, A. (2005). Distinctions between Emotion and Mood. *Cognition & Emotion, 19*(6), 847–878.

22. Gorn, G. J., Goldberg, M. E., & Basu, K. (1993). Mood, Awareness, and Product Evaluation. *Journal of Consumer Psychology, 2*(3), 237–256.

23. Schwarz, N. (1990). Feelings as Information: Informational and Motivational Functions of Affective States. In R. M. Sorrentino & E. T. Higgins (eds), *The Handbook of Motivation and Cognition: Foundations of Social Behavior* (Vol. 2, pp. 527–561). New York: Guilford Press.

24. Puccinelli, N. M., Goodstein, R. C., Grewal, D., Price, R., Raghubir, P., & Stewart, D. (2009). Customer Experience Management in Retailing: Understanding the Buying Process. *Journal of Retailing, 85*(1), 15–30.

25. Zajonc, R. B. (1980). Feeling and Thinking: Preferences Need No Inferences. *American Psychologist, 35*(2), 151–175; Cohen, J. B., & Andrade, E. B. (2004). Affective Intuition and Task-Contingent Affect Regulation. *Journal of Consumer Research, 31*(2), 358–367.

26. Cohen, J. B., Pham, M. T., & Andrade, E. B. (2008). The Nature and Role of Affect in Consumer Behavior. In C. P. Haugtvedt, P. M. Herr, & F. R. Kardes (eds), *Handbook of Consumer Psychology* (pp. 297–348). New York: Psychology Press.

27. Bitner, Servicescapes.

28. Boom, B. H., & Bitner, M. J. (1982). Marketing Services by Management the Environment. *Cornell Hotel and Restaurant Administration Quarterly, 23*(May), 35–39.

29. Bitner, Servicescapes.

30. Kotler, P. (1974). Atmospherics as a Marketing Tool. *Journal of Retailing, 49*(4), 48–64.

31. Baker, The Role of the Environment in Marketing Services.

32. von Helmholtz, H. (1863). *Die Lehre von den Tonempfindungen als physiologische Grundlage für die Theorie der Musik*. von Friedrich Vieweg und Sohn: Brannschweig.

33. Wundt, W. (1874). *Grundzüge der Physiologischen Psychologie*. Leipzig: W. Engelman.

34. Berlyne, D. E. (1970). Novelty, Complexity, and Hedonic Value. *Perception & Psychophysics*, *8*(5), 279–286.

35. Västfjäll, D. (2001). Emotion Induction through Music: A Review of the Musical Mood Induction Procedure. *Musicae Scientiae*, *5*(1 Supplementary), 173–211.

36. MacDonald, R., Kreutz, G., & Mitchell, L. (2013). *Music, Health, and Wellbeing*. Oxford: Oxford University Press.

37. Lesiuk, T. (2005). The Effect of Music Listening on Work Performance. *Psychology of Music*, *33*(2), 173–191.

38. Areni, C. S., & Kim, D. (1993). The Influence of Background Music on Shopping Behavior: Classical versus Top-Forty Music in a Wine Store. In L. McAlister & M. L. Rothschild (eds), *NA – Advances in Consumer Research* (Vol. 20, pp. 336–334). Provo, UT: Association for Consumer Research; North, A. C., Hargreaves, D. J., & McKendrick, J. (1999). The Influence of In-Store Music on Wine Selections. *Journal of Applied Psychology*, *84*(2), 271–276; North, A. C., Hargreaves, D. J., & McKendrick, J. (2000). The Effects of Music on Atmosphere in a Bank and a Bar. *Journal of Applied Social Psychology*, *30*(7), 1504–1522.

39. Berlyne, D. E. (1973). *Aesthetics and Psychobiology*. New York: Appleton-Century-Crofts.

40. Rauscher, F. H., Shaw, G. L., & Ky, C. N. (1993). Music and Spatial Task Performance. *Nature*, *365*, 611.

41. Kellaris, J. J. (2008). Music and Consumers. In C. P. Haugtvedt, P. M. Herr, & F. R. Kardes (eds), *Handbook of Consumer Psychology* (pp. 837–856). New York: Psychology Press.

42. Szabo, A., Small, A., & Leigh, M. (1999). The Effects of Slow-and Fast-Rhythm Classical Music on Progressive Cycling to Voluntary Physical Exhaustion. *Journal of Sports Medicine and Physical Fitness*, *39*(3), 220–225.

43. Leman, M., Moelants, D., Varewyck, M., Styns, F., van Noorden, L., & Martens, J.-P. (2013). Activating and Relaxing Music Entrains the Speed of Beat Synchronized Walking. *PLoS One*, *8*(7), e67932.

44. Roballey, T. C., McGreevy, C., Rongo, R. R., Schwantes, M. L., Steger, P. J., Wininger, M. A., & Gardner, E. B. (1985). The Effect of Music on Eating Behavior. *Bulletin of the Psychonomic Society*, *23*(3), 221–222.

45. Lundin, R. W. (1985). *An Objective Psychology of Music* (third edn). Malabar, FL: Krieger.

46. Davis, W. B., & Thaut, M. H. (1989). The Influence of Preferred Relaxing Music on Measures of State Anxiety, Relaxation, and Physiological Responses. *Journal of Music Therapy*, *26*(4), 168–187.

47. Pietschnig, J., Voracek, M., & Formann, A. K. (2010). Mozart Effect–Shmozart Effect: A Meta-Analysis. *Intelligence*, *38*(3), 314–323.

48. Bruner, G. C. (1990). Music, Mood, and Marketing. *Journal of Marketing*, *54*(4), 94–104.

49. Hevner, K. (1937). The Affective Value of Pitch and Tempo in Music. *American Journal of Psychology*, *49*(4), 621–630.

50. Kellaris, J. J., & Kent, R. J. (1993). An Exploratory Investigation of Responses Elicited by Music Varying in Tempo, Tonality, and Texture. *Journal of Consumer Psychology, 2*(4), 381–401.

51. Moelants, D. (2002). Preferred Tempo Reconsidered. In C. Stevens, D. Burnham, G. McPherson, E. Schubert, & J. Renwick (eds), *Proceedings of the 7th International Conference on Music Perception and Cognition* (pp. 580–583). Adelaide: Causal Productions.

52. Bruner, Music, Mood, and Marketing.

53. Gabrielsson, A., & Lindström, E. (2010). The Role of Structure in the Musical Expression of Emotions. In P. N. Juslin & J. A. Sloboda (eds), *Handbook of Music and Emotion: Theory, Research, Applications* (pp. 367–400). Oxford: Oxford University Press.

54. Van Noorden, L., & Moelants, D. (1999). Resonance in the Perception of Musical Pulse. *Journal of New Music Research, 28*(1), 43–66.

55. Anand, P., & Sternthal, B. (1990). Ease of Message Processing as a Moderator of Repetition Effects in Advertising. *Journal of Marketing Research, 27*(3), 345–353; Peck, J., & Childres, T. L. (2008). Effects of Sensory Factors on Consumer Behavior: If It Tastes, Smells, Sounds, and Feels Like a Duck, Then It Must Be a . . . . In C. P. Haugtvedt, P. M. Herr, & F. R. Kardes (eds), *Handbook of Consumer Psychology* (pp. 193–219). New York: Psychology Press.

56. MacInnis, D. J., & Park, C. W. (1991). The Differential Role of Characteristics of Music on High-and Low-Involvement Consumers' Processing of Ads. *Journal of Consumer Research, 18*(2), 161–173.

57. Chebat, J.-C., Chebat, C. G., & Vaillant, D. (2001). Environmental Background Music and In-Store Selling. *Journal of Business Research, 54*(2), 115–123.

58. Park, C. W., & Young, S. M. (1986). Consumer Response to Television Commercials: The Impact of Involvement and Background Music on Brand Attitude Formation. *Journal of Marketing Research, 23*(1), 11–24.

59. Kellaris, J. J., Cox, A. D., & Cox, D. (1993). The Effect of Background Music on Ad Processing: A Contingency Explanation. *Journal of Marketing, 57*(4), 114–125; MacInnis & Park, The Differential Role of Characteristics of Music; Tom, G. (1990). Marketing with Music. *Journal of Consumer Marketing, 7*(2), 49–53.

60. Dubé, L., Chebat, J. C., & Morin, S. (1995). The Effects of Background Music on Consumers' Desire to Affiliate in Buyer–Seller Interactions. *Psychology & Marketing, 12*(4), 305–319; Dubé, L., & Morin, S. (2001). Background Music Pleasure and Store Evaluation: Intensity Effects and Psychological Mechanisms. *Journal of Business Research, 54*(2), 107–113; North et al., The Effects of Music on Atmosphere in a Bank and a Bar.

61. Alpert, M. I., Alpert, J. I., & Maltz, E. N. (2005). Purchase Occasion Influence on the Role of Music in Advertising. *Journal of Business Research, 58*(3), 369–376.

62. Areni & Kim, The Influence of Background Music on Shopping Behavior: Classical versus Top-Forty Music in a Wine Store.

63. North, A. C., Sheridan, L. P., & Areni, C. S. (2016). Music Congruity Effects on Product Memory, Perception, and Choice. *Journal of Retailing, 92*(1), 83–95.

64. North, A. C., Hargreaves, D. J., & McKendrick, J. (1997). In-Store Music Affects Product Choice. *Nature, 390*(6656), 132.

65. Dubé & Morin, Background Music Pleasure and Store Evaluation.

66. North, A. C., & Hargreaves, D. J. (1998). The Effect of Music on Atmosphere and Purchase Intentions in a Cafeteria. *Journal of Applied Social Psychology, 28*(24), 2254–2273.

67. Areni & Kim, The Influence of Background Music on Shopping Behavior.

68. McElrea, H., & Standing, L. (1992). Fast Music Causes Fast Drinking. *Perceptual and Motor Skills, 75*(2), 362; Milliman, R. E. (1986). The Influence of Background Music on the Behavior of Restaurant Patrons. *Journal of Consumer Research, 13*(2), 286–289.

69. Milliman, R. E. (1982). Using Background Music to Affect the Behavior of Supermarket Shoppers. *Journal of Marketing, 46*(3), 86–91.

70. Alpert, J. I., & Alpert, M. I. (1989). Background Music as an Influence in Consumer Mood and Advertising Responses. In T. K. Srull (ed.), *NA – Advances in Consumer Research* (Vol. 16, pp. 485–491). Provo, UT: Association for Consumer Research.

71. Buckley, C. (2012). Working or Playing Indoors, New Yorkers Face an Unabated Roar. *New York Times.* Retrieved from www.nytimes.com/2012/07/20/nyregion/in-new-york-city-indoor-noise-goes-unabated.html

72. Milliman, Using Background Music to Affect the Behavior of Supermarket Shoppers; Milliman, The Influence of Background Music on the Behavior of Restaurant Patrons.

73. Knoferle, K. M., Spangenberg, E. R., Herrmann, A., & Landwehr, J. R. (2012). It Is All in the Mix: The Interactive Effect of Music Tempo and Mode on In-Store Sales. *Marketing Letters, 23*(1), 325–337.

74. Husain, G., Thompson, W. F., & Schellenberg, E. G. (2002). Effects of Musical Tempo and Mode on Arousal, Mood, and Spatial Abilities. *Music Perception, 20*(2), 151–171.

75. North, A. C., & Hargreaves, D. J. (1999). Can Music Move People? The Effects of Musical Complexity and Silence on Waiting Time. *Environment and Behavior, 31*(1), 136–149.

76. Oakes, S. (2003). Musical Tempo and Waiting Perceptions. *Psychology & Marketing, 20*(8), 685–705.

77. Kellaris, J. J., Mantel, S. P., & Altsech, M. B. (1996). Decibels, Disposition, and Duration: The Impact of Musical Loudness and Internal States on Time Perception. In K. P. Corfman & J. G. Lynch, Jr. (eds), *NA - Advances in Consumer Research* (Vol. 23, pp. 498–503). Provo, UT: Association for Consumer Research.

78. Kellaris, J. J., & Kent, R. J. (1992). The Influence of Music on Consumers' Temporal Perceptions: Does Time Fly When You're Having Fun? *Journal of Consumer Psychology, 1*(4), 365–376.

79. Hul, M. K., Dube, L., & Chebat, J.-C. (1997). The Impact of Music on Consumers' Reactions to Waiting for Services. *Journal of Retailing, 73*(1), 87–104; Kellaris & Kent, The Influence of Music on Consumers' Temporal Perceptions.

80. Cameron, M. A., Baker, J., Peterson, M., & Braunsberger, K. (2003). The Effects of Music, Wait-Length Evaluation, and Mood on a Low-Cost Wait Experience. *Journal of Business Research, 56*(6), 421–430; Yalch, R. F., & Spangenberg, E. R. (2000). The Effects of Music in a Retail Setting on Real and Perceived Shopping Times. *Journal of Business Research, 49*(2), 139–147; Bailey, N., & Areni, C. S. (2006). Background Music as a Quasi Clock in Retrospective Duration Judgments. *Perceptual and Motor Skills, 102*(2), 435–444; North, A.

C., Hargreaves, D. J., & McKendrick, J. (1999). Music and On-Hold Waiting Time. *British Journal of Psychology, 90*(1), 161–164.

81. Kellaris, J. J., & Mantel, S. P. (1996). Shaping Time Perceptions with Background Music: The Effect of Congruity and Arousal on Estimates of Ad Durations. *Psychology & Marketing, 13*(5), 501–515.

82. Bushdid, C., Magnasco, M. O., Vosshall, L. B., & Keller, A. (2014). Humans Can Discriminate More than 1 Trillion Olfactory Stimuli. *Science, 343*(6177), 1370–1372.

83. Herz, R. S. (2007). *The Scent of Desire: Discovering Our Enigmatic Sense of Smell.* New York: HarperCollins.

84. Baron, R. A. (1990). Environmentally Induced Positive Affect: Its Impact on Self-Efficacy, Task Performance, Negotiation, and Conflict. *Journal of Applied Social Psychology, 20*(5), 368–384.

85. Baron, R. A. (1997). The Sweet Smell of… Helping: Effects of Pleasant Ambient Fragrance on Prosocial Behavior in Shopping Malls. *Personality and Social Psychology Bulletin, 23*(5), 498–503.

86. Warm, J. S., Dember, W. N., & Parasuraman, R. (1991). Effects of Olfactory Stimulation on Performance and Stress. *Journal of the Society of Cosmetic Chemistry, 42*(3), 199–210.

87. Ehrlichman, H., & Bastone, L. (1992). The Use of Odour in the Study of Emotion. In S. van Toller & G. H. Dodd (eds), *Fragrance: The Psychology and Biology of Perfume* (pp. 143–159). London: Elsevier Applied Science Publishers.

88. Croy, I., & Hummel, T. (2017). Olfaction as a Marker for Depression. *Journal of Neurology, 264*(4), 631–638.

89. Dazzi, F., de Nitto, S., Zambetti, G., Loriedo, C., & Ciofalo, A. (2013). Alterations of the Olfactory–Gustatory Functions in Patients with Eating Disorders. *European Eating Disorders Review, 21*(5), 382–385.

90. Rahayel, S., Frasnelli, J., & Joubert, S. (2012). The Effect of Alzheimer's Disease and Parkinson's Disease on Olfaction: A Meta-Analysis. *Behavioural Brain Research, 231*(1), 60–74.

91. Herz, R. S. (2010). The Emotional, Cognitive, and Biological Basics of Olfaction: Implications and Considerations for Scent Marketing. In A. Krishna (ed.), *Sensory Marketing: Research on the Sensuality of Products* (pp. 87–107). New York: Routledge.

92. Herz, R. S., & Cupchik, G. C. (1995). The Emotional Distinctiveness of Odor-Evoked Memories. *Chemical Senses, 20*(5), 517–528; Herz, R. S. (1998). Are Odors the Best Cues to Memory? A Cross-Modal Comparison of Associative Memory Stimuli. *Annals of the New York Academy of Sciences, 855*(1), 670–674.

93. Herz, R. S., Beland, S. L., & Hellerstein, M. (2004). Changing Odor Hedonic Perception through Emotional Associations in Humans. *International Journal of Comparative Psychology, 17*(4), 315–338.

94. Bone, P. F., & Ellen, P. S. (1999). Scents in the Marketplace: Explaining a Fraction of Olfaction. *Journal of Retailing, 75*(2), 243–262; Chebat, J.-C., & Michon, R. (2003). Impact of Ambient Odors on Mall Shoppers' Emotions, Cognition, and Spending:

A Test of Competitive Causal Theories. *Journal of Business Research*, 56(7), 529–539; De Luca, R., & Botelho, D. (2019). The Unconscious Perception of Smells as a Driver of Consumer Responses: A Framework Integrating the Emotion-Cognition Approach to Scent Marketing. *AMS Review*, 11(1), 145–161; Michon, R., Chebat, J.-C., & Turley, L. W. (2005). Mall Atmospherics: The Interaction Effects of the Mall Environment on Shopping Behavior. *Journal of Business Research*, 58(5), 576–583; Roschk, H., & Hosseinpour, M. (2020). Pleasant Ambient Scents: A Meta-Analysis of Customer Responses and Situational Contingencies. *Journal of Marketing*, 84(1), 125–145; Spangenberg, E. R., Crowley, A. E., & Henderson, P. W. (1996). Improving the Store Environment: Do Olfactory Cues Affect Evaluations and Behaviors? *Journal of Marketing*, 60(2), 67–80.

95. Lazarus, R. S. (1991). *Emotion and Adaptation*. Oxford: Oxford University Press.

96. Bone & Ellen, Scents in the Marketplace.

97. Roschk, H., & Hosseinpour, M. (2020). Pleasant Ambient Scents: A Meta-Analysis of Customer Responses and Situational Contingencies. *Journal of Marketing*, 84(1), 125–145.

98. Spangenberg, E. R., Crowley, A. E., & Henderson, P. W. (1996). Improving the Store Environment: Do Olfactory Cues Affect Evaluations and Behaviors? *Journal of Marketing*, 60(2), 67–80.

99. Ibid; Doucé, L., & Janssens, W. (2013). The Presence of a Pleasant Ambient Scent in a Fashion Store: The Moderating Role of Shopping Motivation and Affect Intensity. *Environment and Behavior*, 45(2), 215–238.

100. Roschk & Hosseinpour, Pleasant Ambient Scents; Chebat & Michon, Impact of Ambient Odors.

101. Spangenberg et al., Improving the Store Environment.

102. Bone & Ellen, Scents in the Marketplace.

103. Doucé & Janssens. The Presence of a Pleasant Ambient Scent in a Fashion Store; Morrin, M., & Ratneshwar, S. (2000). The Impact of Ambient Scent on Evaluation, Attention, and Memory for Familiar and Unfamiliar Brands. *Journal of Business Research*, 49(2), 157–165.

104. Mitchell, D. J., Kahn, B. E., & Knasko, S. C. (1995). There's Something in the Air: Effects of Congruent or Incongruent Ambient Odor on Consumer Decision Making. *Journal of Consumer Research*, 22(2), 229–238.

105. Roschk & Hosseinpour, Pleasant Ambient Scents

106. Spangenberg, E. R., Grohmann, B., & Sprott, D. E. (2005). It's Beginning to Smell (and Sound) a Lot Like Christmas: The Interactive Effects of Ambient Scent and Music in a Retail Setting. *Journal of Business Research*, 58(11), 1583–1589.

107. Doucé, L., Poels, K., Janssens, W., & De Backer, C. (2013). Smelling the Books: The Effect of Chocolate Scent on Purchase-Related Behavior in a Bookstore. *Journal of Environmental Psychology*, 36, 65–69.

108. Mitchell et al., There's Something in the Air.

109. Bone, P. F., & Jantrania, S. (1992). Olfaction as a Cue for Product Quality. *Marketing Letters*, 3(3), 289–296.

110. Roschk & Hosseinpour, Pleasant Ambient Scents.

111. Ruger, M., Gordijn, M. C. M., Beersma, D. G. M., de Vries, B., & Daan, S. (2006). Time-of-Day-Dependent Effects of Bright Light Exposure on Human Psychophysiology:

Comparison of Daytime and Nighttime Exposure. *American Journal of Physiology: Regulatory, Integrative and Comparative Physiology, 290*(5), R1413–R1420.

112. Badia, P., Myers, B., Boecker, M., Culpepper, J., & Harsh, J. R. (1991). Bright Light Effects on Body Temperature, Alertness, EEG and Behavior. *Physiology & Behavior, 50*(3), 583–588.

113. Chellappa, S. L., Gordijn, M. C. M., & Cajochen, C. (2011). Can Light Make Us Bright? Effects of Light on Cognition and Sleep. *Progress in Brain Research, 190*, 119–133.

114. Smolders, K. C. H. J., & de Kort, Y. A. W. (2014). Bright Light and Mental Fatigue: Effects on Alertness, Vitality, Performance and Physiological Arousal. *Journal of Environmental Psychology, 39*, 77–91.

115. Steidle, A., & Werth, L. (2014). In the Spotlight: Brightness Increases Self-Awareness and Reflective Self-Regulation. *Journal of Environmental Psychology, 39*, 40–50; Zhong, C.-B., Bohns, V. K., & Gino, F. (2010). Good Lamps are the Best Police: Darkness Increases Dishonesty and Self-Interested Behavior. *Psychological Science, 21*(3), 311–314; Kasof, J. (2002). Indoor Lighting Preferences and Bulimic Behavior: An Individual Differences Approach. *Personality and Individual Differences, 32*(3), 383–400.

116. Hirsh, J. B., Galinsky, A. D., & Zhong, C.-B. (2011). Drunk, Powerful, and in the Dark: How General Processes of Disinhibition Produce both Prosocial and Antisocial Behavior. *Perspectives on Psychological Science, 6*(5), 415–427.

117. Johnson, R. D., & Downing, L. L. (1979). Deindividuation and Valence of Cues: Effects on Prosocial and Antisocial Behavior. *Journal of Personality and Social Psychology, 37*(9), 1532.

118. Ilicic, J., & Baxter, S. M. (2019). Hidden in the Dark: Dim Ambient Lighting Increases Game Play Duration and Total Spend. *Journal of Gambling Studies*, 1–16.

119. Hirsh et al., Drunk, Powerful, and in the Dark.

120. Johnson & Downing, Deindividuation and Valence of Cues.

121. Areni, C. S., & Kim, D. (1994). The Influence of In-Store Lighting on Consumers' Examination of Merchandise in a Wine Store. *International Journal of Research in Marketing, 11*(2), 117–125.

122. Summers, T. A., & Hebert, P. R. (2001). Shedding Some Light on Store Atmospherics Influence of Illumination on Consumer Behaviour. *Journal of Business Research, 54*(2), 145–150.

123. Custers, P., de Kort, Y., IJsselsteijn, W., & de Kruiff, M. (2010). Lighting in Retail Environments: Atmosphere Perception in the Real World. *Lighting Research & Technology, 42*(3), 331–343.

124. Wansink, B., & van Ittersum, K. (2012). Fast Food Restaurant Lighting and Music Can Reduce Calorie Intake and Increase Satisfaction. *Psychological Reports, 111*(1), 228–232.

125. Huang, X. I., Dong, P., & Labroo, A. A. (2018). Feeling Disconnected from Others: The Effects of Ambient Darkness on Hedonic Choice. *International Journal of Research in Marketing, 35*(1), 144–153.

126. Biswas, D., Szocs, C., Chacko, R., & Wansink, B. (2017). Shining Light on Atmospherics: How Ambient Light Influences Food Choices. *Journal of Marketing Research, 54*(1), 111–123.

127. Wansink, B. (2004). Environmental Factors that Increase the Food Intake and Consumption Volume of Unknowing Consumers. *Annual Review of Nutrition, 24*, 455–479.

128. Park, N. K., & Farr, C. A. (2007). The Effects of Lighting on Consumers' Emotions and Behavioral Intentions in a Retail Environment: A Cross-Cultural Comparison. *Journal of Interior Design, 33*(1), 17–32; Rea, M. S. (2000). *The IESNA Lighting Handbook: Reference & Application*. New York: Illuminating Engineering Society of North America.

129. Otterbring, T., Löfgren, M., & Lestelius, M. (2014). Let There Be Light! An Initial Exploratory Study of Whether Lighting Influences Consumer Evaluations of Packaged Food Products. *Journal of Sensory Studies, 29*(4), 294–300; Park & Farr, The Effects of Lighting; Tantanatewin, W., & Inkarojrit, V. (2016). Effects of Color and Lighting on Retail Impression and Identity. *Journal of Environmental Psychology, 46*, 197–205; Wansink & van Ittersum, Fast Food Restaurant Lighting and Music Can Reduce Calorie Intake and Increase Satisfaction.

130. Ibid.

131. Gibson, J. J. (1966). Observations on Active Touch. *Psychological Review, 69*(6), 477–490.

132. Klatzky, R. L., Lederman, S. J., & Reed, C. (1989). Haptic Integration of Object Properties: Texture, Hardness, and Planar Contour. *Journal of Experimental Psychology: Human Perception and Performance, 15*(1), 45.

133. Klatzky, R. L. (2010). Touch: A Gentle Tutorial with Implications for Marketing. In A. Krishna (ed.), *Sensory Marketing: Research on the Sensuality of Products* (pp. 33–47). New York: Routledge; Peck, J., & Childers, T. L. (2003). Individual Differences in Haptic Information Processing: The "Need for Touch" Scale. *Journal of Consumer Research, 30*(3), 430–442.

134. Peck, J., & Wiggins, J. (2006). It Just Feels Good: Consumers' Affective Response to Touch and Its Influence on Attitudes and Behavior. *Journal of Marketing, 70*(4), 56–69.

135. Peck, J., & Childers, T. L. (2006). If I Touch It I Have to Have It: Individual and Environmental Influences on Impulse Purchasing. *Journal of Business Research, 59*(6), 765–769.

136. Peck, J. (2010). Does Touch Matter? Insights from Haptic Research in Marketing. In A. Krishna (ed.), *Sensory Marketing: Research on the Sensuality of Products* (pp. 17–31). New York: Routledge; Peck, J., & Childers, T. L. (2003). To Have and to Hold: The Influence of Haptic Information on Product Judgments. *Journal of Marketing, 67*(2), 35–48.

137. McCabe, D. B., & Nowlis, S. M. (2003). The Effect of Examining Actual Products or Product Descriptions on Consumer Preference. *Journal of Consumer Psychology, 13*(4), 431–439.

138. Peck, J., & Childers, T. L. (2005). Self-Report and Behavioural Measures in Product Evaluation and Haptic Information: Is What I Say How I Feel? In G. Menon & A. R. Rao (eds), *NA – Advances in Consumer Research* (Vol. 32, pp. 247). Duluth, MN: Association for Consumer Research.

139. Grohmann, B., Spangenberg, E. R., & Sprott, D. E. (2007). The Influence of Tactile Input on the Evaluation of Retail Product Offerings. *Journal of Retailing, 83*(2), 237–245.

140. Ibid.

141. Peck & Wiggins, It Just Feels Good.

142. Peck, J., & Shu, S. B. (2009). The Effect of Mere Touch on Perceived Ownership. *Journal of Consumer Research*, *36*(3), 434–447; Peck, J., Barger, V. A., & Webb, A. (2013). In Search of a Surrogate for Touch: The Effect of Haptic Imagery on Perceived Ownership. *Journal of Consumer Psychology*, *23*(2), 189–196.

143. Peck & Wiggins, It Just Feels Good.

144. Peck & Shu, The Effect of Mere Touch on Perceived Ownership; Peck et al., In Search of a Surrogate for Touch.

145. Liu, W., Batra, R., & Wang, H. (2017). Product Touch and Consumers' Online and Offline Buying: The Role of Mental Representation. *Journal of Retailing*, *93*(3), 369–381; Peck & Childers, If I Touch It I Have to Have It; Peck & Shu, The Effect of Mere Touch on Perceived Ownership; Peck et al., In Search of a Surrogate for Touch.

146. Ringler, C., Sirianni, N. J., Gustafsson, A., & Peck, J. (2019). Look But Don't Touch! The Impact of Active Interpersonal Haptic Blocking on Compensatory Touch and Purchase Behavior. *Journal of Retailing*, *95*(4), 186–203.

147. Krishna, A., & Morrin, M. (2008). Does Touch Affect Taste? The Perceptual Transfer of Product Container Haptic Cues. *Journal of Consumer Research*, *34*(6), 807–818.

148. Szocs, C., Biswas, D., & Borges, A. (2016). Cheers to Haptic Sensations and Alcohol Consumption: How Glassware Weight Impacts Perceived Intoxication and Positive Emotions. *Journal of the Association for Consumer Research*, *1*(4), 569–578.

149. Ibid.

150. Liu et al., Product Touch and Consumers' Online and Offline Buying.

151. Biocca, F., Kim, J., & Choi, Y. (2001). Visual Touch in Virtual Environments: An Exploratory Study of Presence, Multimodal Interfaces, and Cross-Modal Sensory Illusions. *Presence: Teleoperators & Virtual Environments*, *10*(3), 247–265.

152. Ibid; Kang, N., Sah, Y. J., & Lee, S. (2021). Effects of Visual and Auditory Cues on Haptic Illusions for Active and Passive Touches in Mixed Reality. *International Journal of Human–Computer Studies*, *150*, 102613; Imschloss, M., & Kuehnl, C. (2019). Feel the music! Exploring the Cross-Modal Correspondence between Music and Haptic Perceptions of Softness. *Journal of Retailing*, *95*(4), 158–169.

153. Peck & Shu, The Effect of Mere Touch on Perceived Ownership; Peck et al., In Search of a Surrogate for Touch.

154. Maille, V., Morrin, M., & Reynolds-McIlnay, R. (2020). On the Other Hand...: Enhancing Promotional Effectiveness with Haptic Cues. *Journal of Marketing Research*, *57*(1), 100–117.

155. Papadatou-Pastou, M., Ntolka, E., Schmitz, J., Martin, M., Munafò, M. R., Ocklenburg, S., & Paracchini, S. (2020). Human Handedness: A Meta-Analysis. *Psychological Bulletin*, *146*(6), 481–524.

156. Heller, J., Chylinski, M., de Ruyter, K., Mahr, D., & Keeling, D. I. (2019). Touching the Untouchable: Exploring Multi-Sensory Augmented Reality in the Context of Online Retailing. *Journal of Retailing*, *95*(4), 219–234.

10

EVOLUTIONARY PSYCHOLOGY AND CONSUMER BEHAVIOUR

⸻Learning objectives⸻

To explore, understand, and explain:

- Darwin's theory of evolution and its application to evolutionary psychology
- the survival drives and their applications to consumer behaviour
- the mating drives and their applications to consumer behaviour
- the affiliation drives and their applications to consumer behaviour

10.1 INTRODUCTION

Evolutionary psychology is strikingly different from other schools of psychology, including social, cognitive, and developmental psychology. The research questions of evolutionary psychology focus on answering the "what for" questions, whereas those of other schools of psychology investigate the "how" questions.[1] That is, the "what for" questions examine what the psychological processes are developed for (e.g. why do people crave calorific food?), but the "how" questions look at how the psychological processes operate (e.g. how does exposure to calorific food influence people's behaviour?). These different explanations to the research questions are also called the ultimate explanations (evolutionary psychology) versus proximate explanations (other schools of psychology). Evolutionary psychologists argue that understanding the ultimate reasons behind the operations of psychological processes can provide a more complete picture for the same behaviour, and as a result that evolutionary psychology is not competing with other schools of psychology, but complementing them.

This chapter starts with the basics of evolutionary psychology (Section 10.2), which is rooted in Darwin's theory of evolution. From Section 10.3 to 10.5, the evolutionary roots for innate drives on survival, mating, and affiliation, and how these drives apply to consumer behaviour are discussed. Section 10.6 is a reflection on how we should treat the results of evolutionary psychology with caution, as they may fall into social stereotypes, encouraging the *self-fulfilling prophecy*, a behavioural effect caused by self and social expectations.[2]

10.2 THE BASICS OF EVOLUTIONARY PSYCHOLOGY

Charles Darwin's theory of evolution

Evolution is the process of changes in species over time, and serves as the foundation of biology, in which evolutionary psychology is rooted. The leading figure of the theory of evolution, without a doubt, is Charles Darwin (1809–1882) who developed and advocated the evolutionary theory. At the core of Darwin's theory of evolution are the theory of natural selection and the theory of sexual selection.

The theory of natural selection

Natural selection, also known as survival selection, provides the fundamental thesis of life: every species struggles for existence. The word, struggle, implies challenges the species faces in its environment, where if it fails to adapt to the environmental challenges, the species will die out. As the same species in different environments need to adapt to their respective environments, adaptation has resulted in the same species developing into different species over time. Darwin's natural selection can be summarised by three premises:[3]

1. *variation*: organisms vary
2. *inheritance*: only those variations that can be genetically passed down to offspring play a role in the evolutionary process
3. *adaptation*: some of these inherited (genetic) variations are better adapted to the environment than others

These three premises demonstrate that if the genetic variations are able to provide an advantage in competing for resources for survival, organisms with these variations are able to survive better than others and reproduce more offspring, and consequently these variations in organisms will dominate over time. The theory of natural selection is the foundation of the discussion in Sections 10.3 (the survival drives) and 10.5 (the affiliation drives).

The theory of sexual selection

The theory of sexual selection is the foundation of the discussion in Section 10.4 (the mating drives).

The two sexes often differ significantly in size and structure, despite the fact that both female and male members of the species lived in the same ecological environment, which should have allowed them to have evolved more similarly than different. The theory of sexual selection is able to explain these sex differences: the theory of sexual selection focuses on adaptations for fostering successful mating, which suggests reproduction potential and increased likelihood to pass down the related genetic variations. Over time, these variations will dominate the outlook of the evolvement of the particular species. Darwin identified two primary means by which sexual selection operated: intra-sexual competition and intersexual selection.[4]

Intra-sexual competition

Intra-sexual competition is the competition between members of the same sex for access to mates. They possess varied competitive abilities. For example, males are often larger than females in species in which males engage in physical combat with other males for sexual access to females.[5] Those with the competitive abilities to beat the competition would have access to mates and be able to reproduce, thereby more likely passing down their competitive variations to future generations.

Intersexual selection

Intersexual selection is the preferential mate choice. If members of one sex desire certain qualities in the members of the opposite sex, then members of the opposite sex who possess those qualities will be preferentially chosen as mates, and therefore more likely to pass down those qualities to their future generations.

Female choice

The process of intersexual selection is called "female choice." This is because throughout the animal world, females of many species are choosier than males about whom they mate with as their reproduction resources are more limited, and parental investment is higher than those for males.[6] Research has shown that a female chooses potential mates based on:

1.   the resources the potential mates have,[7] which are direct fitness (to survival) benefits, such as males' ability to provide for the young later on
2.   the quality of heritable personal traits (e.g. attractiveness), which are indirect fitness benefits, such as the male's genetic qualities to pass down to his offspring

What is evolutionary psychology?

Influenced by Darwinism, evolutionary psychology sees psychology as a branch of biology, and focuses on the evolution of the human mind – the human brain. The brain, with only 2% of the human body's mass, consumes 20% of its energy, and this fact implies that the brain takes on important tasks. According to Tooby and Cosmides, the brain's function is to extract information from its environment, interpret that information, and use it to generate behaviour and regulate physiology.[8] The human brain is composed of an integrated assembly of these psychological adaptations that often interact with each other and with physiological mechanisms to generate behaviour.[9] Kplan and Gangestad provide an example of reproductive hormones (physiological mechanisms), psychological mechanisms, and behaviour that illustrates this interaction:[10]

> During puberty, adrenarche initiates cascades of developmental changes in both sexes taking place over almost a decade. In females, ... as mediated by estrogen and other hormones, increased energy is allocated to reproductive traits and functions, including secondary sexual characteristics, while growth ultimately subsides. Males begin producing androgens in substantial quantities, which lead to greater musculature and investment in forms of mating effort, including social competition and physical performance.[11] . . . Pregnancy requires maternal allocation of energy to the developing foetuses, which occurs through chemical communication (e.g. involving gonadotropins) on foetal tissue, uterine tissue, the ovaries, and the brain. . . . Male testosterone levels subside when men become fathers, facilitating relocation of reproductive effort from mating to parenting.

Therefore, evolutionary psychology argues that the brain has been shaped by the same evolutionary process and to the same end, as the rest of our body.[12] That is to say, psychological mechanisms are evolved adaptations by selection.[13] There are three main premises underlying evolutionary psychology:

1.   *Human nature is universal:* An example of this premise is personality.[14] There are, of course, individual psychological variations within universality, but they are superficial variations that do not influence the functions of human nature.
2.   *Psychological adaptations are domain-specific:* Adaptations by definition are to solve fitness problems. Because they focus on problem-solving, adaptations are domain-specific (problem-specific) and content-dependent.[15] For example, learning is evolved psychological adaptations, as in order to learn, the ability of learning the fitness-relevant

tasks needs to be hardwired in our brain. The innate language acquisition device[16] is an example of this idea,[17] and this innate device is domain-specific and can be extended to any choices, practices, and culture, that are attributed to maximizing human reproduction.[18]

3. *The environment in which the psychological adaptations were developed was during the Pleistocene epoch (the hunter-gatherer period):* This is referred to as the environment of evolutionary adaptedness (or EEA). Modern environments and modern selection pressures do not form part of the human EEA mainly because the evolutionary process is slow. However, most aspects of the modern environment still closely resemble our EEA. Therefore, for example, the psychologies underlying mating, parenting, friendship, and status all still work.[19] After all, if a species' current environment diverges too rapidly and too far from its EEA, the species will die out.

10.3 THE SURVIVAL DRIVES - SELF-PROTECTION

The psychological basis

Our ancestors faced many dangers and threats from their environment, predators, and enemies. These evolutionary ancestors who paid attention to these cues of dangers and threats were less likely to be killed, and more likely to pass down their fighting genes to their next generations.[20] As a result of evolution, our self-protection mechanism is activated[21] in the face of such dangers and threats as diseases,[22] angry expressions,[23] snakes and spiders,[24] crime news,[25] strangers,[26] or simply being in the dark.[27] The activation of the self-protection mechanism leads us to seek safety by avoiding loss[28] through taking fewer risks,[29] and paying attention to the information that might suggest dangers and threats, even when it does not.[30] In other words, the self-protection mechanism makes us more vigilant and paranoid[31] – vigilance makes us, for example, have an adaptive memory that better remembers things related to survival,[32] on the one hand; on the other hand, paranoia subjects us to cognitive biases (Box 10.1).

Box 10.1

Cognitive bias - the error management theory

The error management theory, proposed by Haselton and Buss, is the key cognitive bias in evolutionary psychology (and will appear again later in the mating section).[33] The error management theory suggests that people tend to overestimate the dangerous cues by increasing their sensitivity to perceive and interpret the un-dangerous cues to be dangerous. The theory is called error management, because selection pressures result in managing the errors we may make - although the error rates increase when we perceive and interpret the un-dangerous

(Continued)

cues to be dangerous, the net costs decrease as we are able to avoid the deadly threats.[34] The error management theory leads people to over-perceive threats. For example, when seeing others display heuristic disease cues, such as obesity and old age, people are more likely to believe that these people are ill when they are not.[35]

Implications for consumer behaviour

Preference for food variety

The main reasons people like a variety of food are because a variety of food provides different nutrition that we require for survival, and also because, should we eat something toxic, we would not eat much of it when we eat a variety of food.[36] When presented with a variety of food, people eat more,[37] and this effect occurs even when the variety is manipulated via a condiment form, such as ketchup with fries (versus fries alone) and vanilla cream with brownie (versus brownie alone),[38] and via the use of tasteless and odourless features, such as multiple colours (versus single colour) of M&Ms or jelly beans,[39] and multiple shapes (versus single shape) of pasta.[40] Our preference for food variety explains the popularity of all-you-can-eat buffets.[41]

Preference for food taste and smell

Research has shown that people innately prefer fatty, sugary, umami, and salty tastes and smells, and dislike bitter and sour ones.[42] The former suggests nutrition, which our ancestors needed for survival; for example, fighting diseases, such as using spices to combat food-born microorganisms that cause toxins.[43] The latter indicates poison, which our ancestors needed to avoid. This food preference is called Darwinian gastronomy, which explains, for example, why the sales of chocolates, ice-cream, and savoury snacks continue to increase worldwide,[44] and why the top global restaurant chains offer fatty and tasty foods.[45]

Risk-taking behaviour

The activation of the self-protection mechanism leads us to avoid loss and take fewer risks, and loss aversion can be manifested in our preferences and choices following the status quo.[46] For example, in an experiment conducted by Griskevicius et al., when asked to indicate whether the research participants prefer Mercedes-Benz or BMW cars, those with a self-protection motivation choose whichever car brand that the majority prefer, regardless of which brand it is. The self-protection mechanism encourages people to band together with similar others, because they do not wish to draw attention to themselves.[47] As a result, they are more susceptible to compromise[48] and their opinions more easily swayed by those of the majority,[49] subjecting them to be less creative and to stick with options that worked in the past.[50]

Incidental touch from strangers in shops

Cues that signal dangers and threats are evaluated negatively, so that people can quickly get away from those cues. These cues can be as weak as the accidental touch from a stranger when shopping. Research has shown that an accidental touch, especially from a strange man (versus woman), decreases product and brand evaluation, lowers the willingness to pay, and a tendency to spend less time in-store.[51]

Is advertising containing violence effective?

The evolutionary perspective suggests that selection pressures partly form our selective attention; that is, we pay more attention to cues that signify danger and threat.[52] Consequently, people tend to pay attention to violent cues in movies, TV programmes, advertising, video games, et cetera. When people pay attention to these cues, such cues are processed as central cues while surrounding information is processed as peripheral cues.[53] That is, advertisements embedded in violent media contexts are processed as peripheral cues, whereas the violent content is processed as central cues.[54] A meta-analysis of 53 studies confirms that brands advertised in violent media content (violent programmes) are remembered less often, evaluated less favourably, and less likely to be purchased than brands advertised in nonviolent media content.[55] In short, advertisements containing violence renders viewers more likely to focus on the violent content rather than on the brand, and as a result these advertisements are likely to be ineffective.

10.4 THE MATING DRIVES

Mate attraction

The physiological basis

Mate attraction, also known as mate acquisition, suggests that people wishing to attract a mate are motivated to make themselves attractive. Attractiveness, determined by biological factors (e.g. physical appearances, body shape, body odour, skin conditions, voices), are indicators of genetic quality. What we define attractiveness is potentially what can maximise reproduction through, for example, increasing genetic disease resistance for the next generations.[56] For example, due to sex-specific hormonal markers women tend to store fat on the hips and breasts, whereas men tend to store fat in their upper body (shoulders). Consequently, men find women with a 0.7 waist-to-hip ratio attractive because these women are healthy and fertile,[57] whereas women find men with a broad chest with an ideal waist-to-chest ratio of 0.6 attractive because these men are healthy and strong.[58]

In addition, sex-specific hormones influence how women and men behave. That is, a woman's body releases different hormones (estrogen, progesterone, et cetera) over their menstrual cycles, and during the fertile phase women are more beautiful,[59] and also tend to do things that make them even more beautiful, such as wearing sexy clothes.[60] On the other hand, testosterone makes men more impulsive and aggressive.[61] This is the root of *sociobiology*, the biological basis of social behaviour.[62]

The psychological basis

There are sex differences in mate attraction tactics,[63] and these differences exist mainly because of differential *parental investment* between the two sexes in their offspring. According to Trivers, males typically engage less than females in the parental investment of their offspring, and as a result they adopt a reproductive strategy that maximises opportunities for sex.[64] Their evolutionary drive leads them to value those cues indicating reproductive value (i.e. genetic quality) in women, so they focus on beauty and youth for mate selection and attraction.[65] On the other hand, poor mating choices are more costly for females, as there are costs involved in pregnancy, child rearing, and youth, plus all of which may damage their potential future mate value. Therefore, females adopt a strategy that tries to identify the best male by holding back so as to evaluate maximum options of potential mates. That is, females may choose men for men's ability and willingness to invest in areas such as food, shelter, protection, and social status. In fact, female's evaluations of male's physical attractiveness are positively related to the resources and status that the males are able to demonstrate through, for example, their cars or clothes.[66]

Implications for consumer behaviour

Costly signalling theory

Costly signalling theory suggests that the exaggerated traits (e.g. the beautiful plumage of peacocks) used to signal to the potential mates are costly to survival. This theory can also be applied to humans' mating behaviour: people are inclined to show off the characteristics that their potential mates desire. In other words, when the motive of mate attraction is activated, people pay attention to information about their own desirability or the desirability of others as romantic partners.[67] Both men and women want to stand out to attract a mate, but they seek to draw attention to themselves in different ways – see Table 10.1 for the sex difference in their mate attraction strategies and behaviours.

Table 10.1 Sex differences in mate attraction behaviour

	Men	Women
Guiding strategy for mate attraction	• To advertise their strength, resources, and achievement[68]	• To advertise their youth and physical attractiveness[69]

	Men	**Women**
General behaviour	• More independent[70] • More socially dominant[71] • More risk-seeking[72] • More impulsive[73]	• More cooperative and helpful in public than in private[74] • Engage in more beautification practices
Examples from consumer behaviour	• Pay more attention to status goods[75] • Choose more conspicuous and expensive brands[76] • More willing to spend on conspicuous and expensive products/brands[77] • Less willing to choose the status quo product/brand[78]	• Popular products used to immediately accentuate cues of youth include breast padding, push-up bras, high heels, beautiful clothes, and cosmetics.[79] • Different haircuts[80] and hairstyles[81] to amplify alluring characteristics • Higher tendency of risk-taking behaviour in beautification practices, but not in financial risks[82]

Female models in advertising

The ideal female waist-to-hip ratio (0.7) explains why advertisements containing female models with this ratio elicit a more positive attitude in the audience.[83] In fact, the majority of the global online advertisements of female escorts spanning 48 countries use female models/escorts with the same waist-to-hip ratio.[84]

Consumption of perfume

The use of perfume is to amplify body odours that reveal a person's immunogenetics.[85] Recent research has demonstrated that people prefer fragrances that are similar to their own body odour, and prefer their romantic partners to have a similar body odour to themselves.[86] As a result, people use fragrances that best interact with their own body odour to produce an individually specific odour mixture that presents a better personality in the eye of potential mates.[87]

The influence of the menstrual cycle

Women's attention, memory, and behaviour are influenced by their menstrual cycle. When maximally fertile during their menstrual cycle (3–5 days before ovulation), women demonstrate the following cognitive and behavioural tendencies:

1. *Better memory to recall status-related products:*[88] This is because, during this phase, women become more sensitive to cues that signify a good mate, and this sensitivity is transferred to the related cues, such as status-related products.
2. *Spend more money on appearance-related products:*[89] This is because, during this phase, women engage in more beautification practices, as a proxy for sexual signalling. These beautification practices include wearing more sexy, revealing, and tight clothes.[90]

3. *Variety-seeking behaviour*: Variety-seeking behaviour is manifested in choosing products such as yogurts and candy bars.[91] This is because, during this phase, women show greater interest in many more men and a greater probability of having an affair.[92] Their desire for new options in men activates a variety-seeking mind-set that influences choice behaviour also in consumption. However, this variety-seeking mind-set only occurs in those women in a weak romantic relationship that somewhat triggers their mate attraction motive, not in those who are in a committed relationship.[93]

However, women are usually unaware of any change in their cognition or behaviour during this time.[94]

Mate retention

The psychological basis

Once we successfully attract our potential mates, our relationship is not without challenge. Maintaining a successful romantic relationship enhances reproductive fitness,[95] and the main mate retention efforts are to increase our own mate value, for both men and women. That is, men's mate value lies in their resources, and therefore men display their resources to entice their mates, and women's mate retention devotion increases as their mates' incomes and resources increase.[96] On the other hand, women's mate value lies in their youth and physical attractiveness, which is positively related to men's mate retention efforts, as the younger and the more beautiful their mates are, the greater the possibility that their mates could be poached by others.[97] As a result, women's mate retention tactics rely on the enhancement of their physical appearances.

Men, being physically strong, also use verbal or physical dominance-based strategies that focus either on the potential rivals or on their mate to ensure that she remains faithful.[98] For example, regardless of the men's age and the length of the relationship, there is an increasing violence towards other men to fend off intrasexual threats when their mate is young and beautiful.[99] By contrast, women are usually physically weaker than men. Instead of using violence, they pay more attention to potential rivals (i.e. other beautiful women in the vicinity of their mates) and demonstrate public signals of their mates belonging to them;[100] for example, to show off how much they and their men are in love.[101]

Implications for consumer behaviour

Luxury consumption

Women use conspicuous luxury consumption to maintain their relationship by guarding their mates from other potential female rivals. When the mate guarding motive is activated, women desire luxury products (including handbags, T-shirts, cars, and shoes), spend more money on them, and choose products with significantly large-sized logos.[102] Other women who consider pursuing a taken man are less willing to pursue him if his partner had a designer's handbag and expensive jewellery, since these luxury items, if he bought them, represent the man's devotion to his partner.[103]

Joint consumption

Joint consumption, including durable goods (e.g. a house or a car), everyday household goods (e.g. food and toothpaste), and experiential goods (e.g. a vacation or a restaurant), involves balancing the recipient's and the chooser's preferences,[104] and even if people make purchase choices for themselves, their decisions are implicitly or explicitly influenced by their relationship partners.[105] That is, joint consumption is highly relational, and the choosers are aware of the fact that their decisions can impact on their relationships with the co-consumers.[106] How and when does one make compromises in joint consumption? One of the determinants is the relationship goals. First, couples prefer more variety for joint consumption when they believe they will continue the relationship. Variety seeking here suggests varied activities (e.g. going out to dinner, to a movie, and to a concert), as opposed to less varied activities (e.g. seeing several different movies). Variety seeking can inject a sense of excitement to the relationship, which can be maintained more interestingly and easily.[107] Secondly, people would rely on their partner's competencies to effectively make related decisions.[108] For example, men with mates would listen to their wives about what to eat.[109]

Does sex sell?

The error management theory (Box 10.1) also applies in mating drives, and the applications result in men and women reacting differently to sexual images containing sexuality that is unnecessarily explicit. That is, men far prefer the advertisements featuring these sexual images, whereas women report negative attitudes toward these advertisements.[110] As a result, whether or not sex sells depends on who the target audience is. However, even if the target audience is men, this type of advertisement can still be ineffective. This is because, similar to the effectiveness of advertisements containing violence discussed previously in Section 10.3, people tend to pay attention to sexual cues in motives, TV programmes, advertising, video games et cetera.[111] In other words, advertisements embedded in sexual media contexts are processed as peripheral cues, whereas the sexual content is processed as central cues.[112] Therefore, advertising containing sex renders viewers more likely to focus on the sexual content rather than on the brand, and as a result such advertising is ineffective.[113]

10.5 THE AFFILIATION DRIVES

The theory of reciprocal altruism

The psychological basis

The theory of reciprocal altruism argues that adaptations for providing benefits to nonrelatives are evolved mechanisms since the nonrelatives would reciprocate to benefit both parties.[114] Reciprocation means that both benefits and costs are shared between allies and friends, and increases the inclusive fitness for both parties.[115] As a result, people have evolved a psychological adaptation of the need to belong,[116] which motivates us to invest in our friendships by maintaining existing friendships as well as making new friends.[117] When forming groups, people show preferential attitudes towards in-group members versus out-group members,[118] as discussed in Section 8.3.

Implications for consumer behaviour

Gift giving

Research finds that people tend to give more valuable gifts to those who are close friends. In fact, the value of the gifts given to close friends is greater than that given to distant kin.[119]

Need to belong

The need to belong increases when an affiliation motive is activated, and the affiliation motive can be activated by the presence of old friends or by the threat of social rejection.[120] The consumer behaviour implication of the former is gift giving, and of the latter is how they deal with social rejection (or exclusion), which is discussed in Section 8.3.

Status

The psychological basis

Status can bring many benefits, such as access to food (money), territory, and sex. Compared with those with low status, people with high status have greater interpersonal influence, more material resources, higher self-esteem, and better health.[121] For example, wearing high-status, branded clothes versus unbranded clothes can boost compliance with the person's requests from other people as well as the likelihood of being hired for a job.[122] The status-striving motive is more pronounced in men, given the increased possibility to win mates via intrasexual competition (see Section 10.2), and as a result the status motive is closely related to the mate attraction motive, as discussed in Section 10.4.

People with low status seek to approach and imitate prestigious people. People learn prestige criteria, in part, by scrutinising the attention structure. That is, most people typically pay the most attention to those high in prestige.[123] By attending to and imitating the behaviour, such as clothing styles, of those with high status, people learn the prestige criteria of their local culture.[124] Once status is obtained, people focus on preserving their status, such as by being more conservative in their decision making[125] and by prioritising personal goals over group goals.[126]

Implications for consumer behaviour

Costly signalling theory

Costly signalling theory, discussed in Chapter 10.4, suggests that the exaggerated traits (e.g. the beautiful plumage of peacocks) used to signal to the potential mates are costly to survival. This theory can also be applied to humans' status-striving behaviour; that is, humans are willing to pay a high price (or put in great effort) in order to achieve status.[127] The costly signalling theory is manifested in luxury consumption and green consumption.

Luxury consumption

Extensive research has shown that the main purpose of people's buying and using luxury products is to signal their status. The inclination to display luxury products is particularly pronounced for those whose status is low[128] or whose status has been threatened.[129] According to Han et al., not all wealthy people desire status and not all people desiring status can afford luxury products.[130] Those who desire status tend to buy prominent and loud luxury goods so as to display their status to those with inferior status, and to be disassociated from these people, whereas those with low need for status tend to buy inconspicuous and quiet luxury goods only so they can recognise and associate with their own kind. If those with high in status striving cannot afford true luxury, they would then turn to counterfeit luxury products to imitate wealthy people.[131] [132] In addition, the signalling effectiveness using luxury products is greater for those who face others with inferior status than those who face others with superior status.[133] As a result, the showing-off behaviour is frequent only when people deal with other people who have inferior status to theirs.

Green (pro-environmental) consumption

Pro-environmental products are usually more expensive, but buying these so-called green products benefits everyone, not just the self. In a series of experiments, Griskevicius et al. find that the research participants with status-striving motives tend to prefer the green products, including cars, soap, and dishwashers, to the luxury options.[134] In particular, their green preference occurs only when this purchase can be displayed publically (versus privately displayed purchase), and only when this purchase is expensive as opposed to a cheaper option. Similar phenomenon has been observed in consumption of organic foods and sustainable services.[135] For example, in a real-world setting, shoppers of a high-status sustainable grocery chain like to use the branded shopping bags to show off their pro-environmental behaviour.[136]

10.6 REFLECTION

Writing this chapter, I cannot help but notice that the results of evolutionary psychology research "support" social stereotypes such as women are less status-striving than men or that men are more aggressive than women. Although evolutionary perspective indeed provides an additional view of human (consumer) behaviour,[137] it is still alarming. Many evolutionary psychologists keep reassuring us that behaviour is a result of both biological and social factors,[138] and that evolutionary psychology (and sociobiology) only provides explanations of, not justifications for behaviour.[139] From the perspective of objective scientific research, I agree with these evolutionary psychologists: the importance of biological factors is undeniable, and we should not avoid discussing or researching them just because the results might indicate social stereotypes.

Whilst it is important to have an objective scientific attitude, it is equally important to consider the wider impact of "evolutionary explanations" on society (especially if the explanations should be incorrect). We should not forget that the society is also evolving. The recent movement from encouraging women to join STEAM courses (science, technology, engineering, arts, and mathematics), LGBTQ (lesbian, gay, bisexual, transgender, and queer/questioning) rights, to UK's banning brands from using social stereotype depictions in advertisements – all of these illustrate that we, as the human race, try to break stereotypes. To (mis)quote Dawkins, "our brain is evolved enough to be rebellious," rebellious to defy genetic determinism.[140]

10.7 SUMMARY

1. Evolutionary psychology, based on Darwin's evolutionary theory, sees psychology as a branch of biology and focuses on the evolution of the human mind (brain). The human brain has been shaped by the evolutionary process, and as a result psychological mechanisms are also evolved adaptations by selection. There are three premises of evolutionary psychology: (1) human nature is universal (only with differences adapting to local environments), (2) psychological adaptations are domain-specific to solve specific fitness problems, and (3) the environment in which the psychological adaptations were developed was during the Pleistocene epoch (roughly from 2.5 million years to 11 thousand years ago), which is called the environment of evolutionary adaptedness (EEA). The difference between evolutionary psychology and other schools

of psychology is different aspects of the research questions they answer. Evolutionary psychologists are interested in the ultimate explanations, focusing on the "what for" aspect (e.g. what was the behaviour adapted to solve?), whereas psychologists of other schools are interested in the proximate explanations, focusing on the "how" questions (e.g. how or what does the behaviour influence?). Ultimate and proximate explanations are not competing explanations, since they provide different aspects of the same psychological mechanisms.

2. Infectious diseases are one of the important selection pressures; as a result, people have evolved motivation to avoid diseases through the behavioural immune system, such as increasing frequencies of hand-washing with soap. This motivation to avoid diseases is often manifested in consumers' food preferences, which can activate our brain's reward centre. First, people prefer variety. This is because a variety of food can provide a variety of nutrition; also, should we eat something toxic, we would not eat as much of it when we eat a variety of food. Research has shown that people eat more if they are presented with a variety of food. Second, people innately prefer fatty, sugary, umami, and salty tastes and smells, and dislike bitter and sour ones. This is because the former indicates nutrition (which our ancestors needed for survival), whereas the latter implies poison.

3. The motivation to protect one's self is an evolved psychological mechanism because of the many dangers and threats faced by our ancestors. The self-protection motive is activated when we face dangers and threats, including diseases, snakes, crime news, and strangers. Self-protection encourages us to be risk averse by following the status quo. For example, when asked to indicate which car people prefer, Mercedes-Benz or BMW, those with self-protection motive choose whichever car make that the majority prefer, regardless of which brand it is. In addition, if the self-protection motive is activated in a retail setting (e.g. accidentally touched by a male stranger), these shoppers' evaluation of product/brand, willingness to pay, browsing time in the shop decrease.

4. To increase reproduction, people have evolved psychological adaptations to attract and retain mates. Mate attraction and retention have attracted most of the research attention, compared with other evolved adaptations. The mate attraction motive depends on the physical appearances which indicate genetic quality and reproductive potential. In addition, because of differential parental investment between the two sexes in their offspring, men's and women's mate attraction purposes and tactics are different. Men typically engage less than females in parental investment of their offspring, so they focus on maximising opportunities for sex and pay attention to women's reproductive value and genetic quality, which are translated into women's youth and beauty. On the other hand, poor mating choices are costly to women (costs of pregnancy, child rearing, youth), so they try to identify the best mate by holding back to evaluate maximum potential mate options, and pay attention to the potential mates' ability and willingness to invest in, for example, protection and social status.

5. Costly signalling theory is the main theory that explains men's and women's efforts in mate attraction. For example, men tend to advertise their sources, independence,

and achievement, and as a result they pay more attention to status goods, choose more conspicuous and expensive brands, which are not the status quo, become more willing to spend on these products or brands, and buy gifts for their potential mates. On the other hand, women engage in more beautification practices in order to advertise their physical attractiveness. In particular, women's beautification practices are influenced by their menstrual cycle. When maximally fertile during their menstrual cycle, women spend more money on appearance-related products and tend to wear sexy clothes. The women's menstrual cycle plays an important role in their mate attraction motivation.

6. Once we successfully attract our potential mate, we need to maintain a successful relationship, which enhances reproductive fitness. Men's mate retention strategies focus on displaying their resources towards their partner, but aggression towards the potential competitors. On the other hand, women's mate retention relies on enhancing their physical appearances, and in particular they would use a public display of their partner's devotion to themselves to fend off potential rivals. Therefore, men use luxury consumption to display their resources, whereas women use luxury consumption as gifts from their partners to lower a potential rival's mate-poaching intentions.

7. Humans are social creatures, and reciprocal altruism is an evolved adaptation. Altruistic acts can occur between two genetically unrelated people, and such acts suggest that benefits and risks are shared and reduced to increase inclusive fitness. That is why reciprocal altruism is often seen among friends and allies and why humans have a universal need to belong. Reciprocal altruism can be manifested in gift-giving. That is, people tend to give more valuable gifts to those who are close friends than to those who are distant kin.

8. Status can bring many benefits, such as access to food (money) and sex, and can be obtained from dominance (e.g. force) and prestige (e.g. valuable skills). People with high status have greater interpersonal influence, more material resources, higher self-esteem, and better health. The status-striving motive is more pronounced in men, because of increased possibility to win mates via intrasexual competition. As a result, the status motive is closely related to the mate attraction motive. Status can be shown via luxury consumption, and expensive, pro-environmental consumption.

9. There are evolved cognitive biases to increase fitness. People tend to pay more attention to, and better remember, dangers, threats, cheaters, and potential sexual partners. As a result, for example, advertising containing violence or sex are not as effective as we may have believed – the cues of violence or sex are centrally processed, leaving the brand and product information in the advertisement to be processed peripherally.

DISCUSSION QUESTIONS

1. Discuss what evolutionary psychology is and its role in consumer behaviour.
2. Discuss how survival drives apply to consumer behaviour.

3. Discuss the role of parental investment in mating drives and how it applies to consumer behaviour.
4. Explain the role of costly signalling theory and how it applies in consumer behaviour.

FURTHER READING

- Cohen, J. B., & Bernard, H. R. (2013). Evolutionary Psychology and Consumer Behavior: A Constructive Critique. *Journal of Consumer Psychology, 23*(3), 387–399.
- Downes, S. M. (2013). Evolutionary Psychology Is Not the Only Productive Evolutionary Approach to Understanding Consumer Behavior. *Journal of Consumer Psychology, 23*(3), 400–403.
- Griskevicius, V., & Kenrick, D. T. (2013). Fundmental Motives: How Evolutionary Needs Influence Consumer Behavior. *Journal of Consumer Psychology, 23*(3), 372–386.
- Kenrick, D. T., Saad, G., & Griskevicius, V. (2013). Evolutionary Consumer Psychology: Ask Not What You Can Do for Biology, But . . . *Journal of Consumer Psychology, 23*(3), 404–409.
- Saad, G. (2017). On the Method of Evolutionary Psychology and Its Applicability to Consumer Research. *Journal of Marketing Research, 54*(3), 464-477.

NOTES

1. Confer, J. C., Easton, J. A., Fleischman, D. S., Goetz, C. D., Lewis, D. M. G., Perilloux, C., & Buss, D. M. (2010). Evolutionary Psychology: Controversies, Questions, Prospects, and Limitations. *American Psychologist, 65*(2), 110–126; Durante, K. M., & Griskevicius, V. (2018). Evolution and Consumer Psychology. *Consumer Psychology Review, 1*(1), 4–21; Mayr, E. (1961). Cause and Effect in Biology. *Science, 134*(3489), 1501–1506.
2. Eccles, J. S., Jacobs, J. E., & Harold, R. D. (1990). Gender Role Stereotypes, Expectancy Effects, and Parent's Socialization of Gender Differences. *Journal of Social Issues, 46*(2), 183–201.
3. Darwin, C. (1859). *On the Origin of Species: by Means of Natural Selection or the Preservation of Favoured Races in the Struggle for Life*. London: Wordsworth.
4. Darwin, C. (1871). *The Descent of Man, and Selection in Relation to Sex*. London: John Murray.
5. Buss, D. M. (2019). *Evolutionary Psychology: The New Science of the Mind* (sixth edn). New York: Routledge.
6. Trivers, R. L. (1972). Parental Investment and Sexual Selection. In B. Campbell (ed.), *Sexual Selection and the Descent of Man: The Darwinian Pivot* (pp. 136–179). Chicago: Aldine Publishing Company.
7. Howard, R. D. (1978). The Evolution of Mating Strategies in Bullfrogs, Rana Catesbeiana. *Evolution, 32*(4), 850–871; Nisbet, I. C. T. (1977). Courtship-Feeding and Clutch Size in Common Terns Sterna Hirundo. In B. Stonehouse & C. Perrins (eds), *Evolutionary Ecology*

(pp. 101–109). London: Palgrave; Thornhill, R. (1976). Sexual Selection and Nuptial Feeding Behavior in Bittacus Apicalis (Insecta: Mecoptera). *American Naturalist, 110*(974), 529–548.

8. Tooby, J., & Cosmides, L. (2005). Conceptual Foundations of Evolutionary Psychology. In D. M. Buss (ed.), *The Handbook of Evolutionary Psychology* (pp. 5–67). Hoboken, NJ: John Wiley & Sons.

9. Confer et al., Evolutionary Psychology.

10. Page 79, Kaplan, H. S., & Gangestad, S. W. (2005). Life History Theory and Evolutionary Psychology. In D. M. Buss (ed.), *The Handbook of Evolutionary Psychology* (pp. 68–95). Hoboken, NJ: John Wiley & Sons.

11. Ellison, P. T. (2001). *Reproductive Ecology and Human Evolution*. New York: Aldine de Gruyter.

12. Hagen, E. H. (2005). Controversial Issues in Evolutionary Psychology. In D. M. Buss (ed.), *The Handbook of Evolutionary Psychology* (pp. 145–173). Hoboken, NJ: John Wiley & Sons.

13. Tooby & Cosmides, Conceptual Foundations of Evolutionary Psychology.

14. Tooby, J., & Cosmides, L. (1992). The Psychological Foundations of Culture. In J. H. Barkow, L. Cosmides, & J. Tooby (eds), *The Adapted Mind: Evolutionary Psychology and the Generation of Culture* (pp. 19–136). New York: Oxford University Press.

15. Pinker, S. (1997). *How the Mind Works*. New York: Norton.

16. Chomsky, N. (1975). *Reflections on Language*. New York: Pantheon Books; Wexler, K., & Culicover, P. W. (1980). *Formal Principles of Language Acquisition*. Cambridge, MA: MIT Press; Pinker, S. (1984). *Language Learnability and Language Development*. Cambridge, MA: Harvard University Press.

17. Tooby & Cosmides. The Psychological Foundations of Culture.

18. Tooby & Cosmides, Conceptual Foundations of Evolutionary Psychology.

19. Hagen, Controversial Issues in Evolutionary Psychology.

20. Neuberg, S. L., Kenrick, D. T., & Schaller, M. (2010). Evolutionary Social Psychology. In S. T. Fiske, D. T. Gilbert, & G. Lindzey (eds), *Handbook of Social Psychology* (fifth edn, Vol. 2, pp. 761–796). New York: Wiley.

21. Griskevicius, V., & Kenrick, D. T. (2013). Fundamental Motives: How Evolutionary Needs Influence Consumer Behavior. *Journal of Consumer Psychology, 23*(3), 372–386.

22. Schaller, M. (2015). The Behavioral Immune System. In D. M. Buss (ed.), *The Handbook of Evolutionary Psychology* (second edn, Vol. 1, pp. 206–224). New York: John Wiley & Sons; Schaller, M., & Park, J. H. (2011). The Behavioral Immune System (and Why It Matters). *Current Directions in Psychological Science, 20*(2), 99–103.

23. Ackerman, J. M., Shapiro, J. R., Neuberg, S. L., Kenrick, D. T., Becker, D. V., Griskevicius, V., . . . Schaller, M. (2006). They All Look the Same to Me (Unless They're Angry): From Out-Group Homogeneity to Out-Group Heterogeneity. *Psychological Science, 17*(10), 836–840.

24. Öhman, A., & Mineka, S. (2001). Fears, Phobias, and Preparedness: Toward an Evolved Module of Fear and Fear Learning. *Psychological Review, 108*(3), 483–522.

25. Altheide, D. L. (1997). The News, the Problem Frame, and the Production of Fear. *The Sociological Quarterly, 38*(4), 647–668.

26. Scott, H. (2003). Stranger Danger: Explaining Women's Fear of Crime. *Western Criminology Review, 4*(3), 203–214; Foster, S., Villanueva, K., Wood, L., Christian, H., & Giles-Corti, B. (2014). The Impact of Parents' Fear of Strangers and Perceptions of Informal Social Control on Children's Independent Mobility. *Health & Place, 26,* 60–68.

27. Schaller, M., Park, J. H., & Mueller, A. (2003). Fear of the Dark: Interactive Effects of Beliefs about Danger and Ambient Darkness on Ethnic Stereotypes. *Personality and Social Psychology Bulletin, 29*(5), 637–649.

28. Li, Y. J., Kenrick, D. T., Griskevicius, V., & Neuberg, S. L. (2012). Economic Decision Biases and Fundamental Motivations: How Mating and Self-Protection Alter Loss Aversion. *Journal of Personality and Social Psychology, 102*(3), 550–561.

29. Lerner, J. S., & Keltner, D. (2001). Fear, Anger, and Risk. *Journal of Personality and Social Psychology, 81*(1), 146–159.

30. Maner, J. K., Kenrick, D. T., Becker, D. V., Robertson, T. E., Ofer, B., Neuberg, S. L., . . . Schaller, M. (2005). Functional Projection: How Fundamental Social Motives Can Bias Interpersonal Perception. *Journal of Personality and Social Psychology, 88*(1), 63–78.

31. Griskevicius & Kenrick, Fundamental Motives.

32. Nairne, J. S., Pandeirada, J. N. S., & Thompson, S. R. (2008). Adaptive Memory: The Comparative Value of Survival Processing. *Psychological Science, 19*(2), 176–180; Weinstein, Y., Bugg, J. M., & Roediger, H. L., III. (2008). Can the Survival Recall Advantage Be Explained by Basic Memory Processes. *Memory & Cognition, 36*(5), 913–919.

33. Haselton, M. G., & Buss, D. M. (2000). Error Management Theory: A New Perspective on Biases in Cross-Sex Mind Reading. *Journal of Personality and Social Psychology, 78*(1), 81–91.

34. Haselton, M. G., Nettle, D., & Murray, D. R. (2016). The Evolution of Cognitive Bias. In D. M. Buss (ed.), *Handbook of Evolutionary Psychology* (Vol. 2, pp. 968–987). Hoboken, NJ: John Wiley & Sons.

35. Miller, S. L., & Maner, J. K. (2012). Overperceiving Disease Cues: The Basic Cognition of the Behavioral Immune System. *Journal of Personality and Social Psychology, 102*(6), 1198–1213.

36. Saad, G. (2013). Evolutionary Consumption. *Journal of Consumer Psychology, 23*(3), 351–371.

37. Remick, A. K., Polivy, J., & Patricia, P. (2009). Internal and External Moderators of the Effect of Variety on Food Intake. *Psychological Bulletin, 135*(3), 434–451.

38. Brondel, L., Romer, M., van Wymebeke, V., Pineau, N., Jiang, T., Hanus, C., & Rigaud, D. (2009). Variety Enhances Food Intake in Humans: Role of Sensory-Specific Satiety. *Physiology & Behavior, 97*(1), 44–51.

39. Kahn, B. E., & Wansink, B. (2004). The Influence of Assortment Structure on Perceived Variety and Consumption Quantities. *Journal of Consumer Research, 30*(March), 519–533.

40. Rolls, B. J., Rowe, E. A., & Rolls, E. T. (1982). How Sensory Properties of Foods Affect Human Feeding Behavior. *Physiology & Behavior, 29*(3), 409–417.

41. Saad, Evolutionary Consumption.

42. Beauchamp, G. K., & Mennella, J. A. (2009). Early Flavor Learning and Its Impact on Later Feeding Behavior. *Journal of Pediatric Gastroenterology and Nutrition, 48,* S25–S30;

Breslin, P. A. S. (2013). An Evolutionary Perspective on Food and Human Taste. *Current Biology, 23*(9), R409–418; Drewnowski, A. (1997). Why Do We Like Fat? *Journal of the American Dietetic Association, 97*(7, Supplement), S58–S62; Hoover, K. C. (2010). Smell With Inspiration: The Evolutionary Significance of Olfaction. *American Journal of Physical Anthropology, 56*(S51), 63–74.

43. Sherman, P. W. (1999). Darwinian Gastronomy: Why We Use Spices: Spices Taste Good Because They Are Good for Us. *BioScience, 49*(6), 453–463.

44. Statista. (2021). *Confectionery & Snacks Report 2021.* Retrieved from www.statista.com/ study/48835/confectionery-and-snacks-report/; Statista. (2022). *Size of the Global Ice Cream Market from 2013 to 2024.* Retrieved from www.statista.com/statistics/326315/global-ice-cream-market-size/; Euromonitor. (2022). *2016–2021 Global Market Sizes – Ice Cream and Frozen Desserts.* Retrieved from www.euromonitor.com/; Euromonitor. (2022). *2016–2021 Global Market Sizes – Chocolate Confectionery.* Retrieved from www.euromonitor.com/

45. Saad, Evolutionary Consumption.

46. Jost, J. T., & Hunyady, O. (2005). Antecedents and Consequences of System-Justifying Ideologies. *Current Directions in Psychological Science, 14*(5), 260–265; Mok, A., & Morris, M. W. (2012). Bicultural Self-Defense in Consumer Contexts: Self-Protection Motives Are the Basis for Contrast versus Assimilation to Cultural Cues. *Journal of Consumer Psychology, 23*(2), 175–188.

47. Griskevicius, V., Goldstein, N. J., Mortensen, C. R., Cialdini, R. B., & Kenrick, D. T. (2006). Going Along Versus Going Alone: When Fundamental Motives Facilitates Strategic (Non) Conformity. *Journal of Personality and Social Psychology, 91*(2), 281–294.

48. Simonson, I. (1989). Choice Based on Reasons: The Case of Attraction and Compromise Effects. *Journal of Consumer Research, 16*(2), 158–174.

49. Griskevicius et al., Going Along Versus Going Alone.

50. Griskevicius & Kenrick, Fundamental Motives.

51. Martin, B. A. (2012). A Stranger's Touch: Effects of Accidental Interpersonal Touch on Consumer Evaluation and Shopping Time. *Journal of Consumer Research, 39*(June), 174–184.

52. Buss, D. M., & Duntley, J. D. (2006). The Evolution of Aggression. In M. Schaller, J. A. Simpson, & D. T. Kenrick (eds), *Evolution and Social Psychology* (pp. 263–285). New York: Psychology Press.

53. Easterbrook, J. A. (1959). The Effect of Emotion on Cue Utilization and the Organization of Behavior. *Psychological Review, 66*(3), 183–201; Lang, A., Newhagen, J., & Reeves, B. (1996). Negative Video as Structure: Emotion, Attention, Capacity, and Memory. *Journal of Broadcasting & Electronic Media, 40*(4), 460–499.

54.   Bushman, B. J., & Bonacci, A. M. (2002). Violence and Sex Impair Memory for Television Ads. *Journal of Applied Psychology, 87*(3), 557–564.

55. Lull, R. B., & Bushman, B. J. (2015). Do Sex and Violence Sell? A Meta Analytic Review of the Effects of Sexual and Violent Media and Ad Content on Memory, Attitudes, and Buying Intentions. *Psychological Bulletin, 141*(5), 1022–1048.

56. Hamilton, W. D., & Zuk, M. (1982). Heritable True Fitness and Bright Birds: A Role for Parasites? *Science, 218*(4570), 384–387.

57. Singh, D. (2002). Female Mate Value at a Glance: Relationship of Waist-to-Hip Ratio to Health, Fecundity and Attractiveness. *Neuroendocrinology Letters*, *23*(Suppl. 4), 81–91; Singh, D. (1993). Adaptive Significance of Female Physical Attractiveness: Role of Waist-to-Hip Ratio. *Journal of Personality and Social Psychology*, *65*(2), 293–307; Platek, S. M., & Singh, D. (2010). Optimal Waist-to-Hip Ratios in Women Activate Neural Reward Centers in Men. *PLoS One*, *5*(2), e9024; Dixson, B. J., Grimshaw, G. M., Linklater, W. L., & Dixson, A. F. (2011). Eye-Tracking of Men's Preferences for Waist-to-Hip Ratio and Breast Size of Women. *Archives of Sexual Behavior*, *40*(1), 43–50.

58. Maisey, D. S., Vale, E. L. E., Comelissen, P. L., & Tovée, M. J. (1999). Characteristics of Male Attractiveness for Women. *The Lancet Diabetes & Endocrinology*, *353*(9163), 1500; Dixson, A. F., Gayle, East, R., Wignarajah, P., & Anderson, M. J. (2003). Masculine Somatotype and Hirsuteness as Determinants of Sexual Attractiveness to Women. *Archives of Sexual Behavior*, *32*(1), 29–39; Weeden, J., & Sabini, J. (2005). Physical Attractiveness and Health in Western Societies: A Review. *Psychological Bulletin*, *131*(5), 635–653.

59. Roberts, S. C., Havlicek, J., Flegr, J., Hruskova, M., Little, A. C., Jones, B. C., . . . Petrie, M. (2004). Female Facial Attractiveness Increases during the Fertile Phase of the Menstrual Cycle. *Proceedings of the Royal Society B*, *271*(Supplement), S270–S272.

60. Haselton, M. G., Mortezaie, M., Pillsworth, E. G., Bleske-Rechek, A., & Frederick, D. A. (2007). Ovulatory Shifts in Human Female Ornamentation: Near Ovulation, Women Dress to Impress. *Hormones and Behavior*, *51*(1), 40–45.

61. Pavlov, K. A., Chistiakov, D. A., & Chekhonin, V. P. (2012). Genetic Determinants of Aggression and Impulsivity in Humans. *Journal of Applied Genetics*, *53*(1), 61–82.

62. Wilson, E. O. (1975). *Sociobiology: The New Synthesis*. Cambridge, MA: Belknap Press.

63. Buss, D. M., & Schmitt, D. P. (1993). Sexual Strategies Theory: An Evolutionary Perspective on Human Mating. *Psychological Review*, *100*(2), 204–232.

64. Trivers, Parental Investment and Sexual Selection.

65. Buss, D. M. (1989). Sex Differences in Human Mate Preferences: Evolutionary Hypotheses Tested in 37 Cultures. *Behavioral and Brain Sciences*, *12*(1), 1–49.

66. Townsend, J. M., & Levy, G. D. (1990). Effects of Potential Partners' Costume and Physical Attractiveness on Sexuality and Partner Selection. *Journal of Psychology*, *124*(4), 371–389; Dunn, M. J., & Searle, R. (2010). Effect of Manipulated Prestige-Car Ownership on Both Sex Attractiveness Ratings. *British Journal of Psychology*, *101*(1), 69–80.

67. Griskevicius & Kenrick, Fundamental Motives.

68. Buss, D. M. (1988). The Evolution of Human Intrasexual Competition: Tactics of Mate Attraction. *Journal of Personality and Social Psychology*, *54*(4), 616–628; Wiederman, M. W. (1993). Evolved Gender Differences in Mate Preferences: Evidence from Personal Advertisements. *Ethology and Sociobiology*, *14*(5), 331–351.

69. Ibid.

70. Griskevicius et al., Going Along Versus Going Alone.

71. Ainsworth, S. E., & Maner, J. K. (2012). Sex Begets Violence: Mating Motives, Social Dominance, and Physical Aggression in Men. *Journal of Personality and Social Psychology*, *103*(5), 819–829.

72. Baker, M. D., Jr., & Maner, J. K. (2008). Risk-Taking as a Situationally Sensitive Male Mating Strategy. *Evolution and Human Behavior, 29*(6), 391–395.

73. Wilson, M., & Daly, M. (2004). Do Pretty Women Inspire Men to Discount the Future? *Proceedings of the Royal Society B, 271*(Supplement), S177–S179.

74. Griskevicius et al., Going Along Versus Going Alone.

75. Janssens, K., Pandelaere, M., Van den Bergh, B., Millet, K., Lens, I., & Roe, K. (2011). Can Buy Me Love: Mate Attraction Goals Lead to Perceptual Readiness for Status Products. *Journal of Experimental Social Psychology, 47*(1), 254–258.

76. Sundie, J. M., Kenrick, D. T., Griskevicius, V., Tybur, J. M., Vohs, K. D., & Beal, D. J. (2011). Peacocks, Porsches, and Thorstein Veblen: Conspicuous Consumption as a Sexual Signaling System. *Journal of Personality and Social Psychology, 100*(4), 664–680.

77. Griskevicius, et al., Blatant Benevolence and Conspicuous Consumption.

78. Griskevicius et al., Going Along Versus Going Alone.

79. Russell, R. (2009). A Sex Difference in Facial Contrast and Its Exaggeration by Cosmetics. *Perception, 38*(8), 1211–1219; Morris, P. H., White, J., Morrison, E. R., & Fisher, K. (2013). High Heels As Supernormal Stimuli: How Wearing High Heels Affects Judgements of Female Attractiveness. *Evolution and Human Behavior, 34*(3), 176–181; Samson, N., Fink, B., & Matts, P. J. (2010). Visible Skin Condition and Perception of Human Facial Appearance. *International Journal of Cosmetic Science, 32*(3), 167–184.

80. Hinsz, V. B., Matz, D. C., & Patience, R. A. (2001). Does Women's Hair Signal Reproductive Potential. *Journal of Experimental Social Psychology, 37*(2), 166–172.

81. Mesko, N., & Bereczkei, T. (2004). Hairstyle as an Adaptive Means of Displaying Phenotypic Quality. *Human Nature, 15*(3), 251–270.

82. Hill, S. E., & Durante, K. M. (2011). Courtship, Competition, and the Pursuit of Attractiveness: Mating Goals Facilitate Health-Related Risk Taking and Strategic Risk Suppression in Women. *Personality and Social Psychology Bulletin, 37*(3), 383–394.

83. Vyncke, P. (2011). Cue Management: Using Fitness Cues to Enhance Advertising Effectiveness. In G. Saad (ed.), *Evolutionary Psychology in the Business Sciences* (pp. 257–287). Berlin, Heidelberg: Springer.

84. Saad, G. (2008). Advertised Waist-to-Hip Ratios of Online Female Escorts: An Evolutionary Perspective. *International Journal of e-Collaboration, 4*(3), 40–50.

85. Milinski, M., & Wedekind, C. (2001). Evidence for MHC-Correlated Perfume Preferences in Humans. *Behavioral Ecology, 12*(2), 140–149.

86. Lidquist, A. (2012). Perfume Preferences and How They Are Related to Commercial Gender Classifications of Fragrances. *Chemosensory Perception, 5*(2), 197–204; Allen, C., Havlíček, J., Williams, K., & Roberts, S. C. (2019). Evidence for Odour-Mediated Assortative Mating in Humans: The Impact of Hormonal Contraception and Artificial Fragrances. *Physiology & Behavior, 210*, 112541.

87. Lenochová, P., Vohnoutová, P., Roberts, S. C., Oberzaucher, E., Grammer, K., & Havlíček, J. (2012). Psychology of Fragrance Use: Perception of Individual Odor and Perfume Blends Reveals a Mechanism for Idiosyncratic Effects on Fragrance Choice. *PLoS One,*

7(3), e33810; Sorokowska, A., Sorokowski, P., & Havlíček, J. (2016). Body Odor Based Personality Judgements: The Effect of Fragranced Cosmetics. *Frontier Psychology, 7*, 530.

88. Lens, I., Driesmans, K., Pandelaere, M., & Janssens, K. (2012). Would Male Conspicuous Consumption Capture the Female Eye? Menstrual Cycle Effects on Women's Attention to Status Products. *Journal of Experimental Social Psychology, 48*(1), 346–349.

89. Saad, G., & Stenstrom, E. (2012). Calories, Beauty, and Ovulation: The Effects of the Menstrual Cycle on Food and Appearance-Related Consumption. *Journal of Consumer Psychology, 22*(1), 102–113.

90. Grammer, K., Renninger, L., & Fischer, B. (2004). Disco Clothing, Female Sexual Motivation, and Relationship Status: Is She Dressed to Impress? *Journal of Sex Research, 41*(1), 66–74; Haselton, M. G., Mortezaie, M., Pillsworth, E. G., Bleske-Rechek, A., & Frederick, D. A. (2007). Ovulatory Shifts in Human Female Ornamentation: Near Ovulation, Women Dress to Impress. *Hormones and Behavior, 51*(1), 40–45.

91. Durante, K. M., & Arsena, A. R. (2015). Playing the Field: The Effect of Fertility on Women's Desire for Variety. *Journal of Consumer Research, 41*(April), 1372–1391.

92. Durante, K. M., & Li, N. P. (2009). Oestradiol Level and Opportunistic Mating in Women. *Biology Letters, 5*(2), 179–182; Gangestad, S. W., Thornhill, R., & Garver-Apgar, C. E. (2010). Fertility in the Cycle Predicts Women's Interest in Sexual Opportunism. *Evolution and Human Behavior, 31*(6), 400–411.

93. Durante & Arsena, Playing the Field.

94. Durante, K. M., Griskevicius, V., Hill, S. E., Perilloux, C., & Li, N. P. (2011). Ovulation, Female Competition, and Product Choice: Hormonal Influences on Consumer Behavior. *Journal of Consumer Research, 37*(6), 921–934.

95. Hill, K., & Hurtado, A. M. (1996). *The Ecology and Demography of a Foraging People.* New York: Aldine de Gruyter.

96. Buss, D. M., & Shackelford, T. K. (1997). From Vigilance to Violence: Mate Retention Tactics in Married Couples. *Journal of Personality and Social Psychology, 72*(2), 346–361.

97. Ibid.

98. Ibid; Puts, D. A. (2010). Beauty and the Beast: Mechanisms for Sexual Selection in Humans. *Evolution and Human Behavior, 31*(3), 157–175.

99. Buss & Shackelford, From Vigilance to Violence.

100. Ein-Dor, T., Peery-Paldi, A., Hirschberger, G., Birnbaum, G. E., & Deutsch, D. (2015). Coping with Mate Poaching: Gender Differences in Detection of Infidelity-Related Threats. *Evolution and Human Behavior, 36*(1), 17–24.

101. Buss, D. M. (1988). From Vigilance to Violence: Tactics of Mate Retention in American Undergraduates. *Ethology and Sociobiology, 9*(5), 291–317; Buss & Shackelford, From Vigilance to Violence.

102. Wang, Y., & Griskevicius, V. (2014). Conspicuous Consumption, Relationships, and Rivals: Women's Luxury Products as Signals to Other Women. *Journal of Consumer Research, 40*(February), 834–854.

103. Ibid.

104. Liu, P. J., Dallas, S. K., & Fitzsimons, G. J. (2019). A Framework for Understanding Consumer Choices for Others. *Journal of Consumer Research, 46*(3), 407–434.

105. Simpson, J. A., Griskevicius, V., & Rothman, A. (2012). Consumer Decisions in Relationships. *Journal of Consumer Psychology, 22*(3), 304–314.

106. Liu et al., A Framework for Understanding Consumer Choices for Others.

107. Etkin, J. (2016). Choosing Variety for Joint Consumption. *Journal of Marketing Research, 53*(6), 1019–1033.

108. Simpson et al., Consumer Decisions in Relationships.

109. Hasford, J., Kidwell, B., & Lopez-Kidwell, V. (2018). Happy Wife, Happy Life: Food Choices in Romantic Relationships. *Journal of Consumer Research, 44*(6), 1238–1256.

110. Sengupta, J., & Dahl, D. W. (2008). Gender-Related Reactions to Gratuitous Sex Appeals in Advertising. *Journal of Consumer Psychology, 18*(1), 62–78.

111. Geer, J. H., & Melton, J. S. (1997). Sexual Content-Induced Delay with Double-Entendre Words. *Archives of Sexual Behavior, 26*(3), 295–316.

112. Bushman & Bonacci, Violence and Sex Impair Memory for Television Ads.

113. Lull & Bushman, Do Sex and Violence Sell?

114. Trivers, R. L. (1971). The Evolution of Reciprocal Altruism. *The Quarterly Review of Biology, 46*(1), 35–57.

115. Cosmides, L., & Tooby, J. (1992). Cognitive Adaptations for Social Exchange. In J. H. Barkow, L. Cosmides, & J. Tooby (eds), *The Adapted Mind: Evolutionary Psychology and the Generation of Culture* (pp. 163–228). New York: Oxford University Press; Buss, *Evolutionary Psychology*.

116. Baumeister, R. F., & Leary, M. R. (1995). The Need to Belong: Desire for Interpersonal Attachments as a Fundamental Human Motivation. *Psychological Bulletin, 117*(3), 497–529.

117. Maner, J. K., DeWall, C. N., Baumeister, R. F., & Schaller, M. (2007). Does Social Exclusion Motivate Interpersonal Reconnection? Resolving the "Porcupine Problem". *Journal of Personality and Social Psychology, 92*(1), 42–55.

118. Kurzban, R., Tooby, J., & Cosmides, L. (2001). Can Race Be Erased? Coalitional Computation and Social Categorization. *Proceedings of the National Academy of Sciences of the United States of America, 98*(26), 15387–15392.

119. Tifferet, S., Saad, G., Meiri, M., & Ido, N. (2018). Gift Giving at Israeli Weddings as a Function of Genetic Relatedness and Kinship Certainty. *Journal of Consumer Psychology, 28*(1), 157–165; Saad, G., & Gill, T. (2003). An Evolutionary Psychology Perspective on Gift Giving among Young Adults. *Psychology & Marketing, 20*(9), 765–784.

120. Griskevicius & Kenrick, Fundamental Motives.

121. Marmot, M. (ed.) (2005). *Status Syndrome: How Your Social Standing Directly Affects Your Health.* London: Bloomsbury.

122. Nelissen, R. M. A., & Meijers, M. H. C. (2011). Social Benefits of Luxury Brands as Costly Signals of Wealth and Status. *Evolution and Human Behavior, 32*(5), 343–355.

123. Chance, M. R. A. (1967). Attention Structure as the Basis of Primate Rank Orders. *Management Science, 2*(4), 503–518.

124. Henrich, J., & Gil-White, F. J. (2001). The Evolution of Prestige: Freely Conferred Deference as a Mechanism for Enhancing the Benefits of Cultural Transmission. *Evolution and Human Behavior, 22*(3), 165–196.

125. Maner, J. K., Gailliot, M. T., Butz, D. A., & Peruche, B. M. (2007). Power, Risk, and the Status Quo: Does Power Promote Riskier or More Conservative Decision Making? *Personality and Social Psychology Bulletin, 33*(4), 451–462.

126. Maner, J. K., & Mead, N. L. (2010). The Essential Tension between Leadership and Power: When Leaders Sacrifice Group Goals for the Sake of Self-Interest. *Journal of Personality and Social Psychology, 99*(3), 482–497.

127. Nelissen & Meijers, Social Benefits of Luxury Brands as Costly Signals of Wealth and Status.

128. Han, Y. J., Nunes, J. C., & Drèze, X. (2010). Signaling Status with Luxury Goods: The Role of Brand Prominence. *Journal of Marketing, 74*(July), 15–30.

129. Rucker, D. D., & Galinsky, A. D. (2008). Desire to Acquire: Powerlessness and Compensatory Consumption. *Journal of Consumer Research, 35*(August), 257–267.

130. Han et al., Signaling Status with Luxury Goods.

131. Ibid.

132. Wilcox, K., Kim, H. M., & Sen, S. (2009). Why Do Consumers Buy Counterfeit Luxury Brands? *Journal of Marketing Research, 46*(2), 247–259.

133. Gao, H., Winterich, K. P., & Zhang, Y. (2016). All That Glitters Is Not Gold: How Others' Status Influences the Effect of Power Distance Belief on Status Consumption. *Journal of Consumer Research, 43*(August), 265–281.

134. Griskevicius, V., Tybur, J. M., & Van den Bergh, B. (2010). Going Green to Be Seen: Status, Reputation, and Conspicuous Conservation. *Journal of Personality and Social Psychology, 98*(3), 392–404.

135. Puska, P., Kurki, S., Lähdesmäki, M., Siltaoja, M., & Lumoala, H. (2018). Sweet Taste of Prosocial Status Signaling; When Eating Organic Foods Makes You Happy and Hopeful. *Appetite, 121*, 348–359; van der Wal, A. J., van Horen, F., & Grinstein, A. (2016). The Paradox of 'Green to be Seen': Green High-Status Shoppers Excessively Use (Branded) Shopping Bags. *International Journal of Research in Marketing, 33*(1), 216–219.

136. Ibid.

137. Pham, M. T. (2013). The Seven Sins of Consumer Psychology. *Journal of Consumer Psychology, 23*(4), 411–423.

138. Buss. *Evolutionary Psychology*; Dawkins, R. (1989). *The Selfish Gene*. New York: Oxford University Press; Tooby & Cosmides, Conceptual Foundations of Evolutionary Psychology.

139. Hagen, Controversial Issues in Evolutionary Psychology.

140. Dawkins, R. (2016). *The Selfish Gene: 40th Anniversary Edition*. Oxford: Oxford University Press.

11

CONSUMER WELL-BEING

─**Learning objectives**─

To explore, understand, and explain:

- the definition of subjective and objective well-being
- how consumption can increase self-esteem
- how consumption can increase pleasure
- the likely impact of consumption on well-being

11.1 INTRODUCTION

Happiness is the principal criterion of well-being, and hedonic pleasure accounts for happiness. Hedonic pleasure is what we call *subjective well-being*, consisting of the experience of pleasure involving all adjustments concerning the good versus bad elements in life, from small pleasures, such as having an enjoyable afternoon tea with colleagues on a workday, to the attainment of goals.[1] In general, therefore, happiness can be examined via the lenses of life satisfaction, the presence of positive mood, and the absence of negative mood[2] – see Table 11.1.

Table 11.1 Levels of happiness

	Definition	Examples
Biological level[a]	Pleasure as elementary responses A proxy of the survival principles	Tasty food/drinks Sexual orgasm
Psychological level[a]	Preservation and enhancement of positive self-identity	Our competencies and goals
Social level[a]	Internalisation of social goals and values	Quality interpersonal relationships

[a]These levels of happiness are not always compatible. For example, workaholics may obtain happiness at the psychological level because of sense of achievement by perhaps sacrificing happiness at biological (e.g. health) and social (e.g. family life) levels.

Source: Summary based on Averill and More[3]

Consumption, in general, produces pleasure, which is related to subjective well-being, but is subjective well-being a reflection of true wellness? Recent advocacies on environmental and anti-branding issues, focusing on promoting life simplicity and anti-consumption, imply that subjective well-being is not genuine wellness for humans.[4] Whilst some believe that consumers have learnt to fight back with the help of technology advancement and online reviews, providing a pulling force to enhance consumer well-being,[5] the existence of fake reviews[6] and the dependence of far-being-perfect-technology, such as AI,[7] in fact, risk consumer well-being. This chapter does not support the view that consumption is all bad just because it provides pleasure, although it mainly focuses on the negative impact of consumption. Note that some pleasure from consumption is necessary, as a form of defence mechanism, to provide a cushion to protect us from psychological harm and help us move on and move forward in life should there be obstacles in our way. Even so, we should be aware of the likely negative impact of consumption on well-being so the pursuit of pleasure can be more balanced with business's intentions to sell. With this purpose in mind, this chapter concentrates on how consumption can boost self-esteem (Section 11.2) and pleasure (Section 11.3) and examines the potential risks to consumer well-being through such consumption.

11.2 SELF-ESTEEM

The psychological basis

Self-esteem, an emotional component of the self concept,[8] is defined as an evaluation of self-worth[9] usually in the domains that are important to us; for example, appearance, academic or work performance, and social approval.[10] It is derived from our perception of how good we are at things that are important to us[11] and of how we appear in the eyes of others.[12] In other words, self-esteem can be reflected from social comparisons, which demonstrate self-discrepancies between the actual and ideal self and social self (see Higgins's self-discrepancy theory in Section 8.2).

Self-esteem has been found to be crucial for our well-being,[13] because low self-esteem is linked with anxiety and depression,[14] whereas high self-esteem is associated with adaptive attitudes and behaviour leading to self-improvement outcomes.[15] Intuitively, most people would agree with the importance of the positive impact of high self-esteem. However, maintaining self-esteem is not the panacea that most people believe it to be. In fact, maintaining high self-esteem can be counterproductive if that self-esteem is unstable.[16] It is unstable when self-esteem is built on a fragile foundation; that is, unstable self-esteem, also known as vulnerable self-esteem (as opposed to secure self-esteem), which can change very easily according to an individual's most recent situation or experience.[17] In order to protect their vulnerable self-esteem, people tend to engage in self-enhancement (e.g. inflating positive self-views[18]) and self-protection (e.g. less persistence performing difficult tasks[19]) behaviour,[20] behaviour that has been used to characterise narcissists.[21]

It is the secure self-esteem that leads to well-being. People with secure self-esteem tend to maintain an accurate assessment of their own capabilities,[22] accept themselves as they are,[23] and engage in more adaptive behaviour than defensive behaviour.[24] Although they also use self-enhancement strategies, their use is more prudent. For example, they would not sacrifice others in order to puff themselves up.[25] This type of self-esteem is therefore able to foster greater autonomy, positive relations with others, and personal growth.[26]

Implications for consumer behaviour

Exposure to idealised/attractive images in media

Exposure to idealised or attractive images in media triggers an upward social comparison process (Box 11.1), which raises comparison standards for attractiveness, thereby lowering satisfaction with one's own attractiveness and self-esteem for both men[27] and women.[28] This issue is crucial for consumer well-being for two reasons. First, social media are full of these kinds of images, and the popularity of social media becomes detrimental to our society as research has shown that heavy use of social media can lead to decreased self-esteem and well-being.[29] If social media are used to increase social connectedness among friends and family they can transcend the negative impact on well-being,[30] but if they are used for social comparison purposes, such as a passive use of social media by viewing others' photos, updates, and comments on their friends' wall, the effects are more negative than positive for well-being.[31]

Second, the negative impact of social comparison, hence the use of social media, is especially significant for young people,[32] who tend not to realise what is attainable and what is not, and for those who have low or vulnerable self-esteem.[33] In other words, the use of social media and the inclination towards social comparison lowers people's self-esteem, and those whose self-esteem is already low or vulnerable are harmed more significantly.

Box 11.1

Social comparison

The social comparison theory, originally proposed by Festinger, maintains that our evaluations of ourselves influence how we behave, and these evaluations are generated by comparison with other people.[34] In addition, we are motivated to use social comparison to seek self-esteem maintenance,[35] self-enhancement,[36] and self-improvement.[37] Depending on the target of comparison, there are three main types of social comparisons: comparing with a similar other, with an inferior other, and with a superior other.

Similar (or lateral) comparison

Similar comparisons are more frequent with close friends or family than with distant people.[38]

Downward comparison

Downward comparison happens when we compare ourselves to someone who is worse or in a worse situation than us. The downward comparison theory, proposed by Wills, indicates that people typically make downward social comparisons in order to respond to threats to their self-esteem.[39] This is because downward social comparisons are able to bolster our self-evaluation, leading to growing expectations of future success[40] and increasing positive mood,[41] which results in improved subjective well-being. For example, online social comparison during the COVID lockdown that evidenced others suffering similarly, or worse, reduced people's anxiety and stress.[42]

Although downward comparisons are able to improve subjective well-being, the improvement may be illusory or temporary. This is because, when one feels better than others, one's motivation to improve declines.[43] In addition, downward comparison is often used by people with low self-esteem as a way to protect themselves,[44] and this may risk a vicious circle where it becomes difficult for low self-esteem people to stably increase self-esteem without actual improvement.

Upward comparison

Upward comparison occurs when we compare ourselves to someone who is better than us, and there are two possible effects that can result from upward comparison: a contrasting effect and an assimilation effect.

Contrasting effect

The contrasting effect suggests that the comparers believe that they are inferior, as they are different from the superior other. When people feel inferior to others, the negative consequences, such as negative self-evaluation, depressed mood, reduced self-esteem, and decreased subjective well-being, dominate. The negative impact is especially significant for social media users,[45] as social media provide venues for impression management that easily lead to upward comparison and envy.[46] Despite the negative impact, however, people tend to voluntarily choose upward comparisons.[47]

Assimilation effect

The assimilation effect suggests that the comparers believe that they are as good as those who they compare themselves to and that they are able to set appropriate goals to achieve the comparison target's standard. This is because upward comparisons are able to provide useful information for accurate self-evaluation and for inspirations for self-improvement.[48] For example, weight watchers sometimes put photos of thinner people on their refrigerator. Therefore, the decrease in subjective well-being can be temporary. Instead, an increase in subjective well-being becomes possible in the long term because of self-improvement.[49]

Compensatory consumption

Consumption is able to provide meanings, and as a result it can be used to repair our damaged identity by restoring our self-esteem via reducing the gap or self-discrepancies between our actual and ideal self (and social self; see Section 8.2), and when consumption is used in this manner it is called *compensatory consumption*.[50] There are three types of compensatory consumption (Table 11.2):

1. *Symbolic self-completion*: people use products to "symbolically" repair self-threat, which is not an actual repair.
2. *Distraction*: people "bury their head in the sand" in order to avoid, not to repair.
3. *Adaptative consumption*: people face their self-deficits and find ways to improve where they fall short.

Although the first two approaches can be effective (at least in the short term), they bear potentially negative consequences; that is, people tend to use eating, drinking, or shopping to cope with self-deficits.[51] In addition, they are associated with increased materialism (Box 11.2). The most productive and meaningful compensation for self-threat is adaptive compensation, and in order to activate adaptive compensation, first acknowledging and internalising self-deficits is the key; that is, to achieve self-acceptance, a characteristic of those who hold secure self-esteem.[52] Self-acceptance emphasises that people accept and value themselves unconditionally, regardless of whether they have achieved their ideal self.[53] Through self-acceptance, people change the appraisal of their self-deficits in their self-worth from harmful to benign, and as a result they turn to engage in adaptive consumption in order to truly and effectively address their self-deficits.[54]

Table 11.2 Types of compensatory consumption

Types of Compensatory Consumption	Definition	Example
Symbolic self-completion	Threat-specific symbolic self-completion (aka within domain compensatory consumption[a]) When there is an identity deficit that threatens self-esteem, people seek out products that symbolise the specific dimension in which the self falls short.	When our intelligence is threatened, we would purchase products (e.g. fountain pen or the *Economist* magazine) that signify increased intelligence.[55] When our power is threatened, we would choose products that signify status as a means to restore our power.[56]
	Threat-nonspecific symbolic self-completion (aka across domain compensatory consumption or fluid compensation[a]) When one experiences threat in one domain, but compensates from another domain.	When our attractiveness is threatened, we would purchase products that signify other domains of identity, such as intelligence.[57]
Distraction – avoidance behaviour	When an opportunity for symbolic self-completion or for adaptive compensation is not readily available, people engage in any task that can distract their attention from the identity threat, thereby decreasing self-awareness.	When the performance of our presentation is poor, we might increase food consumption.[58]
Adaptive compensatory consumption	When there is an identity deficit, approaches are taken to repair those deficits by improving where one falls short.	When we fail an important exam, we study harder to fill the gaps in our knowledge.

[a.] Across-domain compensation is usually more effective for self-repair,[59] as within-domain compensation is effective only when the connection between the compensatory products/brands and the threatened domains is implicit rather than explicit.[60]

—Box 11.2—

Materialism and well-being

Materialism, associated with low well-being,[61] refers to a devotion to material needs and desires, which can be manifested through the importance we attach to our status and possessions.[62] To materialists, their happiness depends on their status and possessions, and the belief that money can buy happiness. More importantly, materialists buy things as part of their impression management strategy in order to impress others.[63] As a result, materialism often leads to luxury and conspicuous consumption.[64] Because of their tendency to buy more expensive products, the ability to enjoy little pleasures from small purchases, such as a piece of chocolate, may be impaired.[65] In addition, frequent purchases of expensive goods could lead to a detrimental life-style for those who cannot afford them (see impulsive and compulsive buying in Section 11.3), which diminishes their well-being.

The need to engage in compensatory consumption also triggers materialism. For example, materialism is evoked when one feels insecure because of, for example, financial constraints,[66] powerlessness,[67] social exclusion,[68] and low self-esteem.[69] Whilst materialists are able to restore their self-esteem through purchases, thereby drawing joy from this type of consumption, such happiness is of short duration, compared with non-materialists.[70] Moreover, materialists tend to be more neurotic, vain, and selfish,[71] and all of these characteristics reduce their amicability resulting in poor relations with others, and therefore, loneliness.[72] Besides, their well-being is not only harmed at the personal level, but also at the societal level, as using material goods to substitute for social support or becoming selfish reduces their pro-social behaviour.[73]

We are all materialists to some extent, as we cannot deny the pleasure or benefits it brings to us when buying certain things.[74] However, it is the high-level materialism (i.e. over-emphasising what material products can do for us) that we should avoid in order to keep our life balanced and our well-being in-check. Materialism can be triggered by materialistic cues, such as materialistic messages in media or by merely viewing desirable consumer goods.[75] Considering the negative impact of a high degree of materialism, policy makers should think carefully about how to regulate materialistic messages through media and promote messages regarding the potential danger of over-emphasising the benefits material goods can bring.

Social threats

Negative social stereotypes

Facing negative social stereotypes potentially decreases our self-esteem. The three types for compensatory consumption, discussed in Table 11.2, are applicable to offset threats from negative social stereotypes.[76] For example, individuals who belong to a low social class desire to buy high-status products to offset the stereotype threat[77] as a way to symbolically compensate for the threat domain. However, compensatory consumption does not always occur. Its occurrence depends on whether or not those individuals hold strong enough self-esteem for their social groups. If they hold high self-esteem for their groups, they would not need to compensate as they do not see their social group as inferior.[78]

Holding high self-esteem for the social group indicates a strong social identification, which can provide some buffering and to some extent protect people from the stereotype threat. Therefore, the use of aspirational advertisements creating a superior social identity by implying the negative social stereotypes of the audience can be ineffective,[79] as we negatively evaluate the "aspirational" description of the out-group in the advertisement as a defence mechanism to protect our own social identity.[80] In extreme cases, we can selectively ignore the negative information or experience about our own social group.[81]

Social exclusion

There are two strategies that socially excluded people use to increase social inclusion. First, social excluded people are more likely to buy products or brands that can increase their affiliation with other people. For example, socially excluded people tend to buy products or brands that symbolise their group membership and tailor their spending to the preferences of the group, even if such spending is commonly viewed as undesirable, or maybe even illegal.[82] This strategy is often used for socially visible consumption, and not for socially invisible consumption.[83] Socially, people do not wish to advertise their differences from the groups or social partners they wish to affiliate with. However, people's self-esteem can be maintained and self-evaluation can be positive if their decision is consistent with being socially excluded by choosing something distinctive,[84] especially when their social exclusion is long term, instead of temporary.[85]

Secondly, socially excluded people can turn to products or brands for imagined social connections. The most direct way is to choose anthropomorphic products/brands,[86] which, for example, use people-like features (e.g. smiley faces) or person-like descriptions (e.g. use *I*, instead of "it", to refer to the brand/product) in brand communications or product designs. Research shows that interacting with anthropomorphic products generates a similar effect to interacting with real people, thereby reducing their feelings of social exclusion and their needs for compensatory consumption.[87] However, products or brands are not real people – although socially excluded people can derive social connections from their imagination, and such imagination leads to a damaging perception of social inclusion,[88] leading to diminished well-being. That is, using anthropomorphic products or brands reduces socially excluded people's prosocial behaviour, which would otherwise drive them toward social inclusion to satisfy their need for belongingness.[89]

11.3 PLEASURE

The psychological basis

Pleasure, or happiness, is directly linked with well-being. People are motivated to pursuing pleasure, and the pursuit and experience of pleasure is able to activate the commonly known pleasure centres in the brain. However, momentary pleasure does not necessarily equate with meaningful rewards or happiness. For example, pleasure that is extrinsically activated by drugs often results in dissatisfaction, no matter how pleasurable the immediate experience is.[90] The constant struggle between immediate and delayed gratification is often manifested in our decisions, reflected by impulsivity and compulsivity:

- *Impulsivity* is referred to as a strong, irresistible urge to respond to internal or external stimuli without consideration for the negative consequences.[91] We all engage from time to time in impulsive acts, such as blurting out critical comments without thinking.[92] Impulsive behaviour is characterised as immature, irrational, and risky,[93] and severe impulsivity may lead to psychiatric conditions, such as ADHD (attention deficit hyperactivity disorder).
- *Compulsivity*, commonly known as addiction, is defined as repetitive behaviours that are characterised by the feeling that one "has to" perform them in order to avoid negative consequences.[94] The severe cases of compulsive behaviour are clinically categorised as compulsive disorders, such as OCD (obsessive-compulsive disorder) and hoarding disorder.

Impulsivity and compulsivity are two similar but different concepts. Both can be viewed as a predisposed behavioural tendency to behave impulsively[95] or compulsively,[96] and both involve dissociable cognitive functions with the common feeling of a lack of control. However, compulsive acts focus on reducing/avoiding harm, which is in contrast with the reckless or reward-seeking behaviours that characterise impulsive behaviours that disregard risk.[97] In addition, impulsivity and compulsivity are controlled by slightly different parts of the brain – impulsive circuit and compulsive circuit,[98] which contribute to the biological explanation of impulsive and compulsive behaviour.

The biological explanation does not explain the specific forms of impulsive and compulsive behaviour people engage in. Rather, social norms and peer pressures, to some extent, dictate the forms of impulsive or compulsive behaviour that one is exposed to at the start. For example, men are four times more likely than women to become addicted to smoking, and this sex difference becomes more significant in countries where female smoking has been traditionally seen as taboo, for example, in China, there are 24 times more men than women who smoke.[99]

In summary, because of social and psychological reasons, some people are initially exposed to the behaviour and experience that the behaviour can bring, and the failure in the brain functioning makes these people more prone to develop addictions towards the behaviour or to find it more difficult to stop once it is developed. Having said this, not all impulsive and compulsive behaviour involves malfunctioning in the neuron activities in the brain, as these behaviours vary in their degree of severity and not all are clinically recognised.

Implications for consumer behaviour

There are two major types of addictions: addiction to substances and addictive behaviour (Table 11.3), but all of them can be categorised as compulsive behaviour. This section will focus on one example of an addiction to a substance (i.e. smoking) and one addictive behaviour (i.e. compulsive buying), and some of their implications can be applied to other forms of compulsive behaviour. The discussion in this section focuses on the characteristics of the selected behaviour and how it is impacted via marketing efforts; topics on how to reduce or control compulsive behaviours are related to self-regulation and self-regulation failure, which can be found in Section 7.4.

Table 11.3 Types of addictions

Addition to substances[a][b]	Addiction to behaviour[b]
1. Tobacco (nicotine)	1. Compulsive buying
2. Alcohol	2. Gambling
3. Drugs	3. Sex (sexual activities, including sex itself and watching pornography)
	4. Cosmetic surgeries
	5. Binge eating
	6. Video/online gaming
	7. Compulsive exercise
	8. Technology usage (including the Internet, social media, smartphone)

[a.] Substance addiction contains the characteristics that both involve impulsivity and compulsivity.[100]

[b.] Substance addiction is about diminished control over substance intake, in which chemicals from the substances play a part in strengthening the addictive behaviour, whereas addictions to behaviour involves no external chemicals, but only stimulation from the behaviour itself.

Smoking

Tobacco advertising

Most smokers develop an addiction to smoking and the amount they smoke before they reach their adulthood.[101] As a result, the tobacco companies targeted adolescents through their advertising decisions.[102] Advertising does play a role in increasing the likelihood for young people to smoke. To battle with smoking issues, many countries have slowly tightened the ban on tobacco advertising over the years. As the regulations are tightened, the tobacco companies try to use subtler ways to promote their products. For example, Philip Morris and Lorillard sponsored, ironically, anti-smoking advertisements. However, these efforts were more effective in promoting favourable attitudes towards these companies than towards anti-smoking behaviours.[103] In fact, these industry-sponsored advertisements do not at all decrease the likelihood for adolescents to smoke, compared with the anti-smoking advertisements by not-for-profit organisations, such as the American Legacy Foundation.[104] This is because these advertisements, instead of discouraging adolescents from smoking, enhance a positive brand identity of the sponsors, which potentially contributes to the adolescents' intentions to smoke.[105]

Anti-smoking advertising

Research has found that fear appeals are most effective in promoting anti-smoking,[106] so the graphic warning labels on cigarette packs are more effective than the mere, plain packaging.[107] After more than two decades of effort in promoting the knowledge of health risks involved in smoking, adolescents' knowledge has improved,[108] and anti-smoking effort should now focus more on the issues related to addiction.[109]

One motivator for adolescents to not start smoking at all is to instil a correct expectation of how easily they can become addicted and how difficult it is to stop smoking.[110] Research has shown two types of young people are more inclined to experiment with smoking: 1. those who think addiction does not happen so quickly after only several cigarettes believe they can avoid addiction by smoking less,[111] and 2. those who neglect the effect of the substances in addiction.[112]

The promotion of safer tobacco products

Because of anti-smoking efforts, tobacco sales have steadily declined by more than 11% since 2010.[113] To survive, however, tobacco companies have turned their focus to the smoke-free tobacco products, such as e-cigarettes, which is one of the most popular cigarette alternatives. The sales of these smoke-free tobacco products has increased more than 250% since 2010.[114]

Research has shown mixed results on the benefits versus risks of "safer" alternatives. Take e-cigarettes as an example, a recent review has shown that e-cigarettes are 70% more effective than nicotine replacement therapy in helping people to quit smoking.[115] Whilst health experts have endorsed the effectiveness of e-cigarettes in supporting smoking cessation, they also raise a concern that a safer product does not mean it is risk-free (the only risk-free option is not to smoke at all), but the safer claim may encourage smoking.[116] For example, there is evidence to suggest a high level of dual use of e-cigarettes and conventional cigarettes among heavy smokers and an increasing trend towards using e-cigarettes among newer and former smokers.[117] In addition, the "safer" misconception leads to adolescents' experimenting, and later on becoming addicted to, smoking.[118] As a result, in order to minimize the potential negative impacts on prevention and cessation and the undermining of existing tobacco control measures e-cigarette use should be prohibited where tobacco cigarette use is prohibited, and the products should be subject to the same marketing restrictions as tobacco cigarettes.[119]

Compulsive buying

Have you heard of shopping therapy or retail therapy? Acquisition of objects can elevate one's mood, and this elevation of mood serves as positive reinforcement that leads some people to obsess with shopping, and are therefore turned into shopaholics.[120] Compulsive buying is often confused with impulsive buying, but they are different – see Table 11.4. Compulsive buying is a chronic condition that manifests in an obsession for shopping and spending because of over-powering uncontrollable and repetitive urges to buy.[121]

Table 11.4 Differences between impulsive and compulsive buying[a]

	Compulsive Buying	Impulsive Buying[b]
Definition	• Preoccupation and obsession with buying • Chronic loss of impulse control	• Spontaneous, unplanned purchases • Acute loss of impulse control
Trigger	Internally triggered (i.e. negative mood, such as anxiety) • To elevate negative mood	Externally triggered (i.e. the attractiveness of the items to purchase) • To indulge positive mood
Focus (or the source of pleasure)	The act of buying	The items purchased
Amount of purchase	Excessive	Not necessarily excessive
Proportion of people who engage in this form of buying	5-7%	Over 90% of the population buy impulsively at one point
Frequencies	Frequent	Infrequent

[a.] This summary is based on a collection of studies of compulsive and impulsive buying.[122]
[b.] Some extreme cases of impulsive buying are compulsive buying.[123]

Compulsive buying is about the act of buying: compulsive buyers can find comfort and pleas-ure in the act of buying,[124] and their obsession to buy can only be relieved when a purchase is made.[125] After the purchase is made, however, and after the mood is elevated (for a short period of time), negative feelings of shame, guilt, and frustration associated with their compulsive pur-chases set in to activate the continued cycle of compulsive buying;[126] see Figure 11.1.

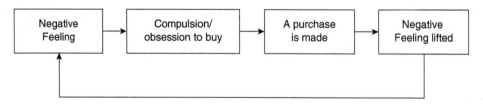

Figure 11.1 Characteristics of compulsive buying

Compulsive buying leads to many detrimental consequences on economic (extreme levels of debt), social (family/marital dissension), and psychological (anxiety and frustration from loss of control) levels.[127] Compulsive buyers tend to shop alone because of these consequences and the disapproval and embarrassment they would potentially experience from others.[128]

Despite these negative consequences, compulsive buying is not recognised as a mental illness by WHO. More and more clinicians, however, have addressed it in their practice and have called for it to be included as a mental illness.[129] Currently, compulsive buying is categorised as a form of either OCD (obsessive-compulsive disorder) or impulse control disorder.[130]

Demographics of compulsive buyers

The onset of compulsive buying occurs when people are aged 18–30, about when they start to live on their own and are able to financially support themselves.[131] The majority of compulsive buyers are women, perhaps because it is women who are usually responsible for shopping for their family.[132] Whilst buying suggests economic power, compulsive buying does not mean compulsive buyers have high income levels. In fact, people at widely varying income levels are equally susceptible to engage in compulsive buying:[133] compulsive buyers with limited income tend to buy low-priced items or at thrift shops, whereas the wealthier compulsive buyers tend to buy large ticket items or in exclusive boutiques.[134]

Triggers for compulsive buying

The main trigger for compulsive buying is negative, depressed mood (Figure 11.1), which may result from low self-esteem[135] or self-discrepancies between the ideal and actual self.[136] As the urge to buy for compulsive buying is internally generated, compulsive buying occurs year round.[137] However, it does not suggest that external, environmental cues are unimportant. In fact, episodes of compulsive buying are worse during, for example, the Christmas holidays and around the birthdays of family members and friends.[138] Buying because of a bargain opportunity is also a trigger for compulsive buying. For example, reports on the record high sales on occasions, like Black Friday in the US[139] and the UK[140] and Singal's day in China,[141] somewhat reflect this phenomenon, especially the Black Friday frenzy, the "have to buy" violence and irrationality, is a reflection of compulsive buying.[142] Therefore, research has supported that the consumption, materialistic culture from the established economy has worsened compulsive buying.[143]

Box 11.3

Compulsive buying versus panic buying

During the early stages of COVID-19, various waves of panic buying for necessities, such as toilet rolls, hand sanitisers, and bleaches, appeared across the globe, despite the reports saying that there were enough supplies.[144] Is panic buying compulsive buying? Not all panic buying is compulsive buying. Panic buying is driven by the fear of short supplies on necessities; for example, people would stockpile food during war. Panic buying would instigate more panic buying, as when we walk into a supermarket but find only empty shelves, our fear deepens, and we behave accordingly to relieve our fear.

(Continued)

For most people, who are not compulsive, being able to obtain a reasonable number of toilet rolls would be sufficient to relieve fear and then stop stockpiling. However, for others, fear may turn into paranoia, which triggers anxiety and depression, which are known comorbidity for compulsive behaviour.[145] As a result, their compulsive behaviour, such as hoarding and compulsive buying, would then be triggered. This explains why some people bought a ridiculous amount of toilet rolls during the COVID panic.[146]

11.4 SUMMARY

1. Self-esteem is an evaluation of self-worth in domains that are important to us, such as appearance, work performance, and social approval, and self-esteem can be determined by the result of social comparison. Depending on whether self-esteem is stable and built on a solid foundation, it can be classified as secure self-esteem and unstable self-esteem. The former promotes personal growth and well-being, whereas the latter engages in self-enhancement and self-protection behaviour (e.g. exaggerating positive self-views and becoming defensive when facing threats) and risks well-being. Idealised images (of facial appearances, body shapes, and lifestyle) in mass media is a form of upward social comparison, which signifies the discrepancies between actual and ideal self and which usually lowers one's self-esteem, especially for those who frequently use social media, which contains plenty of attractive images.

2. Compensatory consumption used to close the gap of discrepancies between the actual and ideal self can help to restore self-esteem. There are three types of compensatory consumption: symbolic self-completion, distraction (avoidance behaviour), and adaptive compensation. Symbolic self-completion suggests that, when there is an identity threat, people seek out products that symbolise either the specific dimension in which the self is threatened (within-domain compensatory consumption; for example, if my status is threatened, I would seek out status-related products to compensate) or in a different dimension in which the self is not threatened (across domain compensatory consumption; for example, if I'm not that beautiful, I would concentrate on how smart I am). However, not all situations where we experience self-threats provide opportunities for symbolic self-completion. In such cases, we may engage in any task to distract ourselves from the threat. Some people use eating as a distraction. Neither symbolic self-completion nor distraction provides a solution. The most productive compensation is adaptive consumption; that is, to repair those self-deficits that cause the self-threat.

3. Social threats may result in reduced self-esteem, and there are two main types of social threats: stereotype threats and social exclusion (rejection). The former is prevalent in our daily life; for example, the stereotypes of women, of people of colour, of the overweight, of the disabled, of recent immigrants, and so on. If these individuals hold high self-esteem for their membership groups, they would not see their groups as

inferior. In this case, no compensatory behaviour would be required. However, if they do not have sufficient self-esteem, they may engage in compensatory behaviour. The three types of compensatory consumption dealing with self-threats are also applicable to those facing stereotype threats. For example, individuals who belong to a low social class desire to buy high-status products. On the other hand, if the social threat is social exclusion, socially excluded individuals are more likely either to buy products or brands that can increase their affiliation with other people or to turn to products or brands for imagined social connections (using brand relationships to offset the lack of interpersonal relationships).

4. The pursuit and experience of pleasure is able to activate the pleasure centres in the brain (the limbic system). However, the immediate gratification reflected by impulsive and compulsive behaviour does not guarantee long-term happiness. For example, addition to substances, such as tobacco (nicotine), alcohol, and drugs is a result of a chemical reaction and the reward from the highs produced by the substances then leads to problems on health, psychology, and financial levels.

5. Impulsivity and compulsivity are two different, but relevant, concepts. The former focuses on the urge to act immediately in order to pursue pleasure, and the latter focuses on the preoccupation of repetitive behaviour in order to avoid harm. Both involve the common feeling of lack of control, but are activated in different regions in our brain (impulsive versus compulsive circuit). However, what starts out as a problem of impulsivity may end up as a problem in compulsivity and vice versa, and this interaction, plus the social factors, determine the form of impulsive and compulsive behaviours. That is, social factors influence the impulsive or compulsive behaviour that one is exposed to at the start, and when the behaviour brings short-term gratification, the gratification encourages people to continue to engage in the same behaviour; for example, compulsive buying, pathological gambling, and addiction to gaming and technologies, such as social media, smartphone, et cetera.

6. Most smokers developed an addiction to smoking and the degree of how much they smoke before they are adults. The tobacco industry, therefore, targets adolescents as their key audience because of profit considerations. Many countries have gradually tightened the regulations of tobacco sales and promotions and promoted health risks information on smoking. The tobacco industry has developed new, safer tobacco products to respond to the decreased demand, and e-cigarettes are among the new products that show the most profit "potential". Although many health experts have found the effectiveness of e-cigarettes in assisting smoking cessation, recent research has shown that they counter effectiveness in anti-smoking because of the "safer" misconception (safer does not indicate safe) that encourages dual use of e-cigarettes and conventional cigarettes among heavy smokers and using e-cigarettes among newer and former smokers.

7. Compulsive buying is an obsession of shopping and spending because of overpowering, uncontrollable, and repetitive urges to buy. The onset of compulsive buying occurs when people are aged 18–30, about when they become financially independent. To compulsive

buyers, the focus is *not* on the items bought, as the compulsion to buy ends with the act of buying. Because of the high frequencies of buying things that they do not need or even want, compulsive buying has many detrimental consequences on economic (extremely high levels of debt), social (family/marital dissension), and psychological (anxiety, frustration, and embarrassment) levels. Research shows that about 5–7% of the population suffers from this condition.

DISCUSSION QUESTIONS

1. What is well-being and what is consumer well-being?
2. How does consumption boost self-esteem?
3. Discuss the impact of compulsive buying on consumer well-being.
4. Discuss the relationship between pleasure, consumer well-being, and addictions.

FURTHER READING

-   Faber, R. J., & O'Guinn, T. C. (2008). Compulsive Buying. In C. P. Haugtvedt, P. M. Herr, & F. R. Kardes (eds), *Handbook of Consumer Psychology* (pp. 1039–1056). New York: Psychology Press.
-   Gilbert, J. R., Stafford, M. B. R., Sheinin, D. A., & Pounders, K. (2021). The Dance between Darkness and Light: A Systematic Review of Advertising's Role in Consumer Well-Being (1980–2020). *International Journal of Advertising, 40*(4), 491–528.
-   Hoffmann, S., & Lee, M. S. W. (2016). Consume Less and Be Happy? Consume Less to Be Happy! An Introduction to the Special Issue on Anti-Consumption and Consumer Well-Being. *Journal of Consumer Affairs, 50*(1), 3–17.
-   Mogilner, C., & Norton, M. I. (2015). Consumer Happiness and Well-Being. In M. I. Norton, D. D. Rucker, & C. Lamberton (eds), *The Cambridge Handbook of Consumer Psychology* (pp. 5–28). New York: Cambridge University Press.
-   Rook, D. W. (1987). The Buying Impulse. *Journal of Consumer Research, 14*(September), 189–199.

NOTES

1. Diener, E., Sapyta, J. J., & Suh, E. (1998). Subjective Well-Being Is Essential to Well-Being. *Psychological Inquiry, 9*(1), 33–37; Diener, E. (1984). Subjective Well-Being. *Psychological Bulletin, 95*(3), 542–575.
2. Lucas, R. E., & Diener, E. (2009). Personality and Subjective Well-Being. In E. Diener (ed.), *The Science of Well-Being: The Collected Works of Ed Diener* (pp. 75–102). Dordrecht: Springer.

3. Averill, J. R., & More, T. A. (2000). Happiness. In M. Lewis & J. M. Haviland-Johnes (eds), *Handbook of Emotions* (second edn, pp. 663–676). New York: Guilford Press.

4. Klein, N. (2000). *No Logo: No Space, No Choice, No Jobs*. London: Flamingo; Lee, M. S. W., & Ahn, C. S. Y. (2016). Anti-Consumption, Materialism, and Consumer Well-Being. *Journal of Consumer Affairs*, *50*(1), 18–47; Cova, B., & D'Antone, S. (2016). Brand Iconicity vs. Anti-Consumption Well-Being Concerns: The Nutella Palm Oil Conflict. *Journal of Consumer Affairs*, *50*(1), 166–192.

5. Hoffmann, S., & Lee, M. S. W. (2016). Consume Less and Be Happy? Consume Less to Be Happy! An Introduction to the Special Issue on Anti-Consumption and Consumer Well-Being. *Journal of Consumer Affairs*, *50*(1), 3–17.

6. Mayzlin, D., Dover, Y., & Chevalier, J. (2014). Promotional Reviews: An Empirical Investigation of Online Review Manipulation. *American Economic Review*, *104*(8), 2421–2455; Luca, M., & Zervas, G. (2016). Fake It Till You Make It: Reputation, Competition, and Yelp Review Fraud. *Management Science*, *62*(12), 3412–3427.

7. Banker, S., & Khetani, S. (2019). Algorithm Overdependence: How the Use of Algorithmic Recommendation Systems Can Increase Risks to Consumer Well-Being. *Journal of Public Policy & Marketing*, *38*(4), 500–515.

8. Heatherton, T. F., & Polivy, J. (1991). Development and Validation of a Scale for Measuring State Self-Esteem. *Journal of Personality and Social Psychology*, *60*(6), 895–910.

9. Coopersmith, S. (1967). *The Antecedents of Self-Esteem*. San Francisco, CA: Freeman.

10. Harter, S. (2015). *The Construction of the Self: Developmental and Sociocultural Foundations* (second edn). New York: Guilford Press.

11. James, W. (1890). *The Principles of Psychology* (Vol. I). New York: Henry Folt and Company.

12. Cooley, C. H. (1902). *Human Nature and the Social Order*. New York: Charles Scribner.

13. Paradise, A. W., & Kernis, M. H. (2002). Self-Esteem and Psychological Well-Being: Implications of Fragile Self-Esteem. *Journal of Social and Clinical Psychology*, *21*(4), 345–361.

14. Sowislo, J. F., & Orth, U. (2013). Does Low Self-Esteem Predict Depression and Anxiety? A Meta-Analysis of Longitudinal Studies. *Psychological Bulletin*, *139*(1), 213–240.

15. Pyszczynski, T., Greenberg, J., Solomon, S., Arndt, J., & Schimel, J. (2004). Why Do People Need Self-Esteem? A Theoretical and Empirical Review. *Psychological Bulletin*, *130*(3), 435–468.

16. Kernis, M. H., Grannemann, B. D., & Barclay, L. C. (1989). Stability and Level of Self-Esteem as Predictors of Anger Arousal and Hostility. *Journal of Personality and Social Psychology*, *56*(6), 1013–1022.

17. Ibid.

18. Baumeister, R. F., Campbell, J. D., Krueger, J. I., & Vohs, K. D. (2003). Does High Self-Esteem Cause Better Performance, Interpersonal Success, Happiness, or Healthier Lifestyles? *Psychological Science in the Public Interest*, *4*(1), 1–44.

19. Jordan, C. H., Spencer, S. J., & Zanna, M. P. (2003). I Love Me... I Love Me Not: Implicit Self-Esteem, Explicit Self-Esteem, and Defensiveness. In S. J. Spencer, S. Fein, M. P. Zanna, & J. M. Olson (eds), *Motivated Social Perception: The Ontario Symposium* (Vol. 9, pp. 117–145). Mahwah, NJ: Lawrence Erlbaum Associates.

20. Alicke, M. D., & Sedikides, C. (2009). Self-Enhancement and Self-Protection: What They Are and What They Do. *European Review of Social Psychology, 20*(1), 1–48.

21. Twenge, J. M., & Campbell, W. K. (2009). *The Narcissism Epidemic: Living in the Age of Entitlement*. New York: Free Press.

22. Epstein, S., & Morling, B. (1995). Is the Self Motivated to Do More than Enhance and/or Verify Itself? In M. H. Kernis (ed.), *Efficacy, Agency, and Self-Esteem* (pp. 9–29). New York: Springer.

23. Paradise & Kernis, Self-Esteem and Psychological Well-Being.

24. Jordan et al., I Love Me... I Love Me Not.

25. Ibid.

26. Paradise & Kernis, Self-Esteem and Psychological Well-Being.

27. Lorenzen, L. A., Grieve, F. G., & Thomas, A. (2004). Exposure to Muscular Male Models Decreases Men's Body Satisfaction. *Sex Roles, 51*(11/12), 743–748.

28. Richins, M. L. (1991). Social Comparison and the Idealized Images of Advertising. *Journal of Consumer Research, 18*(June), 71–83.

29. Schmuck, D., Karsay, K., Matthes, J., & Stevic, A. (2019). "Looking Up and Feeling Down". The Influence of Mobile Social Networking Site Use on Upward Social Comparison, Self-Esteem, and Well-Being of Adult Smartphone Users. *Telematics and Informatics, 42*, 101240; Tazghini, S., & Siedlecki, K. L. (2013). A Mixed Method Approach to Examining Facebook Use and Its Relationship to Self-Esteem. *Computers in Human Behavior, 29*(3), 827–832.

30. Kalpidou, M., Costin, D., & Morris, J. (2011). The Relationship between Facebook and the Well-Being of Undergraduate College Students. *CyberPsychology, Behavior, and Social Networking, 14*(4), 183–189.

31. Tazghini & Siedlecki, A Mixed Method Approach to Examining Facebook Use and Its Relationship to Self-Esteem; Wang, J.-L., Wang, H.-Z., Gaskin, J., & Hawk, S. (2017). The Mediating Roles of Upward Social Comparison and Self-Esteem and the Moderating Role of Social Comparison Orientation in the Association between Social Networking Site Usage and Subjective Well-Being. *Frontiers in Psychology, 8*, 771.

32. Hogg, M. K., Bruce, M., & Hough, K. (1999). Female Images in Advertising: The Implications of Social Comparison for Marketing. *International Journal of Advertising, 18*(4), 445–473.

33. Cramer, E. M., Song, H., & Drent, A. M. (2016). Social Comparison on Facebook: Motivation, Affective Consequences, Self-Esteem, and Facebook Fatigue. *Computers in Human Behavior, 64*, 739–746; Patrick, H., Neighbors, C., & Knee, C. R. (2004). Appearance-Related Social Comparisons: The Role of Contingent Self-Esteem and Self-Perceptions of Attractiveness. *Personality and Social Psychology Bulletin, 30*(4), 501–514.

34. Festinger, L. (1954). A Theory of Social Comparison Processes. *Human Relations, 7*(2), 117–140.

35. Tesser, A. (1988). Toward a Self-Evaluation Maintenance Model of Social Behavior. *Advances in Experimental Social Psychology, 21*, 181–227.

36. Thornton, D. A., & Arrowood, A. J. (1966). Self-Evaluation, Self-Enhancement, and the

Locus of Social Comparison. *Journal of Experimental Social Psychology, 1*(Suppl. 1), 40–48; Wood, J. V. (1989). Theory and Research Concerning Social Comparisons of Personal Attributes. *Psychological Bulletin, 106*(2), 231–248.

37. Collins, R. L. (1996). For Better or Worse: The Impact of Upward Social Comparison on Self-Evaluations. *Psychological Bulletin, 119*(1), 51–69.

38. Brickman, P., & Bulman, R. J. (1977). Pleasure and Pain in Social Comparison. In J. M. Suls & R. L. Miller (eds), *Social Comparison Processes: Theoretical and Empirical Perspectives* (pp. 149–186). Washington, DC: Hemisphere.

39. Wills, T. A. (1981). Downward Comparison Principles in Social Psychology. *Psychological Bulletin, 90*(2), 245–271.

40. Aspinwall, L. G., & Taylor, S. E. (1993). Effects of Social Comparison Direction, Threat, and Self-Esteem on Affect, Self-Evaluation, and Expected Success. *Journal of Personality and Social Psychology, 64*(5), 708–722.

41. Gibbons, F. X., & McCoy, S. B. (1991). Self-Esteem, Similarity, and Reactions to Active versus Passive Downward Comparison. *Journal of Personality and Social Psychology, 60*(3), 414–424.

42. Ruggieri, S., Ingoglia, S., Bonfanti, R. C., & Coco, G. L. (2021). The Role of Online Social Comparison as a Protective Factor for Psychological Wellbeing: A Longitudinal Study during the COVID-19 Quarantine. *Personality and Individual Differences, 171*, 110486.

43. Diel, K., Grelle, S., & Hofmann, W. (2021). A Motivational Framework of Social Comparison. *Journal of Personality and Social Psychology, 120*(6), 1415–1430.

44. Wills, Downward Comparison Principles in Social Psychology.

45. Verduyn, P., Gugushvili, N., Massar, K., Täht, K., & Kross, E. (2020). Social Comparison on Social Networking Sites. *Current Opinion in Psychology, 36*, 32–37.

46. Appel, H., Gerlach, A. L., & Crusius, J. (2016). The Interplay between Facebook Use, Social Comparison, Envy, and Depression. *Current Opinion in Psychology, 9*, 44–49.

47. Gerber, J. P., Wheeler, L., & Suls, J. (2018). A Social Comparison Theory Meta-Analysis 60+ Years On. *Psychological Bulletin, 144*(2), 177–197.

48. Taylor, S. E., & Lobel, M. (1989). Social Comparison Activity under Threat: Downward Evaluation and Upward Contacts. *Psychological Review, 96*(4), 569–575.

49. Collins, For Better or Worse.

50. Mandel, N., Rucker, D. D., Levav, J., & Galinsky, A. D. (2017). The Compensatory Consumer Behavior Model: How Self-Discrepancies Drive Consumer Behavior. *Journal of Consumer Psychology, 27*(1), 133–146.

51. Mandel, N., & Smeesters, D. (2008). The Sweet Escape: Effects of Mortality Salience on Consumption Quantities for High- and Low-Self-Esteem Consumers. *Journal of Consumer Research, 35*(August), 309–323.

52. Paradise & Kernis, Self-Esteem and Psychological Well-Being.

53. Ellis, A. (2003). The Relationship between Rational-Emotive Behavioral Therapy (REBT) to Social Psychology. *Journal of Rational-Emotive and Cognitive Behavior Therapy, 21*(1), 5–20.

54. Kim, S., & Gal, D. (2014). From Compensatory Consumption to Adaptive Consumption: The Role of Self-Acceptance in Resolving Self-Deficits. *Journal of Consumer Research, 41*(August), 526–542.

55. Gao, L., Wheeler, S. C., & Shiv, B. (2009). The 'Shaken Self': Product Choices as a Means of Restoring Self-View Confidence. *Journal of Consumer Research, 36*(June), 29–38.

56. Rucker, D. D., & Galinsky, A. D. (2008). Desire to Acquire: Powerlessness and Compensatory Consumption. *Journal of Consumer Research, 35*(August), 257–267.

57. Sobol, K., & Darke, P. R. (2014). "I'd Like to be that Attractive, but at least I'm smart": How Exposure to Ideal Advertising Models Motivates Improved Decision-Making. *Journal of Consumer Psychology, 24*(4), 533–540.

58. Heatherton, T. F., & Baumeister, R. F. (1991). Binge Eating as Escape from Self-Awareness. *Psychological Bulletin, 110*(1), 86–108.

59. Lisjak, M., Bonezzi, A., Kim, S., & Rucker, D. D. (2015). Perils of Compensatory Consumption: Within-Domain Compensation Undermines Subsequent Self-Regulation. *Journal of Consumer Research, 41*(February), 1186–1203.

60. Rustagi, M., & Shrum, L. J. (2019). Undermining the Restorative Potential of Compensatory Consumption: A Product's Explicit Identity Connection Impedes Self-Repair. *Journal of Consumer Research, 46*(June), 119–139.

61. Dittmar, H., Bond, R., Hurst, M., & Kasser, T. (2014). The Relationship between Materialism and Personal Well-Being: A Meta-Analysis. *Journal of Personality and Social Psychology, 107*(5), 879–924.

62. Richins, M. L., & Dawson, S. (1992). A Consumer Values Orientation for Materialism and Its Measurement: Scale Development and Validation. *Journal of Consumer Research, 19*(3), 303–316.

63. Rose, P., & DeJesus, S. P. (2007). A Model of Motivated Cognition to Account for the Link between Self-monitoring and Materialism. *Psychology & Marketing, 24*(2), 93–115.

64. Hudders, L., & Pandelaere, M. (2012). The Silver Lining of Materialism: The Impact of Luxury Consumption on Subjective Well-Being. *Journal of Happiness Studies, 13*(3), 411–437; Wong, N. Y. C. (1997). Suppose You Own the World and No One Knows? Conspicuous Consumption, Materialism and Self. In M. Brucks & D. J. MacInnis (eds), *NA – Advances in Consumer Research* (pp. 197–203). Provo, UT: Association for Consumer Research.

65. Quoidbach, J., Dunn, E. W., Petrides, K. V., & Mikolajczak, M. (2010). Money Giveth, Money Taketh Away: The Dual Effect of Wealth on Happiness. *Psychological Science, 21*(6), 759–763.

66. Tully, S. M., Hershfield, H. E., & Meyvis, T. (2015). Seeking Lasting Enjoyment with Limited Money: Financial Constraints Increase Preference for Material Goods over Experiences. *Journal of Consumer Research, 42*(1), 59–75.

67. Rucker & Galinsky, Desire to Acquire.

68. Lee, J., & Shrum, L. J. (2012). Conspicuous Consumption versus Charitable Behavior in Response to Social Exclusion: A Differential Needs Explanation. *Journal of Consumer Research, 39*(3), 530–544.

69. Chaplin, L. N., & John, D. R. (2007). Growing up in a Material World: Age Differences in Materialism in Children and Adolescents. *Journal of Consumer Research, 34*(December), 480–493; Sivanathan, N., & Pettit, N. C. (2010). Protecting the Self through Consumption: Status Goods as Affirmational Commodities. *Journal of Experimental Social Psychology, 46*(3), 564–570.

70. Richins, M. L. (2013). When Wanting Is Better than Having: Materialism, Transformation Expectations, and Product-Evoked Emotions in the Purchase Process. *Journal of Consumer Research, 40*(1), 1–18.

71. Górnik-Durose, M. E. (2020). Materialism and Well-Being Revisited: The Impact of Personality. *Journal of Happiness Studies, 21*(1), 305–326; Watson, D. C. (2014). Materialism: Profiles of Agreeableness and Neuroticism. *Personality and Individual Differences, 56,* 197–200; Chang, W.-L., Lu, L.-C., Su, H.-J., Lin, T. A., & Chang, K.-Y. (2011). The Relationship among Consumer Vanity Trait, Materialism and Fashion Anxiety. *African Journal of Business Management, 5*(9), 3466–3471.

72. Pieters, R. (2013). Bidirectional Dynamics of Materialism and Loneliness: Not Just a Vicious Cycle. *Journal of Consumer Research, 40*(4), 615–631.

73. Moldes, O., & Ku, L. (2020). Materialistic Cues Make Us Miserable: A Meta-Analysis of the Experimental Evidence for the Effects of Materialism on Individual and Societal Well-Being. *Psychology & Marketing, 37*(10), 1396–1419.

74. Pandelaere, M. (2016). Materialism and Well-Being: The Role of Consumption. *Current Opinion in Psychology, 10,* 33–38.

75. Bauer, M. A., Wilkie, J. E. B., Kim, J. K., & Bodenhausen, G. V. (2012). Cuing Consumerism: Situational Materialism Undermines Personal and Social Well-Being. *Psychological Science, 23*(5), 517–523.

76. Mandel, et al., The Compensatory Consumer Behavior Model.

77. Mazzocco, P. J., Rucker, D. D., Galinsky, A. D., & Anderson, E. T. (2012). Direct and Vicarious Conspicuous Consumption: Identification with Low-Status Groups Increases the Desire for High-Status Goods. *Journal of Consumer Psychology, 22*(4), 520–528.

78. White, K., & Argo, J. J. (2009). Social Identity Threat and Consumer Preferences. *Journal of Consumer Psychology, 19*(3), 313–325.

79. Dimofte, C. V., Goodstein, R. C., & Brumbaugh, A. M. (2015). A Social Identity Perspective on Aspirational Advertising: Implicit Threats to Collective Self-Esteem and Strategies to Overcome Them. *Journal of Consumer Psychology, 25*(3), 416–430.

80. Chae, B. G., Dahl, D. W., & Zhu, R. J. (2017). "Our" Brand's Failure Leads to "Their" Product Derogation. *Journal of Consumer Psychology, 27*(4), 466–472.

81. Dalton, A. N., & Huang, L. (2014). Motivated Forgetting in Response to Social Identity Threat. *Journal of Consumer Research, 40*(April), 1017–1038.

82. Mead, N. L., Baumeister, R. F., Stillman, T. F., Rawn, C. D., & Vohs, K. D. (2011). Social Exclusion Causes People to Spend and Consume Strategically in the Service of Affiliation. *Journal of Consumer Research, 37*(February), 902–919.

83. Wang, J., Zhu, R. J., & Shiv, B. (2012). The Lonely Consumer: Loner or Conformer? *Journal of Consumer Research, 38*(April), 1116–1128.

84. Dommer, S. L., Swaminathan, V., & Ahluwalia, R. (2013). Using Differentiated Brands to Deflect Exclusion and Protect Inclusion: The Moderating Role of Self-Esteem on Attachment to Differentiated Brands. *Journal of Consumer Research, 40*(December), 657–675.

85. Wan, E. W., Xu, J., & Ding, Y. (2014). To Be or Not to Be Unique? The Effective of Social Exclusion on Consumer Choice. *Journal of Consumer Research, 40*(April), 1109–1122.

86. Chen, R. P., Wan, E. W., & Levy, E. (2017). The Effect of Social Exclusion on Consumer Preference for Anthropomorphized Brands. *Journal of Consumer Psychology, 27*(1), 23–34.

87. Mourey, J. A., Olson, J. G., & Yoon, C. (2017). Products as Pals: Engaging with Anthropomorphic Products Mitigates the Effects of Social Exclusion. *Journal of Consumer Research, 44*(August), 414–431.

88. Waytz, A., & Epley, N. (2012). Social Connection Enables Dehumanization. *Journal of Experimental Social Psychology, 48*(1), 70–76.

89. Mourey, J. A., Olson, J. G., & Yoon, C. (2017). Products As Pals: Engaging with Anthropomorphic Products Mitigates the Effects of Social Exclusion. *Journal of Consumer Research, 44*(August), 414–431.

90. Averill, J. R., & More, T. A. (2000). Happiness. In M. Lewis & J. M. Haviland-Johnes (eds), *Handbook of Emotions* (second edn, pp. 663–676). New York: Guilford Press.

91. Chamberlain, S. R., & Sahakian, B. J. (2007). The Neuropsychiatry of Impulsivity. *Current Opinion in Psychiatry, 20*(3), 255–261; Goldenson, R. M. (1984). *Longman Dictionary of Psychology and Psychiatry*. New York: Longman.

92. Chamberlain & Sahakian, The Neuropsychiatry of Impulsivity.

93. Ainslie, G. (1975). Specious Reward: A Behavioral Theory of Impulsiveness and Impulse Control. *Psychological Bulletin, 82*(4), 463–496; Levy, M. F. (1976). Deferred Gratification and Social Class. *Journal of Social Psychology, 100*(1), 123–135.

94. Faber, R. J., & O'Guinn, T. C. (2008). Compulsive Buying. In C. P. Haugtvedt, P. M. Herr, & F. R. Kardes (eds), *Handbook of Consumer Psychology* (pp. 1039–1056). New York: Psychology Press ; Gillan, C. M., Robbins, T. W., Sahakian, B. J., van den Heuvel, O. A., & van Wingen, G. (2016). The Role of Habit in Compulsivity. *European Neuropsychopharmacology, 26*(5), 828–840; Luigjes, J., Lorenzetti, V., de Haan, S., Youssef, G. J., Murawski, C., Sjoerds, Z., . . . Yücel, M. (2019). Defining Compulsive Behavior. *Neuropsychology Review, 29*(1), 4–13.

95. Whiteside, S. P., & Lynam, D. R. (2001). The Five Factor Model and Impulsivity: Using a Structural Model of Personality to Understand Impulsivity. *Personality and Individual Differences, 30*(4), 669–689.

96. Samuel, D. B., Riddell, A. D. B., Lynam, D. R., Miller, J. D., & Widiger, T. A. (2012). A Five-Factor Measure of Obsessive-Compulsive Personality Traits. *Journal of Personality Assessment, 94*(5), 456–465.

97. Fineberg, N. A., Chamberlain, S. R., Goudriaan, A. E., Stein, D. J., Vanderschuren, L. J. M. J., Gillan, C. M., . . . Morein-Zamir, S. (2014). New Developments in Human Neurocognition: Clinical, Genetic, and Brain Imaging Correlates of Impulsivity and Compulsivity. *CNS Spectrums, 19*(1), 69–89.

98. Robbins, T. W. (2007). Shifting and Stopping: Fronto-Striatal Substrates, Neurochemical Modulation and Clinical Implications. *Biological Sciences, 362*(1481), 917–932.

99. World Bank. (2020). *Prevalence of Current Tobacco Use, Males (% of Male Adults)*. Retrieved from data.worldbank.org/indicator/sh.prv.smok.ma; World Bank. (2020). *Prevalence of Current Tobacco Use, Females (% of Female Adults)*. Retrieved from data.worldbank.org/indicator/SH.PRV.SMOK.FE

100. Fineberg et al., New Developments in Human Neurocognition.

101. U.S. Department of Health and Human Services. (2014). *The Health Consequences of Smoking – 50 Years of Progress: A Report of the Surgeon General.* Retrieved from www.cdc.gov/tobacco/data_statistics/sgr/50th-anniversary/index.htm

102. Cummings, K. M., Morley, C. P., Horan, J. K., Steger, C., & Leavell, N.-R. (2002). Marketing to America's Youth: Evidence from Corporate Documents. *Tobacco Control, 11*(Suppl. 1), i5–i17; Pollay, R. W. (1994). Exposure of US Youth to Cigarette Television Advertising in the 1960s. *Tobacco Control, 3*(2), 130–133.

103. Henriksen, L., Dauphinee, A. L., Wang, Y., & Fortmann, S. P. (2006). Industry Sponsored Anti-Smoking Ads and Adolescent Reactance: Test of a Boomerang Effect. *Tobacco Control, 15*(1), 13–18.

104. Ibid.

105. Ibid.

106. Biener, L., Ji, M., Gilpin, E. A., & Albers, A. B. (2004). The Impact of Emotional Tone, Message, and Broadcast Parameters in Youth Anti-Smoking Advertisements. *Journal of Health Communication, 9*(3), 259–274; Smith, K. H., & Stutts, M. A. (2003). Effects of Short-Term Cosmetic versus Long-Term Health Fear Appeals in Anti-Smoking Advertisements on the Smoking Behaviour of Adolescents. *Journal of Consumer Behaviour, 3*(2), 157–177.

107. White, V., Webster, B., & Wakefield, M. (2008). Do Graphic Health Warning Labels Have an Impact on Adolescents' Smoking-Related Beliefs and Behaviours? *Addiction, 103*(9), 1562–1571.

108. Meienberg, A., Mayr, M., Vischer, A., Zellweger, M. J., & Burkard, T. (2021). Smoking Prevention in Adolescents: A Cross-Sectional and Qualitative Evaluation of a Newly Implemented Prevention Program in Switzerland. *BMJ Open, 11*(12), e048319.

109. Popova, L., & Halpern-Felsher, B. L. (2016). A Longitudinal Study of Adolescents' Optimistic Bias about Risks and Benefits of Cigarette Smoking. *American Journal of Health Behavior, 40*(3), 341–351.

110. Goldberg, M. E. (2008). Assessing the Relationship between Tobacco Advertising and Promotion and Adolescent Smoking Behavior. In C. P. Haugtvedt, P. M. Herr, & F. R. Kardes (eds), *Handbook of Consumer Psychology* (pp. 933–957). New York: Psychology Press.

111. Wang, C., Henley, N., & Donovan, R. J. (2004). Exploring Children's Conceptions of Smoking Addiction. *Health Education Research, 19*(6), 626–634.

112. Ibid.

113. Euromonitor. (2022). *2010–2020 Global Market Sizes – Tobacco.* Retrieved from www.euromonitor.com/

114. Ibid.

115. Hartmann-Boyce, J., McRobbie, H., Butler, A. R., Lindson, N., Bullen, C., Begh, R., . . . Hajek, P. (2020). Electronic Cigarettes for Smoking Cessation. *Cochrane Database of Systematic Reviews, 10*(9), CD01021.

116. Borgida, E., Kim, A., Stark, E. N., & Miller, C. (2008). Consumers and the Allure of "Safer" Tobacco Products. In C. P. Haugtvedt, P. M. Herr, & F. R. Kardes (eds), *Handbook of Consumer Psychology* (pp. 915–932). New York: Psychology Press.

117. Owusu, D., Huang, J., Weaver, S. R., Pechacek, T. F., Ashley, D. L., Nayak, P., & Eriksen, M. P. (2019). Patterns and Trends of Dual Use of E-Cigarettes and Cigarettes among US Adults, 2015–2018. *Preventive Medicine Reports*, *16*, 101009.

118. Soneji, S., Barrington-Trimis, J. L., Wills, T. A., Leventhal, A. M., Unger, J. B., Gibson, L. A., . . . Miech, R. A. (2017). Association between Initial Use of E-Cigarettes and Subsequent Cigarette Smoking among Adolescents and Young Adults: A Systematic Review and Meta-Analysis. *JAMA Pediatrics*, *171*(8), 788–797.

119. Grana, R., Benowitz, N., & Glantz, S. A. (2014). E-Cigarettes: A Scientific Review. *Circulation*, *129*(19), 1972–1986.

120. O'Guinn, T. C., & Faber, R. J. (1989). Compulsive Buying: A Phenomenological Exploration. *Journal of Consumer Research*, *16*(2), 147–157.

121. Faber, R. J., & O'Guinn, T. C. (2008). Compulsive Buying. In C. P. Haugtvedt, P. M. Herr, & F. R. Kardes (eds), *Handbook of Consumer Psychology* (pp. 1039–1056). New York: Psychology Press.

122. Ibid; O'Guinn & Faber, Compulsive Buying; Maraz, A., Griffiths, M. D., & Demetrovics, Z. (2016). The Prevalence of Compulsive Buying: A Meta-Analysis. *Addiction, 111*(3), 408–419; Müller, A., Mitchell, J. E., & de Zwaan, M. (2015). Compulsive Buying. *American Journal on Addictions*, *24*(2), 132–137; Rook, D. W. (1987). The Buying Impulse. *Journal of Consumer Research, 14*(September), 189–199.

123. Rook, The Buying Impulse.

124. Ibid.

125. Black, D. W. (2007). A Review of Compulsive Buying Disorder. *World Psychiatry, 6*(1), 14–18.

126. O'Guinn & Faber, Compulsive Buying.

127. Ibid; Christenson, G. A., Faber, R. J., De Zwaan, M., Raymond, N. C., Specker, S. M., Ekern, M. D., . . . Eckert, E. D. (1994). Compulsive Buying: Descriptive Characteristics and Psychiatric Comorbidity. *Journal of Clinical Psychiatry*, *55*(1), 5–11.

128. Black, A Review of Compulsive Buying Disorder.

129. Burgess, K. (2019, 15 November 2019). Experts Claim Addiction to Shopping is a Mental Illness. *The Times*. Retrieved from www.thetimes.co.uk/article/experts-claim-addiction-to-shopping-is-a-mental-illness-8zptsggjt; Faber, R. J., & O'Guinn, T. C. (2008). Compulsive Buying. In C. P. Haugtvedt, P. M. Herr, & F. R. Kardes (eds), *Handbook of Consumer Psychology* (pp. 1039–1056). New York: Psychology Press.

130. Faber & O'Guinn, Compulsive Buying; Hollander, E., & Allen, A. (2006). Is Compulsive Buying a Real Disorder, and Is It Really Compulsive? *American Journal of Psychiatry, 163*(10), 1760–1762; Lejoyeux, M., & Weinstein, A. (2010). Compulsive Buying. *American Journal of Drug and Alcohol Abuse, 36*(5), 248–253.

131. Christenson et al., Compulsive Buying; d'Astous, A., Maltais, J., & Roberge, C. (1990). Compulsive Buying Tendencies of Adolescent Consumers. In M. E. Goldberg, G. Gorn, & R. W. Pollay (eds), *NA – Advances in Consumer Research* (Vol. 17, pp. 306–312). Provo, UT: Association for Consumer Research; McElroy, S. L., Keck, P. E., Pope, H. G., Smith, J. M. R., & Strakowski, S. M. (1994). Compulsive Buying: A Report of 20 Cases.

Journal of Clinical Psychiatry, 55(6), 242–248; Schlosser, S., Black, D. W., Repertinger, S., & Freet, D. (1994). Compulsive Buying: Demography, Phenomenology, and Comorbidity in 46 Subjects. *General Hospital Psychiatry, 16*(3), 205–212.

132. Coopersmith, S. (1967). *The Antecedents of Self-Esteem.* San Francisco, CA: Freeman; d'Astous, A. (1990). An Inquiry into the Compulsive Side of "Normal" Consumers. *Journal of Consumer Policy, 13*(1), 15–31; Dittmar, H. (2005). Compulsive Buying – A Growing Concern? An Examination of Gender, Age, and Endorsement of Materialistic Values as Predictors. *British Journal of Psychology, 96*(4), 467–491; Heatherton & Polivy, Development and Validation of a Scale for Measuring State Self-Esteem; Schlosser et al., Compulsive Buying; Koran, L. M., Faber, R. J., Aboujaoude, E., Large, M. D., & Serpe, R. T. (2006). Estimated Prevalence of Compulsive Buying Behavior in the United States. *American Journal of Psychiatry, 163*(10), 1806–1812.

133. O'Guinn & Faber, Compulsive Buying; Schlosser et al., Compulsive Buying; Christenson et al., Compulsive Buying.

134. Faber & O'Guinn, Compulsive Buying.

135. DeSarbo, W. S., & Edwards, E. A. (1996). Typologies of Compulsive Buying Behavior: A Constrained Clusterwise Regression Approach. *Journal of Consumer Psychology, 5*(3), 231–262; O'Guinn & Faber, Compulsive Buying.

136. Dittmar, H. (2005). A New Look at "Compulsive Buying": Self–Discrepancies and Materialistic Values as Predictors of Compulsive Buying Tendency. *Journal of Social and Clinical Psychology, 24*(6), 832–859; Japutra, A., Ekinci, Y., Simkin, L., & Nguyen, B. (2018). The Role of Ideal Self-Congruence and Brand Attachment in Consumers' Negative Behaviour: Compulsive Buying and External Trash-Talking. *European Journal of Marketing, 52*(3/4), 683–701.

137. Black, A Review of Compulsive Buying Disorder.

138. Schlosser et al., Compulsive Buying.

139. Naidu, R., & McLymore, A. (2021, 27 November). Black Friday Draws U.S. Shoppers But Many Shun Stores for Online. *Reuters.* Retrieved from www.reuters.com/markets/europe/fearing-empty-shelves-black-friday-early-birds-head-us-stores-2021-11-26/

140. Butler, S. (2021, 26 November). Shoppers Go to Town as UK Rings in Biggest-Ever Black Friday Sales Day. *The Guardian.* Retrieved from www.theguardian.com/business/2021/nov/26/uk-poised-for-record-black-friday-sales

141. Kharpal, A. (2021, 11 November). Alibaba, JD Smash Singles Day Record with $139 Billion of Sales and Focus on "Social Responsibility". *CNBC.* Retrieved from www.cnbc.com/2021/11/12/china-singles-day-2021-alibaba-jd-hit-record-139-billion-of-sales.html

142. Bradford, C. (2021, 26 November). Friday Frenzy: Inside Worst Black Friday Violence from Wal-Mart Worker Trampled to Death to Shooting at Toys 'R' Us. *The Sun.* Retrieved from www.thesun.co.uk/news/16858773/black-friday-violence-walmart-worker-trampled-death/; Kaplan, M. (2020, 27 November). Black Friday's Most Gruesome Injuries and Deaths through the Years. *New York Post.* Retrieved from nypost.com/article/black-fridays-most-gruesome-injuries-and-deaths-through-the-years/; Ayoub, S. (2021, 26 November). Black Friday: How Readers' Shopping Went from Frenzy to Frustration. *The Guardian.*

Retrieved from www.theguardian.com/business/2021/nov/26/black-friday-how-read-ers-shopping-went-from-frenzy-to-frustration

143. Black, A Review of Compulsive Buying Disorder; Dittmar, Compulsive Buying; Mowen, J. C., & Spears, N. (1999). Understanding Compulsive Buying Among College Students: A Hierarchical Approach. *Journal of Consumer Psychology*, 8(4), 407–430; Neuner, M., Raab, G., & Reisch, L. A. (2005). Compulsive Buying in Maturing Consumer Societies: An Empirical Re-inquiry. *Journal of Economic Psychology*, 26(4), 509–522.

144. Mao, F. (2020, 4 March). Coronavirus Panic: Why Are People Stockpiling Toilet Paper? BBC. Retrieved from www.bbc.co.uk/news/world-australia-51731422

145. Black, A Review of Compulsive Buying Disorder; Fineberg, N. A., Chamberlain, S. R., Goudriaan, A. E., Stein, D. J., Vanderschuren, L. J. M. J., Gillan, C. M., . . . Morein-Zamir, S. (2014). New Developments in Human Neurocognition: Clinical, Genetic, and Brain Imaging Correlates of Impulsivity and Compulsivity. *CNS Spectrums*, 19(1), 69–89.

146. Towers, T. (2020, 13 July). Stockpiler Slammed for Storing Hundreds of Toilet Paper Rolls in Garage Next to Posh Car. *Daily Star*. Retrieved from www.dailystar.co.uk/news/world-news/hoarder-slammed-storing-hundreds-toilet-22346247

12

RESEARCH METHODS IN CONSUMER PSYCHOLOGY

To explore, understand, and explain:

- the key qualitative methods: interviews and observations and issues related to sampling, data analysis, and reporting findings
- the key quantitative methods: surveys and experiments and issues related to sampling, data analysis, and reporting findings
- the strengths and weaknesses of the key qualitative and quantitative methods
- frequently asked questions and commonly made mistakes in qualitative and quantitative methods

12.1 INTRODUCTION

Conducting a dissertation project is part of many undergraduate and postgraduate degrees, and the dissertation project forms a significant portion of the final degree that is awarded. Many students with limited research experience often find the dissertation project to be intimidating. Before gaining sufficient experience, this is a common, and completely normal, feeling. This chapter hopes to make doing a research project more accessible.

Choosing and designing a suitable research approach is crucial in all disciplines, and because it is crucial, there are plenty of books dedicated to discussing (specific) research methods. This chapter provides a brief overview of the key research methods that are used in consumer psychology, and highlights the frequently asked questions and commonly made mistakes to provide an initial understanding of research methodology. This can be seen as a shortcut, so it is by no means comprehensive. As a result, when you determine your research strategy, you are urged to refer to the readings about the specific research methods in business, marketing, and psychology. To help you identify suitable readings, some will be recommended along with the discussion of various methods.

12.2 BEFORE CHOOSING A METHOD

There are two main matters to consider in order to make an appropriate decision concerning which method(s) to use. First, at the personal level, are you a person more comfortable with numbers or with words? If you are more comfortable with numbers, a quantitative approach might be more suitable. On the other hand, if you are more comfortable with words, a qualitative approach might be more suitable. Taking advantage of your own strengths as a researcher may optimise the outcome of your research. A related consideration, however, is to think about *what* strengths you wish to further develop. It is difficult to really know whether you have a potential to be good at quantitative or qualitative methods until you try. Higher education provides this opportunity to further develop our skills and ways of thinking. Whilst choosing something you are more comfortable and familiar with is a relatively safe and easy choice, being ambitious by entering an unfamiliar field may open a door that widens your experience and vision. At the personal development level, there is no right or wrong choice in terms of whether you choose a qualitative or a quantitative approach. It is personal. Note this personal choice should ideally reflect the philosophical position you take; however, the philosophy of social science leading to methodology are beyond the scope of this chapter (Box 12.1).

─Box 12.1─

Recommended readings for the philosophy of social science

Chapter 1 Philosophy of Research in Carson, D., Gilmore, A., Perry, C., & Gronhaug, K. (2001). *Qualitative Marketing Research*. London: SAGE.

Benton, T., & Craib, I. (2011). *Philosophy of Social Science: The Philosophical Foundations of Social Thought* (second edn). London: Red Globe Press.

Traditionally, the philosophy of social science is important for qualitative researchers to justify their use of a qualitative method, because their pursuit of knowledge is unavoidably subjective. On the other hand, quantitative researchers, like those researchers in science disciplines, largely follow positivism in their pursuit of knowledge by maintaining objectivity and by being separated from their participants (as much as they can anyway). As a result, a discussion of the philosophy of social science is usually not required in a quantitative study.

Second is at the research level: the decision of which method(s) to use depends on whether your research questions can be answered by using the specific method(s). Some research questions can only be properly researched by certain methods. For example, research on implicit cognition is usually done by experiments. Why? Implicit cognition is about learning without knowing, so how would research participants be able to answer questions about things that they are not aware of? In the following sections where different methods are discussed, their relative strengths and weaknesses will be examined in order to understand which methods are best suited to answer what kind of research question.

─Box 12.2─

Frequently asked question: Which method is "easier" – qualitative versus quantitative methods?

Many students are strategic learners, and as a result, one of the most often asked questions many tutors have come across in supervising dissertation projects is which method is easier, indicating that efforts can be minimised while the quality of the dissertation can be optimised. The simple answer to this question: there is no easy method. There is the most suitable method, depending on the research question(s) you wish to study, as well as on your personal strengths, as discussed earlier in this section.

Qualitative and quantitative methods follow different mindsets, from formulating research questions or hypotheses to research design, data collection, and data analysis. Qualitative methods seem to be easier for formulating research questions, because the research questions are usually broad and can be revised and refined as the research is progressed. On the other hand, when using quantitative methods, one needs to first read the existing literature extensively in order to generate meaningful hypotheses. Good hypotheses are logical, clear about the direction of influence (e.g. product quality positively influences brand loyalty, as opposed to product quality and brand loyalty are related), and sufficiently original – and all of these criteria

(Continued)

require an in-depth understanding of the literature. In addition, hypotheses are less flexible and difficult to change at a later stage. In other words, at the first stage of research, formulating flexible, broad research questions for qualitative methods versus generating specific hypotheses for quantitative methods suggests that qualitative methods would be easier than quantitative methods to carry out.

However, the degree of complexity (or difficulty) is reversed in the data analysis stage. For quantitative methods, data analysis is more like a mechanical process. Identifying which analysis methods and software to use and then finding solutions to interpret the meanings behind the statistical numbers is straightforward. On the other hand, data analysis for qualitative methods is less straightforward, as it is more of a reflective process than a mechanical process. Even though there is software to help with qualitative data analysis, it is the researcher's role to analyse data and interpret findings, as "Computers don't analyse; people do."[1] The effort expended in data analysis for qualitative methods is therefore relatively greater than for quantitative methods.

As researchers, we face ups and downs during the entire research process. Regardless of which method(s) we choose to use, obstacles will appear at one stage or another. Instead of wasting time on finding an "easier" research method, one should consider the suitability of the research method and of personal strengths. Choose one, and stick to it, and when obstacles come, face them. This is how we develop our research skills. Besides, there is no easy way out, so don't waste your time on trying to find one.

—Box 12.3—

Frequently asked question: Which method is superior? Is it the more the better?

Unlike those students seeking an "easier" method discussed in Box 12.2, there are, of course, other motivated students who aim at doing a better job by using a superior method. These students intend to use a "superior" method to improve the quality of their research project. The answer to this question is simple: there is no superior method if you carry out your research with rigour (that is, with good reliability and validity). There is, however, a more suitable method, depending on your research topic as discussed earlier. Different methods have different strengths to tackle different research topics, and these strengths will be uncovered as this chapter continues.

In the following sections, you will also find that reliability and validity of both qualitative and quantitative methods can be checked and confirmed through using multiple methods or triangulating different data sources. Therefore, the second question these motivated students usually ask is whether using more methods indicates better quality. The answer is: it depends. If you are able to carry out each method with rigour, then, in general, the answer is yes. However, it takes time to master the skills required for each method. In other words, it is highly unlikely that you could master multiple methods within the time constraint you face, usually less than six months of concentrating on your research project. Instead of rushing to do more work that is less than mediocre, it would be better to stick to one method, and focus on learning it and on doing it well.

12.3 QUALITATIVE METHODS

The key strengths of qualitative methods lie in their ability to enable you to explore and understand issues in greater depth. Therefore, qualitative methods are best used to address the *how* and *why* research questions. There are three commonly used qualitative research strategies, namely, phenomenological research, ethnographies, and grounded theory. Each research strategy has its unique purposes (Table 12.1).

Table 12.1   The commonly used qualitative research strategies[a]

Qualitative Research Strategies[b]	Purposes & Examples
Phenomenological research	To understand meanings of "lived experiences" brought about by a phenomenon. This research strategy is perhaps the most often seen in consumer research, as the lived experiences range from consumers' experiences with advertising to various types of consumption. Example: Russell and Levy[2]
Ethnographies	To study an intact cultural group in a natural setting over a prolonged period of time by collecting primarily observational data. Example: McAlexander, Schouten, and Koenig[3]
Grounded theory	To discover a general, abstract theory. Example: Hirschman and Thompson[4]

[a] These three strategies are commonly used in consumer research. There are other qualitative research strategies; for example, case studies used by Fournier.[5]

[b] Refer to Goulding for a more detailed comparison and contrast between these three strategies. In addition, depending on the purposes, these strategies can be combined.[6] For example, Schau and Gilly used an ethnographic method for their grounded theory strategy.[7]

Key methods

Methods here refer to the methods of data collection. There are many forms of data, including documents/texts (e.g. consumer diaries) and images/photos, but the most often used methods are interviews and observations, which will be introduced below.

Interviews

Strengths of interviews

The first and foremost strength is that the researcher has some control over the line of questioning to investigate matters of interest in depth. Semi-structured interviews outline the direction of the questions, and even for unstructured interviews researchers are still able to ask questions in their spontaneous conversations. In addition, interviews are particularly useful when participants cannot be observed directly (e.g. participants' feelings, memories, and interpretations). Even when observations are possible, observations focus on ongoing activities, whereas through interviews, participants are able to provide historical information.

Weaknesses of interviews

There are two key weaknesses. First, participants may provide socially desirable responses. That is, the mere presence of the interviewer may bias the participants' responses. The second weakness is the difficulty of "getting into the heads" of those participants who are not eloquent or perceptive. Even if the participants are able to articulate their views well or observe matters acutely, they may unconsciously rationalise their responses. The information is provided by the participants, so unavoidably such information is filtered through their views, and the extent to which the information truthfully reflects their motivations or feelings can be uncertain.

Types of interviews

Semi-structured versus unstructured interviews

The most common form of interviews is semi-structured. *Semi-structured interviews* provide the researcher with a broad direction of questioning, but whether or not the direction changes, and to what extent the depth of questioning goes, depends on the interviewees' responses. On the other hand, *unstructured interviews* do not have pre-arranged questions or directions; they are spontaneous conversations. These conversations or interviews often take place when conducting ethnographic research (Table 12.1). Unstructured interviews are rarely used because of the time constraint and the limited scope of a dissertation project at undergraduate and master's levels.

Depth interviews versus focus groups

Depth interviews are conducted on a one-to-one basis and are the most commonly used form of interviews in academic research. In fact, depth interviews are considered *the* major source of data for many qualitative researchers.[8] A depth interview takes from 30 minutes to more than an hour, and is best suited for research investigating interviewees' attitudes, beliefs, motivations, and feelings on a topic of interest in depth.

Focus groups are small group interviews and are the most popular form of interviews in research carried out by marketing consulting firms or advertising agencies.[9] On average, the length of a focus group is about 1.5–2 hours. Focus groups enable the observation of group interactions, and this is the distinguishing feature of focus groups: their ability to generate insights that are less accessible without group interaction.[10] The ideal composition of group members is homogeneous in its demographic characteristics and the ideal size of a focus group is 5–8 people.

Box 12.4

Online interviews

Thanks to the improvement in the Internet speed and related technology, it is now possible to carry out interviews online. Carrying out online interviews has been critical during Covid-19 lockdowns for many qualitative researchers. The key advantage of online interviews is that there are no geographical constraints. Having no geographical constraints is particularly useful in gaining access to busy participants whose schedule make it difficult for them to participate on site. In addition, another advantage is the possibility of enabling anonymous participation. The possibility to participate in research anonymously helps participants to be more willing to freely discuss issues that are sensitive in nature (e.g. consumption of sex). Despite these key advantages, there are associated limitations with online interviews. The most critical limitation is the potential exposure to distracting stimuli in the participant's environment. People are generally less involved in an online environment. For this reason (and also because of the difficulty in fully capturing body language, facial expressions, and tone of voice), highly emotional issues are better explored in person than through online interviews.[11]

The recommended group size for online focus groups should be smaller than those conducted via face-to-face, as too many voices online can confuse the discussion. The recommended group size for online focus groups is 4-6.[12]

Conducting interviews

Preparation

Three pieces of information need to be prepared before interviews:

1. information to brief participants about the objective of the interview
2. information regarding informed consent to comply with research ethics procedures (see Section 12.5)
3. an interview guide

An interview guide includes the questions or topics that the researchers wish to investigate in the interview. These are general, open-ended interview questions or topics. The interview guide serves as a memory jogger for the researcher during the interview, so it needs not to be a long list of questions. Besides, the point is not the number of questions on the interview guide. Rather, it is more about how you, as an interviewer, can probe deep and rich responses out of your participants.

In some cases, a rolling interview guide can be used. A rolling interview guide is a guide that is revised for the next interview based on the outcome of the previous interview. As the research question(s) might change as the researcher's understanding of the topic increases, the flexibility to change interview questions when the researcher sees fit is necessary. However, the key limitation of using a rolling interview guide is the difficulty of comparing and contrasting between interviews. In order to minimise this difficulty, one can either conduct more interviews when the interview guide is more or less finalised (the guide would usually go through more changes in the first few interviews) or can ensure that the key questions used for comparison remain in every interview.

Key interview techniques

A primary skill of a qualitative researcher is to involve the respondent in a conversation rather than an interview, and the conversation may cover the general topics and associated probes without the respondent knowing they had been planned to be raised.[13]

—Box 12.5—

The rules of good interviewing

- Use the participant's terms, not academic ones. This seems obvious, but many students have the tendency of using academic terms. Most of your participants may not be familiar with academic terms at all, and you should not attempt to use an interview to "educate" your participants.
- Allow the participant's interests and concerns to decide the order of the topics to be discussed. The interview guide provides a general direction of which topics to cover in the interview, but it is not rigid in terms of its order.
- Ask non-directive questions, such as:
  - Could you elaborate that more?
  - Can you give me an example?
  - You mentioned that [repeat in participant's words]. Can you tell me more about that?
- Use the active listening technique. The active listening technique is about using subtle probes (such as "tell me about . . .") in order to get into the mind of your participant. It is not an answer you get from your participant; it is their thoughts, feelings, ideas you

get from your participant.[14] The active listening technique also requires that you check whether your understanding of what the participant has said is what the participant actually means.[15] It can be done by feeding back dialogue in your own words. By so doing, you also remind the participant that what they are saying is very interesting.[16]

- Use subtle language (e.g. a murmur of understanding), body language (e.g. eye contact), or facial expression (e.g. smile) to encourage the participant to continue.
- Never ask questions that may imply what answer is most acceptable or introduce the researcher's own idea into the interview.
  o For example, "Many people believe that you get what you pay for. How important do you think pricing is in deciding which brand to purchase?"
- Never interrupt an answer.

These rules are summarised based on Armstrong's[17] and Carson et al.'s[18] work.

Direct questioning versus indirect questioning

Direct questioning is the most often used form of interviewing technique in consumer research. The key approach to ask questions directly is called laddering. *Laddering* suggests that the researcher asks a broader question first and then moves up the ladder by asking more specific questions based on the participants' responses to the broad question. The benefits of using the laddering technique are twofold. First, broad questions are usually easier to answer, so researchers can ease their participants into a conversation with something the participants can easily respond to. For example, in order to understand what brand of laptops the participants bought and why, the participants' initial responses would be product attributes, including the brand name, the price, the specification, et cetera. Alternatively, you could ask them to talk about their experiences in determining the previous laptops they bought – it is their personal story, which anyone can just tell without worrying whether it is the correct response. Ultimately, the probe would move from product attributes to user characteristics, which could be the underlying emotions, values, or motivators that may not be obvious without sufficient probing, and this is the second benefit of using the laddering technique.

Indirect questioning is categorised as projective techniques. The most often used projective technique in consumer research is Zaltman's metaphor elicitation technique (ZMET), a type of thematic apperception test (TAT), which is a popular, and well-developed, projective technique in psychology. The major benefit of projective techniques is that they are able to provoke responses that participants would be otherwise unwilling or unable to provide. For example, people would be less willing to share their views when the subject under discussion is overly sensitive or personal, and would be unable to when the underlying motivations or attitudes operate at a subconscious level.

In using ZMET, participants are asked to bring about ten pictures of their choice on a specific topic to the interview and to describe the salient content of each picture. The pictures can be from any sources, including magazines, newspapers, or personal photographs. For example, to investigate consumers' perception of advertising, Coulter et al. asked their participants to bring pictures that illustrated the value of advertising,[19] or to investigate consumers' perception of the mobile Internet, Sugai asked his participants to bring pictures that came to their mind when thinking about the mobile Internet.[20]

Box 12.6

Recommended readings for conducting interviews

Depth interviews:

- Chapter 6 In-Depth Interviewing in Carson, D., Gilmore, A., Perry, C., & Gronhaug, K. (2001). *Qualitative Marketing Research*. London: SAGE.
- Morris, A. (2015). *A Practical Introduction to In-Depth Interviewing*. London: SAGE.

Focus groups:

- Chapter 8 Focus Group Interviewing in Carson, D., Gilmore, A., Perry, C., & Gronhaug, K. (2001). *Qualitative Marketing Research*. London: SAGE.
- Krueger, R. A., & Casey, M. A. (2015). *Focus Groups: A Practical Guide for Applied Research* (fifth edn). Los Angeles: SAGE.

Good practices for conducting interviews

Below are three main good practices for conducting interviews:

- *Recordings (voice recordings for depth interviews and video recordings for focus groups)*: Before the interviews, make sure the recording equipment works properly, and don't forget to turn on the equipment after you have gained permission from your participants to record the interview.
- *Taking notes*: It is important to strike a balance between intensive notes taking during the interview and maintaining eye contact with your participants. Intensive notes taking may be distracting for your participants, but occasional pauses during the interview may encourage your participants to think of things that they may have neglected. You could take notes of the interesting points that you wish to probe further during the interview, and then immediately after the interview, when your memory is still fresh, make notes of the important observations you found in the interview. For this reason, you should schedule sufficient time between the interviews for notes taking.

- *Transcribing interviews*: Ideally, transcribing an interview should take place at an early opportunity. This is because transcribing the interviews reveals areas for improvement in the researcher's notes taking and interview probing skills. This is particularly important for an inexperienced researcher for the first few interviews. As a result, do not schedule too many interviews in one day and plan time for listening to the playback or for transcribing the recordings in-between the first three interviews.

Box 12.7

Frequently asked question: Do I have to transcribe interviews?

Transcription can be a tedious job, and transcribing interview data takes a long time. For an inexperienced transcriber, a one-hour interview recording can take about one day to transcribe. However, the time spent on transcription is not wasted, considering the three major benefits the transcriptions may provide:

1. Transcribing interview data helps data analysis.
2. Reading transcriptions is a lot faster than re-listening to the recordings as going through data several times is necessary for analysing qualitative data.
3. It takes much less time to identify the best quotes from the interviews to report and substantiate the findings from the transcriptions than from the recordings.

Observations

Observations are the primary data sources in ethnographic studies (Table 12.1). Entering the field of the selected cultural groups for a prolonged period of time, and the field notes from the researcher's observation on the behaviour and activities of people at the field site comprise the major data source.

Strengths of observations

The main strength is that the researcher is able to share the experience with the participants first-hand and to observe aspects that might escape from notice by the participants. For example, there are things during the course of our life that we, as participants, do not think about, and for those things we do not think about, if the researcher is unaware of them, he or she will be unable to know what to probe in the interview. Similarly, things that might be taken for granted, done without a second thought, or difficult or uncomfortable to elaborate could be revealed via first-hand observation.

Weaknesses of observations

A major weakness of this method is that the presence of the researcher at the research site observing activities as they are revealed may be intrusive.

How long does a researcher need to be in the field for observation?

It depends; it depends on data saturation (see Box 12.9). The minimum time-frame is usually a cycle for the activity you observe, so it can be a month or a year, but classic ethnographers usually spend two to three years immersed in their research sites. Because of the time constraint, most students are unable to conduct a proper ethnographic study for their undergraduate or master's levels of research projects, unless it is a netnography, an online ethnography.

Netnography - online ethnographic studies

Netnography makes ethnographic studies possible for students with time constraints, as it is a research method that uses the traditional, in-person ethnographic research techniques to study the online cultures and communities.[21] This method focuses not on the consumers themselves, but on their behaviour, which translates to the "participating" and "producing" activities carried out online through textual discourse.[22] Activities online leave footprints that can trace back to years of data without the need for the researcher to actually spend the same amount of time in the field, and at the same time, they provide a "powerful window into the naturally occurring reality of consumers" and affords "up-to-the-minute assessments of consumers' collective pulse".[23] Although the researcher might be able to save some time by reading through the texts online at the selected research sites, netnographic data are usually messy and data mining makes data analysis a complicated and time-consuming task.

Conducting observations

The field notes made by the researcher during and soon after observations are the main data collected from the observations, and these field notes should include the following:

1. descriptive notes:
   - description of the physical setting and accounts of particular events under observation
   - portraits of the participants
   - reconstructions of dialogues
2. reflective notes: the researchers' personal thoughts – speculations, feelings, problems, ideas, hunches, impressions, and prejudices

In addition to these field notes, the researcher could utilise data recorded by other means, such as picture/photograph records, video records, and audio records.

Box 12.8

Recommended readings for conducting observations

Those who plan to use observations may refer to the below references:

- Chapter 9 Observation Studies in Carson, D., Gilmore, A., Perry, C., & Gronhaug, K. (2001). *Qualitative Marketing Research*. London: SAGE.
- Kozinets, R. V. (2002). The Field behind the Screen: Using Netnography for Marketing Research in Online Communities. *Journal of Marketing Research, 39*(1), 61-72.

Sampling

Sampling in qualitative studies is selected purposefully. That is, research participants and sites are carefully selected for the suitability of the proposed study. A good sampling design is able to ensure research rigour and should follow the below guidelines:

- Avoid "backyard" research if possible.[24] Backyard research involves studying the researcher's own friends or participants from immediate work or life settings, and easily compromises the researcher's and the participants' ability to disclose information. However, sampling from one's own friends is a common sampling method used by students conducting consumer research because of the advantage of convenience. If backyard research cannot be avoided, then additional types of data (e.g. documents) should be collected in order to cross-validate the findings.
- Set the scope of the study and select a wide range of participants and/or activities within the scope. For example, if you wish to study how people from two different social classes react to different advertising messages, the two different social classes and the specific advertising messages for them to interpret would be the scope. Within the scope, there are many different types of people from the same social class background, for example men versus women, different age groups, and different educational backgrounds, and, if depth interview is the selected method, at least three to four people should be interviewed in order to reduce the possibility of overly relying on a single view to represent the entire sub-group. If, however, the project becomes too big to manage, narrowing the scope would be recommended.

—Box 12.9—

Frequently asked question: What is the minimum sample size for a qualitative study?

Ideally, the best sample size is when data collection achieves saturation, suggesting that the researcher cannot find additional findings from new interviews or new observations, but we do not know what the sample size would be until data are collected and (at least) partly analysed. In addition, due to the nature (and constraints) of a student project, most tutors, if not all, do not require students to follow this guideline.

Qualitative studies do not solely depend on numbers. Richness in the data collected (e.g. how much information one participant can reveal in an interview) is more important than the breadth of the data collected (e.g. how many interviews are conducted). However, richness in data is not always reflected in the length of the interview, as some participants spend much time in thinking what and how to respond to the questions, rather than articulating their thoughts or feelings. In addition, how well participants are able to respond also depends on the researcher's probing ability. Therefore, if your ability to draw out rich responses from your participants is good enough, and if your participants are able to talk about their thoughts and feelings sufficiently, then about five to ten hours' worth of interview data would be able to achieve a decent data analysis.

Data analysis

Qualitative data analysis is not straightforward, as it requires going back and forth from data collection and analysis to reformulation of research questions, which needs further research into the existing literature. It is an ongoing process that involves continuous reflection about the data throughout the study. Only through this continuous reflection can the findings emerge. The key steps in data analysis include the following:

Step 1: Read through all the data to get a general sense of the information and to reflect on its overall meaning.

Step 2: Carry out coding or thematic analysis, which is a form of content analysis by identifying key patterns that appear in the data, until no more important themes appear. On reaching this stage you are said to have reached saturation of data analysis. The themes to be identified include the following:

- themes that readers would expect to find
- themes that are surprising
- themes that address the key theoretical perspective(s) in the research

Step 3: Compare and contrast the identified themes and look for ways to reduce the themes by, for example, understanding how different themes may be related to each other (i.e. whether the themes can be categorised into a hierarchical structure).

Step 4: Interpret meaning of the identified themes based on (1) the researcher's own understanding, culture, and experiences and (2) comparing and contrasting the findings with extant literature.

Box 12.10

Frequently asked question: Is there any software that can help analyse qualitative data?

The short answer is, yes, there is. For example, NVivo is one of the most popular software packages many universities provide for their students and academic staff to use. However, the question that is worth discussing here is whether or not it is worth investing in time in learning and using the software. It depends. If your data are expected to be too rich and diverse to manage, then using one of the software packages would greatly help; however, most undergraduate and master's dissertation projects do not involve data that are too rich or diverse to handle. Using software may actually increase the time required, as the coding process is a manual process. In other words, if your data only contain, say, less than 30-hour interview recordings, going to your data directly without the software assist would be recommended.

Box 12.11

Recommended readings for qualitative data analysis

Spiggle, S. (1994). Analysis and Interpretation of Qualitative Data in Consumer Research. *Journal of Consumer Research, 21*(3), 491-503.

Chapter 12 Organizing, Processing and Visualizing Data in Carson, D., Gilmore, A., Perry, C., & Gronhaug, K. (2001). *Qualitative Marketing Research*. London: SAGE.

Kozinets, R. V., Dolbec, P.-Y., & Earley, A. (2014). Netnographic Analysis: Understanding Culture through Social Media Data. In U. Flick (ed.), *SAGE Handbook of Qualitative Data Analysis* (pp. 262-275). London: SAGE.

Research rigour: How to ensure reliability and validity in qualitative studies

The key strength, but also the key weakness, of qualitative methods largely depends on the researchers' interpretation of meaning derived from their data. As the researchers fill a critical role interpreting data and are inseparable from the subjects (or the social reality) that they study, data interpretation is unavoidably subjective. Pursuing objectivity is not the way to maintain rigour for qualitative methods; however, reducing the researchers' biases is. Qualitative researchers should be mindful not to impose their biases on their findings. As a result, to ensure research rigour, one has to check for reliability and validity.

Reliability and validity are two different concepts. *Reliability* suggests the same key findings would be found by other researchers if they conducted the same research, whereas *validity* indicates the extent to which findings accurately reflect the phenomenon under study. As a result, valid findings are usually reliable, but reliable findings are not necessarily valid. Table 12.2 shows how reliability and validity for qualitative studies can be examined.

Table 12.2   Ways to check reliability and validity of qualitative studies

Reliability	Validity
1. Are consistent themes also identified by different researchers analysing the same data?	1. Discuss with the participants to see if they feel the findings are an accurate reflection of their thoughts or feelings
2. Are consistent themes also identified from the data collected by different researchers or by different methods?	2. Discuss with peers to see if the findings resonate with people other than the researcher
	3. Triangulate different data sources (i.e. use multiple data sources to understand the phenomenon understudy)

Box 12.12

Recommended readings for ensuring reliability and validity for qualitative studies

Riege, A. M. (2003). Validity and Reliability Tests in Case Study Research: A Literature Review of "Hands-On" Applications for Each Research Phase. *Qualitative Market Research: An International Journal, 6*(2), 75-86.

Creswell, J. W., & Miller, D. L. (2000). Determining Validity in Qualitative Inquiry. *Theory into Practice, 39*(3), 124-130.

Cultural issues in data analysis

The main cultural issue that students often encounter is the language issue. That is, the language with which our data are collected and the language in which our results are reported are not necessarily the same language. If your field is in, say China, but your degree requires you write up in English, then how do you analyse your data? Do you translate your data into English before or after data analysis? Translating the whole dataset is not only time-consuming but also unnecessary and could be potentially harmful for data analysis. Language is a product of culture, and if there are things difficult to translate, meaning could be lost in translation. In order to minimise the loss of meaning due to translation, data should be analysed in its original language whenever possible, and only the selected excerpts of data that are to be used in reporting are translated into your final language.

Reporting

Reporting your findings correctly and convincingly is critical to resonate with your readers, who are usually the markers of your dissertation project. To instil credibility into your reporting, what you report and how you report it make a difference.

What you report

You need to demonstrate the manner in which you arrive at your findings is reliable and valid. Therefore, in the *methodology* chapter, you should report the following:

1. the rationale for your choice of method
2. the description of your study design
3. what reliability and validity checks you have employed
4. what bias(es) you might bring to the study and how you deal with these biases
5. an acknowledgement that the ethical procedures have been followed (see Section 12.5)

In the *data analysis* chapter, you should report:

1. the key patterns (themes) that emerged from the data
2. the inconsistent information that emerged that runs counter to your findings. Qualitative studies are not about generalisability, so inconsistent information would not hurt the credibility of your report. In fact, inconsistency, if presented and explained appropriately, can increase credibility, as "real life is composed of different perspectives that do not always coalesce".[25]

How you report

You should imitate how qualitative papers published in journals report their findings. The most common reporting format is to use text-embedded quotations intertwined with the researcher's interpretations, which bring together the findings with the existing literature on the topic; that is, how your findings might confirm, change, or add to our existing knowledge (Figure 12.1). These quotations should be carefully selected from your data as they are used to substantiate your findings. When quotations from your data are used, use indents to call attention to these quotations. Although the majority of the findings are reported via text descriptions, text information can also be summarised in tables or figures where suitable if they are able to help readers better understand your findings by visualising them.

Here, Zoey describes her awe at the first Xena event she attended and her desire to purchase more authentic Xena wear and attend more events. Similarly, Mandy describes how her Xena engagement escalated in tandem with others who started at the conventions when she did:

> The first convention I went to was a fan-run subtext-oriented but main-friendly [run by fans who support the lesbian reading of the show but welcome those who adhere to an action-adventure reading]. I actually went with a boyfriend. We wore clothes we had in our closet:... a mishmash of western leather clothes made to look medieval. Don't ask me how. But the thing is, most other people were dressed like that ... [with] stuff they had already. Not vintage or even authentic replicas.... The elaborate costumes came over time. One person ups the bar and we all really dig it and compliment them, and then we all start upping the ante.... Now, you can't really show up in something you just had in your closet. No one would take you seriously. (interview, 02/10/2001)

Mandy describes how this practice began as a casual nod to medieval attire and became a quest for authenticity and even vintage costumes through competitive, escalating engagement in brand practices. She shows that practices develop; hedonic engagement evolves and deepens over time, and value expands. Mandy's description of the evolution of the practice echoes Warde's (2005, p. 139) assertion that "[p]ractices have a trajectory or path of development, a history."

(1)

Through the mundane act of patronizing local coffee shops, our participants can experience themselves as rebels who are consuming against the grain of corporate-dominated mainstream conformity. Through this formulation, their experiences of authentic cultural difference and social diversity afforded by their favorite coffee shops become a resource for cultivating a sense of personal distinctiveness and defiant individuality. Conversely, their diametric contrast to Starbucks's doppelgänger meanings (i.e., corporate conformity and mass-market standardization) functions as a frame of reference that enhances these experiences of authenticity:

> Frank: Well, yeah, a place like this is unique, which I like. It very much caters to, you know, the population around here. It's very, you know, it's comforting to somebody who lives in the suburbs. It's unique, it's got its artsy sort of thing, but as opposed to Starbucks, you know, everywhere it's still the same corporate kind of cookie-cutter type of place that is more, that I don't see the same uniqueness. You know, you can come in here and get a cup of coffee, and it's going to be different than what you get in [name of another local establishment]; it's going to taste a little bit different, but you know, [in] every Starbucks, the food and drinks are pretty much the same. So, I mean, just a place like this has more personality. I wouldn't go to Starbucks. I'll go out of my way to go all the way to the East Side—for me, a drive from here is about six miles. I'd rather do that, and it's just more of a satisfying experience.

(2)

Figure 12.1 Reporting format for qualitative studies

(1) *Source*: Schau et al.[26]

Reprinted from *Journal of Marketing*, 73(5), Schau et al. How Brand Community Practices Create Value, 30-51, Copyright (2009), with permission from SAGE.

(2) *Source*: Thompson et al.[27]

Reprinted from *Journal of Marketing*, 70(1), Thompson et al. Emotional Branding and the Strategic Value of the Doppelgänger Brand Image, 50-64, Copyright (2006), with permission from SAGE.

12.4 QUANTITATIVE METHODS

Key strengths

Borrowing the concept of science disciplines, such as physics, quantitative psychology, relying on statistics, is able to offer three main strengths:

1. relationships between variables under study can be statistically tested and established
2. these relationships can be generalised
3. objectivity in data collection and data analysis can be achieved

Key weaknesses

However, statistics is not omnipotent. In order to ensure statistics work optimally, quantitative studies require a relatively large sample size. In other words, the extent to which the findings of quantitative studies can be generalised depends on their sample sizes, and a large sample size requires more resources in finance and in time.

Another major weakness is lack of flexibility. That is, quantitative methods mainly use pre-determined scales with a fixed-alternative form (Box 12.13), where respondents select one response, from a predetermined set of responses, that best reflects their thoughts, feelings, and behaviour. In addition, as statistical procedures produce results in the form of garbage-in, garbage-out, so to speak, the quality of the work heavily relies on the quality of these pre-determined scales, which, unlike those in the science disciplines, may change over time and across different cultures.

Key methods

The purpose of quantitative studies is to establish relationships between variables, and there are two main methods: survey and experiment.

Survey

The survey is perhaps the most popular form of quantitative method among students. The strength of this approach is in its simplicity in terms of execution and data analysis, allowing associations to be statistically tested between various variables. However, because the questions are formulated in a fixed-alternative format, the main weakness is its lack of flexibility.

Questionnaire design

There are five main components in a questionnaire:

1. invitation letter, which includes the topic of the research and the ethical steps the research has taken (see Section 12.5)
2. screening question(s) that ensure your respondents belong to the pre-defined sampling frame, if you have a specific type of respondent to recruit
3. behavioural questions, which ask about the respondents' behaviour; questions such as what luxury brands they have bought or how often they use social media belong to behavioural questions
4. attitudinal questions, which ask the respondents' attitudes, including values, beliefs, and opinions; questions such as to what extent they like a certain advertisement or prefer a certain brand belong to attitudinal questions
5. demographic questions, which ask the respondents' age, sex, education level, occupation, ethnicity, and income level

Measurements

Measurements, also known as scales, measurement scales, and inventories, are the proxies that can "measure" a concept (or a variable) under study. To put this more simply, measurements are the attitudinal questions you ask in a questionnaire. The most often used types of measurements are Likert-type scales and semantic differential scales (Box 12.13). A common misconception by students is that they think it is fairly easy and straightforward to develop an appropriate scale of their own, but in fact it is not. As the quality of the measurements determine the quality of your quantitative study as mentioned earlier, the next section will outline steps to follow to ensure the selected measurements are suitable and proper.

Box 12.13

Commonly used measurement types: Likert-type and semantic differential scales

Likert-type scales

The scale, named after its inventor, Rensis Likert (1903-1981), is designed to measure respondents' attitudes by specifying their level of agreement on a symmetric disagree-agree scale for a series of statements - see Figure 12.2 for an example. As there are seven options (also known as response alternatives or response categories) from strongly disagree to strongly agree to choose from, it is a seven-point Likert-type scale.

	Strongly disagree	Disagree	Somewhat disagree	Neither agree nor disagree	Somewhat agree	Agree	Stongly agree
I am committed to this brand.	O	O	O	O	O	O	O
I would be willing to pay a higher price for this brand over other brands.	O	O	O	O	O	O	O

Figure 12.2   An example of a Likert-type scale

Source: a scale extracted from Chaudhuri and Holbrook's brand loyalty[28]

Semantic differential scales

The semantic differential scale, developed by Charles E. Osgood (1916-1991), is designed to measure the meaning (or semantics) of objects, activities, or concepts by placing two opposite adjectives (or descriptions) on each end of a bipolar continuum, such as bad-good, negative-positive, and so on. Respondents select the box according to how close they believe what is being evaluated as, for example, bad versus good, where the box closer to either end of the bipolar continuum reflects an opinion closer to the two extremes of what is being evaluated, with the mid-point representing a neutral position. Figure 12.3 shows an example of how a 7-point semantic differential scale is displayed.

I think the advertisement is . . .

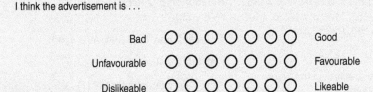

Figure 12.3   An example of a semantic differential scale

Source: a scale extracted from Batra and Stayman's attitudes towards an advertisement.[29] Printed with permission of Oxford University Press.

Optimal number of response categories

One issue that student researchers encounter is how many response categories they should allocate to a scale. The majority of studies use 5, 7, or 9 response categories (i.e. 5-, 7-, or 9-points on a Likert-type or semantic differential scale), and research also shows that these numbers are suitable.[30] You can choose 5-, 7-, or 9-point scales, but you should avoid mixing, for example, 5- and 9-point scales in the same questionnaire.

Research rigour: How to ensure reliability and validity in measurements

Statistical analysis is a garbage-in, garbage-out process. In other words, if the measurements are poor, it is unlikely the analysis can obtain rigorous results. As a result, one way to ensure research rigour is to ensure the measurements are reliable and valid. The most important validity and reliability for a student dissertation project are content validity and internal consistency. *Content validity* ensures the measurements of the items reflect what they are supposed to measure, whereas *internal consistency* suggests that when multiple questions/items are used to measure a concept, they reliably (i.e. consistently) reflect the concept under study. (Multiple items are often used to measure a psychological concept, as psychological concepts are often multi-faceted.)

Below are the steps used to ensure content validity and internal consistency:

Step 1. Choose your measurements from the existing literature. The main reason to use measurements from the existing literature is because they were usually developed by following strict procedures to ensure reliability and validity. You can find these measurements from some papers, such as Richins and Dawson[31] and Thomson, MacInnis, and Park,[32] where the entire paper is about the measurements they developed, whereas other measurements appear in a paper more subtly – see Figures 12.4 and 12.5 for examples.

Measurements

Core Constructs

Desire for Revenge (Time 1: α = .97, AVE = .85; Time 2: α = .96, AVE = .84; Time 3: α = .96, AVE = .82; Time 4: α = .96, AVE = .84)

I want (or wanted) to …

- Take actions to get the firm in trouble.
- Punish the firm in some way.
- Cause inconvenience to the firm.
- Get even with the firm.
- Make the firm get what it deserved.

Desire for Avoidance (Time 1: α = .87, AVE = .66; Time 2: α = .96, AVE = .73; Time 3: α = .91, AVE = .73; Time 4: α = .94, AVE = .81)

I want (or wanted) to …

- Keep as much distance as possible between the firm and me.
- Avoid frequenting the firm.
- Cut off the relationship with the firm.
- Withdraw my business from the firm.

Perceived Betrayal (Time 1: α = .81, AVE = .61; Time 2: α = .86, AVE = .67; Time 3: α = .83, AVE = .71; Time 4: α = .85, AVE = .66)

- I felt (feel) betrayed by the firm.
- The firm broke (breaks) the promise made to me.
- The firm let me down in a moment of need.

Relationship Quality (Time 1: α = .73, AVE = .50)

1. Trust (Time 1: α = .94, AVE = .80)

I felt that the firm was …

- "Very undependable" (1)–"very dependable" (7) "Very incompetent" (1)–"very competent" (7)
- "Of low integrity" (1)–"of high integrity" (7)
- "Very unresponsive to consumers" (1)–"very responsive consumers" (7)

2. Commitment (Time 1: α = .92, AVE = .80)

- I was very committed to my relationship with the service firm.
- The relationship was something I intended to maintain for a long time.
- I put the efforts into maintaining this relationship.

3. Social Benefits (Time 1: α = .94, AVE = .80)

My relationship with the service firm was based on its ability to …

- Recognize who I am as a customer.
- Know my personal needs as a customer.
- Build a "one-on-one" connection.
- Make me feel important and appreciated.

Figure 12.4   How a scale might appear in a paper – Example 1

Source: Grégoire et al.[33]

Reprinted from *Journal of Marketing*, 73(November), Grégoire et al., When Customer Love Turns into Lasting Hate: The Effects of Relationship Strength and Time on Customer Revenge and Avoidance, 18-32, Copyright (2009), with permission from SAGE.

brand commitment (Jacoby and Chestnut 1978). Specifically, purchase loyalty was measured by agreement with the following two statements: "I will buy this brand the next time I buy [product name]" and "I intend to keep purchasing this brand." Coefficient alpha for purchase loyalty was .90. Attitudinal loyalty was measured by two statements: "I am committed to this brand" and "I would be willing to pay a higher price for this brand over other brands." Coefficient alpha for attitudinal loyalty was .83.

Note that at least one of the measures for brand trust and brand affect corresponds closely to the measures cited previously for utilitarian and hedonic value. This correspondence was introduced intentionally to control for the variance due to the product category when effects due to the brand alone are examined. Thus, for example, we capture the variance due to affect toward the product category with the hedonic value item cited previously ("I feel good when I use this product"), and we separately estimate the variance due to affect toward the brand with the brand affect item ("I feel good when I use this brand"). As stated previously, the product-level, category-related variables of hedonic and utilitarian value act as control variables in the sense that they capture product-category effects that might otherwise be subsumed in the brand-level data. By relating the product-category variables to the brand-level variables of trust and affect, we can isolate the variance that is due to the brand alone from the variance that is due to the product category.

As a test of discriminant validity, Fornell and Larcker (1981) have suggested that the average variance extracted for each construct should be higher than the squared correlation between that construct and any other construct. To demonstrate this for the four constructs just described, we conducted a confirmatory factor analysis with LISREL 8.14 (Jöreskog and Sörbom 1996) using the aggregated data for the 149 brands in Phase 3. Fornell and Larcker's (1981) test of discriminant validity held for all four constructs considered separately; specifically, the largest squared correlation between

30 responses for each of 149 brands with the data set from the managerial survey (Phase 2) for the corresponding brands in the 41 product categories covered by both sets of responses. Next, we entered the appropriate product-category data (Phase 1) on hedonic and utilitarian value for each brand in the data set. This resulted in a combined data set for 107 brands with complete observations on all variables except, in a few cases, one or more of the final brand performance outcomes. These brand performance variables were not always provided by the product managers. In Table 1, we provide a list of the 41 product categories in the final data set of 107 brands (with the number of brands in each category shown parenthetically). Confidentiality agreements with the product managers prevent us from divulging the specific brand names in the final data set.

In Table 2, we provide the full set of correlations among the constructs of interest in the study. Note that the two brand performance outcomes, market share and relative price, were essentially independent $(r = .03, n.s.)$, with a vanishingly small shared variance $(r^2 = .0009)$.

Results

Path analysis (LISREL 8.14) was used for testing the model and hypotheses shown in Figure 1. In this path analysis, the multiple indicators were summed together for each construct, and the resulting summated score was used to represent that construct in the simultaneous equation model.[4] Path analysis (LISREL 8.14) testing the proposed model (Figure 1) resulted in the following fit statistics: $\chi^2(18) = 20.32$, $p = .32$, root mean residual (RMR) = .036, goodness-of-fit index (GFI) = .96, adjusted goodness-of-fit index (AGFI) = .89, normed fit index (NFI) = .94, nonnormed fit index (NNFI) = .96, comparative fit index (CFI) = .99, incremental fit index (IFI) = .99. Fourteen structural paths and 13 correlations were estimated for the model containing the ten constructs in Figure 1.

Three of the paths in the proposed model (utilitarian →

Figure 12.5 How a scale might appear in a paper – Example 2

Source: Chaudhuri and Holbrook [34]

Reprinted from *Journal of Marketing*, 65(April), Chaudhuri and Holbrook, The Chain of Effects from Brand Trust and Brand Affect to Brand Performance: The Role of Brand Loyalty, 81-93, Copyright (2001), with permission from SAGE.

Step 2. Carefully choose the measurements that best suit your study. You may find different measurements for the same variable, and if there are multiple measurements, make a decision based on the suitability of the measurement by going through the papers and by comparing the measurement items against the variable that you wish to measure.

Step 3. Pre-test the measurement items with potential participants using a *cognitive interview*, suggesting that respondents think out loud as they fill in the questionnaire. This step is to examine whether the wordings are appropriate and easy to understand, and if not what wordings would be suitable to change into. The reason we need this step is because the measurements were developed in a different time and perhaps within a different culture/country, and the use of the wordings might have evolved over time.

Step 4. Discuss with your peers and/or with experienced researchers to finalise the wordings you propose to change according to your pre-test. We take Step 3 outcomes into consideration with what *should* be measured at the theoretical level in order to determine the final wordings.

Step 5. Once data are collected, check whether internal consistency of each measurement passes the required threshold before hypothesis testing. Cronbach's alphas are the most commonly used benchmark to determine the level of internal consistency; the rule of thumb threshold for acceptable internal consistency is Cronbach's $\alpha \geq .70$.[35]

Box 12.14

Recommended readings for questionnaire design

Questionnaire design:

- Fife-Schaw, C. (2020). Questionnaire Design. In G. M. Breakwell, D. B. Wright, & J. Barnett (eds), *Research Methods in Psychology* (fifth edn, pp. 343-372). Los Angeles: SAGE.
- Brace, I. (2018). *Questionnaire Design: How to Plan, Structure and Write Survey Material for Effective Market Research* (fourth edn). London: Kogan Page.

The following references collected the frequently used measurements from the existing literature:

- Bearden, W. O., Netemeyer, R. G., & Mobley, M. F. (2011). *Handbook of Marketing Scales: Multi-Item Measures for Marketing and Consumer Behavior Research* (third edn). Thousand Oaks, CA: SAGE.
- Bruner, G. C., II. (2021). *Marketing Scales Handbook: Multi-Item Measures for Consumer Insight Research* (Vol. 11). Fort Worth, TA: GCBII Productions.

Cultural issues in questionnaire design

Quantitative research faces language issues at the stage of questionnaire design – that is, translating the measurements. The measurements you find in the literature were mostly developed in English, and if your participants speak a different language, you will have to translate the measurements. In order to maintain validity after these measurements are translated into a different language, Brislin's back-translation procedure should be followed:[36]

Step 1. Someone who is proficient in both languages (ideally who is bilingual and/or a professional translator) translates the measurements from English into the target language.

Step 2. Someone else who is different from the translator in Step 1 translates the translated measurements back into English.

Step 3. Compare the measurements in its original English version and the back-translated version to see whether the meanings both versions convey are the same. If not, then a problem is identified that should be fixed by discussing with the translators and experienced researchers.

Step 4. Pre-test the translated measurements with potential participants by using cognitive interviews to refine the translation.

Box 12.15

Frequently asked question: Do I have to translate my questionnaire if my target participants are proficient in English?

If you believe your target participants to be proficient in English, you might wonder whether it is necessary to translate your questionnaire. You do have an option of *not* translating your questionnaire, if you included a comprehension test in your questionnaire, so those participants whose English is not good enough can be excluded from data analysis. A form of the English comprehension question asks the participants to select a word from a given list that is best related to a target word[37] - see Figure 12.6 for an example. The target words can be chosen from those that are most relevant to the understanding of the questionnaire.

Which of the following words is best related to "moody"?

Happy

Calm

Angry

Emotional

Guilty

Figure 12.6   An example of a basic English comprehension pre-screener

Experiments

Experiments have quickly gained popularity in consumer psychology in leading academic journals. This is because of their ability to test or prove causal relationships. (Surveys can only conceptualise causal relationships, but are unable to test them as statistics do not have the ability to "test" causal relationships.) There are three main different types of experiments, and each type has different strengths and constraints (see Table 12.3).

Table 12.3   Types of experiments

	Strengths	**Weaknesses**
Field experiments *Experiments done in the field.* *Example: Goldstein, Cialdini,* *and Griskevicius*[38]	• Closest to reality, so external validity[a] is enhanced.	• Access to the field may be difficult. • Not all psychological variables can be (easily) manipulated in the field.
Lab experiments *Experiments done in* *a laboratory. Example:* *Ramanathan and McGill*[39]	• Unwanted environmental disturbances are controlled, so internal validity[a] is enhanced.	• Access to a lab may be difficult. • Labs are not a true reflection of reality.
Scenario-based experiments *Scenarios are designed to* *simulate lab/field conditions* *without the ability to control* *unwanted environmental* *disturbances. This is the* *mainstream experiment in* *consumer psychology.*	• Easy and less expensive to implement, compared with the other two types of experiments.	• Unwanted environmental disturbances cannot be controlled. • Scenarios are not a true reflection of reality.

[a] See p. 328-329 for discussion of internal and external validity.

Experimental intervention: Manipulating independent variables (IVs)

Intervention (also known as treatment, manipulation, or priming) designed to manipulate participants in the direction of an experimental design is the key feature of experiments. The best way to learn to design manipulations is to learn from good-quality papers (usually those published in prestige academic journals) that use experiments.

Manipulation can be done in various ways; for example, to induce happy versus sad emotions, researchers can have their participants listen to a specific type of music (Section 9.3), read a short happy [sad] story (or a passage), or write about their most memorable happy [sad] day. In addition, visual stimuli are often used and sometimes embedded in advertising messages that provide descriptions of experimental manipulation. For example, Wan et al. primed their participants to anthropomorphise the target product (dehumidifier) by showing them pictures of products with anthropomorphic features (i.e. human faces on the products).[40]

Alternatively, manipulation can be done more explicitly by asking the research participants to imagine a specific situation. For example, Choi et al. primed hedonic motives by asking their participants to imagine a shopping situation where the participants wanted to buy a new set of headphones because their current ones, while possessing excellent sound quality, were old-fashioned in terms of style.[41] There are two key principles of a good scenario description:

1. a description that the participants can easily relate to
2. the majority of the wording, phrases, and images in the descriptions of different scenarios are the same except for the key wording, phrases, and images that involve the manipulation of the independent variable(s)

Experimental designs

Post-test only control group designs

Post-test only control group designs are the simplest form of experimental designs. An experiment includes two groups: the control group, which does not receive a treatment, and an experimental group, which receives a treatment. Therefore, the control group provides the baseline results that can determine whether the treatment makes a difference. For example, to examine the effectiveness of an advertisement on brand attitude, the participants in the control group rate their brand attitudes without seeing the advertisement, whereas those in the experimental group rate their brand attitudes after seeing the advertisement. In this case seeing the advertisement is the treatment, and if the brand attitudes in the experimental group are significantly different than those in the control group, a conclusion concerning the effectiveness of the advertisement can be drawn.

Factorial designs

Factorial designs are the most often used experimental designs in consumer psychology. Unlike post-test only control group designs that involve only one independent variable (IV), factorial designs have the ability to control and manipulate more than one IV (usually controlling no more than three to four IVs as the design would get overly complicated). As a result, the key strength of a factorial design lies in its ability to observe the effect of the IVs separately (i.e. the main or simple effects of the IVs) as well as interactively (i.e. the interaction effects between the IVs). The interaction effects are also known as the *moderating effects* – see Figure 12.7.

(a) Graphical representation of a factorial design

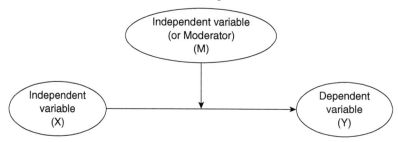

(b) Statistical operation of a factorial design

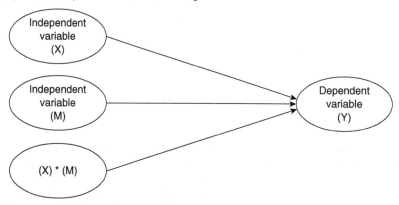

Figure 12.7   Graphical representation and statistical operation of factorial designs – an example

IVs are the factors that cause an impact on a dependent variable (DV), hence, the name, factorial designs. If a factorial experiment has two factors, and each factor has two levels, it is called a 2 x 2 (two by two) factorial design, which forms four experimental conditions. For example, an experiment to study the impact of brand attitude and advertising exposure intensity on purchase intention involves two IVs, brand attitude and advertising exposure intensity, and if there are two levels of brand attitude (positive versus negative) and two levels of ad exposure intensity (high versus low), the 2 x 2 factorial design is stated as 2 (brand attitudes: positive versus negative) x 2 (exposure intensity: high versus low), suggesting four experimental conditions – see Figure 12.8.

You now must understand what is meant by a 2 (body shape: thin v. curvy) x 2 (clothing: conservative v. revealing) x 2 (posture: neutral v. provocative) factorial design to study the perception of the attractiveness of a model in an advertisement.

Brand attitude

	Positive	Negative
Low	*Condition 1* Positive brand attitude with low advertising exposure intensity	*Condition 2* Negative brand attitude with low advertising exposure intensity
High	*Condition 3* Positive brand attitude with high advertising exposure intensity	*Condition 4* Negative brand attitude with high advertising exposure intensity

(Row label on left side: Ad exposure intensity)

Figure 12.8   An illustration of a 2 x 2 factorial design

Between-subjects, within-subjects, and mixed designs

Whether or not each experimental condition is composed of the same or different participants forms different factorial designs: between-subjects (or between-group) design, within-subjects (or repeated-measures) design, and mixed design. Subjects here indicate research participants in experiments. A *between-subjects design* suggests that each participant is assigned to only one of the experimental conditions, and this is the most frequently used design in consumer psychology. A within-subjects design is the opposite of a between-subjects design: a *within-subjects design* indicates that all experimental conditions are tested on the same participants repeatedly. That's why it is also called a repeated-measures design. Because different manipulations are repeated and tested on the same participants, participants may easily get confused or tired from participating in the studies. As a result, a within-subjects design is often avoided if a between-subjects design is possible. Finally, a *mixed design* is a mixed between-subjects and within-subjects design; for example, in a 2 x 2 design, where one IV uses between-subjects design and the other follows a within-subjects design.

—Box 12.16—

Recommended readings for experimental designs

- Morales, A. C., Amir, O., & Lee, L. (2017). Keeping it Real in Experimental Research - Understanding When, Where, and How to Enhance Realism and Measure Consumer Behavior. *Journal of Consumer Research*, 44(2), 465–476.

(Continued)

- Hole, G. (2012). Experimental Design. In G. M. Breakwell, J. A. Smith, & D. B. Wright (eds), *Research Methods in Psychology* (fourth edn, pp. 39-73). Los Angeles: SAGE.
- Chapter 3 Experimental Designs in Field, A., & Hole, G. (2003). *How to Design and Report Experiments*. Los Angeles: SAGE.

Research rigour: How to ensure reliability and validity in an experimental study

The procedure to ensure reliability and validity of the measurements used in an experiment is the same as that used in a survey, so the discussion in this section focuses specifically on the reliability and validity issues in experiments.

Reliability

Reliability of experimental designs concerns replicability, and this is why the majority of academic papers describe their experimental procedures so other researchers are able to replicate them if they so wish. When experiments are reliable, we can be confident in our findings. In order to maximise reliability, an experiment needs to have sufficient sample size and a random assignment of participants to each condition in the experiment. By using many participants, we literally perform many replications of the experimental procedures within the same study, and by randomly assigning participants to different conditions, we are able to balance out systematic differences among the participants, if there are any.

Internal validity

Internal validity refers to the extent to which the observed effect is caused by the hypothesised independent variable. To ensure internal validity, we need to do the following:

1. *Randomly assign participants to different conditions*: Random assignment can balance out systematic differences, and therefore ensures the composition of the participants between conditions is similar. Using similar participants between conditions makes comparisons between conditions meaningful – the observed cause-and-effect is due to the experimental manipulations, not due to the systemic differences in participants between conditions.
2. *Check whether the manipulation works*: Manipulation checks, used to examine whether or not the manipulation of the IV produces statistically significant differences between conditions as intended, are an important stage in an experimental design. If there is no difference after manipulating the IVs, there will be no point in continuing data analysis as the basis of the comparison does not exist.
3. *Rule out other plausible reasons for the effect to have occurred*: We can rule out other plausible causes by (a) conducting an additional experiment to prove that it is not

another plausible cause that produces the effect or by (b) controlling the plausible causes in data analysis. For example, to study the relationship of whether a decreased self-esteem would increase purchase intention of luxury brands, the variable of decreased self-esteem may be manipulated by an insulting service encounter. However, the insulting service encounter may increase the emotion of anger. To rule out anger, one can either conduct an experiment using a manipulation that induces anger but without lowering self-esteem or include anger as a control variable in the data analysis.

External validity

External validity refers to the extent to which the findings can be generalised to other individuals and to other situations. To test external validity, the experimental design could extend the participants, for example, from student participants to non-student participants, and extend the manipulation of conditions, for example, from one product category to other product categories. Ultimately, external validity concerns the extent to which the findings have real-world relevance, and the findings can be validated from lab experiments to field experiments or other types of studies.[42]

Box 12.17

Recommended readings for ensuring research rigour in experiments

- Meyvis, T., & van Osselaer, S. M. J. (2018). Increasing the Power of Your Study by Increasing the Effect Size. *Journal of Consumer Research*, 44(5), 1157-1173.
- Kardes, F. R., & Herr, P. M. (2019). Experimental Research Methods in Consumer Psychology. In F. R. Kardes, P. M. Herr, & N. Schwarz (eds), *Handbook of Research Methods in Consumer Psychology* (pp. 3-16). New York: Routledge.
- Kenny, D. A. (2019). Enhancing Validity in Psychological Research. *American Psychologist*, 74(9), 1018-1028.
- Lin, H., Werner, K. M., & Inzlicht, M. (2020). Promises and Perils of Experimentation: The Mutual-Internal-Validity Problem. *Perspectives on Psychological Science*, 16(4), 854-863.

Sampling

Non-probability sampling versus probability sampling

Broadly speaking, there are two main sampling approaches: probability and non-probability sampling. Probability sampling is considered a superior sampling approach, as via probability sampling, the selected samples are representative of the population. However, probability sampling is expensive to achieve (see Boxes 12.18 and 12.19). As a result, most social science research uses non-probability sampling, and the most common form of non-probability sampling is convenience sampling. In convenience sampling respondents are selected because of their convenience of access; for example, the use of student samples, mall-intercept interviews, and "people on the street" interviews are all classified as convenience sampling.

Box 12.18

Sampling terminology

(Target) population: the collection of elements that a researcher wishes to study. For example, to study women above the age of 18 in the UK, the target population is all women above the age of 18 in the UK or to study women above the age of 18 with minority ethnicity background in the US the target population is all women above the age of 18 with minority ethnicity background in the US.

Sampling frame: a representation of the elements that a researcher is able to reach from the population. For example, to study adult female consumers in the UK, a researcher may be able to access those consumers who are on a consumer survey panel. These consumers from the consumer survey panel constitute the sampling frame. The size of a sampling frame is usually smaller than a target population as there are some members of the target population who are difficult, if not impossible, to reach. The probability, in a probability sampling technique, refers to the equal probability of an individual being selected from the sampling frame, rather than from the population.

Box 12.19

Commonly made mistake: Convenience sampling = random sampling

Students often mistake convenience sampling for random sampling. Convenience sampling is *not* random sampling. The word, "random", has a statistical connotation, but convenience does not. Random sampling indicates that the probability of each participant being selected from the sampling frame is equal. In order to ensure equal probability of sample selection, it is necessary to have a complete list of the names in the sampling frame. For example, selecting participants from a phone book by generating random numbers in order to determine which participants to select is random sampling. Random sampling is difficult and expensive to achieve because one needs to first construct the whole list of potential participants in a sampling frame, and then conduct a random sampling technique to obtain a representative sample.

Sample size

There are many statistical ways to determine a sample size, which is usually based on the precision level you wish to achieve and the maximum error you can tolerate, and interested readers should refer to research method books for more details. However, in addition to the precision level and the allowable error, there are many other factors that influence the decision of a sample size, such as the number of variables included in an analysis, the analysis methods, and the number of groups to be compared. More importantly, a sample size decision is also dependent on the resources one has. As a result, the decision is usually based on judgement. For a student dissertation project, a sample size of around 200 observations is often sufficient.

Online sampling via crowdsourcing websites

Sampling via crowdsourcing websites has become popular in recent years. This trend is driven by its ability to reach non-student adult samples cheaply (compared with the cost of the traditional consumer panels) and quickly, thereby increasing external validity of those studies that largely and traditionally relied on university student samples. The most popular crowdsourcing platform is Amazon's Mechanic Turk (or MTurk for short). Despite its popularity, it comes with some weaknesses, including misrepresented, experienced, and inattentive participants, we need to overcome (see Box 12.20).

Box 12.20

Recommended readings for how to deal with potential risks in crowdsourced sampling

The below papers discuss threats and solutions for using MTurk, which is the most popular (and also most extensively researched) crowdsourcing site for data collection. Although not all of them apply to every crowdsourcing platform (for example, developing an ongoing participant pool within MTurk using their demographic backgrounds[43] is irrelevant to Prolific, which pushes a study only to those who fit the required demographic backgrounds by default[44]), they provide insightful recommendations worth considering when using a crowdsourcing platform for data collection.

- Hauser, D., Paolacci, G., & Chandler, J. (2019). Common Concerns with MTurk as a Participant Pool: Evidence and Solutions. In F. R. Kardes, P. M. Herr, & N. Schwarz (eds), *Handbook in Research Methods in Consumer Psychology* (pp. 319–337). New York: Routledge.
- Kees, J., Berry, C., Burton, S., & Sheehan, K. (2017). An Analysis of Data Quality: Professional Panels, Student Subject Pools, and Amazon's Mechanical Turk. *Journal of Advertising*, *46*(1), 141–155. (In the appendix of this paper, there is a list of recommended

(Continued)

best practices for online data collection. Although the recommendations focus more on advertising experimental research, the majority of the guidance can also apply to consumer psychology.)

- Aguinis, H., Villamor, I., & Ramani, R. S. (2021). MTurk Research: Review and Recommendations. *Journal of Management, 47*(4), 823–837. (This paper provides ten recommendations for using MTurk. These recommendations are proposed for organisation psychology researchers, but most of them can be applied to consumer psychology.)

Data analysis

Quantitative data analysis largely follows a technical process, which is better suited to dedicated books (Box 12.21). The broad guidelines of the three main steps of data analysis: data cleaning, preliminary analysis, and hypothesis testing can be found in Tables 12.4 and 12.5. You can use these tables to identify the analysis methods you may use, and refer to Box 12.21 to find suitable books to guide you through the data analysis procedure.

─Box 12.21─

Recommended readings for quantitative data analysis

Key data analysis methods:

- Hair, J. F., Jr., Babin, B. J., Black, W., & Anderson, R. (2018). *Multivariate Data Analysis* (eighth edn). Andover: Cengage.
- Hayes, A. F. (2018). *Introduction to Mediation, Moderation, and Conditional Process Analysis: A Regression-Based Approach* (second edn). New York: Guilford Press.

A practical guide on using SPSS:

- Pallant, J. (2020). *SPSS Survival Manual: A Step by Step Guide to Data Analysis Using IBM SPSS* (seventh edn). London: Open University Press.

A practical guide on using AMOS:

- Byrne, B. M. (2016). *Structural Equation Modeling with AMOS: Basic Concepts, Applications, and Programming* (third edn). New York: Routledge.

A practical guide on using SmartPLS:

- Hair, J. F., Jr., Hult, T. M., Ringle, C. M., & Sarstedt, M. (2022). *A Primer on Partial Least Squares Structural Equation Modeling* (third edn). Los Angeles: SAGE.

Table 12.4   Guidelines in data analysis steps

Key steps in data analysis	What to examine	Guidelines
1. Data cleaning	• Remove those participants that failed the screening filters, such as attention checks and comprehension checks.	
	• Detect outliers	Outliers are *not* removed by default unless removing them can be justified. Therefore, the removal of outliers should be determined case by case.
	• Missing data analysis	• Remove an observation that contains many missing data (for example, a participant only fills in one third of the questionnaire). • Replace the missing values using missing data analysis for observations that omit a few questions.
2. Preliminary analysis	• Reliability analysis	• Check Cronbach's alpha for each scale to see whether it is above .70 threshold. • If not, check whether a removal of any of the items in the scale would increase Cronbach's alpha. • If Cronbach's alpha is satisfactory, compose a summated scale by averaging the score of the measurement items for each scale.

(Continued)

Table 12.4   (Continued)

Key steps in data analysis	What to examine	Guidelines
	• Manipulation checks	This is applicable only for experimental designs.
	• Descriptive statistics	This includes reporting means, standard deviations, and correlation analysis of the main variables.
	• Tests of assumptions underlying hypothesis testing methods	
3. Hypothesis testing	• Tests of differences • Tests of association	See Table 12.5.

Table 12.5   Main statistical tests for hypotheses

Independent Variable (IV)		Dependent Variable (DV)		Analysis Method	Example and/or Explanation
No. of IV	Type of IV	No. of DV	Type of DV		
Tests of difference: to compare means of DV between two IV groups					
1	Categorical	1	Continuous	Dependent (or paired) sample t-test[a]	To test whether there is a difference between respondents' preferences for Ad A and Ad B by having the respondents evaluate both Ad A and Ad B.
1	Categorical	1	Continuous	Independent sample t-test[a]	Respondents prefer Ad A to Ad B, when respondents are allocated into two separate groups evaluating only Ad A or Ad B.
Tests of differences: to compare means of DV between more than two IV groups					
1	Categorical	1	Continuous	(One-way) ANOVA	Brand attitudes towards luxury brands change according to different life stages (teenage, young adults, mature adults, middle age, and empty nester)

Independent Variable (IV)		Dependent Variable (DV)		Analysis Method	Example and/or Explanation
No. of IV	Type of IV	No. of DV	Type of DV		
2	Categorical	1	Continuous	Two-way ANOVA[b]	Life stages influence people's brand attitudes towards luxury brands, and this relationship is moderated by income levels. See Figure 12.7 for graphical representation.
Tests of association					
1 or more	Continuous	1	Continuous	Simple (if there is one IV) or multiple (if there are multiple IVs) regression[c]	The greater the IV_1, IV_2, IV_3 . . ., the greater (or lower) the DV.
2	Continuous	1	Continuous	Mediation analysis[c]	
> 2	Continuous	> 2	Continuous	Path analysis[d]	Path analysis is able to simultaneously handle multiple IV, DV, and mediators.

[a] If the two groups are related, use dependent sample t-tests. If the two groups are unrelated, use independent sample t-tests.

[b] This is the main analysis method for factorial designs. If it is between-subject design, use two-way ANOVA. If it is within-subject design, use repeated measures for analysis.

[c] These analyses can all be run in SPSS.

[d] Path analysis is run with different software packages. If the sample size is small, the analysis is PLS (partial least square) and can be run with SmartPLS, and if the sample size is sufficiently large, the analysis is SEM (structural equation modelling) and can be run with AMOS.

Reporting

Reporting accurately can demonstrate increased credibility of your research project. In addition to the rationale for your choice of method and the description of your study design, *what* you should report includes the rigorous procedure you have followed in order to arrive at your conclusions. That is, in the *methodology* chapter, you should report the procedures you have gone through to ensure the reliability and validity of your research design. For example:

Table 12.6 What key statistics figures need to be reported?

Type of Analysis	Key Statistics Figures to be Reported[a]	Examples of Reporting[b]
t-test	*Statistical figures:* t (df[*])values and p-values [*] df = degree of freedom *Descriptive figures:* means (M) and standard deviations (SD) of the focal variables or groups for comparison	H1 stated that consumers prefer Ad A to Ad B was tested by an independent t-test, which revealed that respondents preferred Advertisement A (M = 5.49; SD = 1.10) to Advertisement B (M = 4.09; SD = 1.09, t(199) = 14.32, $p < .001$).[c] Thus, H1 is supported.
ANOVA	*Statistic figures:* F (df1, df2[**]) values and p-values [**] df1 = degree of freedom of IV, df2 = degree of freedom in error term *Descriptive figures:* means (M) of the variables of different groups	H2 suggests that consumers' willingness to pay is higher when the advertisement appeal (reason versus feeling) fits with product type (utilitarian versus hedonic product) than when it does not fit. A two-way ANOVA was conducted to compare willingness to pay. Results indicated that consumers' willingness to pay was significantly greater when the advertisement appealed to feeling (vs reason), F(1,118) = 11.39, $p \le .001$, $M_{reasoning\ appeal}$ = \$3.60, $M_{feeling\ appeal}$ = \$4.86, but consumers' willingness to pay did not differ significantly between product types, F(1,118) = 2.45, $p > .05$, $M_{utilitarian\ product}$ = \$4.21, $M_{hedonic\ product}$ = \$4.38).[d] The two-way ANOVA also revealed a significant interaction effect; that is, consumers' willingness to pay was higher when the advertisement appeal fitted with product type, compared when it did not fit with product type, F(1,118) = 9.99, $p \le .01$ (see Figure X[e]). As a result, H2 was supported.
Regression	*Model fit indices:* R², F (df1, df2[***]) values and p-values [***] df1 = degree of freedom in regression term, df2 = degree of freedom in residual term *Statistical figures:* β values, t values, and p-values	H3 states that consumers' brand attitudes determine their purchase intentions of that brand. A simple regression analysis was carried out to test H3, and the results indicated that brand attitude was able to explain 22%[f] of the variance of the respondents' purchase intentions, R² = .22, F(1, 198) = 56.06, $p \le .001$, and that an increase in brand attitude increased .36 purchase intentions, β = .36, t = 7.49, $p \le .001$. Therefore, H3 is supported.
Path analysis	*Model fit indices:* χ^2, df, p; SRMR; RMSEA; TLI; and CFI *Statistical figures:* Regression coefficients and their associated t values	Since the results include many paths, for readability the results are usually presented in a table or diagram (see Figures 12.9 and 12.10)

[a]All the figures can be found from the analysis output generated by the software package, such as SPSS for t-test, ANOVA, and regression, and AMOS for path analysis.

[b]All figures in the examples are fictitious and they are used only to show you how findings are reported.

[c]You can choose to report p-values either as the specific values or as $p > .05$, $p \le .05$, $p \le .01$, or $p \le .001$, but your reporting format should be consistent unless you have a good reason not to. For example, you mainly use the latter format, but when, for example, $p = .06$ is reported, it is because you wish to say it is marginally significant.

[d]A two-way ANOVA reveals both main and interaction effects. Although the interaction effects are usually more interesting than the main effects (and would be included in the hypothesis), it is equally important to report the main effects.

[e]A diagram generated by SPSS (as a bar or line chart) to show the mean values would usually be more accessible to readers.

- if you adopted existing scales or experimental manipulations with some changes, explain what changes you made and why and how these changes are made
- if you translated and back-translated the scales, report how the translation was done, and who were engaged in the translation process

In the *data analysis* chapter, you should report the procedures you have gone through to ensure the appropriateness of your data analysis. These procedures include your data cleaning procedures and the preliminary analyses you conducted prior to your hypothesis testing. In addition, you should explain how you would interpret the results. This detailed information is largely absent from academic papers, but important in a dissertation project to show that you know what you are doing.

The best format of reporting statistical findings is to follow how the academic papers report their results. See Table 12.6 for examples. Treat your readers as statistic experts, and do not worry about the possibility that they might not understand.

The best format of presenting the results in a table or a diagram is similar to how they are presented in academic papers as this is what your markers are used to. Directly copying and pasting tables or diagrams from software that are different from the format your markers are used to should be avoided as it decreases professionalism and readability. Finally, do not overuse tables or diagrams, unless they can increase readability.

	Cool	Uncool
Factor loadings (lambdas)	n = 315	n = 315
Structural Coefficients (Betas)		
Useful/exceptional → Desirability	.75	.86
Energetic → Desirability	.75	.81
Aesthetics → Desirability	.82	.83
Originality → Positive autonomy	.91	.96
Authenticity → Positive autonomy	.87	.83
Desirability → Higher-order cool	I	.98
Positive autonomy → Higher-order cool	.89	.9
Rebelliousness → Higher-order cool	.45	.61
High status → Higher-order cool	.55	.75
Popularity → Higher-order cool	.74	.78
Subculture → Higher-order cool	.53	.61
Iconic → Higher-order cool	.59	.72
Model Fit Statistics	Global	
Chi-square (d.f.)	2,565.8 (I,164)	
NNFI	.98	
CFI	.98	
RMSEA	.064	
SRMR	.072	

Figure 12.9 Results of path analysis demonstrated in a table format – an example

Source: Warren et al.[45]

Reprinted from *Journal of Marketing*, 83(5), Warren et al., Brand Coolness, 36–56, Copyright (2019), with permission from SAGE.

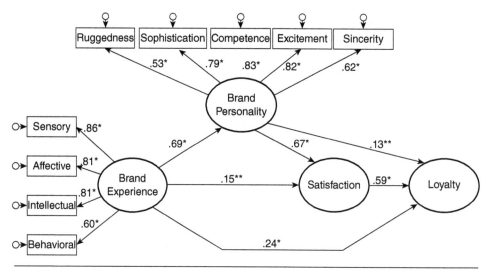

*p < .01.

**p < .05.

Notes: All coefficient values are standardized and appear near the associated path.

Figure 12.10   Results of path analysis demonstrated in a diagram – an example

Source: Brakus et al.[46]

Reprinted from *Journal of Marketing*, 73(3), Brakus et al., Brand Experience: What Is It? How Is It Measured? Does It Affect Loyalty? 52–68, Copyright (2009), with permission from SAGE.

12.5 ETHICAL ISSUES IN RESEARCH

Most universities have developed mature codes of ethics and conduct and require their staff and students to comply with them before contacting potential research participants. In addition to assessing potential risks to the researchers themselves during the research process, the researchers need to assess potential risks to research participants. The researchers have a duty of care to ensure their participants are not harmed by participating in their studies. In the invitation letter (or verbal disclosure) to participants, researchers need to obtain participants' informed consent, which covers your research topic and ensures voluntary participation, confidentiality, and their right to withdraw. Voluntary participation and the right to withdraw are straightforward for participants to activate, but confidentiality with regards to identification of the participants and maintenance of anonymity is more difficult in qualitative studies. It can still be done, for example by using pseudonyms in reporting should quotations from participants be used. If confidentiality cannot be maintained, it is the researchers' responsibility to obtain their participants' consent before the data can be used.

In addition, some forms of data collection would increase risks to research participants, and as a researcher you will need to follow steps to ensure that your participants are not harmed physically or psychologically. For example, if your participants are subjected to potentially harmful manipulations, such as manipulation to temporarily decrease self-esteem or induce negative emotions, you should include additional measures: for example, (1) to include additional manipulation in the end of the study to restore their self-esteem or to induce positive emotions, and (2) to include a debriefing letter to inform the participants of the manipulation that they have been subjected to, the potential risks they might encounter, and information on how to seek help if help is needed.

Finally, if your research involves asking sensitive questions (e.g. sexual questions in a study of consumption of pornography) or vulnerable participants (who are underaged, disabled, or with mental illness), in a way to protect your participants your university would usually require you go through a more comprehensive approval process before you can conduct your study. Follow your university's guideline to seek approval at all times to protect yourself and your participants.

12.6 SUMMARY

1. There is no superior method, as each method has its strengths and weaknesses (Table 12.7), and there is no easier method, as each method is difficult at one stage or another. Choosing the most suitable methods depends on personal strengths, plans for personal development, and research topics.
2. Research rigour can be maintained by ensuring reliability and validity at the stages of research design, data collection, and data analysis (Table 12.7).
3. Reporting should demonstrate the rationale of the choice of the method and the procedure that ensures reliability and validity. The report format should follow the usual format used by academic papers.
4. To protect your participants, you should follow an appropriate ethical procedure to obtain informed consent by providing necessary information through briefing and debriefing your participants.

Table 12.7 Key methods – a summary of strengths, weaknesses, sample size, reliability, and validity

Key Methods	Strengths	Weaknesses	Sample Size	Reliability[b]	Validity[b]
Qualitative methods	General strengths for qualitative methods: • Ability to understand issues in depth • Best at addressing the *how* and *why* research questions	General weaknesses for qualitative methods: • Difficulty in maintaining balance between subjectivity and research rigour		• Similar findings can be found in different data collected by another researchers • Similar findings can be found in the same data analysed by different researchers	• Different data sources are triangulated • Research findings are verified with the participants and peers/experts
In-depth interviews	• Ability to control the line of questioning • Ability to understand feelings, memories, and interpretations that cannot be directly observed	• Possibility of getting socially desirable or unconsciously rationalised responses • Difficulty of getting into the heads of those participants who are not eloquent or perceptive	• About 10 hours' worth of data[a]		
Focus groups	• Ability to observe group dynamics • Ability to draw out creative or inspirational responses through group dynamics (brainstorming)	• Possibility of domination by strong participants	• About 10 hours' worth of data[a]		
Netnography	• Without the constraint of space and time as it is the online footage that is being observed • Ability to share experience with the participants first-hand • Ability to observe aspects that might escape from the participants' notice	• Messy data that can be difficult or time-consuming to analyse	• A complete cycle of the activity under observation (usually 1 year of data)[a]		

[a] The sample size is with a focus on depth of data, rather than breadth of data, and the appropriate sample size depends on data saturation. That is, data collection stops when reaching data saturation, suggesting no more findings can be retrieved from new data collection.

[b] The measures for reliability and validity are applicable to all qualitative methods.

Summary continued

Key Methods	Strengths	Weaknesses	Sample Size	Reliability[b]	Validity[b]
Quantitative methods	General strengths for quantitative methods: • Ability to maintain objectivity in data analysis • Ability to generalise findings • Ability to test and establish relationships between variables under study	General weaknesses for quantitative methods: • Requirement of a relatively large sample size • Lack of flexibility	• Determined based on the following factors: the precision of prediction, the allowance for error, the number of variables, the number of groups, the analysis methods		
Surveys	• Simplicity in implementation and execution		• Around 200 observations	• Adopt measurements from the existing literature • Cronbach's alphas > .70	• Adopt measurements from the existing literature • Pre-test measurements with participants
Experiments	• Ability to study causal relationships • Ability to control unwanted environmental disturbances	• Experimental designs may not always sufficiently reflect reality	• Around 50 observations per group	• Adopt measurements and experimental manipulation from the existing literature • Randomly assign participants to different experimental conditions	

DISCUSSION QUESTIONS

1. What are the key qualitative and quantitative research methods? What are their strengths and weaknesses?
2. Discuss the differences and similarities of depth interviews and focus group interviews.
3. Discuss the differences and similarities of surveys and experiments.
4. Discuss how research rigour can be enhanced for qualitative and quantitative research.

FURTHER READING

*   Breakwell, G. M., Smith, J. A., & Wright, D. B. (eds). (2012). *Research Methods in Psychology* (fourth edn). Thousand Oaks, CA: SAGE.
*   Kardes, F. R., Herr, P. M., & Schwarz, N. (eds). (2019). *Handbook of Research Methods in Consumer Psychology*. New York: Routledge.

NOTES

1. Sayre, S. (2001). *Qualitative Methods for Marketplace Research*. Thousand Oaks, CA: Sage.
2. Russell, C. A., & Levy, S. J. (2012). The Temporal and Focal Dynamics of Volitional Reconsumption: A Phenomenological Investigation of Repeated Hedonic Experiences. *Journal of Consumer Research, 39*(2), 341-359.
3. McAlexander, J. H., Schouten, J. W., & Koenig, H. F. (2002). Building Brand Community. *Journal of Marketing, 66*(1), 38-54.
4. Hirschman, E. C., & Thompson, C. J. (1997). Why Media Matter: Toward a Richer Understanding of Consumers' Relationships with Advertising and Mass Media. *Journal of Advertising, 26*(1), 43-60.
5. Fournier, S. (1998). Consumer and Their Brands: Developing Relationship Theory in Consumer Research. *Journal of Consumer Research, 24*(March), 343-373.
6. Goulding, C. (2005). Grounded Theory, Ethnography and Phenomenology: A Comparative Analysis of Three Qualitative Strategies for Marketing Research. *European Journal of Marketing, 39*(3/4), 294-308.
7. Schau, H. J., & Gilly, M. C. (2003). We Are What We Post? Self-Presentation in Personal Web Space. *Journal of Consumer Research, 30*(3), 385-404.
8. Carson, D., Gilmore, A., Perry, C., & Gronhaug, K. (2001). *Qualitative Marketing Research*. London: Sage.
9. Malhotra, N. K. (2020). *Marketing Research: An Applied Orientation* (seventh edn). Harlow: Pearson.
10. Morgan, D. L. (1997). *Focus Groups as Qualitative Research* (second edn). Thousand Oaks, CA: Sage.

11. Malhotra, *Marketing Research*.
12. Ibid.
13. Carson et al., *Qualitative Marketing Research*.
14. Sayre, *Qualitative Methods for Marketplace Research*.
15. Holstein, J. A., & Gubrium, J. F. (2004). The Active Interview. In D. Silverman (ed.), *Qualitative Research: Theory, Method and Practice* (second edn, pp. 140–161). London: Sage Publications.
16. Carson et al., *Qualitative Marketing Research*.
17. Armstrong, J. S. (1985). *Long-Range Forecasting: From Crystal Ball to Computer*. New York: Wiley.
18. Carson et al., *Qualitative Marketing Research*.
19. Coulter, R. A., Zaltman, G., & Coulter, K. S. (2001). Interpreting Consumer Perceptions of Advertising: An Application of the Zaltman Metaphor Elicitation Technique. *Journal of Advertising*, *30*(4), 1–21.
20. Sugai, P. (2005). Mapping the Mind of the Mobile Consumer across Borders: An Application of the Zaltman Metaphor Elicitation Technique. *International Marketing Review*, *22*(6), 641–657.
21. Jupp, V. (2006). *The Sage Dictionary of Social and Cultural Research Methods*. London: Sage.
22. Kozinets, R. V. (2002). The Field behind the Screen: Using Netnography for Marketing Research in Online Communities. *Journal of Marketing Research*, *39*(1), 61–72; Shao, G. (2009). Understanding the Appeal of User-Generated Media: A Uses and Gratification Perspective. *Internet Research*, *19*(1), 7–25.
23. Kozinets, R. V. (2006). Click to Connect: Netnography and Tribal Advertising. *Journal of Advertising Research*, *46*(September), 279–288.
24. Glesne, C. (2011). *Becoming Qualitative Researchers: An Introduction* (fourth edn). Boston, MA: Pearson.
25. Page 196, Creswell, J. W. (2003). *Research Design: Qualitative, Quantitative, and Mixed Methods Approaches* (second edn). Thousand Oaks, CA: Sage.
26. Schau, H. J., Muñiz, A. M. J., & Arnould, E. J. (2009). How Brand Community Practices Create Value. *Journal of Marketing*, *73*(5), 30-51.
27. Thompson, C. J., Rindfleisch, A., & Arsel, Z. (2006). Emotional Branding and the Strategic Value of the Doppelgänger Brand Image. *Journal of Marketing*, *70*(1), 50-64.
28. Chaudhuri, A., & Holbrook, M. B. (2001). The Chain of Effects from Brand Trust and Brand Affect to Brand Performance: The Role of Brand Loyalty. *Journal of Marketing*, *65*(April), 81–93.
29. Batra, R., & Stayman, D. M. (1990). The Role of Mood in Advertising Effectiveness. *Journal of Consumer Research*, *17*(September), 203–214.
30. Preston, C. C., & Colman, A. M. (2000). Optimal Number of Response Categories in Rating Scales: Reliability, Validity, Discriminating Power, and Respondent Preferences. *Acta Psychologica*, *104*(1), 1–15; Weijters, B., Cabooter, E., & Schillewaert, N. (2010). The Effect of Rating Scale Format on Response Styles: The Number of Response Categories and Response

Category Labels. *International Journal of Research in Marketing, 27*(3), 236–247; Cox, E. P., III. (1980). The Optimal Number of Response Alternatives for a Scale: A Review. *Journal of Marketing Research, 17*(4), 407–422.

31. Richins, M. L., & Dawson, S. (1992). A Consumer Values Orientation for Materialism and Its Measurement: Scale Development and Validation. *Journal of Consumer Research, 19*(3), 303–316.

32. Thomson, M., MacInnis, D., & Park, C. W. (2005). The Ties That Bind: Measuring the Strength of Consumers' Emotional Attachments to Brands. *Journal of Consumer Psychology, 15*(1), 77–91.

33. Grégoire, Y., Tripp, T. M., & Legoux, R. (2009). When Customer Love Turns into Lasting Hate: The Effects of Relationship Strength and Time on Customer Revenge and Avoidance. *Journal of Marketing, 73*(November), 18–32.

34. Chaudhuri & Holbrook, The Chain of Effects from Brand Trust and Brand Affect to Brand Performance.

35. Streiner, D. L. (2003). Starting at the Beginning: An Introduction to Coefficient Alpha and Internal Consistency. *Journal of Personality Assessment, 80*(1), 99–103; Nunnally, J. C., & Bernstein, I. H. (1994). *Psychometric Theory*. New York: McGraw-Hill.

36. Brislin, R. W. (1970). Back-Translation for Cross-Cultural Research. *Journal of Cross-Cultural Psychology, 1*, 185–216.

37. Chandler, J., Rosenzweig, C., Moss, A. J., Robinson, J., & Litman, L. (2019). Online Panels in Social Science Research: Expanding Sampling Methods beyond Mechanical Turk. *Behavior Research Methods, 51*(5), 2022–2038.

38. Goldstein, N. J., Cialdini, R. B., & Griskevicius, V. (2008). A Room with a Viewpoint: Using Social Norms to Motivate Environmental Conservation in Hotels. *Journal of Consumer Research, 35*(3), 472-482.

39. Ramanathan, S., & McGill, A. L. (2007). Consuming with Others: Social Influences on Moment-to-Moment and Retrospective Evaluations of an Experience. *Journal of Consumer Research, 34*(4), 506-524.

40. Wan, E. W., Chen, R. P., & Jin, L. (2017). Judging a Book by Its Cover? The Effect of Anthropomorphism on Product Attribute Processing and Consumer Preference. *Journal of Consumer Research, 43*(6), 1008–1030.

41. Choi, J., Madhavaram, S. R., & Park, H. Y. (2020). The Role of Hedonic and Utilitarian Motives on the Effectiveness of Partitioned Pricing. *Journal of Retailing, 96*(2), 251–265.

42. Winer, R. S. (1999). Experimentation in the 21st Century: The Importance of External Validity. *Journal of the Academy of Marketing Science, 27*(3), 349–358.

43. Wessling, K. S., Huber, J., & Netzer, O. (2017). MTurk Character Misrepresentation: Assessment and Solutions. *Journal of Consumer Research, 44*(1), 211–230.

44. Palan, S., & Schitter, C. (2018). Prolific.ac – A Subject Pool for Online Experiments. *Journal of Behavioral and Experimental Finance, 17*, 22–27.

45. Warren, C., Batra, R., Loureiro, S. M. C., & Bagozzi, R. P. (2019). Brand Coolness. *Journal of Marketing, 83*(5), 36–56.

46. Brakus, J. J., Schmitt, B. H., & Zarantonello, L. (2009). Brand Experience: What Is It? How Is It Measured? Does It Affect Loyalty? *Journal of Marketing, 73*(3), 52–68.

Index

Note: tables and figures are indicated by page numbers in bold print. The letter 'b' after a page number stands for *bibliographical* information in a Further Reading or a Recommended Readings section.

Aaker, J.L. 14, 185, 186
Aaker, J.L. et al 188
active listening 302–7
activity trackers 163–4
actualising tendency (self-actualisation) 6, 157
addiction *see* compulsivity (addiction)
ADHD (attention deficit hyperactivity disorder) 277
advertising:
  aspirational advertising 276
  attention capture 29–30
  and children 100, 101
  and emotional-congruence effect 130
  encouraging environmental behaviour 155
  as entertainment 100, 101
  and fear appeal messages **134**–5
  female models 251
  and happiness 130, 131
  in-game advertisements 101
  Internet:
    banners on webpages 30
    thin-slice information 80
  loss- and gain-frames 155
  and materialistic messages 275
  and processing fluency 155
  recall: primacy and recency effects 32
  repetition 36
  sexual content 253
  and smoking 278–3
  subliminal 86–7
  television 100
  violent content 249
affect and control theory 58, 61, 67–8
affect (feelings) 127, **128**
  see also emotions
affiliation drives 254–60

reciprocal altruism 254
status 254–60
ageing consumers 107–112, 113
  categories and statistics 107, 108
  classification **112**, 113
  ethical issues **111**
  implicit processing 110–111
  information search 110
  physiological changes 108–110, 113
    and marketing implications **109–110**
  research 108
Aguinis, H. et al 328
Ajzen, I.: theory of planned behaviour 11–12
Alba, J.W. et al 43b
Alba, J.W. and Hutchinson, J.W. 43b
alcohol consumption/addiction 229, 278, 283
alignable brand differentiation 57
all-you-can-eat buffets 248
American Legacy Foundation 278
American Psychological Association (APA) 9, 18
Anderson, E. and Simester, D. 64
anger 135–7, 140
  contagious anger 136–7
  coping strategies 136
  incidental anger 137
  and self-control 137
  and service failure 136
Anheuser-Busch Companies 67
Annual Review of Psychology 9
anthropomorphic brands/products 276
Apple 66
Aristotle 1
Association for Consumer Research (ACR) 9, 18
attention:
  banners on webpages 30
  Broadbent's theory 29

capture and transfer **31**
cocktail party phenomenon 29
extrinsic and intrinsic factors 29–30
attitude theories:
   attitude-behaviour linkage 11
   classic attitude theories 11–**12**
   contemporary attitude theories 13
Avis 66

"backyard" research 307
Bagozzi, R.P. et al 141b
Baker, J. 214
Bargh, J.A. 78
Bargh, J.A. and Piertromonaco, P. 84–5
Bartlett, Sir Frederic 7
Baumeister, R.F. et al 161
Bearden, W.O. et al 318b
Beck's beer 66
behaviourism 3, 4–6
   key concepts **5–6**
Belk, R.W. 182, 199b, 214, 216
belonging, need for 254
Benton, T. and Craib, I. 297b
Berlyne, D.E. 36
Bettman 11
bio-psychology 4
Bitner, M.J. (model of servicescape) **216**–19, 231
Black Friday 281
Boom, B.H. and Bitner, M.J. 216
Brace, I. 318b
brands:
   brand exposure 85
   brand-as-person 13–14, 180, 182, 184–90, 197
      anthropomorphic brands 276
   categories 56–7
   communities 14, 158
   differentiation 57
   and digital technology 189
   endorsements 58–60
   evaluation 80–81, 182, 187, 188
      and negative emotions 135
   extensions 56
   familiarity with 39
      and ageing consumers 111
      and children 100, 102, 105–6
   and group membership 193
   knowledge of 194
   luxury brands 194
   names of 82–4
   positioning 33, 66
      and sound symbolism 83
   recognition 81–2
      brand halo effect 81–2
      by children 100, 102

misleading information 82
relationships with 14, 180, 186–91, 197
self-brand congruence 180, 182
self-brand connection 180, 182–4
   antecedents and consequences **183**
   and brand failure 184
and self-identity 181–91
similarity/typicality 56–7
sincere v. exciting brands 188
social ties with 193
storytelling about brands 66–7
transgressions 190
and violent advertising 249
Braun, K.A. 43b
Breakwell, G.M, et al 342b
Broadbent, D.E. 29, 41
Bruner, G.C., II. 318b
Buijzen, M. et al 114b
Byrne, B.M. 328b

Carlston, D. 79
Carson, D. et al 296b, 304b, 307b, 309b
case studies 2
category representations 54
category-based inferences 54–7, 67
   brand categories 56–7
   category representations 54
   cultural/social categories 55
   product categories 55
   similarity-based inferences 55
causal inferences 57–61, 67
   affect and control theory 58, 61, 67–8
   correspondent inference theory 58, 67
   customer satisfaction 61
   endorsements 58–60
   reviews 60–61
CES (consumption emotion set) 126–7
Chaiken, S. 13
Charles, S.T. and Casrstensen, L.L. 114b
children 96–107
   and advertising:
      cognitive defence 101, 113
      developing understanding 104
      as entertainment 100, 101
      vulnerability/susceptibility to 101
   bargaining strategies 105
   brand preferences 100, 105–6
   cognitive development 96–7
      stages **97–8**
   decision-making 104
   group identity 105–6
   knowledge of brands 102
   negotiation skills 102, 105
   peer influence/pressure 102, 106

perception of prices and value 103–**4**
persuasion strategies 105
social development **97–8**
stages of consumer socialisation 98–107,
  99, **106–7**
  perceptual stage: 3-7 years 99–100, 112
  analytic stage: 7-11 years 100–102, 112–13
  reflective stage: 11-16 years 103–6, 113
  understanding of symbolic meanings 102
  use of symbolic meanings 105
  see also ageing consumers
choice overload 33
chunking (recoding) 32
classic consumer decision making 11, **12**
clinical psychology 4
Coca-Cola 84, 86, 158
coding analysis 308
cognition:
  and lighting 225
  and music 218
cognitivism 3, 7–8
  information processing **7**
Cohen, J.B. and Basu, K. 68b
Cohen, J.B. and Bernard, H.R. 259b
collectible products 158–9
compensatory consumption 191, 277–8, 282
  adaptive 277, 278
  distraction - avoidance behaviour 277, 278
  and materialism 275
  and self-threat 191, 277
  symbolic self-completion 277, 278
  types **278**
compulsivity (addiction) 277–2
  and brain 277
  compulsive buying 279–2, 283–4
    and bargain opportunities 281
    characteristics **280**
    demographics 281
    and impulsive buying 279–**0**
    and panic buying 281–6
    triggers 281
  and impulsivity 277, 283
  smoking 277, 278, 278–3
  social pressures 277
  types: substances, behaviour 277–**78**
conditioning:
  classical conditioning **5**, 133–4
  operant conditioning **6**
  and thinking 7
confidentiality 334–5
consciousness 78, 86, 87
  and self-identity 181
consumer development 96–113
  ageing consumers 107–112, 113

children 96–107
consumer familiarity 39
consumer inferences and evaluation 53–68
  category-based 54–7
  causal inferences 57–61
  framing effect 61–7
consumer judgement 81
consumer knowledge 27, 38–41, 42–3
  characteristics 38
  of children 102
  expertise 40
  implicit knowledge 79–84
    brand recognition 81–2
    product/brand evaluation 80–81
    sound symbolism 82–4, 87
    thin-slice information 80–82, 87
  information processing 39–40
  knowledge seeking 194
  objective/subjective knowledge 40
  processing fluency 39
  schema congruity 41, 55
  schemata 38–9
  see also memory
Consumer Psychology Review 9
consumer-brand connection *see* self-brand
  connection
consumer-consumer relationships 14
consumption:
  compensatory consumption 277–**8**
  luxury consumption 132–3, 252–3, 275
    and status 255, 275
    and pleasure 274
    and self-esteem 274, 277
Consumption Markets & Culture 16
contingent view of categorisation 54
correspondent inference theory 58, 67
costly signalling theory 250, 255
counterfactual thinking 137
Creswell, J.W. and Miller, D.L. 310b
cross-cultural psychology 8
crowdsourcing 327
cultural psychology 8
cultural/social categories 55
culture and self 194–9
customer satisfaction 61

Darwin, Charles: theory of evolution 244–50
Dasani water 85
data analysis:
  qualitative research 298, 308–11
    reliability and validity **310**
  quantitative research 298, 328–1
    hypotheses statistical tests **330–1**
    steps **329–30**

Dawkins, R. 256
De Luca, R. and Botelho, D. 233b
Deci, E.L. and Ryan, R.M. 162
development of consumer psychology 9–16, 18
  prior to 1960 11
  1980s-2000s: classic attitude theories 11–**12**
    consumer decision-making model **12**
  1960s-1980s: contemporary attitude
      theories 13
  2000s-present 13–14, 16
  evolution of key theoretical concepts **15**
  journals 9, 16
  timeline since 1960s **10**
developmental psychology 8
Dove 81
Downes, S.M. 259b
Drèze, X. and Nunes, J.C. 169b
drugs addiction 155, 277, 278, 283
Dunn, E.W. et al 130
Dyson vacuum cleaners 57

ecological psychology 213
EKB (Engel-Kollat-Blackwell) model 11
Elliot, R. 141b
emotions 14, 126–41
  and affect and mood 127–**8**
  anger 135–7, 140
  appraisal-tendency framework 128
  CES (consumption emotion set) 126–7
  emotion-congruence effect 128–9, 130
  and evaluations 128
  fear 133–5, 140
  happiness 129–31, 139–40
  PAD (pleasure-arousal-dominance) scale 126
  PANAS scale 126
  positive and negative 126–7
  pride 131–3, 140
  regret 137–9, 140–41
  and sense of smell 223
  see also mood
empirical self 181, 191
endorsements 58–60
  and social media influencers 59–60
environment and psychological adaptations 247
environment-centred theories 213
environmental behaviour 155
  and green (pro-environmental) consumption
      255–56
environmental psychology 212–33
  atmospherics/ambience: music, scent,
      lighting, touch 217–30
  Bitner: model of servicescape **216**–17, 231
  ecological psychology 213
  environment-centred theories 213

key theories **212–13**
  Mehrabian-Russell Model 213–16, **214**, 217,
      223, 225, 231
  stimulation theories 212
error management theory 247–48, 253
ethics and ageing consumers **111**
ethics in research 334–5
  confidentiality 334–5
  duty of care 334
  informed consent 334
  risk to participants 335
  social psychology 8
ethnographies 299, 300, 305, 306
  see also netnography
Evans, J.S.B.T. 78
evolutionary psychology 4, 243–59
  affiliation drives 254–56
  Darwin's theory of evolution 244–47, 256
    brain and adaptation 246–47
    natural selection 244–45, 257
    sexual selection 245–46
  and evolution of society 256
  and male/female stereotyping 256
  mating drives 249–53
    mate attraction 249–52
    and mate retention 252–3
  nature of evolutionary psychology 246–47
  and other forms of psychology 243–4,
      256–57
  survival drives 247–49
exemplar view of categorisation 54
experiments 320–4, 341
  designs:
    factorial designs 321–3
      2 x 2 factorial design 322, **323**
      between-, within-subjects and
          mixed 323
      graphical representation **322**
    post-test only control designs 321
  external validity 324–5
  internal validity 324–5
  intervention 320
  manipulation 320–1, 324, 335
  reliability 324
  types **320**
external (response) efficacy 153
  loyalty programmes **154–5**

Faber, R.J. and O'Guinn, T.C. 284b
fear 133–5, 140
  familiarity with the threat 135
  fear appeal messages **134**–5
  incidental fear 135
  mechanisms

classical conditioning 133–4
  mental processes 134
and self-efficacy 135
Fechner, G.T. 2
feelings 127
  see also emotions; mood
female models in advertising 251
Ferraro, R. et al 85
Festinger, L. 275
Field, A. and Hole, G. 324b
Fife-Schaw, C. 318b
Finkelstein, E.A. et al 164
Fishbein, M. 11
Fishbein, M. and Ajzen, M. 11
Fitzsimons, G.J. et al 88b
focus groups 300, 336
Folkes, V.S. et al 61
food taste and smell 248
food variety 248, 257
Fournier, S. 14, 186, 299
Fox, K.F.A. and Kehret-Ward, T. 103
framing effect (prospect theory) 62–7, 68
  brand stories 66–7
  framing:
    prices 64–6
    product attributes 64
  principles:
    diminishing sensitivity 63
    internal reference points 62–3
    subjective value 63
free association technique 2
free will 5, 6
Freud, Sigmund 2, 11, 14
functionalism 3, 4

Gale, Harlow 9
Galton, Sir Francis 2
gift giving 254, 258
Gilbert, J.R. et al 284b
goals:
  hierarchy 152–**3**
  and loyalty programmes **154–5**
  progress bias 163
  superordinate goals 157–8
Goldstein, N.J. et al 193
Goulding, C. 299
green (pro-environmental) consumption 255–56
Griskevicius, V. et al 248, 255
Griskevicius, V. and Kenrick, D.T. 259b
grounded theory 299

Hair, J.F. et al (2018) 328b
Hair, J.F. et al (2022) 329b
Hallahan, K. 68b

happiness 129–31, 139–40, 273–4
  and advertising 130, 131
  levels **274**
  and materialism 275
  and memory 131
  and shopping 130
  temporal foci 131
  types **129**
  see also pleasure; well-being
haptics *see* touch
Haselton, M.G. and Buss, D.M. 247
Hauser, D. et al 327b
Hayes, A.F. 328b
health behaviour:
  activity trackers 163–4
  goal structure 152–**3**
  obesity and losing weight
    compensation effect 163
    determination 162
    health-halo effect 165
    nutrition labels 165
    resource-depletion theory 161
  smoking 277, 278–79, 283
  see also compulsivity (addiction)
Helmholtz, H. von 217
Herzberg 152
hierarchy of needs 152, 156–9, **157**, 168
Higgins, E.T. 165, 190, 197
history of psychology 1–18
  development of consumer
    psychology 9–16
  qualitative methods 2
  quantitative methods 1–2
  schools of psychology 2–8, **3**
Hoffmann, S. and Lee, M.S.W. 284b
Holbrook, M.B. and Hirschman, E.C. 13
Hole, G. 324b
Hollingworth, Harry 9
human attractiveness *see* mate attraction
human brain 246–47
  impulsivity/compulsivity 277
human nature, universality of 246, 256
humanistic psychology 3, 6
Hutchinson, J.W. and Eisenstein, E.M. 43b
hypotheses 297–98

identity 179–198
  culture and self 194–7
  motivations and actions in identity
    research **180**
  self-identity 181–91
  social identity 191–4
identity-marketing 179
implicit cognition 77–88, 297

ageing consumers 110–111
implicit knowledge 79–84, 87
implicit learning 84–7
implicit-explicit distinction 78–9
    System 1 and 2 **79**
implicit learning 84–7, 88
    limitations 86–7, 88
impulsive buying 160, 275
    and compulsive buying 279–**4**
impulsivity 277
    and compulsivity 277, 283
information overload 33–4
information processing **7**
    elaboration likelihood model 37
    selective information processing 34
informed consent 334
innovation adoption behaviour 156
internal (self) efficacy 153, 155, 155–6
International Marketing Review 9
interviews 300–9, 336
    conducting interviews:
        active listening 302–7
        direct and indirect questions 303–8
            laddering 303, 304
            Zaltman's metaphor elicitation technique
                (ZMET) 303
        leading questions 303
        note-taking 304
        preparation 301–2
        recordings 304
        rules of good interviewing 302–3
        subtle language 303
        transcription 305
    depth interviews 300, 336
    focus groups 300, 336
    interview guide 301–2
    and observations 300
    online 301
    participants and bias 300
    semi-structured 300
    strengths and weaknesses 300
    unstructured 300
intrinsic/extrinsic motivations 162
involvement 156

Jakicic, J.M. et al 164
James, William 180, 182, 191, 197
    Principles of Psychology 181
John, D.R. 114b
joint consumption 253
Jones, E.E. 58, 67
Journal of Consumer Psychology 9, 16, 18
Journal of Consumer Research 9, 16, 18
Journal of Interactive Marketing 9

Journal of Retailing 9
Journal of Services Marketing 9

Kahneman, D. 68b
    Thinking, Fast and Slow 78–9
Kahneman, D. and Tversky, A. 13, 62
Kardes, F.R. et al 325b, 342b
Kardes, F.R. and Herr, P.M. 325
Kassarjian, H.H. and Goodstein, R.C. 19b
Kees, J. et al 327b
Kellaris, J.J. 233b
Kenny, D.A. 325b
Kenrick, D.T. et al 259b
Khan, U. and Dhar, R. 162
Kit Kat 84
Klink, R.R. 83
Koch, Jim 67
Kopetz, C.E. et al 169b
Kotler, P. 217
Kozinets, R.V. 307b
Kozinets, R.V. et al 309
Kplan, H.S. and Gangestad, S.W. 246
Krishna, A. 233b
Krueger, R.A. and Casey, M.A. 304b

language issues in data analysis 310–11
Lazarus, R.S. 223
Lerner, J.S. et al 141b
Levin, I.P. et al 64
LGBTQ rights 256
lighting 225–7
    bright or dim 226
    and cognition 225
    warm and cool 226–7, 232
Likert, Rensis 314
Lin, H. et al 325b
linguistics 8
long-term memory 34–8
    forgetting 35
    rehearsal 35
        memory reconstruction 38
    retrieval 35, 36
    types: declarative and procedural 34–**5**, 42
Lorillard 278
loyalty programmes **154–5**
Luria, A.R. 7
luxury consumption 132–3, 252–7, 275
    and status 255, 275

MacInnis, D.J. and Folkes, V.S. 199b
male-female differences:
    attraction behaviour **250–1**, 252, 257–58
    attractiveness 249–50, 271
    compulsive buying 281

female models in advertising 251
hormones and behaviour 249–50
joint consumption 253
luxury consumption 252–3, 258
reactions to sexual images 253
smoking 277
stereotypes 256, 282
variety-seeking 252
see also evolutionary psychology
Malter, M.S. et al 19b
Mandel, N. et al 199b
Mandela, Nelson 157
Maslow, A.H. 6, 152
hierarchy of needs 156–8, **157**
mate attraction 249–6, 257
costly signalling theory 250, 255, 257–58
and menstrual cycle 251–2
and sex differences 249, **250–1**
parental investment 250
mate retention:
consumption 252–3, 257, 258
male/female mate values 252
material self 181
materialism 273, 275
and compensatory consumption 275
mating drives 249–53
mate attraction 249–52
mate retention 252–3
May, R. 6
Mehrabian, A. and Russell, J.A. (Mehrabian-Russell
Model) 126, 213–16, **214**, 217, 223, 231
mood and emotional responses **215**–16
memory 2, 27–38
and emotion-congruence effect 128–9
false memories 131
and happiness 131
implicit-explicit memory 78
long-term memory 34–8
and menstrual cycle 251
sensory memory 29–31
sensory, short-term and long-term memory **28**
short-term memory 31–4
see also consumer knowledge
menstrual cycle 251–2
mental process and mental experience 79
Meyvis, T. and van Osselaer, S.M.J. 325b
Miller, G.A. 32, 33, 42
Mogilner, C. and Norton, M.I. 284b
mood 127, 128, 139, 215–16
emotional responses (Mehrabian-Russell
model) **215**
and music **218–20**
and scent 223, 224
see also affect (feelings); emotions

Moore, T.E. 88b
Morales, A.C. et al 323b
Morris, A. 304b
Moschis, G.P. 114b
motivation:
and collection behaviour 158–9
expectancy-value theory 152, 153–6
external efficacy 153
loyalty programmes **154–5**
internal efficacy 153
environment behaviour 155
health behaviour 155
innovation adoption behaviour 156
value 154, 156, 168
goals:
commitment to 160
hierarchy 152–**3**, 167
and self-regulation standards 160
superordinate goals 152, 153, 157–8
hierarchy of needs theory 152, 156–9, **157**, 168
and brand communities 158
criticism of 157
subordinate goals 158
intrinsic/extrinsic motivations 162
motivation research 14
motivation theories 152
obesity and losing weight *see under* health
behaviour
and self-identity 179, **180**
self-regulation 159–67, 168
elements:
goal commitment 159, 160
monitoring and feedback 159, 160
standards 159, 160
licensing effect 162–5
mis-regulation 160–61
regulatory focus theory 165–7
foci: promotion and prevention 165–7,
166, 168
regulatory fit 165–6
resource-depletion theory 161
self-determination theory 162
training for self-regulation 160
under-regulation 160
MTurk (Mechanic Turk) 327
Muñiz, A.M. and O'Guinn, T.C. 14
music 217–23, 231
and cognition 218
influence of music **217–18**
and information processing 220
and mood **218–20**
structure **218–20**, 222
and time perception 222–**3**
types of music and fit 220, **221**

narcissism 275
natural selection (evolution) 244–9
netnography 306, 336
neurosciences 4
Nixon, Howard K. 9
non-probability sampling 326
NVivo 309

observations (research method) 305–307
  and interviews 300
  note-taking 306–307
  online (netnography) 306, 336
  strengths and weaknesses 305–306
  time-frame 306
OCD (obsessive-compulsive behaviour) 277
old people *see* ageing consumers
online advertising 30, 80
online ethnography (netnography) 306, 336
online interviews 301
  see also netnography
online retail and touch 229–2
online reviews 60–61
online sampling 327
Oyserman, D. 199b

PAD (pleasure-arousal-dominance) scale 126
Pallant, J. 328b
PANAS scale 126
panic buying 281–6
Pavlov's dogs 5, 213
Pearson, Karl 2
Peracchio, L. and Luna, D. 88b
perception and awareness 84–5
Petty, R.E. and Cacioppo, J.T. 13
Pham, M.T. 19
phenomenological research 299
Philip Morris 278
Piaget, Jean 7, 96–7
Pieters, R. and Wedel, M. 43b
planned behaviour, theory of 11–12
Plato 1
pleasure 276–86, 283
Poffenberger, Albert T. 9
positioning strategy 32
prices:
  children's perceptions of prices and value 103–**4**
  left digit effect 65
  nine-ending effect 64–5
  price-off promotions 65–6
  and quality perception 81
  right digit effect 65
pride 131–3, 140, 162
  authentic and hubristic 131–**2**
  consumption goals 132

  luxury consumption 132–3
  national pride 133
processing fluency 155
product categories 55
product congruence 182
promotion- v. prevention-focused people **166**–7
prospect theory *see* framing effect
  (prospect theory)
prototype view of categorisation 54
"psychology": derivation 1
Psychology & Marketing 9
psychology as branch of biology 246
Puccinelli, N.M. et al 233b

Qualitative Market Research 16
qualitative research 2, 13, 16, 299–312, 336
  commonly used strategies **299**
  compared with quantitative research 296,
    297–99
  cultural/language issues 310–11
  data analysis 298, 308–11
    reflection 308
    reporting 311
    software 309
    thematic analysis 308
  interviews 300–5
  observations 305–307
  reliability and validity **310**
  reporting 311–12
  rigour 309–10
  sampling 307–12
quantitative research 1–2, 312–34, 341
  compared with qualitative research
    296, 297–3
  data analysis 298, 328–5
  experiments 320–9
  reporting 331–8
  sampling 325–32
  strengths and weaknesses 312–17
  surveys 313–23

Ramanathan, S. and McGill, A.L. 193–6, 320
reciprocal altruism 254, 258
reference groups 193, 198
regret 137–9, 140–41
  anticipated regret 139
  consumption regret: types **138**
reliability
  in experiments 324
  in qualitative research 310
replicability 8
reporting:
  qualitative research 311–**12**
    data analysis 311

methodology 311
quotations 311
quantitative research 331, 331–4
key statistics figures **332**, 333
methodology 331
procedures 331, 333
results diagrams/tables **333**, **334**
research methods: choosing 296–299
key methods **336–37**
qualitative or quantitative methods 296, 297–9
research levels 296, 297
see also qualitative research; quantitative research
research questions 297–8
resource-depletion theory 161
response efficacy *see* external (response) efficacy
restaurants 226
retrieval of memory 35
reviews 60–61
Richins, M.L. 126
Riege, A.M. 310b
rigour 298
in experimental studies 324–5
in measurements 315
qualitative research 309–10
and sampling 307
surveys 315
Ringler, C. et al 229
risk to participants 334
risk-taking behaviour 196–9
cushion hypothesis 196–9
and self-protection mechanism 248
Rogers, C.R. 6
Rook, D.W. 284b
Roschk, H. and Hosseinpour, M. 224

Saad, G. 259b
Sam Adams 67
sampling 307–12, 325–32
"backyard" research 307
non-probability sampling 326
online sampling 327
probability sampling 325–26
sample frame 326
sample size 308, 324, 327
scope and range of participants 307
target population 326
scent 223–5, 231–2
and cognition 224
diagnositicity (congruence) 225
influence of scents **224**
and mood 223, 224
and perfume consumption 251
and smell of food 248

Schau, H.J. and Gilly, M.C. 299
schema congruity 41, 55
schemata 38–9
Schumann, D.W. et al 19b
Scott, Walter Dill 9
self-acceptance 277
self-blame 137
self-categorisation 192
self-construal: independence/interdependence
194–5, **196**, 198
decision-making 196
preferences for market messages 195–**6**
self-control 137
self-discrepancy theory 190, 191
self-efficacy *see* internal (self) efficacy
self-enhancement 180, 271
self-esteem 162, 179, 180, 274–80, 282
and compulsive buying 281
and materialism 277, 275
and negative stereotyping 275–80, 282
and social comparison 275, 276
and social exclusion 276, 282
stable and unstable 275
self-identity 181–91, 197–198
actual, ideal and ought self 190–1
and brands:
brand advocacy 182
brand commitment 182
brand evaluation 80–81, 182
and negative emotions 135
brand loyalty 182
brand-as-person: brand personality 13–14,
180, 182, 184–92
and actual/ideal self 190–1
and Big Five **185–6**
and brand evaluation 187, 188
brand relationships 14, 180, 186–7
developments over time 189
and digital technology 189
Cattell's 16 PF **185**
criticism 187
Eysenck three-factor model **184**
Eysenck two-factor model **184**
and individual preferences 188
sincere v. exciting brands 188
transgressions 190
self-brand congruence 180, 182
self-brand connection 180, 182–4, **183**
and brand failure 184
classification: material, social, spiritual self **181**
and consciousness 181
empirical self 181, 191
implicit self-theories 189
self-discrepancy theory 190, 191

self-enhancement 180
self-esteem 162, 179, 180
self-maintenance 180
self-verification 180
and threat to identity 191
self-maintenance 180
self-presentation 192
self-protection 248, 257, 271
self-regulation 159–67, 168
self-threat and compensatory consumption
    191, 273
self-verification 180
semi-structured interviews 300
sensory memory 29–31, 41
servicescape (Boom and Bitner) **216**–17
sexual selection (evolution) 245–46
    and human brain 246
    intersexual selection 245–46
    intra-sexual competition 245
Sheth, Howard 11
short-term memory 31–4, 42
smoking 278
    and alternatives 279
    e-cigarettes 279
    men and women 277
    and tobacco advertising 278–9, 283
So, J. et al 141b
social categorisation 192
social comparison 192, 271–7
    assimilation effect 273
    contrasting effect 272–7
    downward comparison 272
    similar comparison 272
    upward comparison 272, 273
social exclusion 276
social identity 191–2, 198
    actual and ideal social selves 194
    and aspirational advertising 276
    families 191
    groups:
        in-groups and out-groups 192
        reference groups 193, 197
        and social ties 192–3
    key processes **192**
    and negative stereotyping 275–76
    social rejections 194
    strangers 193–4
        mimicking emotions 193–4, 198
        traditional/grouping appeals 193
social media 189
    and social comparison 271, 272–3
social media influencers 59–60
social psychology 3, 8
    and sociology 8

social self 181
social stereotyping 256, 275–76
Society for Consumer Psychology 9
socio-biology 250
Socioemotional Selectivity Theory (SST) 111
software for qualitative analysis 309
sound symbolism 82–4
    and brand positioning 83
    sound and meaning 83
    sound repetition 83–4
Spence, C. 88b
Spiggle, S. 309b
spiritual self 181
Stanford prison experiment (1971) 8
Stanovich, K.E. and West, R.F. 78
Starch, Daniel 9
statistical methods 2
statistical tests **330–5**
status 254–60
    and green consumption 255–60
    and luxury consumption 255, 275
STEAM courses 256
stimulation theories 212
stimulus-organism-response (S-O-R) paradigm
    213–16
storytelling about brands 66–7
Strizhakova, Y. and Coulter, R. 199b
subjective well-being 273, 274
subliminal advertising/messages 86–7
surveys 313–19, 341
    cultural/language issues 318–**9**
    measurements:
        examples: how a scale might appear in a
            paper **316, 317**
        Likert-type scales **314**
        number of response categories 315
        semantic differential scales **315**
        steps to ensure validity 316, 317–8
    question types 313
    rigour 315
survival drives 247–9
symbolic consumption 13

tactile marketing *see* touch
Tajfel, H. and Turner, J. 192
Tay, L. and Diener, E. 157
thematic analysis 308
thematic perception tests (TAT) 303
theories/schools of psychology 2–8
    discussed in this book **16–17**
    main schools **3**
thin-slice information 80–82, 87
Thompson, J. Walter 9
time perception:

and music 222–**3**
and scent 224
tobacco *see* smoking
Tooby, J. and Cosmides, L. 246
touch 227–30
    fit of touch element 228
    from strangers 249
    instrumental and autotelic 227, 232
    and mental imagery 228
    need for **227–28**
    and online retail 229–30
    and quality judgement 229
    when touch is forbidden 229, 232
Touré-Tillery, M. and Fishbach, A. 169b
Tourism Management 9
Trivers, R.L. 250
Tropicana 81
Tseng, T.-H. et al 158
Tversky, A. and Kahneman, D. 68b

validity in qualitative research 310
value 156
Van Gogh, Vincent 157
van Osselaer, S.M.J. and Janiszewski, C. 169b
Vargas, P.T. 87
variation strategy 37
variety-seeking:
    food 248, 257

and joint consumption 253
    women's consumption 252
Verwijmeren, T. et al 87
Vicary, James M. and Thayer, Francis 86
Vohs, K.D. et al 169b
Vroom, V.H. 153

Wang, Y.J. et al 231b
Ward, A. and Mann, T. 161
Washington, W.D. et al 163
Watson, D. et al 126
Watson, John B. 9, 11
Watson, L. and Spence, M.T. 141b
Weber, E.U. and Hsee, C.K. 194
Weiner, B. 58, 61, 67, 68b
well-being 269, 270
    pleasure 276–82
    self-esteem 162, 179, 180, 270–76
Wills, T.A. 272
Wright, P. et al 114b
Wundt, Wilhelm 2, 11, 17, 215

Yang, L.W. et al 88b
Yingling, L.R. et al 163

Zaltman's metaphor elicitation technique
    (ZMET) 302, 304
Zimbardo, P.G. 8

Milton Keynes UK
Ingram Content Group UK Ltd.
UKHW032053100823
426679UK00004BA/70

9 781473 906976